Samuel Bowles

Across the Continent and Back Again

A Summer's Journey to the Rocky Mountains, the Mormons, and the Pacific States

Samuel Bowles

Across the Continent and Back Again
A Summer's Journey to the Rocky Mountains, the Mormons, and the Pacific States

ISBN/EAN: 9783744753920

Printed in Europe, USA, Canada, Australia, Japan

Cover: Foto ©Andreas Hilbeck / pixelio.de

More available books at **www.hansebooks.com**

ACROSS THE CONTINENT:

A SUMMER'S JOURNEY

TO THE

ROCKY MOUNTAINS, THE MORMONS, AND THE PACIFIC STATES,

WITH SPEAKER COLFAX.

By SAMUEL BOWLES,
EDITOR OF THE SPRINGFIELD (MASS.) REPUBLICAN.

SPRINGFIELD, MASS.
SAMUEL BOWLES & COMPANY.
NEW YORK:
HURD & HOUGHTON.
1866.

INTRODUCTORY LETTER

TO THE

HON. SCHUYLER COLFAX,

Speaker of the United States House of Representatives.

MY DEAR MR. COLFAX:—

It was so pleasant and so profitable to travel with you during the summer,—your amiability and your popularity so readily unlocked all mysteries, and made all paths so straight; even Nature gave kinder welcome to your progress than her wont; that I would fain go along with you still farther, and ensure by your presence summer skies for this story of our observations, this record of our experiences. Besides, the book is more yours than mine. Your friendship gave me the opportunity for the travel; your favoring thought first suggested to me the then strange idea that the Letters should be put together into a volume; and your wide and close observation and your quick insight helped me to much of the material and the statistic. So I may rightly claim the favor of your name, and the charm of your company, in this new and unexpected trip into author-land.

You know how strange it seemed to us that our party were almost the first who had ever traveled Across the Continent simply to see the country, to study its resources, to learn its people and their wants, and to acquit ourselves more intelligently, thereby, each in our duties to the public,—you in the Government, and we as journalists. How strange, too, the idea was to the people along our route. They could not well believe that we did not come on a selfish mission of some sort; some secret governmental service; to see how they could best be taxed; to locate the Pacific Railroad; to make a bargain with the Mormons; to regulate the politics of the distant States,—at least to speculate in mines, and buy corner lots. When the fact was realized, while the many felt gratified and flattered, and showed such feeling in a hospitality that had no measure, there were some, you remember, who could not repress the genuine American contempt for whatever is not tangible and real and money-making; and I am afraid we passed in not a few minds for what, in mining vernacular, are known as "bummers."

So I could hardly realize, until I examined the subject, that there was in our literature no connected and complete account of this great Western Half of our Continent. People had visited it in plenty; its whole population, indeed, is drawn from the East; scholars are abundant on the Pacific Coast,—indeed, it is claimed as fact that San Francisco and vicinity hold more college graduates, in proportion to population, than any other city in the country; but they have gone with other objects than to see, to study, and to describe; they are dealing with materialities, and, as a rule, have taken little time to look about them, and observe the fantastic fashions of Nature, to worship the majestic beauty, to comprehend the varied resources of an Empire, that belong to their new Home. Starr King had written home of a few single features in California scenery; Dr. Bellows came back penetrated with wide and deep sense of the marvels he had seen, but the public only got glowing address and magazine article or two from him in detail; Fitzhugh Ludlow created wider interest by his brilliant but few and disconnected papers in the "Atlantic Monthly," on special themes in the journey; and the pencil of his artist-companion, Bierstadt, has caught the glow and the inspiration and the majesty of some chief natural wonders in these distant regions, and spread them on immortal canvass, to excite a world's wonder and whet a world's curiosity. But only enough had been written, only enough was known of the Nature, of the material resources, of the social and industrial development of these vast Plains and Mountains between the Mississippi River and the Pacific Ocean, to make market for more. So we have open field for our story, and hungry market for our harvest. So my Letters are rescued from the destined oblivion of daily journalism to figure in covers.

You will see that they bear substantially their original shape. Here and there is an addition; here and there, an irrelevant paragraph is excised; but they serve better to convey true ideas of the country we passed through, in preserving the freshness of the original composition. They are not a Diary of a personal journey; nor a Guide-Book; nor a Hand-Book of statistics; but they aim to give, with compactness and comprehensiveness, the distinctive experiences of the Overland Journey; to describe, as vividly as I may, the various original scenery that the route and the country offer; to portray the social and material developments of the several States and Territories we visited,—their present and their future, their realization and their capacity; and to develop to the people of the East and to the Government their share in the interests and hopes of the West,—what duties they had to perform, what benefits they might hope to reap. It was a large field to cover with the travel and the study of a single summer; to see, collate and digest the materials of half a Continent; but never did travelers find more generous facilities than we; and to opportunity, such as was never granted to others, we certainly brought intelligent interest and enthusiasm, and the trained eyes and ears and the educated instincts of journalism. We certainly brought, too, independence and integrity to our observation; and in all essential affairs, our conclusions were singularly coincident.

So we have assumed the responsibility and earned the duty of Truth-speaking. And on those great, pressing public themes of the Pacific Railroad, the Mormons, and the Mines, I would have you bespeak for my revelations and discussions the attentive ear of the

B

eastern public. Neither Government nor people seem half alive to the pressing importance of either. The Railroad is, indeed, the great work of the day; the great want, the great revealer, the great creator of this Empire of ours west of the Mississippi. It is cheering to find that, since we went over the Plains, labor upon the eastern end of this Road has had a new impetus; to learn that new elements of capital and enterprise have become engaged; and that on both the two main branches, from Kansas City and from Omaha, the Road is worked for sixty miles west of the Missouri, and by spring will be opened for one hundred. But I find no proper conception in the East of the progress which should and may be attained in the work. A hundred miles a season seems to be regarded as great achievement; whereas the company, that takes more than two years to cross the Plains and reach the Rocky Mountains, is unworthy its charter, recreant to its generous trusts. There *is* no vanity in demanding the completion of the entire line in five years; what is being done on the Sierra Nevadas proves this; there is only wanton waste of wealth, only stubborn disregard and neglect of great national responsibilities in being longer about it.

With regard to the Mormons, too, we all saw that the time had come for a new departure, for a new policy by the Government. The conflict of sects and civilization, growing up there in Utah, will soon solve the polygamous problem,—rightly and without bloodshed,—if the Government will make itself felt in it with a wise guardianship, a tender nursing, a firm principle. You will see I give a supplementary chapter to this subject, to let the Mormon leaders strip off for themselves the thin disguise of loyalty and disposition to succumb, which they wore during our visit.

I rely on you, also, to enforce my cautions on the subject of Mining. That great interest is in danger of real injury from feverish speculation, and false and unwise investments. Of the wealth of the regions we visited, in gold and silver ore, no adequate conception can be formed or expressed; the mind stands amazed before its revelations; but it does not lie around loose on the surface of the ground, and is not to be exploited in brokers' offices in Wall street and "The City." Patient and intelligent labor, in fields well-chosen for their nearness to markets and to supplies, with capital and skill and integrity, are the inevitable laws of great success in mining. The first need of our mining regions is the Pacific Railroad, to equalize prices and enforce morals and system in the business; the second is improved processes for working the ore. These gained, and no interest is likely to make more valuable returns for well-invested capital and labor. A Mining Bureau in connection with the Government is a desideratum, always provided its head shall be a man of special intelligence and divine integrity. A charlatan and a rascal, or one prone to become the victim of such, would make such an institution a curse to both country and Government.

New and valuable mineral discoveries are rapidly being made in all our Pacific States; the season has been one of industrious and successful prospecting; and we are apparently on the eve of a new mining excitement which shall, this time, take in not only the Pacific but the Atlantic as well, and sweep over the seas to Europe. Rightly directed and restrained, this will prove great impetus to our growth, great source to our wealth; but it is a whirlwind, after all, that leaves many a wreck in its passing. And woe be to those of us, who know the perils of the storm, who have seen the fields of its predecessors, if we unworthily fan its power!

I especially commend, on this subject, the exhaustive paper of Mr. ASHBURNER, the Mineralogist of the California Geological Survey, which he has kindly added to my volume. You know we found him the best accredited authority as to mining on the Pacific Coast, and his exposition of Gold Mining in California and Silver Mining in Nevada, will prove applicable to the whole subject; while his detailed scientific examination of the condition of the great Comstock Silver Vein will give encouragement to the many eastern investors in its mines.

In Natural Wonders and Beauties, as in rare gifts of wealth, the country of our Summer Journey stands out prominent and preeminent. Neither the Atlantic States nor Europe offer so much of the marvelous and the beautiful in Nature; offer such strange and rare effects,—such combinations of novelty, beauty and majesty,— as were spread before us in our ride Across the Continent, through the mountains, and up and down the valleys. No known river scenery elsewhere can rival that of the Columbia, as it breaks through the Continental mountains; no inland seas charm so keenly as Puget's Sound; no mountain effects are stranger and more impressive than those the Rocky and the Sierras offer; no atmosphere so fine and exhilarating, so strange and so compensating as California's; no forests so stately and so inexhaustible as those of Washington; no trees so majestic and so beautiful as the Sequoia Gigantea;—aye, and no Vision of Apocalypse so grand, so full of awe, so full of elevation, as the Yosemite Valley! Does not that vision,— that week under the shadows of those wonderful rocks,—by the trickle and the roll of those marvelous water-falls,—stand out before all other sights, all other memories of this summer, crowded as it is with various novelty and beauty? The world may well be challenged to match, in single sweep of eye, such impressive natural scenery as this. Professor WHITNEY tells us that higher domes of rock and deeper chasms are scattered along the Sierras, farther down the range; but he also testifies that, in combination and in detail, in variety and majesty and beauty of rock formations, and in accompanying water-falls, there is no rival to, no second Yosemite. You will be interested in Professor WHITNEY's more detailed account of the Valley, and his suggestions as to its creation, which are appended to my Letters. They are from his just issued second volume of the Reports of the Geological Survey of California, which, if suffered to be completed as begun, will present a complete scientific account, in aggregate and in detail, of that wonderful State, and be the guide to all her future development. The Yosemite Valley ought to be more known in the East, also, through the marvelous photographs of Mr. WATKINS of San Francisco; he has made a specialty of these views, and, besides producing the finest photographs of scenery that I know of anywhere, he gives to those who see them very impressive ideas of the distinctive features of this really wonderful valley.

Other Special Papers accompany the Volume and help to give it completeness on certain points. You will pardon me for taking some extracts from your Speeches on the journey; and I must make my peace with the public for not giving more. There is a valuable Letter by a friend, describing the stage ride through Idaho and its various Mines, which we were forced so reluctantly to omit. A Map, too, is improvised, by which the reader can follow our travels, and see the general "lay of the land" beyond the Mississippi. The Map is corrected according to the latest surveys, and defines the present limits of the Territories, and the locations of the principal Mining Centers.

There will be many to come after us in this Summer's Journey, partly inspired by the pleasure of our experience, chiefly incited by the increased smoothness of the ways. The projecting arms of the Continental Railway will rapidly shorten the distance at both ends. Rival and improved stage lines, new and pleasanter stage routes, surer and better accommodations at the stations, more frequent opportunities for rest, all will speedily come, with protection from the Indians, which Government cannot longer neglect; and even another season, I anticipate such facilities for the Overland Passage, as will invite hundreds where one has heretofore gone, and make the journey as comfortable and convenient for ladies even, as it will be safe and instructive for all. Great as the triumphs of staging which our experience has witnessed this summer, they are but the taste and the forerunner of what will be organized and perfected for the Overland Travel within two years.

But will any of our successors share such welcome, receive such hospitality, as was ours? It can hardly be. The thought of it all, its extent and its unexpectedness, produces a sense of unsatisfying gratitude. I have done what I could, in these Letters, to repay this wide-spread kindness, by making the country, its people and its interests better known to the East. They need nothing but the Truth,—none of them asked us to tell other than the Truth. And yet it were impossible adequately to represent all the strange features, all the rare capacities of this new half of our Nation. So, with a margin still against me, let this book go through you to our friends and benefactors of the Mountains and the Pacific Coast; from bluff Ben Holladay and his gallant knight, Otis, under whose banners we ventured out among the Indians from the Missouri River, on through Saint and Sinner, Gentile and Mormon, Miner and Farmer, gallant men and ladies fair, who gave us everywhere welcome to store of knowledge, to every material comfort, to every divine humanity of head and heart,—on to our tender friends, who dried their wet handkerchiefs in the morning breeze before the fading eyes of my wifeless companions, as we swept out the Golden Gate, on that cool September day; farther on, indeed, to the gallant sailors, who bore us on summer seas down the Continent's side, and back its mate, to Home!

And for you and me, my friend,—

"When you next do ride abroad,
May I be there to see!"

I am, yours, very faithfully,

SAMUEL BOWLES.

SPRINGFIELD, MASS.,
December 25, 1865.

INDEX TO CONTENTS.

LETTER I.

FROM MASSACHUSETTS TO THE MISSOURI.—The Railroad Ride behind; the Stage Ride before—Spanning the Continent—Vitality of Men of the West—The Chicago Wigwam five years ago: History since—Cleveland and Chicago, and their new Life—Atchison and its History and its Position—Pomeroy and Stringfellow—The Trade over the Plains—Speaker Colfax and his party for the Overland Journey—The Indians break the Line—Senator Foster and the Indian Question—Agriculture in the West—Coach off: Good-bye, . . . 1

LETTER II.

FROM THE MISSOURI TO THE PLATTE.—Atchison to Fort Kearney through Kansas and Nebraska—General Connor and no Indians —The "Galvanized Yankee" Soldiers—How we Rode—The Country and its Fascinations—The Scenery and the Atmosphere—The Modern Caravans on the Plains—A Storm of Thunder and Lightning and Hail, and how we weathered it, ... 10

LETTER III.

THROUGH THE PLAINS TO THE ROCKY MOUNTAINS.—A continuous five days' Stage Ride—The Plains the great National Pasture—The Platte River—Climate and Soil—Natural Highway across the Continent—A natural Road-bed—Population of the Region— How we Fared—Prices on the Plains and at Denver—"The noble Red Man," and our Preparations for him—Life and Death on the Plains—The Prairie Dogs and their Companions—The Alkali Water—Parting Breakfast with General Connor at Julesburg—His Position and History—Reception at Denver, ... 18

LETTER IV.

THE ROCKY MOUNTAINS AND THEIR GOLD MINES.—A Week among the Mountains and in the Mines—The Switzerland of America—Long's Peak and Pike's Peak—Bierstadt's "Storm in the Rocky Mountains"—Theater of the Gold Development on Clear Creek—

Central City, Black Hawk, Nevada—Condition and Prospects of the Business—Mysteries of the Sulphurites—Speculating Companies—The Gold Production of Colorado—Reports from Idaho and Montana—The United States the Treasury of the World—Questions of the Future, ... 30

LETTER V.

OF PERSONS, NOT THINGS.—Reception in Colorado—Grand Gala Supper to Mr. Colfax—Pen Portraits of the Party: Mr. Colfax, Governor Bross, Mr. Richardson, Mr. Otis—Social Life in the Rocky Mountains—The Young Men and the Young Women—Ben Holladay and his Stages—Famous Rides across the Plains, ... 43

LETTER VI.

SUNDAY IN THE MOUNTAINS.—Broad Church in the West—Mr. "Lo, the poor Indian"—A Day and a Night at Virginia Dale; its Scenery and its Landlady—Colorado and its People—Movement for State Government—A Mining Story: General Fitz John Porter, Smith and Parmelee, Judge Harding—Lack of "Help" in the Homes—The Blossoming of Eastern Fashions—Lack of Horticulture—Necessity of Irrigation—Canned Fruits and Vegetables—Prices of Food in Colorado and Montana—Vernacular of the Mountains, ... 56

LETTER VII.

FROM DENVER TO SALT LAKE—THROUGH THE ROCKY MOUNTAINS.—The Indians in our Path—Robberies and Murders on the Stage Line—What shall be done with them?—The Quaker Policy *versus* General Connor's Policy—Our Escape and our Faith—Wild Game on the Route: Antelopes, Elk, Trout, Bears, Sage Hens, etc.—The Desert of the Mountains—The Sage Brush—The Bitter Creek Country—Through Bridger's Pass to the Pacific Slopes—A Night Ride over the Pass—The Curious Architecture of Winds and Sands—The "Church Butte," and its Wonders—Fort Bridger—Arrival at Great Salt Lake City, ... 67

LETTER VIII.

THE WAY INTO UTAH: RECEPTION BY THE MORMONS.—Basin of the Great Salt Lake—The Home of the Mormons—Their Triumphs—Ride among the Wasatch Mountains—Playing Snowball among Flowers—Yellow the Favorite Color of Nature—Echo Canyon: its Beauties and its Ruins—The Valley of the Jordan—The City of Salt Lake: its Location and its Promise—Mr. Colfax's Reception by Soldier and Saint—The Hospitality of the Mormons—Excursion to Great Salt Lake—Strawberries and a Mormon Harem—Interview with Brigham Young: How he Looked and Acted—Heber C. Kimball, Dr. Bernhisel and other Church Elders—The Anti Mormons, or Gentiles, and what they are Doing—Death of Governor Doty, ... 79

INDEX TO CONTENTS. xiii

LETTER IX. PAGE.
MORMON MATERIALITIES.—Irrigation and its Results—The Salt Lake City Gardens—Wonderful Crops of Grain—The Mysteries of Great Salt Lake—Extent of the Mormon Settlements—Navigation of the Colorado River—Supplies for Utah by that Route—Policy of the Mormons as to Agriculture and Mines—The Silver Mines in Utah—The Soldiers at Work on Them—Visit to Rush Valley and Stockton, ... 89

LETTER X.
SALT LAKE CITY AND LIFE THERE.—The Chief Commercial City of the Mountains, and the Watering-Place of the Continent—Its Hot Sulphur Springs, and its Salt Lake: their Characteristics and their Uses—The Present Status of the City—Profits of its Merchants—Prices of Goods there—Dinner Party at a Mormon Merchant's—Brigham Young's Theater—A Special Dramatic Performance—Brigham Young on "a Good Thing," 98

LETTER XI.
THE POLYGAMY QUESTION.—Our Opportunities for Studying the Mormons—Testimony from all Interests and Parties—Conclusions—Mormonism not necessarily Polygamy—The Latter sure to fall before the Progress of Democracy—Present Duty of the Government towards the Question—Most of the Federal Officers in the Territory Polygamists—An Important Distinction—Conversation with Brigham Young on Polygamy—Points of the Discussion—Suggestion of a new Revelation against Polygamy—Views of Young as to Slavery and the Rebels—A Sardonic Face, ... 105

LETTER XII.
THE MORMON WIVES: OUR LAST DAY IN SALT LAKE CITY.— The Mormon Women and Polygamy—How they Live Together— The Children and the Schools—The Soldiers Stealing the Surplus Wives—Neglect of their Poor by the Mormons—Character of the Mormon Church Audiences—Services at the Tabernacle—Preaching by Brigham Young—Their Religion a Coarse Materialism—Mr. Colfax's Eulogy on President Lincoln—Elections in Utah—Judge Kinney and Captain Hooper—Good-Bye to Salt Lake, ... 114

LETTER XIII.
SOCIAL LIFE AMONG THE MORMONS.—The Cross Relationships of Polygamy—Brigham Young's Wives—Going to Heaven by the Coat-Tails of the Men—Wives the Reward of Merit—Polygamy "a good thing" for Poor Men—Brigham Young's Retinue—No Handsome Women among the Mormons—Brigham Young's Children— The Soldiers and the Mormons—General Connor and Brigham Young—Porter Rockwell, the Avenger—The Movement towards the Sandwich Islands, ... 123

LETTER XIV.

THE RIDE THROUGH THE SAGE BRUSH AND THE GREAT BASIN.—The Great Desert Basin of Utah and Nevada, and its Characteristics—A Quick Stage Ride through its Alkali Dust and over its Mountains—The Taint of the Alkali—Experiences of the Ride—Greeley and Hank Monk—Problems as to the Culture of this Region—Its Redeeming Beauties in Mountains, in Atmosphere, and in Exhilarating Breeze, ... 131

LETTER XV.

THE SILVER MINES OF NEVADA: AUSTIN AND VIRGINIA CITY.—Nevada the Child of California—Austin: its Location; its Social and Material Development—Classics in a Cellar—The Silver Mines in and about Austin—Character of the Ore—Mills—Improvements and Expenses—New Mining Discoveries—Virginia and its History and Mines—The Famous Comstock Ledge—The Gould & Curry Mine, and its Statistics—Its Superintendent, Mr. Charles L. Strong—The Ophir, Savage, Empire, Yellow Jacket, and other Mines—Cost and Profit of the Virginia Ores—Number of Quartz Mills on the Comstock Ledge—California's Account with Nevada—Conclusions as to the Nevada Mines—Advice to Capitalists—A Rhode Island Example in Colorado—Doubtful Things Very Uncertain—Profanity Discouraged,........................... 141

LETTER XVI.

THE CONTINENT ACROSS.—The Ride over the Sierras—The Great Ride Finished—Still the same Republic, the same Flag—Wonderful Homogeneity of the American People—The Civilization of San Francisco and the Pacific Coast—The Material Prospects of City and Country—The Last Day in Nevada—Valleys of the Truckee, Washoo, and Carson—Steamboat Springs—Reception at Carson City—The Sierra Nevadas and their Beauties—Lake Tahoe—The Stage Ride over the Mountains from Lake Tahoe to Placerville—Hard and Watered Roads and Fast Horses—First Views of California Life, . . 159

LETTER XVII.

OVERLAND TO OREGON.—A Pleasant Revelation in Oregon—The Overland Ride from California—Up the Sacramento Valley—Chico—General Bidwell and his Farm—Red Bluffs and the Family of John Brown—The Trinity, Klamath, Rogue, and Umpqua Rivers—Shasta and Yreka—The Tower House and its Proprietor—Mount Shasta and its Snow Fields—Jacksonville and its Gold Diggings—Pilot Knob—The Forests—Pines and Firs—Oak Groves—The Mistletoe and the Spanish Moss—Joe Lane and Jesse Applegate—Farming in the Umpqua Valley—Entrance to the Willamette Valley—Its Agricultural Wealth and its Rural Beauties—The Agriculture of Oregon—The Rains—The Summers and the Winters—The Towns and the People of the Willamette Valley—Portland: its Location and its Importance, . 169

LETTER XVIII.

THE COLUMBIA RIVER: ITS SCENERY AND ITS COMMERCE.—
The Reach and Importance of the Columbia—Its Breach Through
the Continental Mountains—Fort Vancouver and its History—General Grant as Remembered Here—The Cascades—The Dalles—The
Scenery of Mountain and River—Steamboats on the Upper Columbia—A Bit of Private Fun—The Scenery of the Columbia as compared with the Hudson, the Rhine and the Upper Mississippi—
Mount Hood—The Great Mountain of Oregon—The Highest Peaks
of the United States—The Oregon Steam Navigation Company—Its
Rise, Progress and Purposes—Oregon's Pacific Railroad Cut Off—New
Route to the Carribou Country—Summing Up of Oregon—Its People
and Their Promise, ... 184

LETTER XIX.

THROUGH WASHINGTON TERRITORY.—From Portland to Monticello by Steamer—A Rough Road—A Hard Ride through the Forests—Ferns, Blackberries and Snakes—Skookem Chuck—Olympia
and Reception there—Pacific Tribute to the Stomach—Basis for a
Religious Superstructure—Washington Territory—Its Name and its
Capabilities, ... 196

LETTER XX.

PUGET'S SOUND AND VANCOUVER'S ISLAND.—Great Lumber
Market for the Pacific Coast—Saw-Mills and Ships on the Sound—
Victoria, and its English Features—British Taxes and Expenditures—Frazer River Gold Diggings—Prosperity of Victoria—Depot
of the Hudson Bay Company—Grand Dinner to Mr. Colfax—The
San Juan Boundary Question—Summer Gardens under the Perpetual
Snows—The Pacific Coast Climate *versus* that of New England, ... 204

LETTER XXI.

SAN FRANCISCO: MR. COLFAX, AND HIS RECEPTION IN THE
PACIFIC STATES.—Back to Frisco—Its Fascinations and its Incomparable Climate—The Town always "in the Draft"—The Loss
of the Steamer Brother Jonathan—Speaker Colfax's Tour Complete
—His Reception Described and Analyzed—His Speeches—The Mexican Question—His Speech at Victoria—Governor Bross and Mr.
Richardson, ... 213

LETTER XXII.

THE YOSEMITE VALLEY AND THE BIG TREES.—First Impressions—The Great Natural Wonders and Beauties of the Western
World—Distinguishing Features of the Valley—The Verdure of the
Valley—Where the Zebra and Dr. Bellows' Church were Borrowed
from—Various Shapes of the Mountain Rocks—The Water-falls of
the Valley—The Journey to the Yosemite—Cession of the Valley
and the Big Trees to the State of California—Our Party and its
Experiences—The Excursion to the Big Trees: their Size: their
Age: their Beauty: their Majesty, ... 223

LETTER XXIII.

THE CHINESE ON THE PACIFIC COAST: OUR GRAND DINNER WITH THEM.—Number of Chinese Emigrants—What they Do—Raising Vegetables—Building the Pacific Railway—Servants in Families and Gleaners in the Coal Fields—How the White Men Treat them—Their Habits—Their Religion—Their Vices—How they are to be Reformed—The Chinese *versus* the Irish and the African—Chinese Merchants—Their Intelligence and their Honesty—A Dinner with them—Specimen of Chinese Pigeon-English—How the Dinner Began, and how it Went On—The Chopsticks, and the Food—The Writer Rescued by the Police, and Taken Out to get "Something to Eat,"............................ 236

LETTER XXIV.

THE GREAT THEME: THE PACIFIC RAILWAY.—How its Need is Felt—Anxiety for its Construction—The Hunger for "Home"—The Condition and Prospects of the Enterprise—Where Timber and Fuel are to come from—Routes over the Rocky Mountains—From Salt Lake to the Sierra Nevadas—What the Government has Done—What the People are doing at each End—Lack of Enterprise and Progress at the East—Superior Zeal and Progress at the West—Rival Routes over the Sierras—The Wagon Roads and their Business—Mr. T. D. Judah and his Route for the Railroad—Rapid Progress up the Mountains—Four Thousand Chinese Laborers at Work—Five Years Long Enough to Complete the Whole Line—Appeal to the Men of the East, ... 255

LETTER XXV.

COUNTRY EXCURSIONS: THE GEYSERS, VINEYARDS AND AGRICULTURE.—The Valleys of the Coast Range—How California is Constructed—Oakland—Fred Law Olmsted and Major Ralph W. Kirkham—The San Jose Valley and its Beauties—Excursion to the Geysers—Petaluma—Russian River Valley—Healdsburg—A Rare Whip and a Rare Drive—The Geysers Themselves—The Embodiment of Hell—The Country in the Neighborhood—Napa Valley—Calistoga and Warm Springs—Sonoma Valley and its Vineyards—California Wines—Champagne the Mother's Milk in California—Facilities for Agriculture in California—Illustrative Crops, ... 274

LETTER XXVI.

OF SAN FRANCISCO: BUSINESS MATTERS.—How San Francisco is Located—Its Sand Hills and their Fickleness—Lone Mountain Cemetery—The City Gardens—Contrasts in Business and Social Life—Character of the Business Men—The Bankers—The Bank of California—The Wells & Fargo Express and its Various Business—How it Rivals the Government in Carrying Letters—The Machine Shops and the Woolen Manufacturers—The Mission Woolen Mills and their Success with Chinese Labor—Cotton Manufactory and Other Industrial Enterprises—The Commerce of San Francisco, ... 288

INDEX TO CONTENTS. xvii

LETTER XXVII.
PAG2.

MINING IN CALIFORNIA: ITS VARIETIES, RESULTS, AND PROSPECTS.—Present Yield of the Mines of the Pacific States—Processes and Progress of Gold Seeking—The Soil Washings, the Deep Diggings, and Hydraulic Mining—Great Enterprises of the Latter—The Large Results—The Waste of Nature by Mining—"Yuba Dam" and its Anecdote—The Quartz Mining and its Status—Grass Valley—Lola Montez, and the Horse Milkman—Condition of Mining in Mariposa County—The Fremont Estate Come to Grief—General Prospects and Condition of Mining in California—The Idaho Mines —Mining in the Various States Compared—The Advantage for California—Personal Experiences in Visiting Mines—How We Went Into the Gould & Curry Mine, and How We Got Out, ... 302

LETTER XXVIII.

SOCIAL LIFE IN SAN FRANCISCO: THE WOMEN: RELIGION AND MINISTERS.—Visit to the Cliff House—The Pacific Ocean—The Seals and the Pelicans—A Ride along the Beach—The Chaos of Society in San Francisco—Domination of Materialism and Masculinism—The Women Savored with it—How the Ladies Dress—A Feminine Lunch Party—Activity in Public Morals—Education and Religion—Churches and School-houses—Ambition for Small Preachers—Rev. Dr. Wadsworth, Rev. Dr. Scudder, Rev. Mr. Stebbins—The Country Parishes—Wide Field for Missionary Labor—The Pacific Railroad the Great Missionary of All—Rev. Mr. Stebbins' Views of California Life, ... 321

LETTER XXIX.

CLIMATE AND PRODUCTIONS: COST OF LIVING: THE CURRENCY QUESTION: THE MINT—Advantage of the Pacific Climate for Invalids—Effects of the Climate upon the Race—The Fruits and Vegetables of California, Compared with those of the East—Beauty of the California Spring—The Best Time to Visit the Pacific States—Comparative Prices of Living—The What Cheer House—Prices in the Markets—Gold and Silver the only Currency—Question of Introducing Paper Money—The Mint at San Francisco —The World's Settling House at San Francisco, ... 335

LETTER XXX.

THE MINING QUESTIONS AGAIN: GENERAL REVIEW.—A New Word of Caution to Eastern Capitalists—Speculators and Swindlers in the Field—Other Authority for these Views; Professor Whitney and Mr. Ashburner—Double Injury of Deception—Importance of the Geological Survey of California—The Superior Richness of the Colorado Gold Mines—New Mining Discoveries in California—Latest Phase of the Comstock Ledge—The Gold and Copper Mines in Arizona—Last News from Idaho—The Oil Fever of the East and the Gold Fever of the West—The Copper and Quicksilver Mines of California—The Petroleum Speculation in California—Vineyards Growing on the supposed Oil Beds, ... 348

LETTER XXXI.

THE FAREWELL FESTIVITIES; POLITICS AND POLITICIANS.—
The Pathos of Parting—Our Final Visit in San Francisco—A
Crowded Week—Magnificent Dinner Party—Brilliant Farewell Ball
and Banquet, with Orthodox Belles and Hot Beef Tea—Politics of
the Pacific States—Their Rescue from Secession—Their Affiliation
with the Union Party—Governors Blaisdell, Lowe and Gibbs—Senators Stewart and Conness—T. Starr King's opportunity—His Sacred
Fame on the Pacific Coast—The California Congressmen—Large
Emigration of Rebels from Missouri to Oregon—Anecdote of Senator Nesmith of Oregon—Pacific Loyalty a Passion, and its Intolerance—The Indians of the Pacific States—The Indian Question
Briefly Summed Up—The Slang Phrases of the Coast—A Parting
Word for California and her Sister States, ... 358

LETTER XXXII.

THE VOYAGE HOME BY STEAMSHIP AND THE ISTHMUS.—
An Unique Sea Trip—Your Companions on the Voyage—The Accommodations and Food on the Steamer—The Crowd—The Mixture—
The Babies—Down the Coast on Smooth Seas and in Sight of Land
—Tropical Weather and its Effects—Stopping at Acapulco—The
Town and its Mexican Inhabitants—The Evening on Shore—Interview
with General Alvarez—Poor Prospects for Mexican Independence—
The Bartering for Fruits and Shells—Down the Coast Again—Guatemala and its Volcanoes—San Salvador and Nicaragua—Arrival at
Panama—Scenes in the Harbor—Burial of one of our Passengers—
Day Upon the Isthmus—Panama and its Idiosyncrasies—The Railroad Across the Isthmus—The Ride and its Tropical Revelations—
The Natives and their Nudity—Chagres River and the Isthmus
Fever—Aspinwall and its Barrenness—The Steamship Service on
the Atlantic Side—A Fortunate Run to New York—The Trip Summed
Up—The Pacific Mail Steamship Company and its new Career—
Prices of Passage—The Moral Unhealth of the Crowd on the Steamers—The Summer Journey Ended: Its Limits Reviewed: Its Triumphs Stated: Its Results Measured, ... 370

INDEX TO CONTENTS. xix

SUPPLEMENTARY PAPERS.

I. PAGE.

THE MORMONS.—Their Present Attitude towards the Government—
Defense of Polygamy—A Specimen of Mormon Preaching—The
Emigration of 1865, ... 391

II.

MINES AND MINING.—The Mines in Montana—The Uncertainties of
Mining, by PROFESSOR WHITNEY—The Mining Laws and their Operation, by Mr. CHARLES ALLEN of Boston—How the Metal is Extracted
from the Reese River Quartz, by Mr. ALLEN—Eastern Investment in
Reese River Mines—GENERAL ROSECRANS on the Mines of Nevada, .. 399

III.

MR. COLFAX'S SPEECHES.—Mr. Lincoln's Message to the Miners,
at Central City, Colorado—The Respective Duties of Government
and People: Suggestions to the Mormons, at Great Salt Lake City—
The Mines and their Taxation. at Virginia City. Nevada—The Pacific
Railroad, at Virginia City, Nevada—The Republic and Peace: The
Mexican Question, at San Francisco—California's Past and Future,
at San Francisco—America and Britain, at Victoria, Vancouver's
Island—Farewell Speech, at Parting Banquet in San Francisco, ... 405

IV.

IDAHO AND ITS MINES: WITH AN ACCOUNT OF THE OVERLAND JOURNEY
FROM OREGON TO SALT LAKE CITY.—Up the Columbia—Walla Walla—
Over the Blue Mountains—The Grand Ronde Valley—The Upper
Snake River—Thomas & Ruckel's Stage Line, and its Proprietors—
Idaho Territory—Boise City—Idaho City—The Various Gold Dig-
gings—South Boise—Owyhee—Illustrations of Mining Life—The
Great Falls of Snake River—Road Agents—Sage Plains—Salt Lake, 418

V.

THE YOSEMITE VALLEY.—Its Marvels and its Beauties, Scientific-
ally Described, by Professor J. D. WHITNEY, ... 429

VI.

THE BIG TREES.—The Grove in Calaveras County—Exact Measurements of some of the Largest Trees—The Species and the Name, . 436

VII.

CALIFORNIA'S WEALTH.—Statistics from an Agricultural Address
by Dr. HOLDEN of Stockton, ... 438

VIII.

THE GOLD MINES OF CALIFORNIA. AND THE SILVER MINES OF NEVADA—A Special Paper. by Mr. WILLIAM ASHBURNER. Mining Engineer.—The Gold Producing Regi n of California—Placer Mining —The Quartz-Mines: their History and Condition—The Silver Mines of Nevada—The Comstock Vein and its various Mines: the Gould & Curry, the Ophir, the Chollar-Potosi the Savage. the Imperial. etc. —How they have been Managed—The Problem of their Future, and its Probable Solution, ... 439

LETTER I.

FROM MASSACHUSETTS TO THE MISSOURI.

ATCHISON, Kansas, May 21, 1865.

A WEEK of leisure traveling ends the first or railroad stage of the great overland trip across the Continent. It is 1,425 miles by railroad from Springfield to Atchison, via Buffalo, Cleveland, Chicago, and the Hannibal and St. Joseph Railroad through northern Missouri. Here, the outmost post of our eastern railway system, we commence a coach ride of two thousand miles before we meet the projecting arm of the California railways at Placerville. Thence a day takes us down to San Francisco, and the Continent is spanned, the national breadth is measured. How this Republic, saved, reunited, bound together as never before, expands under such personal passage and footstep tread; how magnificent its domain; how far-reaching and uprising its material, moral and political possibilities and promises! There is no such knowledge of the nation as comes of traveling it, of seeing eye to eye its vast extent, its various and teeming wealth, and, above all, its purpose-full people—growing only greater in personal power and activity as they grow fewer in numbers. We think our Yankee leaders have active brains and comprehensive hands; but the pioneers in the commerce and in the civilization of the West impress you as men of broader grasp and more intense vitality. The very breadth of their field expands them.

It is five years since I was last in the West. Then I came to attend the Convention that nominated Mr. Lincoln for President. How long ago that seems! How dim the almost tragic scenes and excitements and struggles of the Wigwam! Personal preferences were lost and won there, life-long ambitions wrecked, new combinations created, and old ones shattered, whose significance was little understood then. What century of other history has held such revolutions, has wrought such influences on the present and the future of the world, as these five years! What five years of all life, of ours or anybody's else, would you or I exchange for even our witness of these?

We had an afternoon and evening in Cleveland, and a day in Chicago. I gathered new impressions of the beauty of the former city. No other place, East or West, unites such a business street as Superior to such a residence avenue as Euclid. It is the gem of the western cities. Springfield has similar union of business convenience and breadth with beautiful rural homes; but the scale is smaller— our Main street is narrower, our Maple and Chestnut shorter and less magnificently studded with palatial country residences.

Chicago is still great—to all Chicagoians. She has indeed made herself the commercial center of all the North-west. Milwaukee gives up the contest, and even her own State, to her old rival; and St. Louis looks on with envy at the more rapid strides of the metropolis of the free North-west. There is less building in progress, however, than I ever have seen before, and fewer new structures are noticed on the business streets than are usually observed between visits; though there be spots enough still needing reconstruction. Chicago is getting esthetically ambitious, however; she talks less of corner lots and corn and new blocks than of yore; and turns her thoughts more to art, to literature and to philanthropy. Already with the great journal of the North-west, she is founding another, and draws from New York, in Mr. Dana, to lead it, one of the most eclectic of American scholars, one of the most executive of American minds. Just now, too, she is vain over a new and beautiful opera-house—reared from the profits on alcohol—and a season of undiluted Italian opera; and earnest, moreover, with a grand Soldiers' Fair. Fitting it is that Chicago, which led in these monster fairs for the benefit of the army, should also close their glorious and holy procession. Their history is a proud chapter in our war; and in it the American women write their own nobility and patriotism.

This border town of Atchison is memorable in Kansas experiences. It was first settled and possessed by border ruffians of the worst type. The famous Buford Company of South Carolinians made it head-quarters. Stringfellow was its *pater familias*. But Mr. Pomeroy, the agent of the New England Emigrant Aid Company, finally got possession of it by strategy—he bought up its newspaper and threw a force of free state men into town during one night, and thenceforth defied the old settlers. Since then Pomeroy and Stringfellow have joined hands, bought up the town as a speculation, and are now growing rich together by its development and prosperity. Stringfellow lives here, and has become gentlemanly and loyal since the war broke out, and Pomeroy is United States Senator from Kansas, and also resides here when not in Washington. The town lies rather incoherently along some broken bluffs on the west bank of the Missouri River, five hundred miles from St. Louis, about twenty above Leavenworth, and the same distance below St. Joseph, the metropolis of northern Missouri. A railroad runs along the opposite bank of the river, and gives communication with St. Joseph and Leavenworth. Lawrence lies off to the south-west say fifty miles, Atchison being in fact in the north-eastern corner of the State. It is now the starting point of the overland mail for the mining regions and California, and the head-quarters of the stage company; also one of the chief points on the border for the trans-shipment, from cars and steamboats to wagons, of goods of all sorts bound to the mines of Colorado, Idaho, Montana, &c., and the saints of Utah. Nebraska City, Omaha, St. Joseph, Leavenworth and

Lawrence are rivals in this great business of freighting to the far West—how great nobody can realize who does not look upon it directly at this the busy season of the year;—but Atchison lies best as to the roads west, being both upon the river, and, through a great bend in its course, the most western of any town upon it, in the State or in Missouri, and perhaps does more of the outfitting and forwarding than any other one town. Most of the goods are only sent through the town, being bought by the shippers or territorial merchants in Philadelphia, New York, St. Louis and Chicago; yet a single firm here, in a modest building, is selling one million dollars yearly to small traders, or to fill up forgotten places in large trains. Long trains of heavily loaded wagons, drawn by mules and oxen, are moving out daily, now; but immense warehouses and large yards are still stored full with massive machinery for working the mines, and goods for feeding and clothing the miners, and agricultural implements to cultivate the prairies, waiting for their turn. The mule trains have been in progress for a month, but the ox-teams have had to wait till now, so that the animals could be fed on the grass *en route*. The Indians made such havoc last year that food for man or beast has been very scarce on the road across the Plains all the winter and spring; the Overland Stage and Mail Company has been very much crippled thereby; and the grain that it is now feeding out to its horses on the road has cost it, in purchase and transportation, something like eight dollars a bushel, or eight and ten cents a pound!

Speaker Colfax and his friends are gathered here for their long and inviting yet rather rough journey to the Pacific Coast. The party embraces the Speaker, Lieutenant-Governor Bross of Illinois, senior editor of the Chicago Tribune, Mr. Albert D. Richardson of the New York Tribune, and myself. Mr. George K. Otis of New York, special agent of the Overland Stage Line, accompanies us; and we have laid in every possible mitigation of the fatigues and discomforts of the long ride. There are rifles and revolvers for Indians and game; sardines for those who cannot digest bacon; segars for the smoking Speaker; black tea for the nervous newspaper men; crackers for those fastidious stomachs that reject saleratus biscuit; and soap for those so aristocratic as to insist on washing themselves *en route.*

Something of fillip is given to our ride by the overland stage from the West, due yesterday noon, coming in only this morning, and with the news that it had been attacked by the Indians about one hundred and forty miles back, or some half way to Fort Kearney. It is the first raid of the red-skins this season; and so thorough precautions had been made by General Connor, who has charge of the troops along the route, that it was believed there would be no trouble; the stages had assumed their old certainty and regularity, came in here every day within half an hour of the schedule time, and left precisely at eight every morning, and timed their arrivals at the stations along the route so certainly that the keepers had the meals all cooked and warm as the stages drove up, all the way from here to Salt Lake City. But to-day's news shows that some of the Indians had broken through or run around the military lines. They commenced by ambushing a party of some twelve to twenty soldiers, mostly converted rebels, on their way up from Leavenworth to Fort Kearney, but without arms. Two of these they killed outright, and most of the rest they wounded so savagely that they will probably die. The next day they assaulted the incoming stage, which had some six or eight passengers, men, women and children, circling around and around the vehicle on well-mounted horses, and shooting their arrows fast and sharp—only one had a musket, and another a pistol—at horses and passengers. The horses were whipped up, the men on the coach had two rifles and kept them in play, and thus the Indians were held at bay until the protection of a station and a train was secured, when the attacking party, finding themselves baffled, retired. They numbered about twenty-five in all, and their appearance on what was supposed to be the safest part of the route, and the one least protected by soldiers, has made some excitement.

Senator Foster of Connecticut, (Vice-president, *ex-officio)* and Senator Doolittle of Wisconsin, have just started south-west on an expedition to Santa Fe in New Mexico. They take a body guard of over one hundred cavalrymen, and will sweep around through Colorado, across the Overland Route to the upper Missouri, and come down through Nebraska. The two Senators are a part of a joint committee of Congress to visit all our Indian territories, examine into the condition of the Indians and their relations to the whites, and report facts and suggestions, with a view to a more intelligent and effective Indian policy. This is the occasion of their journey, the section they are visiting being their allotted space of the committee's work. It is an important, and, it is to be hoped, will prove a beneficent mission, that is thus undertaken. Whoever shall discover and cause to be put in practice a policy towards our Indian tribes, that shall secure protection alike to them and the whites, and stop indiscriminate massacre on both sides, will prove the greatest of national benefactors. But the almost universal testimony of the border men is that there can be no terms made with the Indians—the only wise policy, they aver, is extermination. This is dreadful if true; and I cannot believe it. The Indians have great provocation for their bad faith and their massacres in our own bad faith to them, in the systematic manner they have been plundered and cheated and every way abused by officers of the government, and the coarsest of the border men. But if the policy of extermination is the only possible one, the sooner it is adopted, and carried out, the better. It is cruelty to all parties, it is loss to people and nation, to let affairs drift along in the present way, exposing settlers and travelers to unexpected assaults and robbery, and interrupting the course of the subjugation and civilization of the continent.

The season lags, and plowing and planting are

greatly belated in the West. There is evident lack of labor, and nature kindly prolongs the springtime. A few fields of corn are up; but more still are yet being plowed. A steam plow, cheap, simple, but effective, is still the great need of our western agriculture, for plowing is its greatest, most wearing, most delaying burden. The other labor-saving machines are in use to an extent that would amaze New England farmers—planters, mowers, reapers;—you see them by the dozens in every little village, and they are the prominent feature of freight at the depots all along the railroads. The "Buckeye" is the favorite mower and reaper out -here. The caterpillars are ruining the orchards along our route through Illinois and Missouri as painfully as at the East, and the farmers seem as indifferent to their ravages. It is a sad sight—a thrifty young orchard of apples, otherwise, with half its trees stripped of all life by these pests, and the rest going in the same direction.

But the overland coach waits; General Connor has taken command of our party; and so, dear friends all, we sail out into this vast ocean of land. I shall think of you with every joy, and, possibly with selfish longing, with every pain. Do you think of me when the June roses open, with the dew of July mornings, with the fragrant cool of an August evening shower, when the katy-dids sing in September; and, God willing, I shall be with you again ere the maples redden in October.

LETTER II.

FROM THE MISSOURI TO THE PLATTE.

FORT KEARNEY, Nebraska, May 24.

A TRIFLE short of two days has borne us two hundred and fifty miles, riding night and day, to this point, which is the junction of the Omaha, Nebraska City and Atchison roads for the grand central Overland Route to Colorado and Utah and the Pacific Territories. Our road lay through the northern counties of Kansas and the southern of Nebraska; across the valleys of the Big and Little Sandy and the Big and Little Blue rivers; and here we strike the Platte River, up which and its southern branch we continue till we reach Denver. We came through the region of the Indian surprises and attacks of last week, but met no hostile red-skin. We found abundant evidences, however, of their last year's swoop through the line, in ruins of houses and barns which they then burned, and stories of their terrible massacres. General Connor and his aid, Captain Jewett, are riding out with us on their way to Julesburg, the General's head-quarters, two hundred miles farther west; and through the exposed parts of the line we had, as all the stages now have, a guard of two to four cavalrymen. A few soldiers, with a half-dozen cool and well-armed passengers, are always enough to frighten off or drive away any number of Indians less than a hundred. The red-skin fights shy, and only attacks where he is sure of little or no resistance; and he is despised, as a foe, by all the military men and old stagers along the Plains. But the necessity of keeping up steady mail and travel communication through this region, and of protecting the immense traffic in provisions, goods and machinery now in progress between the East and far West, enforces upon the government the duty of placing a strong military force all along the various leading roads, and then of sending out troops enough to drive the Indians to the far North and South, and keeping them there, or else of wholly exterminating them.

Among the present limited number of troops on the Plain are two regiments of infantry, all from the rebel army. They have cheerfully re-enlisted into the federal service. We passed one of these regiments on the road yesterday, it having just come upon the line. They were all young but hardy looking men; and the Colonel, who is of course from the old federal army, testified heartily to their subordination and sympathy with their new service. They are known in the army as "whitewashed rebs," or as they call themselves, "galvanized Yankees."

Aside from the Indian question—which, indeed, gave only a pleasant zest to our progress, and taught us novices at which end to hold our pistols and rifles,—we have had a most delightful ride so far. The weather has been clear and warm; the company intelligent and good natured; the food at the meal stations more excellent than that of the hotels and restaurants on the railroads west of Chicago; the country and its scenes most novel and inspiring. We drove at an average of six miles an hour, including all stops, sometimes making full ten miles an hour on the road, in an easy and commodious new Concord stage, such as are in use all through this route, and with horses as sprightly and in as good condition as you ever rode after in the good old days of staging in the Connecticut River valley. Every ten or twelve miles we come to a station, sometimes in a village of log and turf cabins, but oftener solitary and alone, where we change horses; and every two or three stations, we change drivers; but except for meals, for which half an hour is allowed, our stops do not exceed five minutes each.

The country up to fifty miles of this point, presents the characteristics of the finest prairie scenery of the West—illimitable stretches of exquisite green surface, rolling like long waves of the sea, and broken at distances of miles by an intervale with a small stream, along whose banks are scattered trees of elm and cotton-wood. Here and there is a "ranch" or farm with cultivated land, but these grow rarer and rarer—the uniform view is one wide rolling prairie, freshly green, spreading out as far as the eye can reach, with the distant fringe of thin forest by the water-course, and sending forth and receiving the sun at morning and evening, as the ocean seems to discharge and accept it when we travel its trackless space.

No land could be richer; no sight could more deeply impress you with the measureless extent of our country, and its unimproved capacities, than that which has been steadily before us for these two days. Within the last fifty miles, the soil grows thinner, the grass less rich, the sand hills of the Platte rise before the eye, and Plain, rather than Prairie, becomes the true descriptive name. The streams are few and scant, and the water muddy; but wells give good drinking water all along the route, though oftentimes they have to be sunk as deep as fifty or seventy-five feet. It is too early yet for many of the prairie flowers; but the rich, fresh green of the grass satisfies the eye. Scattered through it we catch frequent glimpses of the prairie hen, multiplying for the hunter's harvest in November; from its bare, last year's stalks floats out the liquid music of the larks; the plover, paired as in Paradise, and never divorced even in this western country of easy virtue and cheap legislation, bob up and down their long necks, or flutter their wide wings in flight at every rod; little blackbirds accompany you in great shoals; a lean, hungry-looking wolf steals along at a distance with one eye on you, and the other on the carcass of a horse or ox, dropped in sickness or fatigue from some passing train; away off near the horizon scamper most daintily and provokingly a half-dozen antelopes—too near for restful palates, too far for waiting rifles; and over all and illuminating all floats an atmosphere so pure, so rare, so ethereal, as pictures every object with a pre-Raphaelite distinctness, makes distant things appear near, and sends the horizon far away in an unbounded stretch of slightly rounding green earth. Add to these a constant breeze, tempering the sun to a most grateful softness, and bearing an inspiring tonic to lungs and heart; sunsets and sunrises that rival Italy or the Connecticut valley; a twilight prolonged as in England; and a dryness and purity to the atmosphere, that you certainly know not in New England, and guards the most exposed against colds,—and you may form some idea of the life of our senses and sensibilities so far on this excursion.

But I omit one great feature in the constant landscape—the long trains of wagons and carts, with their teams of mules and oxen, passing to and fro on the road, going in empty, coming out laden with corn for man and beast, with machinery for the mining regions, with clothing, food and luxuries for the accumulating populations of Colorado, Utah and Montana,—for all these territories and the intermediate populations draw their supplies from this quarter, and not from the California shore. The wagons are covered with white cloth; each is drawn by four to six pairs of mules or oxen; and the trains of them stretch frequently from one-quarter to one-third of a mile each. As they move along in the distance, they remind one of the caravans described in the Bible and other Eastern books. Turned out of the road on the green prairie, for afternoon rest or a night's repose, the wagons drawn around in a circle, as a sort of barricade against Indians or protection against storm, and the animals turned loose to feed, and wandering over the rounding prairie for a mile—"cattle upon a thousand hills;" at night their camp fires burning;—in any position, or under any aspect, they present a picture most unique and impressive, indeed. I have seen nothing like it before; and it summons up many a memory of oriental reading. Just now, these trains are moving more compactly than usual, for protection against Indian attacks; but their numbers and the amount of goods they are hauling, give you an idea of the magnitude and importance of the commerce across these Plains, that neither bare figures, nor parts of speech can impart. The mule trains make from fifteen to twenty miles a day; and the oxen about twelve to fifteen. They depend entirely upon the prairies for food as they go along; and indeed the animals grow stronger and fatter as they move on in their summer campaign of work, coming out of their winter rest poor and scrawny, and going back into it in the fall, fat and hearty.

The chief sensation and experience of our ride so far was a storm of thunder and lightning, hail and rain, upon the Plains. Such storms are memorable in all travel or life in this country for severity; and we had one of the very best of them. It struck us this morning, about six miles back, and just as we had come to the banks of the Platte. First came huge, rolling, ponderous masses of cloud in the west, massing up and separating into sections in a more majestic and threatening style than our party had ever before seen in the heavens. Then followed a tornado of wind. Horses, coach and escort turned their backs to the breeze, and bending, awaited its passing. It stripped us of every loose bit of baggage; and we sent out scouts for their recovery. Next fell the hail, pouring as swift rain, and as large and heavy as bullets. The horses quailed before its terrible pain. Our splendid quartette of blacks careered and started over the prairie; we tumbled out of the coach to save ourselves one peril, and so met the other—the fire of the heavenly hail; it bit like wasps, it stunned like blows. But horses and coach were to be saved; and after a long struggle, in which the coach came near overturning, and the horses to running away, in dismay and fright, and our driver and military friends proved themselves real heroes, and everybody got wet, the hail subsided into a pouring rain, the horses were quieted and restored to their places, and we got into a drowned coach, ourselves like drowned rats, and hastened to refuge, over a prairie flooded with water, in this hospitable station. We are remaining here a few hours to dry our clothes and baggage, receive and send dispatches, see the quarters of the military establishment, over which Colonel Livingston presides, and put ourselves in order for another two days' ride to Julesburg, half way to our first grand destination at Denver.

Speaker Colfax is receiving every attention possible from such people as there are along this line; everybody seems to know him—many to be his old personal friends in Indiana; the stage proprietors and their agents are extending to him and his party every hospitality and courtesy; and the military officials only such protection as they are now according to all passengers, and such politeness as their good breeding is sure to suggest. For myself, I enjoy the grand ride much better than I expected; but for the remaining twinges of sciatica, it would be unalloyed pleasure; and the anticipated sleepless night rides prove but small inconvenience.

LETTER III.

THROUGH THE PLAINS TO THE MOUNTAINS.

DENVER, Colorado, May 29.

OUR coach rolled into this town, the leading one of Colorado Territory, and lying under the very shadow of the Rocky Mountains, on Saturday noon, exactly "on time," and in less than five days from the Missouri River. It was a magnificent, uninterrupted stage ride of six hundred and fifty miles, much more endurable in its discomforts, much more exhilarating in its novelties, than I had anticipated. From Fort Kearney, where we struck the Platte River, and finished the first third of the distance, we found the soil growing thinner and thinner; the sand hills rose and rolled away in regular serial form, north and south; and we passed on to and through the great Central Desert of the Continent, stretching from the far distant north to the Gulf of Mexico, and separating by four hundred miles of almost uninhabitable space the agriculturally rich prairies of the Mississippi valley, from the minerally rich slopes and valleys of the Rocky Mountains. Yet not a desert, as such is commonly interpreted—not wörthless, by any means. The soil is fat, indeed, compared with your New England pine plains. It yields a coarse and thin grass that, green or dry, makes the best food for cattle that the Continent offers. It is, indeed, the great Pasture of the nation. This is its present use and its future profit. Now it supports the machinery of the commerce of the two great wings of the nation, that it both separates and connects. Then—when railroad shall supersede cattle and mules—it will feed us with beef and mutton, and give wool and leather immeasurable. Let us, then, not despise the Plains; but turn their capacities to best account.

The Platte is a broad, shallow but swift river, furnishing abundant good water for drinking and for limited irrigation, but offering no possibilities of navigation—not even for ferriage. When it is too swift and strong for fording, it must be let alone, and a route on either shore kept, or the falling waters waited for. The soil of the valley and of the Plains, which it crosses, is not by any means mere sand, but rather a tough, cold, sandy loam, with an admixture of clay. It is too cold and dry for corn and vegetables. Wheat and barley may be raised on its best acres, with the help sometimes of a simple irrigation; but the pasture is its manifest destiny and use. There is a steady, imperceptible rise from the Missouri to the Rocky Mountains; half way, we get above the dew-falling point; and here at Denver, at the base of the mountains, we are five thousand feet above the level of the sea. The days are warm, however; the sun pours down over its shadeless level with a hot, burning power; but a cool wind tempers its bitterness, and at night the air is absolutely cold. This is the universal rule of all our western country, beyond the Mississippi valley, and distinguishes the summers of its whole extent from those of the East.

This valley of the Platte, through these Plains, is the natural highway across the Continent. Other valleys and routes have similar advantages, but in minor degree: this unites the most; for it is central—it is on the line of our great cities and our great industries, East and West, and it is the longest, most continuous. A smooth, hard stage road is made by simply driving over it; a railroad awaits only sleepers and rails. Here and there, at rare intervals, is a gully or dry creek or petty stream to cross; but this, the longest and best stage road in the world, has not to-day a quarter of a mile of simplest bridging; and a railroad of six hundred and fifty miles would not need a mile. There is an occasional stretch of heavy sand; after a rain also of temporary mud; but at this season of the year a speed of ten miles an hour could easily be attained by horses, with proper relays and a light load, throughout the whole distance. This would reduce the transit to three days; but with ponderous mails, a heavy coach, and six to fourteen passengers, the five days occupied in the journey constitutes a great triumph of stage management and horse-flesh capacity.

The region is substantially uninhabitable; every ten or fifteen miles is a stable of the stage proprietor, and every other ten or fifteen miles an eating-house; perhaps as often a petty ranch or farmhouse, whose owner lives by selling hay to the trains of emigrants or freighters; every fifty or one hundred miles you will find a small grocery and blacksmith shop; and about as frequently is a military station with a company or two of United States troops for protection against the Indians. This makes up all the civilization of the Plains. The barns and houses are of logs or prairie turf, piled up layer on layer, and smeared over or between with a clayey mud. The turf and mud make the best houses, and the same material is used for military forts and for fences around the cattle and horse yards. Their roofs, where covered, are a foot thickness of turfs, sand, clay, and logs or twigs, with an occasional inside lining of skins or thick cloth. Floors are oftenest such as nature offers only; and, as at some of the Washington hotels, the spoons at the table do not always go around. Mexican terms prevail: an inclosure for animals is called a "corral;" a house of turf and mud is of "adobe;" and a farm-house or farm a "ranch."

Our meals at the stage stations continued very good throughout the ride; the staples were bacon, eggs, hot biscuit, green tea and coffee; dried peaches and apples, and pies were as uniform; beef was occasional, and canned fruits and vegetables were furnished at least half of the time. Each meal was the same; breakfast, dinner and supper were undistinguishable save by the hour; and the price was one dollar or one dollar and a half each. The devastations of the Indians last summer and fall, and the fear of their repetition, form the occasion and excuse for enormous prices for everything now upon the Plains and in the Territories on this side the mountains. Twenty-five cents a pound has been charged the past year for transporting any sort of goods. The government and the stage company have paid ten and twelve dollars a bushel for corn, all of which has to be brought up from the Missouri and Mississippi valleys, and from seventy-five to one hundred dollars a ton for hay. But General Connor means to emancipate himself from the hay speculators hereafter; he has bought twenty-five mowing machines, which are to be distributed among the military stations, and used by the soldiers upon the generous common grass of the river bottoms for gathering a winter supply of hay. The stage company is also pursuing the same policy. Wood costs on the Plains seventy-five dollars a cord, so distant are the thin forests that furnish it; lumber, when it is used at all, which is rarely, for it must be freighted from one end or the other of the route, one hundred and fifty to two hundred dollars a thousand; a wagon and team of oxen (five pairs) twenty to twenty-five dollars a day; common labor two and three dollars a day and board. And at Denver, the end of the route, here is a specimen of the prices to-day: potatoes twenty-five cents a pound or fifteen dollars a bushel; flour fifteen and twenty cents a pound; corn eighteen cents a pound or ten dollars a bushel; mechanics and laborers eight and ten dollars a day; beef forty cents a pound, and hams forty-five to fifty cents; girls as house servants ten dollars a week. These rates are likely to be cut down one third or one half during the present season, however, as General Connor gives security to transportation across the Plains, and competition in freighting and merchandising works its legitimate influences.

The ride from Fort Kearney gave us but few new experiences. The "noble red man" disappointed both fear and hope. He gave us a wide berth; perhaps he had intuitive knowledge of our brave hearts and our innumerable Colts', Smith & Wessons', Remingtons', Ballards', and double-barreled shot-guns—certainly we bristled with the munitions of war like a fortification prepared for assault; more likely he saw the four cavalrymen that constantly galloped by our side from station to station, with pistols at holsters and rifles slung in the saddles,— for bloodthirsty as our red brethren are, when defenseless men or women or children come in their way, they have a holy horror of well-armed soldiers, breech-loading rifles, and magazine pistols. They easily learn and most faithfully practise the maxim of civilization, that discretion is the better part of valor.

Animal and vegetable life, too, grew scantier; the antelope eluded all rifle shot; only a prairie hen was brought down; We were too early for the buffalo, and not one crossed our path: as the Plains grew more barren, the prickly pear and the sage bush became plenty in their tough unfruitfulness; the road was marked more frequently with the carcasses of oxen and horses—scarcely ever were we out of sight of their bleaching bones; occasionally the pathos of a human grave gave a deeper touch to our thoughts of death upon the Plains, deepened, too, by the knowledge that the wolf would soon violate its sanctity, and scatter the sacred bones of father, mother or child over the waste prairie;—the wiser instinct of the Indian showed itself, once in a while, in the sepulture of their kindred above ground—for, rolling his dead in a blanket, he places the body in mid-air between two forked poles, six or eight feet high, and so, if not poised for an upward flight, at least safe from vulture profanation;—and anon we grew gay over the lively little prairie dogs, looking half rat and half squirrel, as they scampered through the grass or dove, with a low, chirruping bark, back into their holes. These animals are smaller and more contemptible than I had expected; their holes, marked by a hillock of sand, are congregated in villages, sometimes extending a quarter or half a mile along the roadside. Only a pair occupy each hole, but we hear the same story, that earlier travelers record for us, that a snake and an owl share their homes with them. The snakes we did not see; but the owl, a species no larger than a robin, solemn, stiff and straight, stood guard at many of the holes.

We passed through an alkali region, where the soil for two or three feet seemed saturated with soda, and so poisons the fallen water that, if drank by man or beast after a shower, it is sure to be fatal. All the water of this region and the Plains has a savor of alkali or sulphur in it, but not to an unhealthy degree. We stopped at Fremont Spring, named for its discovery and use by the great explorer, on his original trip through this region, and found it pure, sweet water, slightly marked with sulphur. We were not without our daily paper; for we stopped the incoming stage and had the latest California journals, but, though they gave us fresh news from the Pacific shore, their eastern intelligence was indeed a twice-told tale. At the telegraph stations, however,—for those bare but wonder-working poles and wires ran in sight all along the road, and kept us in their mysterious sympathy with friends and home,—we had a special privilege of reading the news as it ran East and West, and so we were up with the world, though so far out of it in all material circumstance.

We dropped General Connor, who had been our fellow passenger from Atchison, early Friday morning, at Julesburg, where he has his head-quarters for the summer, and where the Platte River forks, one branch extending north to Fort Laramie and the South Pass through the mountains, and the other marking our southerly line to Denver. Julesburg is only a village of tents and turf forts and barns, affording no facilities for a luxurious military life; but it is well located for General Connor's plans for protecting the commerce of the Plains from the Indians, and for punishing them for their past offenses and present threatenings against it. We took a parting breakfast with him in camp, just at sunrise, eating canned chicken and oysters off tin plates, and drinking our coffee with the brownest of sugar and the most concentrated of milk, all in the simplest and most barren of border life. But we parted from him with real regret and a large respect. He had shown himself to us both a genuine gentleman and a valuable commandant; and we found reason in our personal acquaintance to confirm the judgment of the people of all this region, that he is of all men, whom the government has assigned to the duty, the most fit and efficient for restraining the Indians, for protecting and developing the interests of government and people, for settling the Mormon problem, for giving order and unity to the incoherent and chaotic social and material life of all this vast region.

General Connor has been for two years in command at Utah, and of his administration there and his views of the Mormons, I shall have occasion to speak when I am on the spot. It is only two months since he had assigned to him, also, the protection of the Overland Routes across the Plains; but everybody hereabouts notes with pride and confidence the change already introduced. The soldiers have ceased to be thieves and bullies; a new and better social tone is visible in all the mining region; the laws are better respected; soldiers guard the whole central line of travel, and cavalrymen escort every stage—there is no longer any real danger, or will not be, so soon as a few more troops can be put in their places, in traveling or freighting over the main road from the river to the mountains; the Indians will speedily be driven back to their reservations, and forced to submit to whatever terms the government may dictate; prices will fall along the Plains and in the Territories on the eastern slopes of the mountains; and all the business of this vast and rich region will receive, under certainty and safety, an impetus, and gain an uniformity, that have never before marked their history. Whether the Indians shall be wholly exterminated; or forced into submission and half civilization in limited territories, undisputed for the present by the white; or set to work upon the Pacific Railroad—these are not points for General Connor to decide. The choice belongs to the government at Washington. But General Connor will certainly restrain them from violence, and punish them for their barbarities. He believes they may be made useful in building the Pacific Railroad; and he has proposed to furnish two thousand of one or two tribes, who have already submitted to his authority, and whom he is now supporting at an enormous expense far distant from his base of supplies, to the railroad company for an experiment.

General Connor has a personal history characteristic of America. He was born in Ireland, came early to New York with his parents, enlisted in the United States cavalry, when a young man, for service in our Indian territory, served out his regular term, lived in Texas, rejoined the army during the Mexican war, and became a captain, removed to California, prospered in business as a farmer and otherwise, again took up arms for his country when the rebellion broke out, and was appointed colonel of a California regiment, and thence, by his well-recognized experience and his services in this region, was advanced to a brigadiership, and assigned, some two or three years ago, to the command of the military district of Utah. He is an intelligent and accomplished gentleman, in the prime of life and power, strict in discipline, clear and strong in thought and in its expression; and if willing to continue in the service, as I am sure the government ought to be most earnest to have him, and sustained in his policy, he will most honorably and usefully connect his name with the disposition of the two great questions of our national responsibility and duty in this quarter—the Mormons and the Indians. Twenty-five years ago, General Connor left Fort Leavenworth, on the Missouri River, a private in the United States regular army. Last week he visited it a second time, a Brigadier-general and the Commander of the District of the Plains, comprising a larger territory, and embracing more delicate and important responsibilities than any other single military district in the country. The contrast of the two facts tells the whole story of his character and his history, and sustains my judgment of him.

The reception of Speaker Colfax and his party on their arrival here was very enthusiastic and flattering. They were met and welcomed by Governor Evans and other territorial officers and a committee of the citizens of Denver; in the evening there was a large popular gathering to pay personal respect to the visitors; and Mr. Colfax, Mr. Bross, and Mr. Richardson made eloquent and effective speeches.

Mr. Colfax was especially happy and felicitous; public speaking is as natural and easy to him as swimming to a duck; and he repeated President Lincoln's parting suggestions and messages to the miners with pathetic fidelity, and they were received with mournful interest and deep pleasure. Public and private courtesies are showered upon him and his friends. They start this morning for a visit to the mines and the mountains, which will occupy four days, when they will return here, and again take up their progress westward, in the long ride to Utah, next Saturday. They are all in good health and the best of spirits—not alcoholic—and very glad they came; especially your S. B.

LETTER IV.

THE ROCKY MOUNTAINS AND THEIR GOLD MINES.

DENVER, Colorado, June 2.

WE have been spending an interesting week among the Rocky Mountains; riding and driving up and down their rugged sides, through their narrow valleys, and over their occasional plains; fording their turbulent streams; gazing with never-ceasing delight upon their various forms of beauty, under cloud and storm and sunshine, their snow-capped peaks, their deep ravines and narrow gorges, their purpling, shadowed sides and tops, their high pinnacles of rock, monuments of Creation and History; and then, descending into the golden mines, following tortuous veins of precious rock, hundreds of feet beneath the surface, tracing the specks of gold among the comparative dross of iron and copper and lead, hobnobbing with the dusty miners in their dreary workshops, faintly illuminated with occasional candles, and then, ascending to day and light again, watching the processes for extracting the wealth from the ore,—the irresistible grinding of the stamps, the washing with much water, the securing with copper and mercury, the after-delaying with blankets: all the rarest wonders and beauties of Nature, all the divinest patience of Labor and the faith of Knowledge, all the mysteries of Science and the intricacies of Art have been spread before us during these crowded days among the mines and the mountains of Colorado.

How the mind runs back to one's youthful, vague, mythical knowledge of the Rocky Mountains in their actual presence! How difficult to realize that, whereas, twenty years ago, they and their location and character and the region about them were almost unknown, now, two weeks from home, I am sporting familiarly under their shadows, following tediously up their sides, galloping in the saddle around their summits, drinking from their streams, playing snow-ball in June with their imperishable snow banks, descending into their very bowels, and finding companionship and society as various and as cultured and as organized as in New England; cities of thousands of inhabitants, not only at their base, but away up in their narrow valleys, eight and nine thousand feet above the sea level! All this seems dream-like, yet weary head and sore feet and stern statistics testify to the reality.

As to the mountains, as a natural spectacle, they are first cousins to the Alps. When the Pacific Railroad is done, our Switzerland will be at our very doors. All my many and various wanderings in the European Switzerland, three summers ago, spread before my eye no panorama of mountain beauty surpassing, nay none equaling, that which burst upon my sight at sunrise upon the Plains, when fifty miles away from Denver; and which rises up before me now as I sit writing by the window in this city. From far south to far north, stretching around in huge semi-circle, rise the everlasting hills, one upon another, one after another, tortuous, presenting every variety of form and surface, every shade of cover and color, up and on until we reach the broad, snow-covered range that marks the highest summits, and tells where Atlantic and Pacific meet and divide for their long journey to their far distant shores. To the North rises the king of the range, Long's Peak, whose top is fourteen thousand six hundred feet high; to the South, giving source to the Arkansas and Colorado, looms up its brother, Pike's Peak, to the hight of thirteen thousand four hundred feet. These are the salient features of the belt before us; but the intervening and succeeding summits are scarcely less commanding, and not much lower in hight. Right up from Denver stands the mountain top that was the scene of Bierstadt's "Storm in the Rocky Mountains," and up and down these mountain sides were taken many of the studies that he is reproducing on canvas with such delight to his friends and fame for himself. No town that I know of in all the world has such a panorama of perpetual beauty spread before it as Denver has in this best and broadest belt of the Rocky Mountains, that rises up from the valley in which it is built, and winds away to the right and to the left as far as the eye can see—fields and woods and rocks and snow, mounting and melting away to the sky in a line often indistinguishable, and sending back the rays of the sun in colors and shapes that paint and pencil never reproduced, that poetry never described. These are sights that the eye never tires of—these are visions that clear the heart of earthly sorrow, and lead the soul up to its best and highest sources.

Leaving nature for the material, beauty for booty, fancy for fact, I come to speak of the mineral wealth and development of this section of the Rocky Mountains. And, unless I deny the evidence of the senses, and the testimony of experience and knowledge, I must coincide in the inexhaustibleness of the one and the wonderfulness of the other. This whole vast range of mountains, that divides our Continent, seems indeed crowded with veins of rich mineral ore. They run into and through the hill-sides as the bars of a gridiron,—every hundred feet, every fifty feet, every twenty feet. There is no end to them in number; there is no apparent limit to their depth; one hundred feet, three hundred feet, and four hundred feet have the miners sunk shafts, and did we descend, but the veins of ore hold their course and their richness undiminished, oftenest enlarged.

The chiefest development of these mines in this territory lies along and up the Clear Creek, and centers around its sources some forty miles up and in the mountains west from Denver. Here, along the creek and some narrow gulches leading into it, within the space of five miles, is gathered a population of some six to seven thousand. The principal villages are Central City, Black Hawk and Nevada, holding rank in the order named. These are most uncomfortably squeezed into little narrow ravines, and stuck into the hill-sides, on streets the narrowest and most tortuous that I ever saw in America; some houses held up in dizzy hights on stilts, others burrowed into the stones of the hill, with a gold "lode" in the back yard, and often a well issuing from a rock of precious metals. But here these towns are, thriving, orderly, peaceable, busy, supporting two of them each its daily paper, with churches and schools, and all the best materials of government and society that the East can boast of. Down in the close valleys, and up the steep hill-sides to the very top, rise the mills for grinding out the gold, or the shanties that cover the shafts that lead down after the ore. Farther away, on the mountains, thick as ant-hills or prairie-dog-holes, and looking the same, are "lodes" or leads of mineral, discovered, dug into, pre-empted, but not worked—hundreds, thousands of them, with fortunes or failures involved in their development, ready to be tried when the discoverer gets time or money, or turned over to a Wall street stock company of five millions capital.

Forty or fifty miles below Denver, near what is called the South Park, a beautiful table-land of meadow and wood between Pike's Peak and the main range, is the second center of mineral development in Colorado territory; but this one upon Clear Creek is, as yet, the scene of largest improvement and population. Other sections of the territory are probably as rich in valuable ore; some are well believed to be much more so; no part of the mountains may be held wholly barren; it happens only that these localities were most attainable, and were first lit upon by the early comers. What is called gulch mining, or washing the sand and soft and pulverized rock of the valley, for the gold that ages of rains have filtered out of the solid rock of the mountains, is about over in Colorado—we see only now its abundant ruins in sluices, piles of worked over earth, and the rotting simple machinery sometimes used; yet in some of the fresher gulches, this work is still profitable; and we saw pan washings that turned out one, two and three dollars to the pan. I have a dollar's worth of gold dust that I saw washed out from about three quarts of earth, in less than ten minutes of time.

The chief attention now is given to the solid mining; but for various causes, principally from the high prices of labor and provisions, all mining here has been dull for nearly a year. Not more than twenty or twenty-five of the one hundred stamp mills in the territory are now at work. With labor and food from three to four times as high as at the East, growing mainly out of the interruption to communication by the Indians, and the inflation of the currency last year, and, the short supply of laborers because of the war, and with gold now reduced to nearly par, mining hardly pays expenses. When expenses get back, as they are soon likely to do, to the currency standard, the business will again become profitable, and be actively resumed. Preparations are fast making for this now, and mills and mines are being set in order, and resuming work.

Another reason of the dull times is that much of the best property has been changing hands, passing from the early or original owners and workers into joint stock companies, owned mainly in the East, which in some cases are not conducting the business so wisely as their predecessors, and in others are stopping for a better labor and supply market, or to enlarge and improve their works. Again, it is believed the mining interest is on the eve of great improvements in the processes of extracting the gold from its associate metals and sulphides, and owners of mines and mills are experimenting in this direction, or are content to wait for the results of others' experiments.

The common process of crushing the ore into fine powder, and then washing the same upon copper plates coated with quicksilver, which collects the disintegrated gold, or is supposed to, it is well ascertained gets but about twenty-five per cent. of all the precious metal. Three-quarters goes off in the "tailings," or refuse, as they are called. With such a waste, only the most valuable of the ore pays expenses at such times as these. Good ore yields about one hundred dollars in gold per cord, or twelve dollars per ton, under the stamping and quicksilver process. This leaves a fair margin under favorable management, for getting out the ore costs about forty dollars a cord, hauling five dollars, and crushing and extracting twenty dollars. Choice ores yield three hundred dollars a cord; but these are rare. The difficulty is not in separating the gold from the pure copper, iron or lead, or the quartz with which it is compacted; but the sulphurets of these metals, which suffuse and coat the whole, are the plague and mystery. These cover and hold the gold in a stern chemical lock, how to break which in a simple, effective way is the great study of the mineral chemists and mining capitalists. Various processes are on trial; one which we saw applies a hot flame and a brisk wind to all the pulverized ore, which changes its chemical character, burns up the sulphurets, and leaves the metals all free; then they are scoured, so as to brighten the gold, and then washed, as originally, in copper pans coated with quicksilver, which, better than any other article in these days of paper currency and forgotten coin, knows the gold when it sees it, and sticks to it with fraternal embrace. This process was getting twenty-five dollars a ton from the "tailings" or refuse of the old or common process, or twice as much as was originally obtained. Another process has obtained three hundred and seventy-five dollars from less than a ton of "tailings," which is probably many times what the original ore produced by the common stamping and washing. The object desired is to "desulphurize" the ore; both these inventions do this, though in different ways. When the thing is done, and this season can hardly pass until it is satisfactorily accomplished, we shall see the Colorado mines yielding from five hundred to eight hundred dollars per cord of ore, instead of from fifty to two hundred and fifty dollars as now. (A cord is rated at about eight tons, though different ores vary very much in weight.) This rate of production will at once put a new phase upon the business, afford almost any price for labor and supplies, redeem all the mining companies from whatever present embarrassments they feel, stimulate the investment of capital in these mines with great rapidity, and even, by generous dividends, go far to excuse that vicious system of putting up a mining company's stock to one, two, three and five millions, when the actual cash investment was not over as many hundreds of thousands.

This last habit of parties interested in the mining business has had a most fatal influence upon the whole interest; the small dividends upon large, many times watered capitals have erroneously represented the state of the business; and the suspicions and distrust, that the operation has surely scattered among outside capitalists, have hindered if not forbidden investments. Few or none of the companies now operating here have spent over two hundred and fifty thousand or three hundred thousand dollars for their mines, machinery and mills, yet their capitals are reckoned by millions; and of course in hard times like these they can afford no adequate, seductive dividends on such swollen sums. How much better it would be to have the shares in a half million company, worth twice the par value, and receiving dividends of twelve to fifty per cent., than with a nominal capital of two or three millions, the stock selling for seventy-five dollars per share, and receiving small dividends with doubt and irregularity, no honest, sensible man can fail to see. I meet no manager of a mine here, whether an old miner or an agent from the home capitalists, who does not condemn, as foolish in itself, a fraud upon the public, and a damage to the whole mining interest, this practice of making the nominal capitals from two to ten times the actual, in the generally vain hope of gulling the flats in Wall street or in New England country towns. This mining business of the West is too promising in real profit, too legitimate and necessary to the national wealth and development, to be trifled with in this weak and wretched way.

The gross production of the Colorado gold mines is not correctly known. The United States mint reports only ten millions in all up to July first of last year. This puts the Territory next to California in total product, ranking her above North Carolina or Georgia in all their history; but it gives her only a small proportion of the whole production of the nation from the beginning till now,—ten millions out of six hundred millions, California being accredited with all but about forty millions of the gross amount. Other authorities give Colorado's total production as over fifty millions, accrediting her with twenty millions in a single year (1864;) but these figures are certainly as far the other way. An intelligent authority here (General Pierce, the surveyor-general of the Territory,) gives me the following estimates: 1862, ten millions; 1863, eight millions; 1864, five millions. The falling off indicates nothing as to the real wealth of the mines, only changes in the business of producing, and the natural results of high prices. The year 1862 embraced successful gulch mining, and the first of the quartz mining, under most favorable circumstances, following a year (1861) of depression and non-production far more fruitful of croakers than 1864 and the first half of 1865 have been. Just now the new Territories of Idaho and Montana, in the far North, are drawing off the floating population, the gulch miners, and those eager for fortunes at a jump. The day of these is over here. Slow and sure is now the motto for Colorado, as for California. Her capacity is proven, admitted; capital, science, labor and machinery will return twenty-five, fifty and one hundred per cent. on their investments; but gold eagles are no longer picked up by the basketsfull, and hundred thousand dollar fortunes in a day or a month, are not to be had here,—but further on, if at all.

The reports from Idaho and Montana, particularly the latter, are indeed astonishing; the gulch mining, discovered and developing in Montana, is reliably reported to me as far richer than any ever realized in California or Colorado, paying steadily an ounce of gold (sixteen to eighteen dollars) a day to the man, and in some gulches two and three ounces a day. But these placers will soon be worked out; these Territories, like their predecessors, will speedily come down to the hard-pan, and have to pick and powder and stamp and melt out their gold from the solid mountains that hold the original deposits. Montana and Idaho, too, must hold out greater inducements at first, in order to secure their peopling and development, for the one is dependent on Oregon for supplies, and eight hundred miles away from a base at that; while Montana has to come this way for everything to eat and work with, and is at least one thousand six hundred miles away from railway and water communication.

All reports, all facts, whether floating in the air from mouth to mouth, or ground out by hard experience, and put down in black and white, go to sustain the broadest and fullest meaning of the dying statement of President Lincoln, that *the United States hold the treasury of the world;* and establish beyond reasonable doubt, that the countries of and adjacent to the Rocky Mountains are freighted with the most precious of ores—gold first, next silver, in which Nevada and Utah are most conspicuous, and Colorado not found wanting, and then copper (with which the Colorado mineral veins are richly loaded), and also lead, iron and coal. On the Plains, near the foot of the mountains, coal and iron are already found in abundant quantities, and are being mined and put to practical use. Found, too, just where they are most needed, to take the place of the wood, now fast being drained from the mountains, and furnish the material for the machinery necessary to work over the ore and make available the finer metals. Irrigation, already entered upon on a large scale, even here, will supply agriculture with its lacking; and through and by all these means combining, and worked with the energy and enterprise of the American people, stimulated by the great profits sure to be realized from wise and persevering use of the opportunities, the western half of the American nation will fast move forward in civilization and population; this wilderness will blossom as the rose, and the East and the West will stand alike equal and together, knowing no jealousy, and only rivaling each other in their zeal for knowledge, liberty and civilization." But of what effect upon the currencies and the values of the world will be all this tide of gold and silver pouring into the lap of nations? Will their commerce and populations grow in extent and want in equal proportions, and absorb what is to be so lavishly fed out to them? Perhaps so. But these promises of the American nation and these resulting queries are rich in thought and study.

LETTER V.

OF PERSONS, NOT THINGS.

DENVER, Colorado, June 3.

OUR week in Colorado is ended; we are off this morning for the seven days' stage ride north and west along the base of the Rocky Mountains, and through them at Bridger's Pass, to Salt Lake City, where we expect to worship with Brigham Young in his tabernacle on Sunday week. While here and in the adjacent mountains, Mr. Colfax has made half a dozen speeches, and redelivered his Chicago eulogy upon President Lincoln, the latter at the request of Governor Evans on the occasion of the national mourning (June 1st,) for the loss of our lamented chief magistrate. He has been received with distinguished honor, made a most favorable impression, and encouraged the miners and people of the Territory in many ways by his presence and his words. Their compliments to him ended last evening by a grand gala supper at the principal hotel in this town, in which the leading officials of the Territory, General Connor, and the ladies and gentlemen of the village to the number of over one hundred participated. Though the tickets were twelve dollars each, which is a fair specimen of prices this way, they were soon in earnest demand at an advance of three dollars. The entertainment proved a brilliant one in every respect; various and bountiful and elegant as a feast; graceful and gracefully rendered by both ladies and gentlemen as a compliment; and humorous, eloquent, interesting, and inspiring in its speeches. We go on in our journey with a rich sense of the hospitality and the kindness, the enterprise and the intellectual and social culture of the people of Colorado, both in its City of the Plains and its Cities of the Mountains. Never was progress in wealth, in social and political organization, in the refinements of American home life, more rapid and more marked than in the brief history thus far of Colorado. Soon she will enter the Union as a State, holding not only the elements but the acquired realities of a noble and proud one, and contributing largely, as she has steadily done even as a Territory, to the common profit of the nation. From the beginning, Colorado has always sent more gold to the East than she has brought back in goods; and she is destined to be permanently a profitable partner in the household.

Your readers may like to know more of my companions on this long journey before we go farther on. Let me introduce them. As a public man, everybody knows about Mr. Colfax; how prominent and useful he has been through six terms in Congress, and how, by virtue of his experience, ability and popularity, he has come to be Speaker, and stands before the country one of its best and most promising statesmen. But this is not all, nor the best of the man. He is not one of those, to whom distance lends enchantment; he grows near to you, as you get near to him; and it is, indeed, by his personal qualities of character, by his simplicity, frankness, genuine good nature, and entire devotedness to what he considers right, that he has principally gained and holds so large a place on the public arena. Mr. Colfax is short, say five feet six, weighs one hundred and forty, is young, say forty-two, has brownish hair and light blue eyes, is a childless widower, drinks no intoxicating liquors, smokes *a la* General Grant, is tough as a knot, was bred a printer and editor, but gave up the business for public life, and is the idol of South Bend and all adjacencies. There are no rough points about him; kindliness is the law of his nature;—while he is never backward in differing from others, nor in sustaining his views by arguments and by votes, he never is personally harsh in utterance, nor unkind in feeling, and he can have no enemies but those of politics, and most of these find it impossible to cherish any personal animosity to him. In tact, he is unbounded, and with him it is a gift of nature, not a studied art; and this is perhaps one of the chief secrets of his success in life. His industry is equally exhaustless; —he is always at work, reading, writing, talking, seeing, studying—I can't conceive of a single unprogressive, unimproved hour in all his life. He is not of brilliant or commanding intellect, not a genius, as we ordinarily apply these words; but the absence of this is more than compensated by these other qualities I have mentioned,—his great good sense, his quick, intuitive perception of truth, and his inflexible adherence to it, his high personal integrity, and his long and valuable training in the service of the people and the government. Without being, in the ordinary sense, one of the greatest of our public men, he is certainly one of the most useful, reliable and valuable; and in any capacity, even the highest, he is sure to serve the country faithfully and well. He is one of the men to be tenaciously kept in public life; and I have no doubt he will be. Some people talk of him for president; Mr. Lincoln used to tell him he would be his successor; but his own ambition is wisely tempered by the purpose to perform present duties well. He certainly makes friends more rapidly and holds them more closely than any public man I ever knew; wherever he goes, the women love him, and the men cordially respect him; and he is sure to be always a personal favorite, even a pet, with the people.

The other official of the party, Lieutenant-Governor Bross of Illinois, is indeed our *pater familias*, our "governor." Hale and hearty in body and mind; ripe with say fifty-five years and a wide experience and culture in school, college and journalism; cheery in temperament, enjoying rough, out-door life like a true, unspoiled child of Nature; sturdy in high principles; unaffected and simple in manners and feeling as a child; a ready and most popular stump speaker; enthusiastic for all novel experience, we all give him our heartiest sympathy and respect, and constitute him the leader of the party. Our best foot, we always put him foremost, whether danger, or dignity, or fun is the order of the occasion. Governor Bross was born in New Jersey,—and so says he never can be president, as the Constitution requires that officer to be a native of the nation; lumbered on the Susquehannah; went to Williams College, Massachusetts; taught school in Franklin and Berkshire counties; ditto and married in New York; and, following the star of empire, went to Chicago, and, entering on the editorial profession, has gone on from small to great things, until he is now the senior proprietor and editor of the leading journal of the North-west, and the second officer in the State government of Illinois.

Mr. Richardson of the New York Tribune has lived on the borders of Bohemia for many years, sometimes on one side, sometimes on the other, and presents all the contradictions of such an existence. Of eastern Massachusetts birth and early education, (with a brother who is the able conductor of the Boston Congregationalist) he learned while young to love the smell of the printing office and the romance of the reporter's life, and ran the round of editorial experience in nearly all our western cities; then was bitten by the passion for travel and border life; came out to Kansas for the Boston Journal; then to Colorado with Mr. Greeley, edited a newspaper out here during the early days of bowie knives and Colt's revolvers; crossed the Plains half a dozen times; went to Texas and New Mexico; and finally, as the war came on, after making a secret tour of the South as a special correspondent for the Tribune, became the head of the western and south-western army correspondents of that paper, and in undertaking to run the gauntlet of the rebel batteries at Vicksburg, when General Grant opened his final campaign in that quarter, was captured by the enemy;— as their pet and special prisoner he went the rounds of their jails and pens, and after twenty months' servitude made his escape, and in a wonderful journey of one month through the rebel country in winter, reached our lines in safety, and became a hero. Notwithstanding this long Bohemian life, amid rough people and in out-of-the-way places, Mr. Richardson imposes on you with the style and air of a man who has had a very narrow escape from the pulpit, and cherishes a natural hankering for it yet. Certainly you never would recognize in him a true child of Bohemia. He wears black broadcloth and "biled shirts," (the western phrase for white under-clothes,) does not chew tobacco, disdains whiskey, but drinks French brandy and Cincinnati Catawba, carries a good deal of baggage, does not know how to play poker, and shines brilliantly among the ladies. He is a young widower of less than thirty-five, of medium size, with a light complexion and sandy hair and whiskers, and is a very companionable man. His large and peculiar experience in the West and in the South by field and flood, gives him a rich store of anecdote and illustration, with which he entertains us on our long stage rides. He is already famous before the country; and his new book of experiences in the South will make him much more so. It is probable he will stay longer on the Pacific shore than the rest of the party, and perhaps revisit Utah, the Mining Regions and Mountains, with the view of making a book upon them another season.

Looking-glasses are banished from overland baggage, and the fourth member of the party must, therefore, remain unsketched. But there is a number five, who is occupying too important a share in our experience, to be forgotten in any call of the roll. This is Mr. George K. Otis of New York, the special agent and representative of our host, Mr. Holladay of the Overland Mail and Stage Line. He accompanies us in the capacity of guide, philosopher and friend, which he most generously fulfills. Himself, under Mr. Holladay, the organizer and manager of the stage line, he is acquainted with all this region and its people; and being a man of infinite jest and of free and generous nature, we lack nothing under his protecting care, which a thoughtful generosity, nor a practical experience, nor abounding humor and wide intelligence can give us. His puns are sometimes "fearfully and wonderfully made"; but he earns forgiveness by making himself a large share of our daily comfort and pleasure. Happy those who fall to the traveling companionship of Otis!

Accompanying so distinguished and popular a public officer as Mr. Colfax, we share mutually in the hospitalities extended to him; we have access to the most intelligent sources of information; we see and learn in a short time what ordinary private travelers could only gain by long and careful observation and examination. Everywhere, so far, the people of the towns visited are bountiful in their courtesies; the journey is one continued ovation; public receptions and entertainments, and the choicest of private hospitalities are showered upon us; and we find that neither the graces nor the culture of life are confined to the East. They flourish here among the Rocky Mountains as beautifully as in the parlors of Boston, or the sweet groves of the Connecticut valley.

Most agreeable of all our experiences here are the intelligent, active, earnest, right-minded and right-hearted young men and women we meet; people, many of whom have been here for years, but, instead of losing anything of those social graces that eastern towns and cities are wont to think themselves superior in, have not only kept even pace in these, but gained a higher play for all their faculties, and ripened, with opportunity and incentive and necessary self-reliance, into more of manhood and womanhood. Everywhere, too, I find old friends and acquaintances from the Connecticut valley; and nowhere do I find them forgetting old Massachusetts, or unworthy her parentage. I see less drunkenness; I see less vice here among these towns of the border, and of the Rocky Mountains, than at home in Springfield; I see personal activity and growth and self-reliance and social development and organization, that not only reconcile me to the emigration of our young people from the East to this region, but will do much to make me encourage it. To the right-minded, the West gives open opportunity that the East holds close and rare; and to such, opportunity is all that is wanted, all that they ask.

The great Overland Stage Line, by which we are traveling, was originated by Mr. William H. Russell of New York, and carried on for a year or two by himself and partners, under the name of Russell, Majors and Waddell. They failed, however, and some three years ago it passed into the hands of their chief creditor, Mr. Ben Holladay, an energetic Missourian, who had been a successful contractor for the government and for great corporations on the Plains and the Pacific. He has since continued the line, improving, extending and enlarging it until it is now, perhaps, the greatest enterprise owned and controlled by one man, which exists in the country, if not in the world. His line of stages commence at Atchison, on the Missouri River: its first section extends across the great Plains to Denver, six hundred and fifty miles; from here it goes on six hundred miles more to Salt Lake City, along the base of and through the Rocky Mountains at Bridger's Pass. From there to Nevada and California, about seven hundred and fifty miles farther, the stage line is owned by an eastern company, and is under the management of Wells, Fargo & Co., the express agents. All this is a daily line, and the coaches used are of the best stage pattern, well known in New England as the "Concord coach." From Salt Lake, Mr. Holladay runs a tri-weekly coach line north and west nine hundred and fifty miles through Idaho to the Dalles on the Columbia River in northern Oregon, and branching off at Fort Hall, also a tri-weekly line to Virginia City in Montana, four hundred miles more. From Denver, too, he has a subsidiary line into the mountain centers of Central City and Nevada, about forty miles. Over all these routes he carries the mail, and is in the receipt for this service of six hundred and fifty thousand dollars per annum from the government. His whole extent of staging and mail contracts—not counting, of course, that under Wells, Fargo & Co., from Salt Lake west,—is two thousand seven hundred and sixty miles, to conduct which he owns some six thousand horses and mules and about two hundred and sixty coaches. All along the routes he has built stations at distances of ten to fifteen miles; he has to draw all his corn from the Missouri River; much of his hay has also to be transported hundreds of miles; fuel for his stations comes frequently fifty and one hundred miles; the Indians last year destroyed or stole full half a million dollars' worth of his property,—barns, houses, animals, feed, &c.; he pays a general superintendent ten thousand dollars a year; division superintendents a quarter as much; drivers and stable-keepers get seventy-five dollars a month and their living; he has to mend and in some cases make his own roads—so that, large as the sum paid by the government, and high as the prices for passengers, there is an immense outlay, and a great risk in conducting the enterprise. During the last year of unusually enormous prices for everything, and extensive and repeated Indian raids, Mr. Holladay has probably lost money by his stages. The previous year was one of prosperity, and the next is likely to be. But with so immense a machine, exposed to so many chances and uncertainties, the returns must always be doubtful. Only a great man would assume such an enterprise; only a strong man could carry it through, over such obstacles as are constantly presented; and the regularity, the promptness and the uniform high state of the entire service, in general and particular, make of the whole a matter of real wonder, and an occasion of great credit to Mr. Holladay. It is very natural that he should be unpopular along his route, and be denounced as a monopolist, taking advantage of his monopoly to extort high prices and give small accommodations; this is the universal experience of such great enterprises in a new country. But it would be difficult, if not impossible, through these infant and struggling years of this country,—where travel and business of all kinds are uncertain and irregular, and prices fluctuating, and the risk of losses from Indians and robbers very great,—to discover here or elsewhere the man or the means for the performance of this great service so perfectly as Mr. Holladay does it; and I am inclined to reckon him high among the agencies that are so fast developing the great western Territories of the Republic, and to doubt if many others in the community are doing their share in the work more fairly to the public than he is. The passenger fares by his stages are now, from Atchison to Denver one hundred and seventy-five dollars, to Salt Lake three hundred and fifty dollars, to Nevada five hundred dollars, to California five hundred dollars, to Idaho five hundred dollars, to Montana five hundred dollars. These are much higher than they were two years ago, and will probably be reduced during the season, as safety from the Indians and lower prices for food and corn are assured, from thirty-three to fifty per cent.

Mr. Holladay now resides in New York City, and is reported to be immensely wealthy,—say five millions. He owns and runs, also, lines of steamships in the Pacific Ocean from San Francisco, north to Oregon and British Columbia, and south to Mazatlan, Mexico, with contracts for the mails on both routes from our government or from Maximilian of Mexico. He conducts all this immense business successfully by the choice of able and trusty managers to whom he pays large salaries. Mr. John E. Russell, formerly of Greenfield, Massachusetts, is his confidential secretary and financier at New York; Mr. George K. Otis is his special agent at Washington; Mr. William Reynolds, a life-long stage manager, dating his education as such back to Chester W. Chapin, Horatio Sargent and Frank Morgan in Springfield, but since with large experience in the South and California, is the general manager of the overland line, resident at Atchison; and his (Mr. Holladay's) brother resides at San Francisco in charge of his steamships. Mr. Holladay visits his overland line about twice a year, and when he does, passes over it with a rapidity and a disregard of expense and rules, characteristic of his irrepressible nature. A year or two ago, after the disaster to the steamer Golden Gate on the Pacific shore, by which the only partner he ever had, Mr. Edward Rust Flint, son of old Dr. Flint of Springfield, lost his life, and himself barely escaped a watery grave, he made the quickest trip overland that it is possible for one man to make before the distance is shortened by railway. He caused himself to be driven from Salt Lake to Atchison, twelve hundred and twenty miles, in six and one-half days, and was only twelve days and two hours from San Francisco to Atchison. The trip probably cost him twenty thousand dollars in wear and tear of coaches and injury to and loss of horses by the rapid driving. The only ride over the Plains, at all comparable with this, was that made by Mr. Aubrey, on a wager, from Santa Fe to Independence, seven hundred miles, in six and one-half days. But this was made on horseback, and when the rider reached his destination, he was so exhausted that he had to be lifted from his horse. How exciting the thought of such rides as these across these open fields and through these mountain gorges, that make up the half of our Continent!

LETTER VI.

A SUNDAY IN THE MOUNTAINS.

VIRGINIA DALE, Colorado, June 5.

THERE are no aristocratic distinctions between the days of the week west of the Missouri. The Broad Church rules here, and so broadly that even Saint Burleigh of your modern Florence would find hearty welcome, particularly from our red brethren, who would rate his scalp with its ornaments at the value of a dozen of the ordinary sort. Sundays are as good as other days, and no better. Stages run, stores are open, mines are dug, and stamp mills crush. But our eastern prejudices are not yet altogether conquered by the "spirit of the age;" and so, on reaching here yesterday morning at sunrise, we commanded a twenty-four hours' halt. Possibly our principles had a point put to them by learning from the down stage that Mr. "Lo, the poor Indian" had got loose up the line, stolen the horses, and interrupted communication. At any rate,—be the motive fear for our scalps or fear for our souls,—we followed the fashion of our forefathers, and slept through the day, some of us in the coach, the rest stretched out on the piazza of the only house in

Virginia Dale; clambering up a high rock in the evening to view the landscape o'er of valley, stream, snow-clad mountain, and far-distant plain, and closing out our observances with a more hearty than harmonious rendering of our small repertoire of psalm tunes.

Lodgings are not extensive in this locality; the Speaker borrowed a bed; two slept in the coach; and two of us rolled ourselves up in our blankets and took the floor. I hit upon a board whose hard side was accidentally put up; and what with this, and hungry and dry and noisy stage drivers coming in at from two to four A. M., and less vociferous but quite as hungry invaders of our bodily peace in the form of vermin, the night brought more of reflection than refection—to us. But we are off early this morning, having satisfied our Christian consciences, and learned that the Indians were certainly still one hundred and fifty miles away, but leaving behind for a Monday's rest a fresh stage load of eager gold seekers and Salt Lake merchants, whom our scruples on the subject of Sunday traveling had thrown one day behind. But they were solaced by the arguments that we would make the paths straight for them above, that they must stop somewhere, and that here was the best food and the prettiest cook on the line.

Virginia Dale deserves its pretty name. A pearly, lively-looking stream runs through a beautiful basin, of perhaps one hundred acres, among the mountains,—for we are within the embrace of the great hills,—stretching away in smooth and rising pasture to nooks and crannies of the wooded range; fronted by rock embattlement, and flanked by the snowy peaks themselves; warm with a June sun, and rare and pure with an air into which no fetid breath has poured itself,—it is difficult to imagine a more lovable spot in nature's kingdom. It is one hundred miles north from Denver, half of the way along the foot of the hills, crossing frequent streams, swollen and angry with the melting snows, and watering the only really green acres we have seen since leaving Kansas; and half the road winding over and around and between the hills that form the approaches to the Rocky Mountains. Only the station of the stage line occupies the Dale; a house, a barn, a blacksmith shop; the keeper and his wife, the latter as sweet, as genteel and as lady-like as if just transplanted from eastern society, yet preparing bountiful meals for twice daily stage-loads of hungry and dirty passengers; the stock-tender and his assistant,—these were all the inhabitants of the spot, and no neighbors within fifteen miles. For the day, our party and its escort,—the soldiers lying off on the grass by the water with their camp fire and their baggage wagon,—made unusual life, and gave a peculiar picturesqueness to the sequestered spot.

How women, especially, can live contentedly in these out-of-the-way places on the borders, working hard and constantly, among rough and selfish men, and preserve their tender femininity, keep themselves neatly and sometimes even gracefully dressed, and not forget their blushes under free compliments, would be passing strange, if we did not see it daily in our journey, and know it by the whole history of the sex. I certainly have seen young women out here, miles away from neighbors, knowing no society but their husbands and children and the hurried travelers,—depending on the mails for their chief knowledge of what the world is doing,—who could pass without apology or *gaucherie* to presiding over a Boston dinner party or receiving in state at Washington. Not all, indeed, are such, but they are frequent enough to be noted with both surprise and pleasure.

This is the northern border of Colorado. We pass to-day into Dacotah. Before parting with the former Territory, let me note a few facts about it and its people. Colorado has now not over twenty-five to thirty thousand population, which is five to ten thousand fewer than in 1860. The adventurers are gone. What remain are the substantial, the earnest, who have cast in their lot with the Territory, are satisfied with its promise, and are wisely working for the construction of a State and their own estate. A very large proportion are men who came here four, five and six years ago, and have a reason for the faith that is in them. Last year, a movement to become a State failed, mainly because of the unpopularity of the men prominent in it, and candidates for its principal offices. It will be renewed this year, under more favorable and promising auspices. The population is too small, indeed, for a State; but there are advantages in it, and necessities, almost, for it, that justify both the people in seeking and the general government in recognizing the change. The Territory has great interests, national indeed in character, needing more vigorous interpretation and espousal at Washington than can be secured by a delegate. The population is compact and enterprising and ambitious; willing to assume the burdens of a government for themselves; and appreciating the advantages they will get from it.

One especial motive with the Coloradians for making a State government is to get a judiciary of their own, that shall be both more intelligent and independent than that furnished by the Washington authorities. The men sent out to these new Territories as judges are not apt to be of a very high order either of morals or intellect. They are often hungry adventurers; and their salaries bearing generally no comparison to the cost of living in these remote regions, and large pecuniary interests often being involved in the questions brought before them,—as is especially the case in the mining Territories,—they are too apt to yield to the temptations offered to them, and sell their judgments for a price. However this may be in Colorado's recent experience, her best citizens are convinced that they can get a higher morality, a stricter justice, and a more intelligent law from judges of their own selection and paying, than from those sent out here and paid by "Uncle Sam."

A case has just occurred in the mining districts, not illustrating, as I know of, the venality of the federal judiciary, but calculated, at least, to bring it into contempt. General Fitz John Porter, famous as General McClellan's pet, and notorious as having loved his patron and his spite against General Pope, better than his country and her service, is out here as superintendent of some mines. He claimed a vein, that belonged to Smith & Parmalee, as the latter thought, and began working it. The other party resisted; Judge Harding sustained Porter by an injunction against Smith & Parmalee; but whenever Porter's men undertook to work in the vein, they found it filled with such sulphurous and offensive smoke that they could not stay in it, and had to come out. How the smoke came there, no one could tell; but, as the vein connected with the Smith & Parmalee mine, everybody could guess. Thereupon Smith & Parmalee were brought before Judge Harding on alleged "contempt of court," for smoking out the party of the other part: nothing could be proven against them, however; but the most learned judge decided that the defendants had not *disproven* the alleged contempt, and so held them in five thousand dollars bail! The judicious grieved, the unskillful laughed, and everybody said there could be no contempt too great for such a court as that. This Judge Harding is from Indiana, and was first sent by Mr. Lincoln to be Governor of Utah, but becoming offensive and ineffective there, he was recalled, and given this judgeship to break his fall. But beside a broken character as a public officer, he brought hither such scandalous, Mormon ways of living, as to shock all shades of public opinion, which is now uniting to drive him out of the Territory.

As the great need of the business men and miners in Colorado is male laborers, so that of the housekeepers is female laborers or "help." Housekeeping in large families—and children do accumulate surprisingly here—is a very serious burden to the wives and mothers. Their eastern sisters, in their direst woes with poor servants, can have but faint appreciation of the burdens of living and entertaining here, where cooks and waiting girls are not to be had at any price. We go to rich dinners and bountiful teas at the homes of distinguished and wealthy citizens, and sit and eat without the company of hostess or any other ladies. She and her friends are busy in the kitchen, and come out only to stand behind our chairs, and change the plates and pass the viands. There is an uncomfortable feeling in being thus entertained; but it is the necessity of the country, and all parties make the best of it. The price of the commonest of female labor is two dollars a day and board. But the Colorado ladies have their compensations; their husbands complain that they can get no goods, no machinery out from the States under a year from the time of ordering—that all business, all progress must wait this long delay; yet the ladies shine in the latest fashions of millinery and dressmaking. Modes that were but just budding when I left home, I find in full blossom here. How it is done I do not understand—there must be a subtle telegraph by crinoline wires; as the southern negroes have what they call a grape-vine telegraph.

The burden laid upon all agriculture, the absolute

want of all horticulture as yet in all this country, are among its serious drawbacks. The winds, the sun, the porous yet unfriable soil, the long seasons of no or inadequate rain, leave all vegetation gray and scanty, except it is in direct communication with the water-courses. Trees will not live in the house yards; house owners can have no turf, no flowers, no fruits, no vegetables—the space around the dwellings in the towns is a bare sand, relieved only by infrequent mosses and weeds. The grass is gray upon the plains; cotton-wood and sappy pine are almost alone the trees of the mountain region; no hard wood is to be found anywhere; and but for the occasional oases by the streams, and the rich flowers that will spring up on the high mountain morasses, the country would seem to the traveler nearly barren of vegetable life. But what there is is rich in quality; the coarse and gray bunch grass of plain and prairie, of hill-side and rocks, affords the best of nutriment for horses, cattle and sheep; they grow fat fast upon it in summer, and exist upon it in winter. Even here, where, in June we see snow on the hill-sides close to us, and shiver under double blankets at night, the cattle live out of doors through the long winter. It is, indeed, a rich grazing country, and will support its herds of thousands.

Irrigation is a necessity for all extensive cultivation of the soil, however; and the extent to which this is already being employed, and the amount of money invested in it, are occasions of surprise. But with the far distance of all competing production, and the great fertility of the soil when thus developed, it will richly pay to carry water from the mountain streams miles on miles from their natural courses, and spread it by little artificial rivulets over acres on acres of grains, potatoes and the other vegetables. A plan is in progress of execution for bringing a large water-course some fifteen miles around Denver, and letting it out in gentle, fructifying streams all over the town and its adjacent farms and gardens. Then will this now barren wilderness of store and house and sand blossom like the rose; then can door-yards be green with grass, shaded with trees, and beautiful with flowers. Meantime, the people must live on canned fruits and vegetables from the East; and possess their esthetic souls in patience, for the rest, in magnifying their mountain view of charming yet constant beauty. The extensive and common use of these imported productions of our eastern orchards and gardens in all the country west of the Missouri River, is most astonishing. They are on every table; few New England housekeepers present such a variety of excellent vegetables and fruits, as we find everywhere here, at every hotel and station meal, and at every private dinner or supper. Corn, tomatoes, beans, pine apples, strawberry, cherry and peach, with oysters and lobsters, are the most common; and all of these, in some form or other, you may frequently find served up at a single meal. These canned vegetables and fruits and fish are sold, too, at prices which seem cheap compared with the cost of other things out here. They range from fifty cents to one dollar a can of about two quarts. Families buy them in cases of two dozen each at twelve to fifteen dollars a case; while away up in Montana, they are sold at only twenty-seven dollars a case.

Colorado has four daily and four weekly papers, two each at Denver, and one each at Black Hawk and Central City, in the mining region; and though their circulation is small—some five to seven hundred each—the large prices they get for subscriptions, for advertising and for printing, serve to support them all liberally. Let me close with the current Colorado rates of staples and luxuries: Flour twenty cents a pound, meal twenty-three cents, hams fifty cents, lard forty cents, syrup five dollars per gallon, cheese seventy-five cents, coffee seventy-five cents, brown sugar forty-five cents, butter sixty cents, milk fifty cents per quart, best cigars fifty cents each, printing paper sixty-eight cents per pound, daily paper, per year, twenty-four dollars, weekly seven dollars, brooms one dollar, molasses four dollars and a half per gallon, boots fourteen dollars per pair, common labor, per day, five dollars. And here are some of the latest Montana prices, twelve hundred miles farther on: Flour fifty to sixty cents a pound, hams seventy-five cents, golden syrup eight dollars, cheese one dollar, crackers ninety cents, beans fifty cents, wood twelve to fifteen dollars per cord, lumber one hundred dollars per thousand. The high price and terrible quality of whisky and other liquors in all these distant Territories are operating as a very effective temperance agent. I see very little of them or of their effects anywhere.

Some of the vernacular of the mountains is sufficiently original and amusing to be reported, also. A "square" meal is the common term for a first rate one; "shebang" means any kind of an establishment, store, house, shop, shanty; "outfit" has a wider range, your handkerchief, your suit of clothes, the cut of your hair, your team, your whole possessions, or the most infinitesimal part or item thereof; and "affidavit" signifies anything else that these other terms do not cover.

LETTER VII.[1]
FROM DENVER TO SALT LAKE—THROUGH THE ROCKY MOUNTAINS.

SALT LAKE CITY, June 12.

WE finished early yesterday (Sunday) morning the second and severest third of the great stage-ride across the Continent. We are now two-thirds the way to California, and the rest of the journey seems easy compared to what has been passed over. It is through a more peopled country, freer from Indian raids, and will be relieved to us by more frequent resting-places. The distance from Denver to Salt Lake City is six hundred miles; we should have driven it in five days but for the Indians, who broke in upon the line before us and cleaned it out of horses for fifty miles, threw the country into confusion and travel into anxiety, and delayed our progress for two or three days, so that we were in all seven days in the trip. But we just escaped more severe possible disaster; for the "pesky sarpints," as they are not unnaturally reckoned by everybody in the West, hovered close upon both our front and our rear; our escort drove off a band of them who were attacking a train of repentant and returning Mormons, right in our path; and they swooped in upon a stage station the night after we passed it, stole all its horses, killed the two stock-tenders, also three of the five soldiers who were located there as guard, and severely if not mortally wounded the other two. But though our escort was small over this line, never over ten cavalrymen, and sometimes none at all, our coach came through unmolested.

Whether these fresh Indian inroads in this quarter presage a general Indian war, are by pretended friendly tribes or those known to be inimical, are mainly for getting supplies of horses, which has seemed to be the principal object, or inspired by general hate and bloodthirstiness, or, so far as they have fallen upon the "Josephites" or deserting Mormons, have been directed by some of the leaders of the Latter Day Saints here to put a stop to this sort of depletion of their power and population; whether they are by petty straggling bands, led by desperate white robbers, or are the advance couriers of all the warlike tribes of the Plains and the Mountains,—there is only one course to be pursued with regard to them, and that General Connor is now doing with new energy. He will guard and patrol the whole main overland road, as he has been doing the lower part of it, with cavalrymen and infantry, and give an escort to every stage; from the military posts, every one hundred to two hundred miles along the route, he will send out scouting parties to track up the marauders; if the raids and murders can be traced to friendly tribes, as has been done in one or two cases, he will demand those engaged in it, and failing to get them will seize and hang some of the principal chiefs;—he will retaliate quickly and sharply; and then, with a large force, now gathering at Fort Laramie, he will go in pursuit of the great body of the hostile Indians in the North, and inflict upon them a sharp punishment;—and so conveying to them all the knowledge of our power and purpose to make them peaceable, do the best and only thing to secure their friendliness. The government is ready to assist in their support, to grant them reservations, to give them food and make them presents; but it must and will, with sharp hand, enforce their respect to travel, their respect to lives and property, and their respect to trade throughout all this region.

And if this cannot be secured, short of their utter extermination, why extermination it must be. Else, we may as well abandon this whole region; give up its settlement, its subjugation to civilization, its development to wealth and Christianity. It is the old eternal contest between barbarism and civilization, between things as they have been and are, and material and moral progress; and barbarism and barbarity must go to the wall, somewhat too roughly perhaps, as is always the case with new, earnest, material communities, but yet certainly. The Mormons have exhausted the Quaker policy towards the Indians; have fed and clothed them for years, paying them in all ways heavy subsidies, in consideration of being let alone; but they are growing tired of it, both because it is expensive, and is not sure of success. Only a few days ago, some Indians attacked the Mormons at a settlement about eighty miles south of here, and killed eighteen or twenty persons. Brigham Young and other officials of Church and State went down to investigate the matter and restore peace; they have just come back, reporting success, and laying part of the blame on the whites, but still with less of the old disposition to subsidize the barbarians.

Montana is disturbed with reports of Indian outrages; this whole region of mountains and plains is sensitive and suffering with the apprehensions or the realities of their general recurrence; commerce suffers; prices go up; emigration stops; and all the development of the great West is clogged. No wonder is it, then, that the entire white population of the Territories clamors for positive measures of restraint and punishment. The red man of reality is not the red man of poetry, romance, or philanthropy. He is false and barbaric, cunning and cowardly, attacking only when all advantage is with him, horrible in cruelty, the terror of women and children, impenetrable to nearly every motive but fear, impossible to regenerate and civilize. The whites may often be unjust and cruel in turn; but the balance is far against the Indian; and the country must sustain the government and General Connor in pursuing a vigorous offensive and defensive policy towards him.

Do not suppose, however, we lost sleep or rations, or eyes for passing scenery, as we rolled over the mountains, and passed the divide between the great oceans of America. We rested proudly on our own prowess and the rifles of our escort. We had immense faith in the double-barreled shot-gun of Governor Bross; and we created terrible alarm among some emigrants in our rear by firing at a mark in our front. So we ate our antelope, when we could get it, and our "mountain chicken" (fried bacon) regularly, with faith in its undisturbed digestion, and cuddled up each in his corner at night for equally reliable sleep. The canned fruits and vegetables and clean table-cloths disappeared for a time after Virginia Dale, but the antelope came in to soften the fall; one of our escort shot one of the bounding beauties as he stopped, five hundred yards away, to gaze through his limpid, liquid eyes in wonder on our turn-out; and we found him and his successors most luscious eating—very delicate deer, tender, melting and digestible.

The antelopes weigh from sixty to eighty pounds, are fawn-like in color and appearance, have short, branching horns, and are plenty at all seasons upon the high plains and in the mountains of the region. The elk, as large as a small cow, and with horns four to six feet long, and the black-tailed deer are rarer game; this is not the season for shooting them; and they cling closer to the mountains. Of fish we had but few; trout were as abundant as fever and ague in Indiana, but always a little way off, at the next brook or station. The soldiers at Fort Halleck had just made captive a cinnamon bear, which strayed down into camp from an adjoining mountain; and our stage gave a wide berth to a grizzly bear, which was taking his midnight nap in the middle of the road. The grizzly was the only animal that our courage and our double-barreled shot-gun were not equal to; and he is, indeed, next to the Indian, the terror of all hunters. We missed, too, the sage hen, a favorite game of the region, but not of the season; rabbits scented our approach and scooted away out of shot; the retreat of the hungry, thievy-looking wolf was hastened by our balls; only the ridiculous little prairie dogs and the funnier and littler squirrels—beautifully striped with black, and hardly bigger than a mouse—sported carelessly in our warlike presence.

The scant, coarse vegetation of the Plains and of Denver's neighborhood grew green and rich in our memory, as we came on north and west from Virginia Dale, entered the Laramie Plains, passed along on the snow line, crossed the mountain range at Bridger's Pass, and went out upon the country of the Bitter Creek. The Desert of the Mountains is far drearier and more barren than the Desert of the Plains. That seems redeemable and has its uses; this is only for trying the patience and taxing the ingenuity of man. There is very little to redeem the middle two hundred miles of our ride from utter worthlessness for human service. The soil is sand, so saturated with alkali as to poison its water, and to give the earth the appearance, in spots, sometimes for large areas, of a fresh hoar frost or a slight snow. Grass is only a spasmodic tuft. The sage bush is the chief, almost only vegetation— a coarse, wild form of our garden sage, growing rugged and rough from one to three feet high; yet mules and cattle sometimes will eat it because they must or die, and it does make quick, hot fire for the emigrants' and wagon-drivers' kettles—but think of savoring your food with soap and sage tea; think of putting a soap factory and an apothecary shop into one room, and that your kitchen! Through all this inhospitable, barren region, there are no buildings save the stage stations; no inhabitants but the stock-tender and the station-keeper; an occasional tented wigwam of half-breed or father of half-breeds stands by a stream: we pass with pity the emigrant's slow wagon and the mule train—hot and dusty and parched by day, cold and shivering and parched by night;—it is a wonder how people can go alive through this country at the rate of only twelve and fifteen miles a day, and finding food and drink as they go. But they do, year by year, thousands by thousands. Shall the Indian still add to the horrors of the passage, as he has and does?

The road, too, grows rough; sluices and gulches are frequent and deep; rocks begin to abound; and the stage staggers about in a way frightful to all exposed parts of the body. Yet we do not seem to be going over the highest range of mountains in the country; we are passing rather through hardly perceptible rising valleys; and though the mountains that guard us on either side grow nearer and lower to us, they always seem to be above us rather than under us. Striking the North Platte, as it first comes out of the mountains, but rough and rapid as are all the streams of the mountains at this season of melting snow, and some thousand miles from where we parted company with it at Julesburg on the Plains, to follow its southern sister to Denver; we enter upon the night ride through Bridger's Pass, from the Atlantic to the Pacific slopes of the Rocky Mountains. You need to be told what you are doing. There is no slow hill-climbing; the horses trot the stage along; and the soldier escort gallop behind. Not through valleys still, but apparently along and up the beds of departed rivers, with mountain walls on either hand,—sometimes ten or twenty miles wide, and again narrowing to rods, but oftenest miles in width; on one side bare, perpendicular walls of rock, thrown into all imaginable and unscientific combinations of the original or sub-original formations, and since carved and fluted by wind and sand and rain into all and every shape that architecture ever created, or imagination fancied; on the other, rounded hill-side with scant verdure and occasional stunted tree and frequent snow-bank. Not in one continuous bed or valley, was our upward course, but a succession of such, leading one into another.

So we rode on through the clear twilight, that lingers till nine and ten o'clock in this region, into the rich moonlight that only gave new form and beauty to the rocks, and out into the morning dawn that hastens on at two to three; watching the water to see which way it ran, and building Pacific Railroads along these easy grades back to home and forward to fame and fortune. I was in the saddle, galloping with the captain of the escort; but the earlier and more enthusiastic lieutenant-governor of Illinois, who kept guard with the driver on the box, shouted out the passage over the line—it was no more than a "thank-ye-marm" in a New England's winter sleigh-ride, yet it separates the various and vast waters of a Continent, and marks the fountains of the two great oceans of the globe. But it was difficult to be long enthusiastic over this infinitesimal point of mud; the night was very cold, and I was sore in unpoetical parts from unaccustomed saddles, and I got down from all my high horses, and into my corner of the stage, at the next station.

The effect of the high winds and blowing sands and sharp rains of this region upon the soft rock and clay of some of these hills, is certainly very curious. These agencies have proved wonderful miracle-workers. Wind-augers Mr. Fitzhugh Ludlow called them, I believe; but some of his stories as to their performances are purely imaginative, and only excite ridicule among the mountaineers. But the tall, isolated rocks, that surmount a hill, sometimes round, but always even and smooth as work of finest chisel; the immense columns and fantastic figures upon the walls of rock that line a valley for miles; the solitary mountains upon the plain, fashioned like fortresses, or rising like Gothic cathedral, and called *buttes* (a French word signifying isolated hill or mountain), separated from their family in some great convulsion of nature; the long lines of rock embankment, one above another, formed sometimes into squares like a vast fort, and again running along for miles, a hundred feet above the valley, looking like the most perfect of railroad embankment, with the open space occasionally for a water course;—these and kindred original fashions of nature, with details indescribable and picturesque, constitute the sole redeeming feature for scenery of the country I have been describing, and are a constant excitement and inspiration to the traveler.

One of the most curious single specimens of this natural architecture, that we passed on our road down the Pacific slope, is called "The Church Butte," and is familiar to all overland travelers. At a distance, it looms up on the level plain, a huge, ill-shapen hill; near by, it appears the most marvelous counterfeit of a half-ruined, gigantic, old-world Gothic cathedral, that can be imagined. We stopped before it just as the sun had gone down in the west, and as the full moon came up the eastern horizon, and the soft, contrasting lights, deepening slowly into shadowy dimness, gave exquisite development to the manifold shapes and the beautiful and picturesque outlines, that rock and clay had assumed. The Milan or the Cologne cathedral, worn with centuries, ill-shapen with irregular decay, could not have looked more the things they are or would be, than this did. Everything belonging to the idea was there in some degree of preservation. Porch, nave, transept, steeple, caryatides, monster animals, saints and apostles, with broken columns, tumbled roof, departed nose or foot, worn and crumbling features, were all in their places, or a little out, but recognizable and nameable. We walked around this vast natural cathedral of sandstone and clay—a full half mile—and greater grew our wonder, our enthusiasm. The hour and the light were certainly propitious; but viewed under any light, it is certainly one of the great natural wonders of the Continent, and is chief among three or four things that have already abundantly repaid me for this long journey.

Flowing out from the Butte on all sides was a thick solid stream of fine stone and clay, that told how the work was done, how it was going on still, refining, pointing, carving, chiseling, but gradually and surely leveling, as all mountains, the world over, are being leveled, and the whole surface of the globe made one vast plain. The share which the high winds and the sand they take up and blow with powerful force in right lines, and in curves, and in whirls, have in this great work, both in its fantasies and in its destruction, is such as can hardly be realized by those who have not experienced or witnessed them. Sand showers or sand whirlpools are of almost daily occurrence. They load the atmosphere with sand; they carry it everywhere; among rocks, into houses, through walls, into the bodies of everything animate and inanimate, and there keep it at its work of destruction and reconstruction. There is a window among the mountains of Colorado that a single storm of this sort has changed from common glass into the most perfect of ground glass; and the fantastic architecture of its creation among the rocks of the country, from the North Platte to Fort Bridger, can only be understood and appreciated by being seen.

As we approached Fort Bridger, the country grew fairer—sage bush gave way to grass; the streams became purer; timber lined the water courses; and the land became bearable indeed. Fort Bridger is an old and pleasantly located post; a fresh river runs through the camp yard; the valley looks sweet and green in June; and back rise the always beautiful and always snow-covered mountains. Here we stopped, had kind greeting at two o'clock in the morning, went to bed for the first time in a week, and after a sumptuous breakfast with Judge Carter, the merchant and magistrate of the precinct, passed on and over into the basin of the Great Salt Lake. But that day's ride, and our reception and experiences among the Mormons must wait another letter.

We remain here for a full week. The grass is too green; the trees too new to our eyes; the roses too red and refreshing; the strawberries and green peas too tempting to our carnal appetites; the curious social and wonderful material developments of this city and Territory too rare and remarkable; and the hospitality of the people, Mormon and Gentile, too generous and inviting, to permit us to leave hurriedly.

LETTER VIII.

THE WAY INTO UTAH: RECEPTION BY THE MORMONS.

GREAT SALT LAKE CITY, Utah, June 14.

LEAVING Fort Bridger for our last day's ride hither, we leave the first Pacific slopes and table-lands of the Rocky Mountains, drained to the south for the Colorado River and to the north for the Columbia, and go over the rim of the basin of the Great Salt Lake, and enter that Continent within a Continent, with its own miniature salt sea, and its independent chain of mountains, and distinct river courses; marked wonderfully by nature, and marked now as wonderfully in the history of civilization by its people, their social and religious organization, and their material development. This is Utah—these the Mormons. I do not marvel that they think they are a chosen people; that they have been blessed of God not only in the selection of their home, which consists of the richest region, in all the elements of a State, between the Mississippi valley and the Pacific shore, but in the great success that has attended their labors, and developed here the most independent and self-sustaining industry that the western half of our Continent witnesses. Surely great worldly wisdom has presided over their settlement and organization; there have been tact and statesmanship in the leaders; there have been industry, frugality and integrity in the people; or one could not witness such progress, such wealth, such varied triumphs of industry and ingenuity and endurance, as here present themselves.

We enter Utah over and among a new series of hills, the belongings of the Wasatch Mountains, the first of the subsidiary ranges of the Rocky Mountains, and the eastern guard and parent of the Salt Lake valley. We have our finest day's ride yet along the crests of hills eight thousand feet high, and through valleys and gorges guarded by perpendicular walls of rock, all rich with a spring verdure that is fresh and grateful to our eyes. . We play at snow ball from the large white drifts that lie along our road; and we pick abundant flowers at the same time. These spring up quickly with the grass, watered by melting snow, and inspired by the sun's hot heat; for twice hot it is compared with our eastern sun, in these high western regions. Some are new to mine eyes; many wear familiar faces, though greatly modified by change of soil and climate; and above all other colors, the yellow predominates. Did you ever think this the favorite color of nature? What other clothes your meadows and these hills with buttercups and dandelions till green is out-borne by yellow? What other has more varieties of plants in its list—more shades in its blossoming? Here I find new ones; among others little sun flowers, a foot high, three or four blossoms to a plant, and plants as thick as plantains by the pasture path. Let us treat yellow, then, with more respect, since it is nature's chosen; and learn, as we may, what variety and range of beauty there is in its shades.

So we rolled rapidly through summer and winter scenes, with sky of blue and air of amber purity, and when the round moon came up out from the snowy peaks, giving indescribable richness and softness to their whiteness, we kept on and on, now up mountain sides, now along the edge of precipices several hundred feet high, down which the stumble of a horse or the error of a wheel would have plunged us; now crossing swollen streams, the water up to the coach doors, now stammering through morass and mire, plunging down and bounding up so that we passengers, instead of sleeping, were bruising heads and tangling legs and arms in enacting the tragedy of pop-corn over a hot fire and in a closed dish; and now from up among the clouds and snow, we tore down a narrow canyon at a breakneck rate, escaping a hundred over-turns and toppling on the river's brink until the head swam with dizzy apprehensions. Most picturesque of all the scenes of this day and night ride was the passage through Echo Canyon, a very miniature Rhine valley in all but vines and storied ruin. The only ruins in it were those of feeble fortifications which the Mormons set up when President Buchanan marched his army against them, but halted and went away without attack, leaving stores of provisions, wagons and ammunition, and a contempt for the government, neither of which the Mormons have quite exhausted yet. Early "sun-up" brought us to the last station, kept by a Mormon bishop with four wives, who gave us bitters and breakfast, the latter with green peas and strawberries, and then, leaving wife number one at his home, went on with us into the city for parochial visits to the other three, who are located at convenient distances around the Territory.

Finally we came out upon the plateau or "bench," as they call it here, that overlooks the valley of the Jordan, the valley alike of Utah Lake and the Great Salt Lake, and the valley of the intermediate Great Salt Lake City. It is a scene of rare natural beauty. To the right, upon the plateau, lay Camp Douglas, the home of the soldiers and a village in itself, holding guard over the town, and within easy cannon range of tabernacle and tithing-house; right beneath, in an angle of the plain, which stretched south to Utah Lake and west to the Salt Lake—"and Jordan rolled between,"—was the city, regularly and handsomely laid out, with many fine buildings, and filled with thick gardens of trees and flowers, that gave it a fairy-land aspect; beyond and across, the plain spread out five to ten miles in width, with scattered farm-houses and herds of cattle; below, it was lost in dim distance; above, it gave way, twenty miles off, to the line of light that marked the beginning of Salt Lake—the whole flat as a floor and sparkling with river and irrigating canals, and overlooked on both sides by hills that mounted to the snow line, and out from which flowed the fatness of water and soil that makes this once desert valley blossom under the hand of industry with every variety of verdure, every product of almost every clime.

No internal city of the Continent lies in such a field of beauty, unites such rich and rare elements of nature's formations, holds such guarantees of greatness, material and social, in the good time coming of our Pacific development. I met all along the Plains and over the mountains, the feeling that Salt Lake was to be the great central city of this West; I found the map, with Montana, Idaho, and Oregon on the north, Dacotah and Colorado on the east, Nevada and California on the west, Arizona on the south, and a near connection with the sea by the Colorado River in the latter direction, suggested the same: I recognized it in the Sabbath morning picture of its location and possessions; I am convinced of it as I see more and more of its opportunities, its developed industries, and its unimproved possessions.

Mr. Colfax's reception in Utah was excessive if not oppressive. There was an element of rivalry between Mormon and Gentile in it, adding earnestness and energy to enthusiasm and hospitality. First "a troop cometh," with band of music, and marched us slowly and dustily through their Camp Douglas. Then, escaping these, our coach was waylaid as it went down the hill by the Mormon authorities of the city. They ordered us to dismount; we were individually introduced to each of twenty of them; we received a long speech; we made a long one—standing in the hot sand with a sun of forty thousand lens-power concentrated upon us, tired and dirty, with a week's coach-ride: was it wonder that the mildest of tempers rebelled?— transferred to other carriages, our hosts drove us through the city to the hotel; and then—bless their Mormon hearts—they took us at once to a hot sulphur bath, that nature liberally offers just on the confines of the city, and there we washed out all remembrance of the morning suffering and all the accumulated grime and fatigue of the journey, and came out baptized in freshness and self-respect. Clean clothes, dinner, the Mormon tabernacle in the afternoon, and a Congregational ("Gentile") meeting and sermon in the evening, were the other proceedings of our first day in Utah.

Since, and still continuing, Mr. Colfax and his friends have been the recipients of a generous and thoughtful hospitality. They are the guests of the city; but the military authorities and citizens vie together as well to please their visitors and make them pleased with Utah and its people. The Mormons are eager to prove their loyalty to the government, their sympathy with its bereavement, their joy in its final triumph—which their silence or their slants and sneers heretofore had certainly put in some doubt—and they leave nothing unsaid or undone now, towards Mr. Colfax as the representative of that government, or towards the public, to give assurance of their rightmindedness. Also they wish us to know that they are not monsters and murderers, but men of intelligence, virtue, good manners and fine tastes. They put their polygamy on high moral and religious grounds; and for the rest, anyhow, are not willing to be thought otherwise than our peers. And certainly we do find here a great deal of true and good human nature and social culture; a great deal of business intelligence and activity; a great deal of generous hospitality—besides most excellent strawberries and green peas, and the most promising orchards of apricots, peaches, plums and apples that these eyes ever beheld anywhere. They have given us a serenade; and Mr. Colfax has addressed them at length with his usual tact and happy effect, telling them what they have a right to expect from the government, and reminding them that the government has the right to demand from them, in turn, loyalty to the Constitution and obedience to the laws, and complimenting them on all the beauty of their homes and the thrift of their industry. Governor Bross and Mr. Richardson also made happy addresses, and the crowd of the evening, and the "distinguished guests" gave every sign of being mutually pleased with each other.

We have been taken on an excursion to the Great Salt Lake, bathed in its wonderful waters, on which you float like a cork, sailed on its surface, and picnicked by its shore,—if picnic can be without women for sentiment and to spread table-cloth, and to be helped up and over rocks. Can you New Englanders fancy a "stag" picnic? We have been turned loose in the big strawberry patch of one of the saints—very worldly strawberries and more worldly appetites met and mingled; and we have had a peep into a moderate Mormon harem, but being introduced to two different women of the same name, one after another, was more than I could stand without blushing.

In Mormon etiquette, President Brigham Young is called upon; by Washington fashion, the Speaker is also called upon, and does not call—there was a question whether the distinguished resident and the distinguished visitor would meet; Mr. Colfax, as was meet under the situation of affairs here, made a point upon it, and gave notice he should not call; whereupon President Brigham yielded the question, and graciously came to-day with a crowd of high dignitaries of the church, and made, not one of Emerson's prescribed ten minute calls, but a generous, pleasant, gossiping sitting of two hours long. He is a very hale and hearty looking man, young for sixty-four, with a light gray eye, cold and uncertain, a mouth and chin betraying a great and determined will—handsome perhaps as to presence and features, but repellent in atmosphere and without magnetism. In conversation, he is cool and quiet in manner, but suggestive in expression; has strong and original ideas, but uses bad grammar. He was rather formal, but courteous, and at the last affected frankness and freedom, if he felt it not. To his followers, I observed he was master of that profound art of eastern politicians, which consists in putting the arm affectionately around them, and tenderly inquiring for health of selves and families;

and when his eye did sparkle and his lips soften, it was with most cheering, though not warming, effect—it was pleasant but did not melt you.

Of his companions, Heber C. Kimball is perhaps the most notorious from his vulgar and coarse speech. He ranks high among the "prophets" here, and is as unctuous in his manner as Macassar hair oil, and as pious in phrase as good old Thomas a Kempis. He has a very keen, sharp eye, and looks like a Westfield man I always meet at the agricultural fairs in Springfield. Dr. Bernhisel has an air of culture and refinement peculiar among his associates; he is an old, small man, venerable, and suggestive of John Quincy Adams, or Dr. Gannett of Boston, in his style. Two or three others of the company have fine faces—such as you would meet in intellectual or business society in Boston or New York,—but the strength of most of the party seems to lie in narrowness, bigotry, obstinacy. They look as if they had lived on the same farms as their fathers and grandfathers, and made no improvements; gone to the same church, and sat in the same pew, without cushions; borrowed the same weekly newspaper for forty years; drove all their children to the West or the cities; and if they went to agricultural fairs, insisted on having their premiums in pure coin.

But the hospitality of Utah is not confined to the Mormons. The "Gentiles" or non-Mormons are becoming numerous and influential here, and, citizens and soldiers, comprise many families of culture and influence. They are made up of officers of the federal government, resident representatives of telegraph and stage lines, members of eastern or California business firms having branches here, and a very fair proportion, too, of the merchants of the city. Some of the more intelligent of the disgusted and repentant Mormons swell the circle. They have organized a literary association, established a large and growing Sunday school, largely made up of children of Mormon parents, have weekly religious services led by the chaplain at Camp Douglas, conduct an able and prosperous daily paper (the Union Vedette,) and in every way are developing an organized and effective opposition to the dominant power here. These people, united, earnest and enthusiastic as minorities always are, claim a share in entertaining Mr. Colfax and his friends, and gave them a large and most brilliant social party last night. They are not reluctant to show us their ladies, as the Mormons generally seem to be, and their ladies are such, in beauty and culture, as no circle need be ashamed of. The enjoyment of this social entertainment of music, conversation, dancing and refreshments, was sadly and only broken by the announcement during the evening of the sudden death of the territorial governor, Judge Doty, formerly of Michigan and Wisconsin.

LETTER IX.

MORMON MATERIALITIES.

SALT LAKE CITY, June 16.

THE Necessity of all Agriculture, on the Plains, among the Mountains, on the Pacific shore, nearly all the western half of our Continent, is Irrigation. The long, dry summers, frequently months without rain, the hot sun and dry winds, the clayey character of the soil, all ensure utter defeat to the farmer's business, except he helps his crops to water by artificial means. But in Utah, agriculture is the chief business; its population of one hundred and twenty thousand inhabitants, live by it, prosper by it, have built up a State upon it. Irrigation is, therefore, universal and extensive; the streams that pour down from the mountains are tapped at various elevations, the water carried away by canals, big and little, to the gardens and meadows cultivated, and thence, by numerous little courses, one in three or four feet, spread over the whole extent, over the grain, between the rows of corn, of trees, of vegetables. Individuals, villages, companies perform this work, as a less or greater scale of it is required. The water is apportioned among the takers according to their land or their payments. Each one gets his share; and when the supply is scant, as is often the case, each one suffers in like degree.

Salt Lake City is thus irrigated, mainly from one mountain stream; bright, sparkling brooks course freely and constantly down its paved gutters, keeping the shade trees alive and growing, supplying drink for animals and water for household purposes, and delightfully cooling the summer air; besides being drawn off in right proportion for the use of each garden. Once a week is the rule for thus watering each crop; to-day a man takes enough for one portion of his garden; to-morrow for another; and so through his entire possessions and the week. Under this regular stimulus, with a strong soil made up of the wash of the mountains, the finest of crops are obtained; the vegetable bottom lands of your own Connecticut and of the western prairies cannot vie with the products of the best gardens and farms of these Pacific valleys, under this system of irrigation. There needs to be rain enough in the spring or winter moisture remaining to start the seeds, and there generally is; after that, the regular supply of water keeps the plants in a steady and rapid growth, that may well be supposed to produce far finer results, than the struggling, uneven progress of vegetation under dependence upon the skies— a week or a month of rain, and then a like prolongation of sunshine. The gardens in the cities and villages are tropical in their rich greenness and luxuriance. I do not believe the same space of ground anywhere else in the country holds so much and so fine fruit and vegetables as the city of Salt Lake to-day.

The soil of these valleys is especially favorable to the small grains. Fifty and sixty bushels is a very common crop of wheat, oats and barley; and over ninety have been raised. President Young once raised ninety-three and a half bushels of wheat on a single acre. I should say the same soil located in the East, and taking its chances without irrigation, would not produce half what it does here with irrigation. Laborious and expensive as the process must be, the large crops and high prices obtained for them make it to pay. Over all this country, that is forced to have an irrigated farming, there is no business that now pays so well, not even mining, and nowhere else in the whole Nation is agriculture so profitable. But the mountain snows do not provide half the water the valleys need. Many a broad and beautiful valley goes unredeemed from a dry, half-barren vegetation, for the lack of water to be put upon it. Salt Lake City has exhausted its present supply, and now contemplates a grand canal from Utah Lake, thirty miles off, to provide water for its extending gardens and the wide valley below and beyond the city,—the most of which is now only a poor and growing poorer pasture, but which with irrigation will become as productive farming land as lies under the shadow of the Republic.

The country drained by the Great Salt Lake is about one hundred and fifty miles east and west, and two hundred and fifty north and south. Four or five large streams of fresh water pour into it; but it has not a single visible outlet, and its water is one-fourth solid salt—two mysteries that mock science and make imagination ridiculous. Other salt is found in the country; there is a mountain of rock salt a few miles away; and below in Arizona is a similar mountain whose salt is as pure as finest glass. President Young showed us a brick of it to-day, that excited our surprise and delight as much as any novelty we have seen on our journey. The Territory of Utah covers the region drained by the Salt Lake, and perhaps one hundred miles more both in breadth and length. But the Mormon settlements extend one hundred miles farther into Idaho on the north, and perhaps two hundred miles into Arizona on the south, clinging close, through their entire length of six hundred to seven hundred miles, to a narrow belt of country hardly more than fifty miles wide; for on the east of this are the mountains, and to the west, the great Central American Desert, that forms part of the great internal basin of this section of the Continent, and leads the traveler on to the Sierra Nevada mountains of the Pacific States.

These settlements are mostly small, counting inhabitants by hundreds, gathered about the course of a mountain stream; but there are several places of considerable importance, as Provo at the South and Ogden City at the North. Their extension south into the valley of the Colorado, paves the way to the successful working of a favorite commercial idea of the leading business men here, which is the use of the Gulf of California and the Colorado River, which empties into it, for the great avenue of trade;

for bringing in the supplies of goods needed here, and for sending out such surplus products, agricultural and mineral, as these interior valleys are offering. The Colorado is found to be navigable for steamboats for four hundred miles, or to within six hundred miles of this city, and the substitution of this reduced distance of land carriage, open all the year, through their own Territory, and up valley roads, for seven hundred miles to San Francisco or over one thousand miles to the Missouri River, through deserts and over mountains, and often interrupted by rivers, is a manifest improvement and advantage for the commerce of this country, that can hardly be overestimated. There are already steamers on the Colorado, and some of the merchants are having goods come over the route by way of experiment. If it succeeds, as seems quite certain, then the heavy trade of Utah and its dependencies will come and go from New York by way of the Isthmus of Panama and around Cape Horn, and merchants here, instead of having to buy a year's supply of goods at once, can market several times a year, and do business with much less capital and at much greater advantage otherwise.

The policy of the Mormon leaders has been to confine their people to agriculture; to develop a self-sustaining, rural population, quiet, frugal, industrious, scattered in small villages, and so manageable by the church organization. So far, this policy has been admirably successful; and it has created an industry and a production here, in the center of the western half of our Continent, of immense importance and value to the future growth of the region. A few of the simpler manufactures have been introduced of late, but these are not in conflict with the general policy. There are three cotton mills, confined to cotton yarns, however, almost exclusively, and one woolen mill. Probably there are a hundred flouring mills in the Territory also. Flour, the grains, butter, bacon, dried peaches, home-made socks and yarn, these are the chief articles produced in excess and sold to emigrants and for the mining regions in the North. Probably two hundred thousand pounds of dried peaches were sold for Idaho and Montana last year. Hides are plenty; there is a good tannery here; and also a manufactory of boots and shoes. Cotton grows abundantly in the southern settlements; and experiments with flax, the mulberry tree and the silk worm are all successful.

As to mining, the influence of the church has been against it. There have been no placer or surface diggings discovered to offer temptations to the mass of the people; and the leaders affect to believe that the ores so far found are not valuable enough to pay for working. They have a reason for discouraging mining, of course, in the sure conviction that it would introduce a population and influences antagonistic to the order and power of the church. Iron, they admit, exists in large quantities, especially in the southern mountains, and they have made some attempts to develop it, but without great success, for the reason, as they say, that they had not the proper workmen and materials to do it with. But as to gold and silver, they are incredulous; and not only that, but President Young argues that the world has many times more of both than it needs for financial purposes; that the country is poorer to-day for all the mining of gold and silver in the last twenty years; and that for every dollar gained by it, four dollars have been expended.

But these views are not likely to gain wide acquiescence. There is no reason to doubt that the mountains of Utah are rich in the precious metals—perhaps not so much so as other States and Territories, but still enough so to tempt miners and capitalists to invest in the business of developing them in rivalry with Nevada and Colorado. So far, the discoveries have been chiefly of silver, in connection with large deposits of lead and copper. Our party have spent two interesting days this week in an excursion about forty miles into an adjoining beautiful valley, where some valuable developments have been made in this line. Most of the discoveries have been made by soldiers in General Connor's command—volunteers from the mining regions of California and Nevada—who have been stationed in this vicinity for the last two years; and most of those whose terms have expired have gone to work to improve and develop them. We found among the various canyons or ravines of the Rush Valley a hundred or two of mines freshly discovered and worked out to various depths of ten to one hundred feet. Colonel George, who, in the absence of General Connor to fight the Indians, is in command of the camp here, accompanied us, and saw the lodes for the first time. He is an old Nevada miner, and he says these promise much better—fifty per cent. better—than the famous silver mines of that young State. There, fifty to one hundred dollars of silver from a ton of ore is considered highly profitable and satisfactory; here, the surface ore assays from one hundred to five hundred dollars a ton, and in several cases lodes have been opened that assay from one thousand to four thousand dollars to the ton. The last figure is obtained from one just opened and named the New York lead. The farther the mines are worked, the richer grows the ore. The Mormons say they will soon work out; but the miners have faith, and are working away with all the capital and labor they can command. At present, the ore is easily worked, and does not demand expensive machinery like stamp mills and steam or water power. Smelting furnaces are the chief necessity to reduce the ore to its elements, and separate the metal from the dross. As the mines are further worked, the ore will probably grow harder, and require more elaborate processes.

General Connor, who is an old Californian, has large faith in these prospectings, has taken much interest in their development, and has located and is building up a town, called Stockton, near them, in the Rush Valley. Here we found a population of perhaps two hundred, all "Gentiles," many of them old soldiers, and all full of faith and zeal in their new enterprise. Major Gallagher, formerly of General Connor's California regiment, is living here as the general's agent, and as farmer and miner on his own responsibility. We spent the night at the "government reserves," two miles beyond Stockton, by the shore of Rush Lake; these reserves being valuable lands selected some years ago by Colonel Steptoe, as likely to be needed for government uses, and now thus appropriated for supplies of wood for the camp in town and to pasture surplus horses. Here we met a rough but generous hospitality, a midnight supper, a roaring open fire, and beds on the floor and in the stable-yards; but we slept soundly, ate heartily, and gathered sweetest of flowers amid a snow-storm on the hill-sides the next day, as we wandered about in search of the silver lodes.

In the more remote parts of the Territory, other silver mines have been discovered, and are being worked with success. Their distance from markets, the necessity of more or less machinery for their profitable operation, and the lack of capital among those who have discovered the lodes, are obstacles to their rapid development; but judging from all I can see and learn, there is no good reason to doubt their great value, and sufficient cause to regard them as offering one of the best fields for wisely investing capital and labor in all the mining regions, and to predict ere long such an interest and excitement in regard to them, as will give Utah a new population and rapid growth, and place her among the first of the mining States. The antecedent, achieved development of her agricultural capacities, her settled population and her gathered and organized civilization will then prove of a great advantage, and be properly appreciated.

LETTER X.

SALT LAKE CITY AND LIFE THERE.

SALT LAKE CITY, Saturday, June 17.

IN the "great and glorious future" of our Fourth of July orations, when polygamy is extinct, the Pacific Railroad built, and the mines developed, Salt Lake City will be not only the chief commercial city of the mountains, the equal of St. Louis and Chicago, but one of the most beautiful residence cities and most attractive watering-places on the Continent. Its admirable location and early development secure the one; its agreeable climate for eight months in the year, at least, and the surpassing beauty of its location, with its ample supply of water, its fruits and vegetables, will add the second; and joining to all these circumstances, its snow-capped mountains, its hot sulphur springs, and its Great Salt Lake, and we have the elements of the third fact. There are two principal sulphur springs, one hot enough (one hundred and twenty degrees) to boil an egg, which is four miles from the center of the city, and the other just the right temperature for a hot bath, (ninety degrees,) which is close to the city, and is already brought into a large enclosure for free bathing purposes. Both these streams are large enough for illimitable bathing; the water is as highly sulphurized and as clear as that of the celebrated Sharon Springs; and its use, either for drinking or for baths, most effective in purifying the blood and toning up the.system. Other and smaller springs of the same character have been found in the neighborhood.

Then the Lake opens another field of attractions; it is a miniature ocean, about fifteen miles from the city, fifty miles wide by one hundred long,—the briniest sheet of water known on the Continent,—so salt that no fish can live in it, and that three quarts of it will boil down to one quart of fine, pure salt,—but most delicious and refreshing for bathing, floating the body as a cork on the surface,—only the brine must be kept from mouth and eyes under the penalty of a severe smarting;—with its high rocky islands and crestfull waves and its superb sunsets, picturesque and enchanting to look upon; while its broad expanse offers wide space for sailing, and every chance for sea-sickness. Count up all these features for a watering-place; and where will you find a Newport, a Saratoga or a Sharon that has the half of them? So, ye votaries of fashion, ye rheumatic cripples, ye victims of scrofula and ennui, prepare to pack your trunks at the sound of the first whistle of the train for the Rocky Mountains, for a season at Salt Lake City.

The city is regularly laid out into squares of ten acres each, and these into lots of one acre and a quarter, only farther subdivided in the business or more thickly populated streets. The building material is mostly sun-dried bricks, (called adobe,) covered with plaster, and the houses are generally of one story, covering much space and with as many front doors as the owner has wives. A few of the newer stores are built of stone, and are elegant and capacious within and without. Brigham Young's establishment occupies a full square, and embraces several dwellings, a school house for his forty or fifty children, extensive stables, a grist mill, a carpenter's shop, and the "tithing" office. An opposite square is devoted to church purposes; and here is the old Tabernacle, a new and larger one partly done, and the foundations of the great Temple, which, if ever completed, according to the design, will be the finest church edifice in America. Nothing is doing upon it now. Within the same enclosure is the "Bowery," an immense thatch of green boughs, covering space for an audience of several thousands. Here the general Sunday services are held during the warm weather. Both these squares, President Young's and the church grounds, are enclosed by solid walls of mud and stones, twelve feet high, and walls of a like character are even used for fences about many of the residences.

There are very large mercantile interests here. Several firms do a business of a million dollars or more each, a year, and keep on hand stocks of goods of the value of a quarter of a million. They frequently have subsidiary stores in other parts of the Territory to the number of four or six. Their freights are enormous, and sometimes their goods are a year on the way hither. One firm has just received a stock of goods, costing one hundred thousand dollars, that was bought in New York last June. It got caught on the Plains by early snow, last fall, and had to winter on the way. Another leading merchant paid one hundred and fifty thousand dollars for freights last year. One lot of goods, groceries, hardware, dry goods, everything, was found to have cost, on reaching here, just one dollar a pound, adding to original purchase the cost of freighting, which from New York to this point averages from twenty-five to thirty cents a pound. It of course requires large capital and courage to enter upon the mercantile business here under such circumstances. Prices, too, must rule high; and when the supply is short, as it was last year, and the demand large, great profits are realized; and again, with an overstocked market and a small sale, there is danger of heavy losses. One concern made seventy-five per cent. profit last year, but this season promises poorly; and the stocks on hand cannot, in many cases, be sold for their cost. I give the ruling rates for some of the leading articles, both of native production and imported : beef twelve to twenty cents, mutton twenty to twenty-five cents, pork fifty cents, bacon seventy-five cents, hams one dollar, wood eighteen dollars per cord, lumber one hundred dollars per thousand, butter fifty cents, sugar seventy-five to eighty-five cents, coffee one dollar to one dollar and ten cents, green tea (almost universal on the Plains and in the mountains) three and a half to five dollars, tobacco two to two dollars and a half, axes four dollars and a half, heavy brown sheetings eighty-five to ninety cents, fine seventy-five to ninety cents, prints twenty-five to forty cents, dried apples sixty cents, dried peaches fifty cents, molasses three to three dollars and a half, gunpowder two dollars, day labor three dollars, mechanics three to five dollars, clerks twelve hundred to three thousand dollars a year. The only coal mines yet developed in the Territory lie forty miles over the mountains east, on our road hither, and it costs twenty-five to thirty dollars a ton to transport it to the city, so that the price for it is thirty-five to forty dollars. It is a bituminous coal, and of very fair quality.

Your readers would mistake if they supposed that these prices enforced any poverty in living among these people. There are not many absolutely poor; and the general scale of living is generous. In the early years of the Territory, there was terrible suffering for the want of food; many were reduced to the roots of the field for sustenance; but now there appears to be an abundance of the substantial necessaries of life, and as most of the population are cultivators of the soil, all or nearly all have plenty of food. And certainly, I have never seen more generously laden tables than have been spread before us at our hotel or at private houses. A dinner to our party this evening by a leading Mormon merchant, at which President Young and the principal members of his council were present, had as rich a variety of fish, meats, vegetables, pastry and fruit, as I ever saw on any private table in the East; and the quality and the cooking and the serving were unimpeachable. All the food, too, was native in Utah. The wives of our host waited on us most amicably, and the entertainment was, in every way, the best illustration of the practical benefits of plurality, that has yet been presented to us.

Later in the evening we were introduced to another, and perhaps the most wonderful, illustration of the reach of social and artificial life in this far off city of the Rocky Mountains. This was the Theater, in which a special performance was improvised in honor of Speaker Colfax. The building is itself a rare triumph of art and enterprise. No eastern city of one hundred thousand inhabitants,—remember Salt Lake City has less than twenty thousand,—possesses so fine a theatrical structure. It ranks, alike in capacity and elegance of structure and finish, along with the opera-houses and academies of music of Boston, New York, Philadelphia, Chicago and Cincinnati. In costumes and scenery, it is furnished with equal richness and variety, and the performances themselves, though by amateurs, by merchants and mechanics, by wives and daughters of citizens, would have done full credit to a first-class professional company. There was first a fine and elaborate drama, and then a spectacular farce, in both which were introduced some exquisite dancing, and in one some good singing also. I have rarely seen a theatrical entertainment more pleasing and satisfactory in all its details and appointments.

Yet the two principal male characters were by a day-laborer and a carpenter; one of the leading lady parts was by a married daughter of Brigham Young, herself the mother of several children; and several other of his daughters took part in the ballet, which was most enchantingly rendered, and with great scenic effect. The house was full in all its parts, and the audience embraced all classes of society, from the wives and daughters of President Young,—a goodly array,—and the families of the rich merchants, to the families of the mechanics and farmers of the city and valley, and the soldiers from the camp. President Young built and owns the theater, and conducts it on his private account, or on that of the church, as he does many other of the valuable and profitable institutions of the Territory, such as cotton, saw and flour mills, the best farms, etc.; and, as he is at no expense for actors or actresses, and gets good prices for admission, he undoubtedly makes a "good thing" out of it. During the winter season, performances are given twice a week; and the theater proves a most useful and popular social center and entertainment for the whole people. Its creation was a wise and beneficent thought.

LETTER XI.

THE POLYGAMY QUESTION.

SALT LAKE CITY, June 18.

OUR visit here closes in the morning. It has been very interesting, instructive and gratifying to us. We have had unusual opportunities for learning the opinions of the Mormons, for studying their institutions, for measuring their culture and capacity, for observing their social, material and religious development, and for informing ourselves as to the conflict fast growing up between them and the non-Mormons who are rapidly accumulating in the community. The leaders in the church and in society have been generous and constant in their hospitality, and frank in their conversation, partly, I will not doubt, from a hearty, human good feeling, and partly, no doubt, also, from anxiety as to the future policy of the government towards them and their institutions, and eagerness to propitiate political and public opinion in their favor. We have attended the services at the Mormon Tabernacle on two successive Sabbaths, on one of which Brigham Young himself preached in exposition and defense of the doctrines of his church. Mr. Colfax and his friends have also had two long interviews with Brigham Young and the other leaders of the church, in one of which the peculiar institution of the people was freely and frankly but most earnestly discussed by all. The testimony and opinions of the "Gentiles," and of intelligent citizens, men and women, who, once Mormons, have now left the church, have been freely offered to us, and gladly heard. Valuable facts and opinions have also been gathered from old and intelligent citizens, who have held a sort of independent and neutral position, who are neither polygamists in theory or practice, nor members of the church, but who, either from motives of policy or qualities of temperament, have taken no part with the pronounced and denouncing "Gentiles." Nor have the opinions and feelings of women in polygamy been wholly denied to us; though we have not been offered their society by their husbands with any particular generosity;—this, indeed, being the only feature of their hospitality that has been measured and chary.

The result of the whole experience has been to increase my appreciation of the value of their material progress and development to the nation; to evoke congratulations to them and to the country for the wealth they have created and the order, frugality, morality and industry that have been organized in this remote spot in our Continent; to excite wonder at the perfection and power of their church system, the extent of its ramifications, the sweep of its influence; and to enlarge my respect for the personal sincerity and character of many of the leaders in the organization;—also, and on the other hand, to deepen my disgust at their polygamy, and strengthen my convictions of its barbaric and degrading influences. They have tried it and practised it under the most favorable circumstances, perhaps under the mildest form possible; but, now as before, here as elsewhere, it tends to and means only the degradation of woman. By it and under it, she becomes simply the servant and serf, not the companion and equal of man; and the inevitable influence of this upon all society need not be depicted.

But I find that Mormonism is not necessarily polygamy; that the one began and existed for many years without the other; that not all the Mormons accept the doctrine, and not one-fourth, perhaps not one-eighth practise it; and that the Nation and its government may oppose it and punish it, without at all interfering with the existence of the Mormon church, or justly being held as interfering with the religious liberty that is the basis of all our institutions. This distinction has not been sufficiently understood heretofore, and it has not been consistently acted upon by either the government or the public of the East. Here, by the people, who are coming in to enjoy the opportunities of the country for trade and mining, and there, by our rulers at Washington and by the great public, this single issue of polygamy should be pressed home upon the Mormon church,—discreetly and with tact, with law and with argument and appeal, but with firmness and power.

Ultimately, of course, before the influences of emigration, civilization and our democratic habits, an organization so aristocratic and autocratic as the Mormon church now is must modify its rule; it must compete with other sects, and take its chance with them. And its most aristocratic and uncivilized incident or feature of plurality of wives must fall first and completely before contact with the rest of the world,—marshalled with mails, daily papers, railroads and telegraphs,—ciphering out the fact that the men and women of the world are about equally divided, and applying to the Mormon patriarchs the democratic principle of equal and exact justice. Nothing can save this feature of Mormonism but new flight and a more complete isolation. A kingdom in the sea, entirely its own, could only perpetuate it; and thither even, commerce and democracy would ultimately follow it. The click of the telegraph and the roll of the overland stages are its death-rattle now; the first whistle of the locomotive will sound its requiem; and the pick-ax of the miner will dig its grave. Squatter sovereignty will speedily settle the question, even if the government continues to coquette with it and humor it, as it has done.

But the government should no longer hold a doubtful or divided position toward this great crime of the Mormon church. Declaring clearly both its want of power and disinclination to interfere at all with the church organization as such, or with the latter's influence over its followers, assuring and guaranteeing to it all the liberty and freedom that other religious sects hold and enjoy, the government should still, as clearly and distinctly, declare, by all its action and all its representatives here, that this feature of polygamy, not properly or necessarily a part of the religion of the Mormons, is a crime by the common law of all civilization and by the statute law of the Nation, and that any cases of its extension will be prosecuted and punished as such. Now half or two-thirds the federal officers in the Territory are polygamists; and others bear no testimony against it. These should give way to men who, otherwise equally Mormons it may be, still are neither polygamists nor believers in the practice of polygamy. No employes or contractors of the government should be polygamists in theory or practice.

Here the government should take its stand, calmly, quietly, but firmly, giving its moral support and countenance, and its physical support, if necessary for fair play, to the large class of Mormons who are not polygamists, to missionaries and preachers of all other sects, who choose to come here, and erect their standards and invite followers; and to that growing public opinion, here and elsewhere, which is accumulating its inexorable force against an institution which has not inaptly been termed a twin barbarism with slavery. There is no need and no danger of physical conflict growing up; only a hot and unwise zeal and impatience on the part of the government representatives, and in the command of the troops stationed here, could precipitate that. The probability is, that, upon such a demonstration by the government, as I have suggested, the leaders of the church would receive new light on the subject themselves,—perhaps have a fresh revelation, and abandon the objectionable feature in their polity. No matter if they did not,—it would soon, under the influences now rapidly aggregating, and thus reinforced by the government, abandon them.

In this way, all violent conflict would, I believe, be successfully avoided; and all this valuable population and its industries and wealth may be retained in place and to the Nation, without waste. Let them continue to be Mormons, if they choose, so long as they are not polygamists. They may be ignorant and fanatical, and imposed upon and swindled even, by their church leaders; but they are industrious, thriving, and more comfortable than, on an average, they have ever been before in the homes from which they came hither; and there is no law against fanaticism and bigotry and religious charlatanry. All these evils of religious benightment are not original in Utah, and they will work out their own cure here, as they have done elsewhere in our land. We must have patience with the present, and possibly forgiveness for supposed crimes in the past by the leaders, because we have heretofore failed to meet the issues promptly and clearly, and have shared by our consent and protection to their authors in the alleged wrongs.

The conversation I have alluded to with Brigham Young and some of his elders, on this subject of polygamy, was introduced by his inquiring of Mr.

Colfax what the government and people of the East proposed to do with it and them, now that they had got rid of the slavery question. The Speaker replied that he had no authority to speak for the government; but for himself, if he might be permitted to make the suggestion, he had hoped the prophets of the church would have a new revelation on the subject, which should put a stop to the practice. He added further that, as the people of Missouri and Maryland, without waiting for the action of the general government against slavery, themselves believing it to be wrong and an impediment to their prosperity, had taken measures to abolish it, so he hoped the people of the Mormon church would see that polygamy was a hindrance and not a help, and move for its abandonment. Mr. Young responded quickly and frankly that he should readily welcome such a revelation; that polygamy was not in the original book of the Mormons: that it was not an essential practice in the church, but only a privilege and a duty, under special command of God; that he knew it had been abused; that people had entered into polygamy who ought not to have done so, and against his protestation and advice. At the same time, he defended the practice as having biblical authority, and as having, within proper limits, a sound, moral and philosophical reason and propriety.

The discussion, thus opened, grew general and sharp, though ever good-natured. Mr. Young was asked how he got over the fact that the two sexes were about equally divided all over the world, and that, if some men had two, five, or twenty wives, others would have to go without altogether. His reply was that there was always a considerable proportion of the men who would never marry, who were old bachelors from choice. But, retorted one, are there any more of such than of women who choose to be old maids? Oh yes, said he, most ungallantly; there is not one woman in a million who will not marry if she gets a chance! One of the saints, who was pressing the biblical usage and authority for many wives as above all laws and constitutions, was asked as to the effect of the same usage and authority for human sacrifice,—would you, he was asked, if commanded by God, offer up your son or your enemy as a sacrifice, killing them? Yes, he promptly replied. Then the civil law would lay its hands upon you and stop you, and would be justified in doing so, was the apparently effective answer.

In the course of the discussion, Mr. Young asked, suppose polygamy is given up, will not your government then demand more,—will it not war upon the Book of the Mormons, and attack our church organization? The reply was emphatically No, that it had no right, and could have no justification to do so, and that we had no idea there would be any disposition in that direction.

The talk, which was said to be the freest and frankest ever known on that subject in that presence, ended pleasantly, but with the full expression, on the part of Mr. Colfax and his friends, of their hope that the polygamy question might be removed from existence, and thus all objection to the admission of Utah as a State be taken away; but that, until it was, no such admission was possible, and that the government could not continue to look indifferently upon the enlargement of so offensive a practice. And not only what Mr. Young said, but his whole manner left with us the impression that, if public opinion and the government united vigorously, but at the same time discreetly, to press the question, there would be found some way to acquiesce in the demand, and change the practice of the present fathers of the church.

The conversation was continued on the subjects of punishing the leading rebels, and of slavery in the abstract. Mr. Young favored slavery *per se* as established by Divine authority, but denounced the chattel system of the South; and he opposed the hanging of any of the rebel chiefs as an unwise and aggravating policy. Now that peace is established, let all be pardoned, he said; but early in or during the war, he would have disposed of the rebel chiefs that fell into the hands of the government without mercy or hesitation. Had he been President when Mason and Slidell were captured, he would have speedily put them "where they never would peep," and negotiated with England afterwards. He uttered this sentiment with such a wicked working of the lower jaw and lip, and such an almost demon-like spirit in his whole face, that, quite disposed to be incredulous on those matters, I could not help thinking of the Mountain Meadow massacre of recusant Mormons, of Danites and Avenging Angels, and their reported achievements.

LETTER XII.

THE MORMON WIVES: OUR LAST DAY IN SALT LAKE CITY.

SALT LAKE CITY, June 18.

How do the Mormon women like and bear polygamy? is the question most people ask as to the institution. The universal testimony of all but their husbands is, that it is a grievous sorrow and burden; only cheerfully submitted to and embraced under a religious fanaticism and self-abnegation rare to behold, and possible only to women. They are taught to believe, and many of them really do believe, that through and by it they secure a higher and more glorious reward in the future world. "Lord Jesus has laid a heavy trial upon me," said one poor, sweet woman, "but I mean to bear it for His sake, and for the glory He will grant me in His kingdom." This is the common wail, the common solace. Such are the teachings of the church; and I have no doubt both husbands and wives alike often honestly accept this view of the odious practice, and seek and submit to polygamy as really God's holy service, calculated to make saints of themselves and all associated with them in the future world.

Still a good deal of human nature is visible, both among the men in embracing polygamy, and in their wives in submitting to it. Mr. Young's testimony on this point is significant. Other signs are not wanting in the looks and character of the men most often anointed in the holy bonds of matrimony, and in the well-known disagreement of the wives in many families. In some cases they live harmoniously and lovingly together; oftener, it would seem, they have separate parts of the same house, or even separate houses. The first wife is generally the recognized one of society, and frequently assumes contempt for the others, regarding them as concubines, and not wives. But it is a dreadful state of society to any one of fine feelings and true instincts; it robs married life of all its sweet sentiment and companionship; and while it degrades woman, it brutalizes man, teaching him to despise and domineer over his wives, over all women. It breeds jealousy, distrust, and tempts to infidelity; but the police system of the church and the community is so strict and constant that it is claimed and believed the latter vice is very rare.

The effect upon the children cannot help being debasing, however well they may be guarded and educated. But it is a chief failing, even a scandal to the Mormons, that, plentifully as they are providing children, who swarm everywhere as did the locusts in Egypt, they have organized no free school system. Schools are held in every ward of the city, and probably in every considerable village, in buildings provided for evening religious meetings under the direction of the local bishops, but a tuition fee is exacted for all who attend, and the poor are practically shut out. The anti-polygamists should agitate at once and earnestly to reform this evil,—it is a strong point against the dominant party, and a weak point in the welfare of the Territory. It is a good and encouraging sign to learn from intelligent sources that, as the young girls, daughters of Mormons, grow up to womanhood, they are indisposed to polygamy, and seek husbands among the "Gentiles" rather than among their own faith.

The soldiers at Camp Douglas, near this city, are illustrating one of the ways in which polygamy will fade away before the popular principle. Two companies, who went home to California last fall, took about twenty-five wives with them, recruited from the Mormon flocks. There are now some fifty or more women in the camp, who have fled thither from town for protection, or been seduced away from unhappy homes and fractional husbands; and all or nearly all find new husbands among the soldiers. Only to-day a man with three daughters, living in the city, applied to Colonel George for leave to move up to the camp for a residence, in order, as he said, to save his children from polygamy, into which the bishops and elders of the church were urging them. The camp authorities tell many like stories; also of sadder applications, if possible, for relief from actual poverty and from persecution in town. The Mormons have no poorhouse, and say they have no poor, permitting none by relieving all through work or gifts. But the last winter was so long and so severe, with wood at thirty and forty dollars a cord, that there was much real suffering, and the soldiers yielded to extensive demands upon their charity, that the church authorities had neglected to fulfill, or absolutely denied.

Your readers are aware, I suppose, that a large proportion, perhaps the majority, of the people of Utah are foreigners,—recruits by missionaries sent out over the whole world. The larger proportion are English, from the factory towns of Great Britain. But Germans, Swedes, Finns, Scotch, Icelanders, and even East Indians, are here. Mr. Young boasts that fifty different nationalities are represented among his people. The bulk of them all are of the peasantry, the lower classes of working people at home; and so the congregations of the Mormons do not exhibit the marks of high acuteness and intelligence. The audiences at the Tabernacle to-day and last Sunday, and at the theater last night, were what would be called common-looking people. The handsome girls were few; the fine-looking women even fewer; intelligent, strong-headed men were more numerous; but the great mass, both in size, looks and dress, was below the poorest, hardest-working and most ignorant classes of our eastern large towns.

The gatherings and the services, both in speaking and singing, reminded me of the Methodist camp-meetings of fifteen or twenty years ago. The singing, as on the latter occasions, was the best part of the exercises, simple, sweet, and fervent.

"Daughters of Zion," as sung by the large choir last Sunday, was prayer, sermon, song and all. The preaching last Sabbath was by Mr. Samuel W. Richards, who was of Massachusetts origin, but a Mormon leader and missionary for many years. Beyond setting forth the superiority of the Mormon church system, through its presidents, councils, bishops, elders and seventies, for the work made incumbent upon Christians, and claiming that its preachers were inspired like those of old, his discourse was a rambling, unimpressive exhortation, such as you may hear from a tonguey deacon in any country Baptist or Methodist meeting-house. The Bible, both old and new testament, is used with the same authority as by all Protestants; the Mormon scriptures are simply new and added books, confirming and supplementing the teachings of the original Scriptures. The rite of the sacrament is administered every Sunday, water being used instead of wine, and the distribution proceeding among the whole congregation, men, women and children, and numbering from three to five thousand, while the singing and the preaching are in progress. The prayers are few and simple, undistinguishable, except in these characteristics, from those heard in all Protestant churches, and the congregation all join in the Amen.

Brigham Young's preaching to-day was a very unsatisfactory, disappointing performance. There was every incentive to him to do his best; he had an immense audience spread out under the "bowery" to the number of five or six thousand; before

him was Mr. Colfax, who had asked him to preach
upon the distinctive Mormon doctrines; around
him were all his elders and bishops, in unusual
numbers; and he was fresh from the exciting discussion of yesterday on the subject of polygamy.
But his address lacked logic, lacked effect, lacked
wholly magnetism or impressiveness. It was a curious medley of scriptural exposition and exhortation,
bold and bare statement, coarse denunciation and
vulgar allusion, cheap rant and poor cant. So far as
his statement of Mormon belief went, it amounted
to this: that God was a human, material person,
with like flesh and blood and passions to ourselves,
only perfect in all things; that he begot his son
Jesus in the same way that children are begotten
now; that Jesus and the father looked alike and
were alike, distinguishable only by the former being
older; that our resurrection would be material, and
we should live in heaven with the same bodies and
the same passions as on earth; that Mormonism
was the most perfect and true religion; that those
Christians who were not Mormons would not necessarily go to hell and be burned by living fire and
tortured by ugly devils, but that they would not
occupy so high places in heaven as the Latter Day
Saints; that polygamy was the habit of all the
children of God in the earlier ages, and was first
abolished by the Goths and Vandals who conquered
and constructed Rome; that Martin Luther approved of it in a single case at least; that a clergyman of the church of England once married a man
to a second wife while his first wife was living; and

that in England now, if a man wanted to change his wife, he had only to offer her at auction and knock her off for a pot of beer or a shilling, and marry another. (This last statement called out a voice of dissent from an English working-face in the audience.) A good deal of boasting of the success of the Mormons, their temperance, frugality and honesty, and a sharp denunciation of the "few stinking lawyers who lived down in whiskey street, and for five dollars would attempt to make a lie into a truth," were the only other noticeable features of this discourse of the president of the church of the Latter Day Saints. It was a very material interpretation of the statements and truths of scripture, very illogically and roughly rendered; and calculated only to influence a cheap and vulgar audience. Brigham Young may be a shrewd business man, an able organizer of labor, a bold, brave person in dealing with the practicalities of life,—he must, indeed, be all of these, for we see the evidences all around this city and country; but he is in no sense an impressive or effective preacher, judged by any standards that I have been accustomed to.

His audience, swollen one or two thousand more, could not have helped drawing a sharp contrast,—dull in comprehension and fanatically devoted to him as most of them probably are,—between his speech and his style, and those of Mr. Colfax, who, at a later hour this evening, delivered in the same place, by invitation of the church and city authorities, his Chicago Eulogy on the Life and Principles of President Lincoln. He spoke it without notes, and with much freedom and fervor to an audience unused to so effective and eloquent a style, and more unused, we fear, to such sentiments; and he received rapt attention and apparently delighted approval throughout the whole. Mr. Colfax's other and informal speeches here, and his whole intercourse with the authorities and people of all parties, considerate always, but frank and ever consistent with his principles, had won him the respect of all and the affection of many; but the pronouncing of this eulogy has increased the feeling in his favor to a high enthusiasm.

The election for territorial delegate to Congress from Utah occurs in August. Judge Kinney, who was sent here as judge by President Buchanan, and becoming agreeable to the Mormon leaders, was sent to Congress by them when superseded in his judgeship by Mr. Lincoln, has recently come back from Washington, and seeks re-election. But it is doubtful if Mr. Young decides to have him go again. He has indicated a purpose of returning Captain Hooper, an old and prosperous merchant here, who served the term before Judge Kinney, and who has lately sold out his business here, in order to go on a mission for the church to England.* He was popular and useful in Congress before, is an intelligent, able man, and though a Mormon of many years' standing, has the principle and good sense to be content with one most excellent wife. These and other selections for office are of course nominally made by the people voting as in other States and

* Mr. Hooper has since been chosen to Congress.

Territories; but the real choice is made beforehand by the church authorities, and the vote is usually quite small. Only one case is known of the bishop's ticket ever having been defeated. This was at a small country village in the choice for mayor; but the fact was not suffered to go abroad,—it was too dangerous an example.

But adieu to Salt Lake and many-wive-and-much-children-dom; to its strawberries and roses; its rare hospitality; its white crowned peaks, its widespread valley, its river of scriptural name, its lake of briniest taste. I have met much to admire, many to respect, worshiped deep before its Nature,—found only one thing to condemn. I shall want to come again when the railroad can bring me, and that blot is gone.

LETTER XIII.

SOCIAL LIFE AMONG THE MORMONS.

AUSTIN, Nevada, June 22.

I GO back to the Mormons, to add some facts and gossip, because their civilization is so remarkable, and because they and their institutions are about to come into new and final conflict with the people and the government of the country. Polygamy introduces many curious cross-relationships, and intertwines the branches of the genealogical tree in a manner greatly to puzzle a mathematician, as well as to disgust the decent-minded. The marrying of two or more sisters is very common; one young Mormon merchant in Salt Lake City has three sisters for his three wives. There are several cases of men marrying both mother (widow) and her daughter or daughters; taking the "old woman" for the sake of getting the young ones; but having children by all. Please to cipher out for yourselves how this mixes things. More disgusting associations are known,—even to the marrying of a half-sister by one Mormon. Consider, too, how these children of one father and many mothers,—the latter often blood relations,—are likely to become crossed again in new marriages, in the second or third, if not the first, generations, under the operation of this polygamous practice; and it is safe to predict that a few generations of such social practices will breed a physical, moral and mental debasement of the people most frightful to contemplate. Already, indeed, are such indications apparent, foreshadowing the sure and terrible realization.

Brigham Young's wives are numberless; at least no one seems to know how many he has; and he has himself confessed to forgetfulness in the matter. The probability is he has from sixteen to twenty genuine or complete wives, and about as many more women "sealed" to him for heavenly association and glory. The latter are mostly pious old ladies, eager for high seats in the Mormon heaven, and knowing no surer way to get there than to be joined on to Brigham's angelic procession. Some of these sealed wives of his are the earthly wives of other men; but, lacking faith in their husbands' heavenly glory, seek to make a sure thing of it for the future by the grace of gracious Brigham. Down East, you know, many a husband calculates on stealing into heaven under the pious petticoats of his better wife; here the thing is reversed, and women go to heaven because their husbands take them along. The Mormon religion is an excellent institution for maintaining masculine authority in the family; and the greatness of a true Mormon is measured, indeed, by the number of wives he can keep in sweet and loving and especially obedient subjugation. Such a man can have as many wives as he wants. But President Young objects to multiplying wives for men who have not this rare domestic gift. So there is no chance for you and I, my dear Jones, becoming successful Mormons!

In many cases, the Mormon wives not only support themselves and their children, but help support their husbands. Thus a clerk or other man, with similar limited income, who has yielded to the fascinations and desires of three or four women, and married them all, makes his home with number one, perhaps, and the rest live apart, each by herself, taking in sewing or washing, or engaging in other employment, to keep up her establishment and be no charge to her husband. He comes around, once in a while, to make her a visit, and then she sets out an extra table and spends all her accumulated earnings to make him as comfortable and herself as charming as possible, so that her fraction of the dear sainted man may be multiplied as much as possible. Thus the fellow, if he is lazy and has turned his piety to the good account of getting smart wives, may really board around continually, and live in clover, at no personal expense but his own clothing. Is not this a divine institution, indeed!

When President Young goes on a journey through the Territory, on private or public business, he takes a considerable retinue with him, and always a wife and a barber. The former is more his servant than his companion in such cases, however. His household is said to be admirably managed. A son-in-law acts as commissary; the wives have nothing to do with the table or its supply; and whenever they want new clothes or pocket money, they must go to this chief of staff or head of the family bureau. Considering his opportunities, the head of the Church of Latter Day Saints has made a rather sorry selection of women on the score of beauty. The oldest or first is a matronly-looking old lady, serene and sober; the youngest and present pet, who was obtained, they say, after much seeking, is comely but common-looking, despite the extra millinery in which she alone of the entire family indulges. The second president and favorite prophet of the church, Heber Kimball, who in church and theater keeps the cold from his bare head and the divine afflatus in by throwing a red bandanna handkerchief over it, is even less fortunate in the beauty of his wives; it is rather an imposition upon the word beauty, indeed, to suggest it in their presence.

Handsome women and girls, in fact, are scarce among the Mormons of Salt Lake,—the fewer "Gentiles" can show many more of them. Why is this? Is beauty more esthetic and ascetic? Or, good-looking women being supposed to have more chances for matrimony than their plainer sisters, do they all insist upon having the whole of one man, and leave the Mormon husbands to those whose choice is like Hobson's? The only polygamist, into whose family circle we were freely admitted, had, however, found two very pretty women to divide him between them; and I must confess they appeared to take their share of him quite resignedly, if not amicably. They were English, and of nearly equal years; appeared together in the parlor and in public with their husband, and dressed alike; but they had the same quiet, subdued, half-sad air that characterized all the Mormon women, young and old, that I saw in public or private. There is certainly none of that "loudness" about the Mormon ladies, that an eastern man cannot help observing in the manners of our western women generally. And I hardly think the difference is to be attributed to the superior refinement and culture of the sisters of the Salt Lake Basin; it rather and really is the sign and mark of their servitude, their debasement.

Brigham Young's younger children, as seen in his school, to which we were admitted, look sprightly and bright and handsome; and some of his grown up daughters are comely and clever; but his older sons give no marked sign of their father's smartness. The oldest, Brigham Jr., is mainly distinguished for his size and strength,—he weighs two to three hundred pounds, and is muscular in proportion. He has now taken one of his wives and gone to England with her, on business for the church. The next son, John, is a poor, puny looking fellow, with several wives and an inordinate love for whiskey. Brigham's dynasty will die with himself.

There is no more love lost between the soldiers and the Mormons than between the soldiers and the Indians. The "boys in blue" regard both as their natural enemies, and the enemies of order and the government; and the feeling is cordially reciprocated. General Connor, the commander of the military force in Utah, has never even seen Brigham Young; and the latter, it is quite certain, has no desire ever to see him. There is a provost guard of soldiers in Salt Lake City, but the rent of the building which it occupies is about expiring, and, according to a Mormon way of getting rid of an uncomfortable presence, none other is now to be had in its place. Every building singularly happens to be occupied or engaged just now; and the Mormons have evidently hoped to thus drive all these standing menaces, and seducers of their women, as they add the soldiers all are, out of town and into the camp, two miles distant. But when Mr. Colfax suggested to two or three of the elders that such a result could only be interpreted at Washington as a compact and contrivance to embarrass the soldiers and defy the government, they seemed to be incited to a new and original line of thought; and the probability is that the provost guard will be able to find some unoccupied building, that had not been before thought of.

One of the characters of Mormondom is Porter Rockwell, the accredited leader of the Danites or "Avenging Angels" of the church. We were presented to him, and were invited to eat strawberries and cream at his "ranch," but our engagements did not permit our accepting and partaking. Though given to heavy whiskey drinking of late years, he is as mild a mannered man as ever scuttled ship or murdered crews; and I really do not think that any anxiety for our lives entered into our declination of his hospitality, inexplicable as it may seem that for any less reason we should have omitted any opportunity at strawberries. There is a difference of opinion, even among the "Gentiles," as to his real share in the mysterious and terrible takings-off of parties in bad odor with the saints of the church; though unlettered, he is strong-minded and strong-hearted, and, unless under the influence of a shocking fanaticism, I can hardly believe, from his appearance and manners, he could be guilty of such crimes as are laid at his door by the more implacable and suspicious of the "Gentile" residents. I should not be willing, however, to see Mr. Fitzhugh Ludlow fall in his way again; there might not be murder, but the author of the largely imaginative articles in the Atlantic Monthly on this western journey would certainly feel the sharp vengeance of the injured and irate "Avenger." Mr. Ludlow tells the worst stories about Rockwell, such as that he had committed about fifty murders for the church and as many more on private account, as if accepted, proved facts; at the same time that he acknowledges being his guest, and availing himself of his courtesies to see the country. Porter shuts his teeth hard when the subject is now mentioned, and mutters that he supposes "it is all wheat," this being Utah idiom for all right. Which means, of course, that he don't suppose any such thing.

There is little or no immigration to the Mormons this season, at least not yet. They have been sending out fresh relays of missionaries and recruiting agents to England and the Continent of Europe, and expect great returns next year. On the Sandwich Islands they seem to have established a permanent colony, also, to which has just been contributed a new company of about fifty, men, women and children from Utah. Some of the "Gentiles" believe this Sandwich Island movement is towards a new and contingent base; and that if hard pressed here by the progress of civilization and the hand of authority, the Mormon leaders will gather up all their available forces and wealth, and retreat thither. It is certain that they must make a change of base of one sort or another before long, either in the matter of polygamy, or else in the location of their earthly tabernacles and kingdom. Even without the interference of government, they must soon give way here, in their peculiar sway and their revolting institution, before the progress of population and the diversification of civilized industry that comes along with it. Our bachelor stage-driver out of Salt Lake, who said he expected to have a revelation soon to take one of the extra wives of a Mormon saint, is a representative of the Coming Man. Let the Mormons look out for him.

LETTER XIV.

THE RIDE THROUGH THE SAGE BRUSH AND THE GREAT BASIN.

VIRGINIA, Nevada, June 28.

WE are nearly out of the Sage Brush! Nearly into a "white country," where the grass grows green, and water runs, and trees mount skyward and spread sweet shade. Like some of the dry, barren plains that lead up to the Rocky Mountains on the east, the six hundred miles we have come over from Salt Lake to this point, pass through a region whose uses are unimaginable, unless to hold the rest of the globe together, or to teach patience to travelers, or to keep close-locked in its mountain ranges those rich mineral treasures that the world did not need or was not ready for until now. The Basin of the Great Salt Lake, that I briefly described in a late letter as the center of the Mormon development, is but the south-eastern and most fertile corner of an immensely large intra-mountain basin, that has no water outlet to the ocean, that absorbs all the water developed within its limits, and cries, oh how hungrily for more, whose chief natural vegetable product is Sage

Brush, and which holds within its bounds the great, if not the sole, silver mines of the nation.

This Great Desert Basin,—but desert only because comparatively waterless,—lies on the very central and commercial line of the Republic,—the line of greatest population and thrift and wealth both east and west of it,—stretches three hundred miles from north to south and six hundred miles from east to west, is about equally divided between the two states of Utah and Nevada, and is walled in on the one side by the Rocky Mountains and on the other by the Sierra Nevadas. Not a wide, unbroken plain, however, is this vast basin desert of the West. Through it, north and south, run subsidiary ranges of mountains, averaging at least one to every fifty miles, and the intervening valleys or plains all dip, though almost imperceptibly, to the center, which gratefully suggests that they were once not altogether so tearless as now. Mountain and plain are alike above dew point; rain is a rarity,—near neighbor to absolute stranger; and only an occasional range of the hills mounts so high as to hold its winter snows into the summer suns, and yield the summer streams that give, at rare intervals, sweet lines of green, affording forage for cattle and refreshment and rest for traveler. Springs are even more infrequent, but not altogether unknown, and water may sometimes, though very hardly, be got, when all else fails, by digging deep wells. Such streams as rise from springs or snow-banks in the mountains, begin to shrink as they reach the Plains, and end in salt lakes, or sink quietly into the famishing earth. Humboldt River, the largest and longest of the basin, runs west and south from three hundred to five hundred miles, and then finds ignominious end in a "sink," or, in a very natural big disgust at the impossibility of the job it has undertaken, quietly "peters out." So of the Carson River, which comes from the Sierra Nevadas on the west, and finds its home in a lagoon within sight of its parent peaks. Reese River, now so famous as localizing the new and extensive silver mining operations about Austin, is but a sluggish brook that the shortest-legged man could step across at its widest, and yields itself up to the hot sands without greening but a narrow line in the broad plain in which it runs. And yet it is the largest and almost only stream that we met in traveling westward from the Jordan which waters the valley of Salt Lake; and the two are four hundred miles apart!

Through this wide stretch of treeless mountain and plain, at its center,—fifty to one hundred miles below the old and more fortunately watered emigrant route along the valley of the Humboldt,—on a nearly straight line west, we have made the most rapid stage ride yet achieved on the great overland line, and the equal perhaps of any ever made of like distance on the Continent. Mr. Holladay's ownership ceases at Salt Lake; from there hither, the stages are run by the Overland Mail Company, whose stockholders are New Yorkers, and mainly the same as those of the great express company of Wells, Fargo & Co., which monopolizes the express business in all these western States and Territories, having its offices in every town and village, and extending its routes as fast and as far as the most enterprising prospectors successfully push their hunt for the precious metals. At Salt Lake City, therefore, we parted with our protector and companion, thus far, Mr. Otis,—with many a rare memory of his good fellowship,—and found new friends and careful protection on our farther journey in the officers and drivers of the Overland Company. Their part of the line has been happily exempt, for now two years, from the inroads of the Indians; it is all nearer to good markets than most of Mr. Holladay's; and so we naturally found it in better condition, and able to run more promptly and regularly. Ambitious to see how fast they could send Mr. Colfax and his friends over their route, they took us up at Salt Lake on Monday morning week, and set us down at Austin, four hundred miles distant, in fifty hours, or two-thirds the time usually taken. Awaiting our examination of the mining region about Austin, we were again put over the road on the double quick, and landed in Virginia, two hundred miles farther off, in twenty-two hours more, or fourteen less than the schedule time; and so came into this town at six o'clock Sunday morning, while all the elements of a magnificent popular reception, that had been arranged for the night before, were fast asleep in bed, and totally undreaming of the march that we were stealing upon them. Here, we are near the foot of the Sierra Nevadas, on the borders of California, and will be transferred, for our farther progress, to still another line of coaches.

But our fast ride by the Overland Mail stages from Salt Lake will always be a chief feature in the history and memory of our grand journey across the Continent. The stations of the company are ten to fifteen miles apart; at every station fresh horses, ready harnessed, took the places of the old, with a delay of from two to four minutes only; every fifty miles a new driver took his place on the box; wherever meals were to be eaten, they were ready to serve on arrival; and so, with horses ever' fresh and fat, and gamey,—horses that would shine in Central Park and Fifth Avenue equipages,—with drivers, gentlemanly, intelligent and better dressed than their passengers, and a division superintendent, who had planned the ride and came along to see it executed, for each two hundred miles,—we were whirled over the rough mountains and through the dry and dusty plains of this uninhabited and uninhabitable,region, rarely passing a house except the stage stations, never seeing wild bird or beast, for there were none to see, as rapidly and as regularly as we could have been over macadamized roads amid a complete civilization. The speed rarely fell below eight miles an hour, and often ran up to twelve. But so wisely was all arranged, and so well executed, that not an animal suffered; to horses and men the ride seemed to be the work of every day, as indeed it was in everything but our higher rate of speed.

But the passengers are content that it should be

a single experience for them; they are glad to have had it, but will spare their friends a repetition,—at present. The alkali dust, dry with a season's sun, fine with the grinding of a season's stages and freight trains, was thick and constant and penetrating beyond experience and comparison. It filled the air,—it was the air; it covered our bodies,—it penetrated them; it soared to Almighty attributes, and became omnipresent, and finding its way into bags and trunks, begrimed all our clean clothes and reduced everything and everybody to a common plane of dirt, with a soda, soapy flavor to all.

This alkali element in the soil of all this region, as of much of the country on the other side of the Rocky Mountains, I have heard no explanation of. In some spots it prevails to such a degree as to clean the ground of all, even the most barren vegetation; and wide, smooth, bare alkali plains stretch out before the eye sometimes for miles, and white in the distance like a snow-bank. In some places so strong is it that the earth when wet rises like bread under yeast. It taints the water everywhere, and sometimes so strongly that bread mixed with it needs no other "rising." Yet I find no evidence of any general unhealthy effect from its presence; animals eat the grass and drink the water flavored with it; and though the dust chokes all pores and makes the nose and lips sore, the inconvenience and annoyance seem to be but temporary from even large doses of it.

Then the jolts of the rocks and the "chuck holes" of the road, to which the drivers in their rapid progress could give no heed, kept us in a somewhat perpetual and not altogether graceful motion. There was certainly small sleep to be enjoyed during this memorable ride of three days and nights; and though we made the best of it with joke and felicitation at each other's discomfort, there was none not glad when it was over. The drivers all had the same consolation to administer to us for the rough riding, and that was the story, memorable all along this route, of Mr. Greeley's experience upon it some six years ago. He had met rather a dull driver, was behind time, and became impatient, as he had a lecture engagement just over the mountains in California. So when he struck the mountain road, and a noted driver then and still,—for stage driving is a trade that men follow through their lives,—by name Hank Monk, Mr. Greeley suggested that he would like to get over the road a trifle faster. "Yes," said Hank, as he gathered up the reins of six half-wild mustangs, then in common use on the road,—"keep your seat Mr. Greeley, and I will get you through in time." Crack went his whip; the mustangs dashed into a fearful pace, up hill and down, along precipices frightful to look at, over rocks that kept the noted passenger passing frantically between seat and ceiling of the coach;—the philosopher soon was getting more than he bargained for; and at the first soft place on the road, he mildly suggested to the driver that a half an hour more or less would not make much difference. But Monk was in for his drive and his joke, and replied again, with a twinkle in his left eye, after a fresh cut at his mustangs, "Just keep your seat, Mr. Greeley, and you shall be through in time." Mr. Greeley kept his seat so well as he could, got through on time, and better, unharmed, though greatly to his surprise, in view of the dangers and roughness of the drive, and rewarded the driver, who had served him the rough joke, with a new suit of clothes. The story is now classic with all the drivers and all travelers on the road; and Monk wears a watch with his reply to Mr. Greeley engraved on the case,—the present of some other passengers, whom he had driven both rapidly and safely over his perilous route. The road is better now; and the horses tamer; but the driving is hardly less fearful.

It is an interesting problem whether these unpromising valleys, gray and brown with an unnatural sunshine, can ever be subdued to the service of the population that the mineral wealth of their hills invites and will inevitably draw into them. Save a sandy desert of sixty miles wide, which comes after the fertile strip of eastern Utah is passed, there is nothing in the soil itself that forbids valuable uses. It is made up of the wash and waste of the Rocky Mountains, and wherever even moderately watered is very productive. Some theorists contend that with the occupation and use of the country, rains will multiply; and the observations of the Mormons give a faint encouragement to this idea. Another theory is, that by plowing during the later rains of spring, and sowing during the long, dry summer rest, the smaller and hardy grains will sprout with the fall rains, strengthen in the winter, and quickly ripen in the early spring. Such treatment involves a year's fallow, as the harvest would be too late for another plowing the same spring. This culture is doubtless practicable, as it has been proven, in the high sage brush plains in California; but it would seem as if these alkaline valleys of the great interior basin were too cold, and go dry too long, for like successful treatment. It is worthy intelligent and persistent experiment, however; for I observe that wherever the sage bush can grow, other things can and will with the addition of water.

Do not think such a country is altogether without beauty or interest for a traveler. Mountains are always beautiful; and here they are ever in sight, wearing every variety of shape, and even in their hard and bare surfaces presenting many a fascination of form,—running up into sharp peaks; rising up and rounding out into innumerable fat mammillas, exquisitely shapen, and inviting possibly to auriferous feasts; sloping down into faint foot-hills, and mingling with the plain to which they are all destined; and now and then offering the silvery streak of snow, that is the sign of water for man and the promise of grass for ox. Add to the mountains the clear, pure, rare atmosphere, bringing remote objects close, giving new size and distinctness to moon and stars, offering sunsets and sunrises of indescribable richness and reach of color, and accompanied with cloudless skies and a south wind, refreshing at all times, and cool and exhilarating ever in the afternoon and evening; and you have large compensations even for the lack of vegetation and color in the landscape. There is a rich exhilaration, especially, in the fresh evening air, dry, clear and strengthening, that no eastern mountain or ocean breeze can rival. In looking out through it at sunset on the starry heavens, and in taking in its subtle inspiration, one almost forgets alkali, and for the nonce does not remember flowers and grass and trees.

LETTER XV.

THE SILVER MINES OF NEVADA—AUSTIN AND VIRGINIA CITY.

VIRGINIA, Nevada, June 27.

CALIFORNIA, mature at eleven, plants a colony in 1859-60, which ripens into a new State in 1864. Nevada is the first child of California. As bachelor uncles and fond friends sometimes think children are born in order to wheedle them out of silver cups; so Nevada sprang into being under like metallic influence. And if she promised to give, rather than to get, she fails yet to keep full faith; for though in her six years of life, she has yielded sixty millions of material for pure coin of the realm, she has absorbed much more than that amount of California capital and labor. Coming west out of the barren plains of the great interior basin,—even in their midst,—we strike the first wave of Pacific coast life at Austin. Five hundred miles from San Francisco, two hundred miles from the Sierra Nevadas, in middle Nevada, huddled and incoherent along the steep hill-sides of a close canyon, running sharply up from the Reese River valley, lies the easternmost and freshest mining town of the State and the section.

Two years old, Austin has already had a population of six or eight thousand, cast one thousand nine hundred votes at the presidential election, and, now, experiencing its first reaction, falls back to four thousand inhabitants. It bears family likeness to Central City and Black Hawk in Colorado; houses are built anywhere and everywhere, and streets are then made to reach them; one side of a house will be four stories and the other but two,—such is the lay of the land; not a tree nor a flower, nor a grass plot does the whole town boast,—not one; but it has the best French restaurant I have met since New York, a daily newspaper, and the boot-blacks and barbers and baths are luxurious and aristocratic to the continental degree;—while one of the finest specimens of feminine physical beauty and grace presides over a lager beer saloon; gambling riots openly in the large area of every drinking shop,—miners risking to this chance at night the proceeds of the scarcely less doubtful chance of the day; and weak-minded and curious strangers are tempted by such advertisements as this:—

Mammoth Lager Beer Saloon, in the basement, corner Main and Virginia streets, Austin, Nevada. Choice liquors, wines, lager beer and cigars, served by pretty girls, who understand their business and attend to it. Votaries of Bacchus, Gambrinus, Venus or Cupid can spend an evening agreeably at the Mammoth Saloon.

Both inquisitive and classical, we went in search of this bower of the senses; and we found a cellar, whitewashed and sawdusted; two fiddles and a clarionet in one corner; a bar of liquors glaring in another; and a fat, coarse Jew girl proved the sole embodiment and representative of all these proclaimed gods and goddesses. We blushingly apologized, and retired with our faces to Mistress Venus, Cupid, etc., as guests retire from mortal monarchs,— lest our pockets should be picked; and we shall take our mythology out of the dictionaries hereafter.

All up the Austin hill-sides, among the houses, and beyond them, are the big ant-hills that denote mines or the hopes of such. Down in the valley are the mills for crushing and separating the ore. Back and around the corners, and over the mountains for many miles, are similar though less frequent signs. The main Austin belt, however, has been successfully traced for but five miles, and one in width. The veins of ore lie thick in the rotten granite of the hills, like the spread fingers of some mineral giant. They are also comparatively small, sometimes as inches, rarely widening to more than three or four feet. But to compensate for this disadvantage, they are exceeding rich and generally reliable. But then again, the metal is so compounded with sulphurets of other metals, with antimony and arsenic, that it is hard to extract, and requires a roasting, burning, or smelting process, like the gold ores of Colorado, in addition and intermediate to those of crushing and amalgamating, to successful operation. About fifty veins are now being worked successfully, and as many more have been satisfactorily prospected, and are being put in condition for operating, or are awaiting the coming of capital and its machinery. Water flows into all the veins freely, and much labor is required to pump it out. The first necessity of every mine, indeed, is a steam engine and hoisting apparatus, to draw up water and ore from the bottom of the shaft or tunnel. But few of the mines have mills connected with them; several of the older and strong companies only combine both operations, and make the two profits. The mills are located with regard to wood and water, rather than to the ore, and the latter is carted sometimes for miles to be worked. Half a dozen mills, working some seventy-five stamps in all, are already put up in the Austin and neighboring canyons; but only about fifty stamps are now at work. The number will speedily be doubled by mills going up or undergoing repair. The ore yields from one hundred to four hundred dollars in silver and gold per ton; but at present prices, it costs nearly or quite one hundred dollars to mine and work it, so that which yields only one hundred dollars cannot be profitably worked. Consequently miners, who have no mills, separate their ores, and hire worked out only the most valuable, saving the rest up until competition brings down the price of milling, or they erect mills of their own. The charge for working the ores at the mills is eighty dollars a ton, about half of which is profit. The same description of work can be hired done here at Virginia for thirty to forty dollars per ton. The ore of one mine near Austin has averaged one hundred and eighty dollars a ton for many months, and yields a net profit of at least eighty dollars a ton to its owners. Another company,

CASES OF SUCCESSFUL MINING. 145

owning both mill and mines, finds its ores yielding one hundred and fifty dollars a ton without assorting, and the cost of getting out and working is but fifty dollars; so that, working six tons a day, their steady profits are six hundred dollars daily, on an expenditure, in investments, of less than two hundred thousand dollars, and the employment of about thirty men.

New York companies are now coming in here and putting up fine new establishments. One hundred thousand dollars will pay for a fine large mill with fifteen to twenty stamps. Promising, prospected mines can be bought for from ten thousand to one hundred thousand dollars, depending upon the extent of their claims on the surface, and the notoriety they have attained, as well as upon the gullibility of the purchasers. It is not advisable for new enterprises to erect mills, first because there will probably soon be enough in the region to supply present wants at a fair price, and second, because so soon as a cheaper and more speedy communication can be obtained, the ores will be transferred to other places, where fuel and water are more abundant, for milling. Even now, with freight ten to twelve cents a pound from Austin to San Francisco, all the ore from one mine in Austin is sent to England to be worked. It is so valuable and yet so refractory that it pays to send it this long distance in order to give it a cheap but complete manipulation.

New discoveries of valuable ore are constantly making both in the immediate neighborhood of

Austin, and far south and north on the same range of mountains. In both directions veins equally rich and much larger have been found; and many parties are busy prospecting. Scattered mills are also in operation in these more remote localities; and many a mining village is struggling for notoriety among the Humboldt mountains to the northwest. But Austin is the chief point of mining population and development in central Nevada, as Virginia is in western; and the two are by far the most conspicuous and representative points of the silver mining interest on the Pacific Coast.

But Virginia presents many contrasts to Austin. It is three or four years older; it puts its gambling behind an extra door; it is beginning to recognize the Sabbath, has many churches open, and closes part of its stores on that day; is exceedingly well built, in large proportion with solid brick stores and warehouses; and though the fast and fascinating times of 1862–63 are over, when it held from fifteen thousand to twenty thousand people, and Broadway and Wall street were not more crowded than its streets, it has a thrifty and enterprising air, and contains a population of ten thousand, besides the adjoining town or extension of Gold Hill, which has about three thousand more.

The situation of Virginia is very picturesque; above the canyon or ravine, it is spread along the mountain side, like the roof of a house, about half way to the top. Right above rises a noble peak, fifteen hundred feet higher than the town, itself about six thousand feet high; below stretches the foot-hill, bisected by the ravine; around on all sides, sister hills rise in varying hights, rich in roundness and other forms of beauty, but brown in barrenness, as if shorn for prize fight, and fading out into distant plain, with a sweet green spot to mark the rare presence of water and verdure.

Different, too, in its mines is Virginia from Austin. Instead of numerous little veins, the wealth of Virginia lies in one grand ledge of ore, running along the mountain side, just within the upper line of the town, for three miles; of width, from fifty to one hundred feet, and of depth incalculable. This is the famous Comstock Ledge; and no silver mines worth working have yet been found off from it, in the neighborhood of Virginia; though thousands of dollars and years of labor have been spent in the search. Nor has the working of this ledge at its various points been attended with uniform success. At least as many companies have failed upon it as have succeeded. Only fourteen out of about thirty companies formed and still at work upon the Comstock Ledge have paid dividends. One company has spent over a million dollars in the vain pursuit of "pay ore;" the vein it has, the ore it finds, but the latter is not rich enough to pay for milling. But it still goes on, seduced by the hope of finding the valuable streak which its neighbor had yesterday, but may have lost to-day. Other companies have spent hundreds of thousands for vain expectations; but still hold on, some of them at least, in the belief that a lower point in the lode will develop sure and recompensing wealth. The success of other companies has been more marked even than these failures, though they be fewer in number.

The Gould & Curry is the largest and most famous enterprise here. It has twelve hundred feet in length on the surface of the ledge, has dug down six hundred to eight hundred feet in depth, and back and forth on its line twenty or thirty times; its whole excavations foot up five millions of cubic feet, and afford some two miles of underground travel, and it has consumed more lumber to brace up the walls of its tunnels than the entire city of Virginia above ground has used for all its buildings. This company own the largest and finest mill probably in the world, costing nearly a million of dollars, and running eighty stamps. This mammoth enterprise has only drawn one hundred and eighty thousand dollars from its stockholders, and has paid them back four millions in dividends. Altogether, it has produced twelve millions of bullion, and but for extravagance in management and the necessity for many a blind and expensive experiment, its profit share of this sum would have been at least fifty, instead of thirty-three, per cent. In one year the yield of this mine was four and a half millions, and its profits one million, but with a railroad to San Francisco, the latter would have been swollen to three millions!

This immense development was secured under the energetic superintendence of Mr. Charles L. Strong, a native of Easthampton in Hampshire County, Massachusetts, brother of the brave General Strong who fell in leading the black troops upon the forts of Charleston, and the nephew and adopted son of Mr. A. L. Strong of that village. Mr. Strong took charge of the Gould & Curry mine in its infancy, and carried it on to its perfection and triumph, when, about a year and a half ago, his constitution gave way under its great responsibility and work, and he was forced to retire. At one time, the mine sold at the rate of six thousand dollars a foot, but now it is down to about eighteen hundred; for, though it is producing bullion at the rate of two millions a year, and pays handsome monthly dividends uninterruptedly, it has about exhausted all the valuable ore in its mine at the present depth, and is working up mainly the poorer ore that it rejected in its first progress through the vein. The company is now making an important experiment to find richer ore at a lower depth; and by means of a tunnel, started half a mile off down the hill, and a shaft one thousand feet deep, will soon open the mine that distance down. The future fortunes of the company hang mainly upon the result of this enterprise. Not only, indeed, that of the Gould & Curry, but of most of the enterprises upon the Comstock Ledge. Many of them have reached, or seem to be reaching, a like point of exhaustion with the Gould & Curry, and are either making a similar experiment, or are awaiting the results of this. The promises of a successful finding are certainly quite encouraging, and they are strengthened by the recent success of some small experiments in the same direction on distant parts of the ledge, which seem to indicate improved ore at the greater depths.

The Ophir Company is another of the mammoth enterprises. That, too, has taken out twelve millions of bullion, but the stockholders have not got much as their share, in consequence of extravagant and fickle management, and experiments that proved expensive failures. The Savage Company, owning another large and successful mine, has taken out six millions bullion.

That part of the Comstock Ledge lying on Gold Hill is divided up into smaller properties, such as one hundred and two hundred feet, and one as low as ten feet, measuring on the surface; and these have been worked generally to better advantage than the sections in Virginia. The Empire Company's claim has sold as high as eighteen thousand dollars per foot, the highest price ever obtained for any mine here; but it has grown less profitable and interrupted its dividends since, and has fallen to from three thousand to four thousand dollars a foot. This company never took any money from its stockholders, and in only one month through its operations of some years has it failed to pay expenses. Another successful and now popular company in Gold Hill is the Yellow Jacket, which has taken out about two millions of bullion, and paid its stockholders three hundred and thirty thousand dollars, or thirty-five thousand dollars more than all their assessments. But among its heavy expenditures, which suggests one cause of the ruin of many of these mining companies, is an item of two hundred and seventy thousand dollars for "legal services and quieting title."

The Comstock Ledge ore is, with small exceptions, much more simple in its combinations than that at Austin, and requires only to be crushed and amalgamated to extract the bullion. These two processes will produce from sixty to eighty per cent. of all the precious metal. It is also less rich than the Austin ore; fifty dollars is a good average per ton, and is about what the Gould & Curry claims for what it works of its own ore. But the average of all the mines is even less than that; one mine reports an average yield for the year of but $30.26 per ton; and the product of the whole ledge for the first three months of the present year is given to me as about one hundred thousand tons, yielding nearly four millions dollars, and averaging a fraction less than forty dollars. To meet this lower yield per ton, however, is a greatly decreased cost of working the ore, which does not need the roasting or smelting process, and the whole expense of mining and reducing does not exceed twenty-five dollars a ton, and is even brought as low as eighteen and twenty dollars by the Gould & Curry company. The probability is that even this cost may be much reduced, and that ore which will yield but ten and fifteen dollars to the ton can soon be worked with profit. A choice selection of the Gould & Curry ore, such as promises one thousand dollars a ton or over,—for there are streaks of such in all the mines,—is sent to Swanzey, Wales, for working;—this amounts to say fifty tons a year; a next lower quality, which will yield two hundred or three hundred dollars a ton, and amounts to some fifty or sixty tons a month, is sent over into the neighboring valley of Washoe to be treated by the Freiburg process, which includes the roasting, and is the same as is necessary for all the Reese River ores. The balance or bulk of the product is treated at their own mill, which disposes of about one hundred tons a day, or, if there is an excess, as there often is, it is worked at some neighboring custom mills.

There are, in all, seventy-seven quartz mills working on ore from the Comstock Ledge, twenty-two of which are connected with mines, and fifty-five are custom mills. They are located in four different counties, only about half being in the same county with the mines whose ores they crush. Fifty-four of them are run by steam, twelve by water, and eleven by water and steam combined. They have in all one thousand and nineteen stamps, and their capacity is one thousand eight hundred and forty-two tons daily, which is only about two-thirds employed now. The mines have been running down in daily production, from one thousand six hundred and forty tons last October to one thousand in June, but they are now increasing again; and if the present search for paying ore at lower depths in the leading mines is realized, it will speedily go up to a higher point than it ever before reached. The present product of the whole State is probably nearly twenty millions dollars a year, of which Austin is sending forward a million and a quarter, and Virginia and Gold Hill fifteen to sixteen millions. Though the bullion, as perfected here, looks like pure silver, nearly or quite one-third of it in value is really gold; and this is extracted after it gets to market, in England, or by the United States mints at San Francisco and in the East.

During the great excitement of 1862, when the Austin mines were first discovered, and the Comstock Ledge was doing its best, there was a wild speculation in mining properties, and many bogus or wildcat claims were bought and sold, and numerous companies organized that never did any business. Some statistics before me give seven hundred as the number of companies incorporated to operate on the Comstock Ledge alone; yet of these but one hundred had prospected mines, and only fourteen have operated so successfully as to pay dividends.

Most of the capital invested in the Nevada mines so far has been Californian; as most of the men engaged upon the mines, either in managing or working them, are from that State. The leading companies are owned and controlled in San Francisco, and have been to a considerable extent the victims of vicious stock gambling, which the real uncertainties of mining and the ease with which bogus uncertainties can be plausibly manufactured have tended to facilitate. As yet, though many great fortunes have been made, both from the mines and the commerce they have developed, California' has not got the money back which she has sent over the Sierras into Nevada; some say she has invested many times as much as she has received, and that not one-twentieth, not one-fiftieth, indeed, of all the mining enterprises in the silver State have succeeded; but a probably wiser judgment is that, taking the conceded values of the newly created property in Nevada, she pays a fair profit to-day; and that while one hundred millions have been invested in mills and mines, and only sixty millions taken out in bullion, the mills and mines are worth much more than the balance. Then California has taught herself and the country how to mine intelligently and economically by her Nevada experience; mining here has been carried to greater perfection than ever before on this Continent; and the wisdom thus acquired is already going back to profit California's own gold mines, and remains and extends over all the mining region as a sure and safe basis for all future operations.

Eastern capital and eastern men are now coming hither in force, and promise soon to start up anew the rather dormant life of the State, and give rapid and profitable development to its great mining wealth. One small circle of New York capitalists have already invested about two millions dollars in mills and mines here and in Austin, and by the help of a liberal faith and the employment of first-class agents, are doing well in all their enterprises. In view of this fact and example, and the wide interest manifest throughout the East, as to this mining wealth and the chances for realizing from it, let me organize some conclusions from my various observations and statistics:—

1. The eastern slopes of the Sierra Nevadas in both California and Nevada, and the mountain ranges of Nevada, are undoubtedly rich in copper,

silver and gold, silver being the predominating and most available metal.

2. In spite of the scarcity of wood and water, and the high cost of labor and food, consequent upon the great distance from supplies, and the lack of railroad communication, the extraction of these metals will pay generously for the wise, careful, honest and persevering employment of capital and labor.

3. The Comstock Ledge in Virginia and its neighborhood is being fully developed, and offers no opportunities for new enterprises; though as Pacific capital is not satisfied with less than fifty or seventy-five per cent. per annum, and eastern is happy with twenty-five, purchases of some of its mines, or of interests in them, might be favorably effected from the latter quarter without the risk of new enterprises. But those who undertake such purchases, or indeed any investments in this quarter, must not think to find these people out here wanting in sharpness at a bargain. Wall street is easily out-managed by Montgomery street, and an old miner, who is generally a traditional Yankee with large improvements, will fool a dozen spectacled professors from your colleges in a single day. The latter sort of people are, indeed, at a great discount in this region, as all the rules of science with which they come equipped, are outraged and defied by the location and combination of ores, rocks, oils and soils on this side of the Rocky Mountains.

4. The mines of the Reese River district (Austin, &c.,) though of narrow veins, offer a very promising field for new enterprises. They are richer,

and seem to be more certain to hold out than those of the Comstock Ledge; though in the matter of continuance they need yet further testing. But no such enterprise should be entered upon without first sending an intelligent agent out to examine the condition of things, the location of the mines, their improvements and promises; and, if not himself a miner, he should call to his aid here one of that class upon whom he can rely for experience and integrity.

5. Beginners in the business should not be in haste to buy or erect mills. There is a superabundance to-day of that sort of property on the Pacific Coast. Those at Virginia and its neighborhood are not worth what they cost (six millions) by at least twenty-five or thirty per cent.; and stamps and engines can probably be bought cheaper on this Coast than they can be bought in New York and shipped around or across the mountains. The first business is to work the mine and get out the ore, which can be crushed at the custom mills, already or soon to be plenty, in the neighborhood of all the mining centers; and then measuring the profits thus realized, and finding them sure and reliable, the managers can decide whether it is best to extend operations with them, by buying and working more mines or by running their own mills.

6. Everything depends upon an intelligent and faithful superintendent. I meet many such here, experienced Californians, Englishmen from the Mexican mines, Germans of both practice and theory at home, New York and Boston merchants. Fore-

men of mills and mines, first promoted from pick and shovel, are good material for such positions, and are gaining them. The miners as a class are of a higher grade than eastern laborers, and they offer many individuals fit for the upper places in the business. I was impressed with the wisdom of an organization which a party of Rhode Island capitalists had made in Colorado. They combined four or five different mines and mills, each distinct in its affairs, under the general management or overseership of an experienced scientific miner from California, and sent along with him from home a common treasurer and accountant. In this way they got the benefit of the best talent and experience, and the most reliable guardianship over the expenditures, without making the cost thereof too heavy.

7. Do not make the capital of your mining company out of all proportion to the cost of the enterprise. Avoid putting up a property, that has cost one hundred thousand dollars and needs a working capital of as much more, to two millions, because you may hope sometime to pay a ten per cent. dividend on such a sum. And then, again, do not insist on having a dividend at the end of the first thirty days, unless you are ready to pay an assessment at the beginning thereof to meet it.

8. When somebody offers you a mine, whose ore assays one thousand or ten thousand dollars a ton, you need not necessarily disbelieve him, but do not necessarily conclude that all its ore, for an indefinite distance into the earth, is of equal value. The Comstock Ledge was opened with a chunk that

yielded twenty thousand to thirty thousand dollars per ton, or at that rate; but as I have told you, the mines on that ledge that are paying at all, do not average forty dollars from their ore. Every day new discoveries are being made, south and north, in the State, of lodes whose surface ore pays, according to report, any amount this side of one hundred thousand dollars a ton! yet it does not follow that the mine below it will even pay for working. For these are among the doubtful things that are very uncertain in their progress. Even the poorest mines have their streaks and chunks of rich ore; do not, therefore, judge by a single fist-full nor by an assay; but invest your money only after you have ascertained how much your mine will practically work out, cart-load by cart-load, without culling.

9. And if you have neither time nor money enough, nor disposition, perhaps, to go largely into these mining enterprises, and follow their management intelligently, but still would like to make some small ventures to fortune in this direction, seek out some company that are in or going into the business, on these principles, and that have got a reasonably sure thing of it, and make your investment with them; and then be content with twenty-five per cent. return for your money. If it yields more, give it away in charity,—if less, or even nothing, don't swear nor mention it to your wife.

10. And finally,—though the subject, like the veins, is inexhaustible,—if you read so far as this, and make profitable use of these suggestions, "remember the printer," when the dividends come in.

LETTER XVI.

THE CONTINENT ACROSS: THE RIDE OVER THE SIERRAS.

SAN FRANCISCO, July 4.

Across the Continent! The Great Ride is finished. Fifteen hundred miles of railroad, two thousand of staging, again sixty miles of railway, and then one hundred and fifty miles by steamboat down the Sacramento River, and the goal is reached, the Continent is spanned. Seven weeks of steady journeying, within hail of a single parallel line from east to west, and still the Republic! Still the old flag,— the town is gay with its beauty to-day,—still the same Fourth of July;—better than all, still the same people, with hearts aglow with the same loyalty and pride in the American Union, and the same purpose and the same faith for its future.

Greater the wonder grows at the extent of the Republic; but larger still our wonder at the mysterious but unmistakable homogeneity of its people. San Francisco, looking westward to the Orient for greatness, cooling its summer heats with Pacific breezes, thinks the same thoughts, breathes the same patriotism, burns with the same desires that inspire New York and Boston, whose outlook is eastward, and which seem to borrow their civilization with their commerce from Europe. Sacramento talks as you do in Springfield; Nevada, over the mountains, almost out of the world, anticipates New England in her judgments, and makes up her verdict, while those close to the "Hub of the Universe" are looking over the testimony.

It is this that is the greatest thing about our country; that makes it the wonder of nations, the marvel of history,—the unity of its people in ideas and purpose; their quick assimilation of all emigration,—come it so far or so various; their simultaneous and similar currents of thought, their spontaneous, concurrent formation and utterance of a united Public Opinion. This is more than extent of territory, more than wealth of resource, more than beauty of landscape, more than variety of climate and productions, more than marvelous material development, more than cosmopolitan populations, because it exists in spite of them, and conquers them all by its subtle electricity.

It is very interesting, indeed, to stand amid this civilization of half a generation; to see towns that were not in 1850, now wearing an old and almost decaying air; to walk up and down the close built streets of this metropolis, and doubt whether they look most like Paris or New York, Brussels or Turin; to count the ocean steamers in the bay, or passing out through the narrow crack in the coast hills beautifully called the Golden Gate, and wonder as you finish your fingers where they all came from and are going to; to find an agriculture richer and more various than that of Illinois; to feast the senses on a horticulture that marries the temperate and torrid zones, and makes of every yard and garden and orchard one immense eastern green-house; to observe a commerce and an industry that supply every comfort, minister to every taste and fill the shops with every article of convenience and luxury that New York or Paris can boast of, and at prices as cheap as those of the former city to-day; to find homes more luxurious than are often seen in the eastern States, and to be challenged unsuccessfully to name the city whose ladies dress more magnificently than those of San Francisco.

None of this surprises me. I had large ideas of the Pacific Coast and its development; and I long ago gave up being surprised at any victories of the American mind and hand over raw American matter. Still, Nevada and California, with towns and cities of two to fifteen years' growth, yet to-day all full-armed in the elements of civilization, wanton with the luxuries of the senses, rich in the social amenities, supplied with churches and schools and libraries, even affecting high art, are wonderful illustrations of the rapidity and ease with which our people organize society and State, and surround themselves with all the comforts and luxuries of metropolitan life. The history of the world elsewhere offers no parallels to these.

At present, and in comparison with the flush times of their first creative years, the States and towns of the Pacific Coast are but slowly growing, and business is dull. Many mining towns are indeed falling back, if not approaching desertion. Founded on temporary interests,—the sands of their streams all washed out, they are deserted for fresher fields. But new interests, as agriculture and manufactures, and new and closer modes of extracting their mineral wealth will sooner or later restore most of these; in some instances are already beginning to do so. The general comparative dullness is but a natural and temporary reaction from a hot and stimulated development. Our great war and its interests have occupied the Nation's life and thought, and centered it in the East, absorbing its capital and offering rare opportunities, also, for new industries and speculations. California was too far away to share in this stimulus; and by rejecting the national currency that was one of its elements, she has even denied herself the benefits of its overflow. But by drouth in her agriculture, by losses in many of her mining operations, by the cessation of the heavy tide of emigration, and by the narrow policy of her bankers and capitalists, she has been gathering valuable lessons of experience; she has learned both how to farm and mine; she has come to appreciate her great wants of capital and labor; and she is in fine condition to receive and accept the new stimulus, that is already drawing out of her own trials a more economical and intelligent prosperity, and bringing in a new tide of means and men from the East. Farmers may be poor; country merchants may be bankrupt; gambling may be at a low ebb in the mining towns; labor comparatively low, and pan washings unremunerative; San Francisco brokers and bankers may, as is charged, have sucked the life out of the interior;—here, indeed, may rents be falling and houses unoccupied: but the real industries of the Pacific Coast were never more productive and promising than now,—never so much, in any previous year, of hay and grain; of vegetables and fruit, of gold and silver brought out of the ground, as is and will be in this year of -1865. This is the test and promise of prosperity; and this year will date a renewal of life and growth to California and its adjacent States,—not so hot and feverish and rabid as that of '49 and '50 and '59 and '60, but strong enough to satisfy a just ambition, and sure enough to encourage permanent investments and permanent citizenship,—the real foundations and security of a State.

But to go back on the record of our journey: Our last day in Nevada was passed among its pleasantest and richest valleys, under the shadows of the Sierra Nevada mountains, and rejoicing in the fertilizing streams from their springs and snows. Here, in the valleys of the Truckee, the Washoe, and the Carson, is the garden of the State; here were a few agricultural settlers, fifteen and twenty years ago, colonists from Utah, to which all this region was originally attached. Now, the Mormons are displaced by a more vigorous and varied population, prosperous with farming, with lumbering among the rich pines of the Sierras, and with quartz mills, seeking proximity here to wood and water, and fed by the mines over the hills in Virginia and Gold Hill

Skirting the hill-sides from Virginia at early morning, on a capital toll road, that runs from mountain to mountain on a common level, we breakfasted at Steamboat Springs, where the phenomenon of an immense natural tea-kettle is in operation. For a mile or more along a little stream, underneath a thin crust of earth, water immeasurable is seething and boiling, and occasionally breaking through in columns of steam and in bubbling spouts and streams,—too hot to bear the hand in ;—the waste drawn off to a neighboring bath-house where chronic rheumatisms and blood affections are successfully treated, or tempering the cool river below. The boiling springs are flavored with sulphur and soda, and are similar to the more celebrated Geysers in California. In the winter the vapor fills the valley, and from this and the rumbling, bubbling noise of the seething waters, comes the name of Steamboat Springs. Down the valleys we drove to Washoe Village and Lake,—here speeches and lunch,—and then farther on to Carson City, the capital of the young State, where the inevitable brass band, a militia company of twelve privates, "and nary two alike," more speeches and a dinner from Governor Blaisdell were the programme.

Here we confronted the long-looked-for, the even long-seen Sierra Nevadas, the Andes of North America, the distinctive range of our Pacific States, fountain of their streams, source and bearer of their mineral wealth, chief element and parent of their beauty of landscape, and replenisher of their fertility of soil. To us, too, long on the desert plain and the barren mountain,—sad-eyed with weeks away from forests and sparkling waters, and the verdure of grass and vines and flowers,—they offered indeed the golden pathway to the Golden Gate of the Pacific.

The ride over the mountains, down their western valleys, on to the ocean, was a succession of delights and surprises. The surging and soughing of the wind among the tall pines of the Sierras came like sweetest music, laden with memories of home and friends and youth. Brass bands begone, operas avaunt! in such presence as we found ourselves on the mountain top of a moonlight night, by the banks of Lake Tahoe, among forests to which the largest of New England are but pigmies, lying and listening by the water to the coming of the Pacific breeze and its delicate play upon the high tree-tops. All human music was but sound and fury signifying nothing, before such harmonies of high nature. The pines of these mountains are indeed monsters,—three, four, five feet through, and running up to heaven for light, straight and clear as an arrow by the hundred feet,—suggestive forerunners of *the* "big trees" of Calaveras and Mariposa, that we are yet to see. Rich green-yellow mosses cling to many a trunk; and firs and balsams fill up the vacant spots between the kingly pines; while laughing waters sport lustily before our unaccustomed eyes, among the rocks in the deep ravines, along and far below the road on which our horses gallop up hill and down at a fearful pace.

The initial trip of a little steamer upon Lake

Tahoe (formerly Lake Bigler) was among the novelties of our mountain experience. This is one of the beautiful lakes of the world, richly ranking with those of Scotland and Swiss-Italy, and destined to arouse as wide enthusiasm. It is located up among the mountains, itself six thousand five hundred feet high, overlooked by snow-capped peaks, bordered by luscious forests; stretches wide for eight to fourteen miles in extent, with waters clear and rare almost as air,—so rare, indeed, that not even a sheet of paper can float, but quickly sinks, and swimming is nearly impossible; and abounds in trout:—where, indeed, are more elements of lake beauty and attraction? Already, though far from heavy populations, it has its mountain and lake hotel, and draws many summer visitors from California and Nevada.

From Lake Tahoe to Placerville, the first considerable town in California, is seventy-five miles of well-graded road, up to the mountain summits, and down on the western side; and the drive over it, made in less than seven hours, even surpassed any that had gone before in rapidity and brilliancy of execution. With six horses, fresh and fast, we swept up the hill at a trot, and rolled down again at their sharpest gallop, turning abrupt corners without a pull-up, twisting among and by the loaded teams of freight toiling over into Nevada, and running along the edge of high precipices, all as deftly as the skater flies or the steam car runs; though for many a moment we held our fainting breath at what seemed great risks or dare-devil performances. The road is excellent, hard and macadamized, constructed by private enterprise and imposing heavy tolls, and therefore far different from that, whose rough remains and steep passages are occasionally met on the mountain side, over which Mr. Greeley made his famous ride six years ago.

But there is no stage-riding, no stage-driving, left in the States,—I doubt if there ever was any,—at all comparable to this in perfection of discipline, in celerity and comfort, and in manipulation of the reins. Mr. Colfax well said, in one of his speeches, that as it was said to require more talent to cross Broadway than to be a justice of the peace in the country, so he was sure much more was necessary to drive a stage down the Sierras as we were driven, than to be a member of Congress. For a week, at least, we worshiped our knights of the whip. Think, too, of a stage-road one hundred miles long, from Carson to Placerville, watered as city streets are watered, to lay the dust for the traveler! Yet this luxury is performed through nearly the entire route, day by day, all the summer season.

All over the Sierras in our road, the scenery is full of various beauty; some of its features I have mentioned; but another chief one was the high walls of rock, rising abruptly and perpendicularly from the valley for many hundreds of feet. Many a rich boulder, anon a hill, and a frequent mountain peak of pure rock, thousands of feet high, like pyramids of Egypt, are seen along the passage. The whole scenery of the Sierras is more like that of the Alps than any other in America, and has even features of surpassing attraction.

At Placerville, among vineyards and orchards and flower gardens, a night; three speeches from Speaker Colfax, and a grand midnight dinner;—at Sacramento, sixty miles hence by a railroad, which is seeking the mountains,—a superb breakfast and two speeches and more roses,—and thence by steamboat, large and elegant as the best of Sound and North River boats, and all built in San Francisco, through wide grain fields, yellow with harvest and sun, we came to refreshing halt in the luxurious halls of the Occidental Hotel, of famous Leland creation and supervision, late on the last Saturday night.

My memory is crowded with observations in California and Nevada, yet to be compacted for your reading; but the journey cannot wait now for them. My steps move faster than my pen. Next Monday,—after a crowded week of sight-seeing and hospitality in San Francisco and vicinity,—we retrace our steps as far as the mountains on a more northern route, and thence into the most interesting gold-quartz mining region, and on along the valleys on the eastern slope of the Sierras north to Oregon, and back, through British Columbia, and by the ocean, the first of August.

LETTER XVII.

OVERLAND TO OREGON.

PORTLAND, Oregon, July 20.

I WAS prepared for California. But Oregon is more of a revelation. It has rarer natural beauties, richer resources, a larger development, and a more promising future than I had learned of. The dazzle of gold and silver has made California more conspicuous in eastern eyes. Our visit here has therefore had the always delicious element of unexpectedness in its pleasures. There was some rebellious flesh among us, when we were told that to see Oregon we must take another week of day and night stage riding; much of it on rough mountain roads, and in a "mud wagon" at that. We thought to have been through with that sort of travel. But no week's riding has given us greater or richer variety of experience; more beauty of landscape; more revelation of knowledge; more pleasure and less pain, than this one up through northern California and middle Oregon, between the coast mountains and the Sierra Nevadas.

Our point of departure was Sacramento, and the distance to Portland from there is six hundred and fifty miles, due north. Two short bits of railroad put us forward in the Sacramento valley about fifty miles; at Oroville we began the stage ride proper, up still for another one hundred miles in the broad and generally rich and beautiful valley of the Sacramento and its tributaries,—sometimes rolling in waves of earth, then flat and wide as flattest and widest of Illinois prairies, often treeless and uncultivated, though not uncultivatable; and again charming with old oak groves, and fruitful with grain fields and orchards, that yield an increase unknown in all eastern or western valleys. At Chico, we took supper with General Bidwell, one of the pioneers of the Pacific Coast, and one of the new members of Congress from California. Jilted by a young woman who chose a lover with more acres, he turned rover, and came out here from Missouri as early as 1841 as one of a secret filibustering party, that intended to get up a revolution against Mexico, then the parent of this region, and join California to the then lone star republic of Texas. The scheme was fruitless, but General Bidwell became the owner of one of the famous Spanish grants of land in the richest part of this valley, and now has a farm of twenty thousand of its acres, of which one thousand eight hundred are under cultivation. His crop of wheat, in 1863, was thirty-six thousand bushels, from nine hundred acres of land, or at the average rate of forty bushels to the acre. This is a poorer grain year, and his wheat will average but thirty bushels per acre. The general average of the valley is twenty-five bushels. Of barley and oats, his other principal crops, he usually harvests fifty bushels to the acre. His garden and orchard cover one hundred acres. A large flouring mill is among his concerns, and its product is the favorite brand of the State. Add to these illustrative facts of his wealth, and of the beauty and productiveness of the country, that General Bidwell still seems a young man, is fresh and handsome and of winning manners,—a bachelor, and intends to keep house in Washington during his congressional term, and do I not equally interest farmers, statisticians and the ladies of our capital's society?

On through a like productive country, crossing streams whose banks are lined with an almost tropical growth of trees and vines, along roads bordered with fences and trees, by farms and orchards rich in grains and fruits, we make our first night ride, passing in the gray morning the prosperous little town of Red Bluffs, which is noteworthy as the head of navigation on the Sacramento River,—some three hundred miles from its mouth,—and so a central point of commerce for all northern California and southern Oregon, and as the present home of the widow and daughters of the immortal John Brown. They straggled in here, weary and poor, from their overland journey, but found most hospitable greeting from the citizens and have secured a permanent home. A subscription among the Californians generally will give them soon a nice cottage; Mrs. Brown earns both love and support as a successful nurse and doctor, particularly for children; her two older daughters are teachers in the public schools; and the younger one is herself a pupil.

Now the valley grows narrow, the mountains east and west chassez across and in among each other, and for the remaining two hundred miles of California, and the first two hundred of Oregon, we are winding among the hills and following up and down narrow valleys, first of tributaries of the Sacramento, and then of minor though earnest streams,—Trinity, Klamath, Rogue and Umpqua,—that steal their way, among the now scattered and mingling ranges of coast and Sierra Nevada, west to the ocean.

Shasta and Yreka are the two remaining villages of importance in California, with perhaps fifteen hundred inhabitants each. Born of rich placer gold diggings in neighboring valleys and gulches, but bereft of half of their former population by the discovery of more tempting fields elsewhere, and the inherent migratory character of gold seekers, they present a sad array of unoccupied stores and houses, like, indeed, to nearly every other of the interior mining towns of California. Their second reactionary stage now seems beginning, however; a more careful and intelligent working of the gold sands and banks proves them still profitable,—in some cases richly so; the Chinese are coming in to work over the neglected courses, satisfied with smaller returns than the whites; and best of all, agriculture, hitherto despised, is asserting its legitimate place as the base of all true and steady prosperity. The valleys, though small, are fruitful, and many of the hill-sides are equally rich for grain and fruit. These hills of northern California and southern Oregon seem, indeed, the true home of apple, pear and grape, and are sure to have a large place in the future fruit-growing and wine-making prosperity of the Pacific Coast.

Beyond Shasta, just out of the valley, we stopped to dine at a most inviting hotel, amid garden and orchard of great fruitfulness, which I found to be "The Tower House," and the proprietor Mr. Levi H. Tower, whom you Springfield people of fifteen and twenty years' residence will remember as a prominent armorer, foreman of the Eagle Engine Company, and a popular young man, up to 1849, when he cast in his fortunes with the first emigration to California. After years of the ups and downs that belong to nearly every experience on this Coast, he has become prosperous, and grown stout, but keeps his Springfield memories green, and is yet a bachelor. Two of his sisters and a brother-in-law live upon his place. He owns a toll-road over the mountain, and his orchard, only five years old, produced last year three thousand bushels of peaches, one thousand five hundred bushels of apples, and grapes by the ton, for which he finds market among the miners in the mountains around, and in the villages north and south.

Along here, individual mountains assumed a rare majesty; snow peaks were visible, ten thousand and eleven thousand feet high; and soon, too, Mount Shasta, monarch of the Sierras in northern California, reared its lofty crown of white, conspicuous among hills of five thousand and six thousand feet,* both for its vast fields of snow, its perfect shape, and its hight of fourteen thousand four hundred feet above the sea level. We saw it from various points and all sides, and everywhere it was truly a King of the Mountains, and is entitled to rank among the first dozen mountain peaks of the world.

Jacksonville was the first conspicuous town in Oregon, and showed obvious first-cousinship to Yreka and Shasta. But its neighboring gold diggings made better report; many of the five hundred men engaged upon them in the county were very prosperous, and all were making good wages; promising quartz mines were also discovered; and we found, everywhere almost in these mountain counties of northern California and southern Oregon, gathering evidences of much gold yet uncrushed or undug, that would still form the basis, with cheaper and more abundant labor and capital, of a large population and a new material growth for this region. The northern county of California (Siskiyou) counts no fewer than two thousand Chinese among its population, and of these, eleven hundred are engaged in gold digging, from whom as foreigners the State gathers a tax of four dollars a month each, or from fifty thousand to sixty thousand dollars a year. That they pay this enormous tribute, and still keep at work, shows well enough that it pays them to wash and re-wash the golden sands of these valleys.

The scenery of this region is full of various beauty. Of conspicuous single objects, Pilot Knob, a great chunk of bare rock standing on a mountain top, ranks next to Mount Shasta; it must be eight hundred to one thousand feet high in itself, and seen from all quarters, it has been famous as a pilot to the early emigrants in their journey across the mountains. The hills are rich with pine forests, and these grow thicker and the trees larger and of greater variety, as also the valleys widen and seem more fertile, as the road progresses into Oregon. Firs rival the pines and grow to similar size, one hundred and two hundred feet high and three to five feet in diameter. Farther up in Oregon, about the Columbia River, the fir even dominates, and is the chief timber, and specimens of it are recorded that are twelve feet through and three hundred feet high! The oak, too, has its victories in the valleys, and we ride through groves and parks of it that are indescribably beautiful. That fascinating parasite of British classics, the mistletoe, appears also, and shrouds the branches of the oak with its rich, tender green, and feeds on its rugged life. Many an oak had succumbed to the greedy bunch boughs of the mistletoe, that fastened themselves upon it, and despite its beauty and the sentimental reputation it brings to us from British poets, I came to shrink from its touch and sight. More graceful and inviting and less absorbing of life,—rather token of death,—was the pendant Spanish moss, hanging gray and sere and sad from the pine branches and trunks, along our way in southern Oregon.

The birch, the ash, the spruce, the arbor vitae, and the balsam, all contribute to these forests.

But they do not rob your Connecticut valley of its precious elms; to their individual beauty no tree here can offer successful rivalry. In aggregates, however, for forests of trees, for size and beauty of pines and spruces and firs, for amount and quality of timber as timber, and for groves of oaks, there can be no competition in the East to the Sierra Nevadas and the Coast Mountains and their intermediate valleys in California and Oregon. They become the perpetual wonder and admiration and enthusiasm of the traveler.

The cross valleys of the Rogue and Umpqua rivers present many rich fields for culture. The soil is a gravelly loam, warm and fertile, and more favorable for fruits, especially the grape and the peach, than the more northern valleys of Oregon. But the way to market is long and hard; and the products of agriculture here must mainly go out to the world on the hoof or in wool. So that the temptation to the farmer is not yet very strong. Yet we found a few rich farms and prosperous gentleman farmers. "Joe" Lane, famous in Oregon politics, lives in one of these valleys; his occupation of public life is gone; he fell out with a portion of his own party, and was put out by the uprising volume of loyal and anti-slavery sentiment, wherein he has never shown any sympathy. He was an able but low, coarse and groveling politician.

A man of another description and history is Mr. Jesse Applegate, whose fame as an old pioneer, an honest, intelligent gentleman, incorruptible in thought and act, and the maker of good cider, kept increasing as we neared his home in the Umpqua; and we made bold to stop and tell him we had come to see him and eat our breakfast out of his larder. We did all to our supreme satisfaction, finding a vigorous old man, who had been here twenty-five years, participated largely in the growth and history of the country, and the conversion of its people to right political principles; clear and strong and original in thought and its expression, with views upon our public affairs worthy the heed of our wisest; every way, indeed, such a man as you wonder to find here in the woods, rejoice to find anywhere, and hunger to have in his rightful position, conspicuous in the government. Oregon ought surely to send Jesse Applegate to Washington, and the general testimony is that she would, were he not so implacably hostile to all the helping arts of politician and place-seeker, which is of course only another reason why she should do what she yet does not. Mr. Applegate has sent his three sons to the war, and remains in their place to carry on his farm of two thousand acres. But farming here, he says, is but a cheap, careless process; labor is so dear, and grain grows so easily, and the market is so distant, that there is no incentive for real cultivation and care, in the business. Grass grows naturally, abundantly; timothy seed thrown upon the unbroken soil, gives the best of permanent mowing; and so mild are the winters, and so abundant the feed upon hill and plain, that even that is only improved as a precaution against exceptional snow.

Though he feeds cattle by the hundreds and thousands, he has now one hundred and twenty-five tons of hay that he cut two years ago, but for which he has had no use.

Two days and a night of rough riding from Jacksonville over rather unmilitary roads, built some years ago by the since famous General Hooker, brought us out, of a sweet, June-like afternoon, upon the hill that overlooks the head of the Willamette (Wil-*lam*-ette) Valley. Here the mountain ranges cease their mazy dancing together, and take their places east and west, feeding a river that runs midway north one hundred and twenty-five miles to the Columbia River, and watering a valley through that length and for fifty miles wide. This is the Willamette River and valley,—the garden of Oregon,—itself Oregon; that which led emigrants here years before the gold discoveries on the Pacific Coast; the holder of nearly two-thirds of all the inhabitants of the State; the chief source of its present strength and prosperity, and its sure security for the future; lifting it above the uncertainties of mining, and giving guaranty of stability, intelligence and comfort to its people.

We were led down into this indeed paradisiacal valley through richest groves of oak; the same are scattered along the foot hills on either side, or people the swelling hills that occasionally vary the prairie surface of its central lines; while the river, strong and free and navigable through the whole valley a part of the year, and through the lower half at all times, furnishes a deep belt of forest through the very middle of the valley. Never beheld I more fascinating theater for rural homes; never seemed more fitly united natural beauty and practical comforts; fertility of soil and variety of surface and production; never were my bucolic instincts more deeply stirred than in this first outlook upon the Willamette valley. The soil is a strong, clayey, vegetable loam, on a hardpan bottom, holding manures firmly, and yielding large crops of the small grains, apples and potatoes. Wheat and apples are the two great crops at present; much of the improved land being set out with apple orchards, that come into full bearing in from two to three years after planting. Wool and beef are, also, as in the lower valleys, leading items in the agricultural wealth of the Willamette. The hills and valleys of interior Oregon furnish almost inexhaustible and continuous pasture grounds. The spring is too cold and wet for peaches; the summer nights are too cold for corn, though it is grown to a limited degree; but Isabella and Catawba grapes ripen perfectly; it is the home of the cherry; and pears, plums and all the small berries reach high perfection. The average yield of wheat in the valley is twenty-five bushels to the acre; but fifty is often obtained with careful cultivation.

Though this valley supports a population of fifty thousand by agriculture only, probably not one-tenth of its area has yet felt the plow, and certainly not over one-half is under fence. Its best lands can be bought for from five to twenty-five dollars an acre, depending upon improvements, and nearness to villages and river. Only specially favored farms go higher, as some do to fifty and even one hundred dollars an acre. Much of the farming is unwisely done; the farms are generally too large, the original locations being mostly of six hundred and forty acres each; and the agricultural population are largely Missourians, Kentuckians and Tennesseeans, of that class who are forever moving farther west, and only stop here because there is no beyond but the ocean. The eastern men proper in Oregon, of whom there are indeed many, are mostly in the villages and towns, leaders in trade, and commerce, and manufactures, as well as in the professions.

The agriculture of Oregon knows no such drawback and doubt as the long summer drouths, that hang over that of all the rest of the country west of the Rocky Mountains, and render expensive irrigation a necessity to certainty in culture. Her fertile region,—so made fertile, indeed,—between the Coast Mountains and the Sierras, or the Cascades, as the interior range of mountains is called in Oregon, is abundantly supplied with rain the year round. There is enough in summer to ripen the crops, and not too much to interfere with harvesting; and the winter is one long shower of six months. The Californians call their northern neighbors the Web Feet; and from all account there is something too much of rain and mud during the winter season; but the fertility and perfection which its agriculture enjoys in consequence leave the practical side of the joke with the Oregonians.

There is no snow in the valleys of middle and western Oregon; only rain and mist deaden the dormant season; but February is usually a clear and warm month, and the work of the farmer then actively begins. The summers are long and favorable, with warm days but cool nights,—more endurable for the human system than New England summers, and kinder for all vegetation, with the single exception, perhaps, of Indian corn. The average temperature of the Willamette valley for the six summer months is from sixty-five to seventy, and of the six winter months from forty to forty-five degrees. And grass grows through all the so-called winter.

Eugene City, Corvallis, Albany, Salem, Oregon City and Portland are the chief centers of population in the Willamette valley, in the order in which we passed them, coming down to the Columbia. Salem is the State capital, and is a beautifully located, thriving, inland town. Here our party had a state reception; here I met our old democratic brother editor of Westfield, Massachusetts, Mr. Asahel Bush, who has made a fortune here, and wielded large power in the politics of the State, dethroning on the Douglas breach Joe Lane as senator, but failing to keep progressing in the right direction, is now himself dethroned by the Union and republican possession of the State, and is in retirement from newspaper and business, and meditating eastern migration; here, too, Mr. Reuben Boies, of Blandford origin and Chicopee residence, has grown into just distinction, and is one of the supreme judges of the State, but has his present residence on a beautiful farm in one of the neighboring foothills, where also he has erected and put in successful operation a woolen mill;—and from here, also, we took steamboat passage, fifty miles, to this town, the commercial and business center of the State, half rival to San Francisco itself, and the only other town, indeed, of prominence on the Pacific Coast, that shows signs of steady, uninterrupted prosperity at this moment. At Oregon City, on our way hither, we paid respect to the original capital of the Territory, inspected a new and extensive woolen mill that cost seventy-five thousand dollars in gold, and were railroaded around the falls of the Willamette, which, though not a brilliant feature in the natural scene, offer temptations and almost inexhaustible water-power for the manufactures that the agricultural productions of the State invite, and the enterprise of its citizens is already wisely and eagerly reaching forward to.

Portland, by far the largest town of Oregon, stands sweetly on the banks of the Willamette, twelve miles before it joins the Columbia River, and one hundred and twenty miles from where the Columbia meets the Pacific Ocean. Ships and ocean steamers of highest class come readily hither; from it spreads out a wide navigation by steamboat of the Columbia and its branches, below and above; here centers a large and increasing trade, not only for the Willamette valley, but for the mining regions of eastern Oregon and Idaho, Washington Territory on the north, and parts even of British Columbia.

Even Salt Lake, too, has taken groceries and dry goods through this channel, and may yet find it advantageous to buy more and continuously; such are the attained and attainable water communications through the far-extending Columbia.

The population of Portland is about seven thousand; they keep Sunday as we do in New England, and as no other population this side of the Missouri now does; and real estate, as you may infer, is quite high,—four hundred dollars a front foot for best lots one hundred feet deep on the main business street, without the buildings. In religion, the Methodists have the lead, and control an academic school in town and a professed State university at Salem; the Presbyterians are next with a beautiful church and the most fashionable congregation, and favor a struggling university under Rev. S. H. Marsh, (son of President Marsh of the Vermont university,) located twenty miles off in the valley; perhaps the Catholics rank third, with a large Sisters of Charity establishment and school within the city. Governor Gibbs, the present chief magistrate of the State, resides here, and though a lawyer, owns and runs a successful iron foundry that imports its material from England, though undeveloped iron mines are thick in neighboring hills;—a single daily paper has two thousand five hundred circulation, with a weekly edition of three thousand more; and altogether Portland has the air and the fact of a prosperous, energetic town, with a good deal of eastern leadership and tone to business and society and morals.

LETTER XVIII.

THE COLUMBIA RIVER—ITS SCENERY AND ITS COMMERCE.

PORTLAND, Oregon, July 23.

WHEN an enthusiastic Oregonian told me the Columbia River was the largest of the Continent, and watered a wider section of country than any other, I thought of the St. Lawrence and the Mississippi, and smiled with mild incredulity. But unroll your map, and trace its course into the heart of this north-western interior, through the Cascade Mountains, back into the great basin between them and the Rocky Mountains, and then, by its main branches, stretching up north and winding out through all British Columbia, and south and west into Idaho and over into the bowels of the Rocky Mountains, touching with its fingers all the vast area north of the great desert basin and west of the Rocky Mountains; then sail with me up and down its mile and a half wide sweep of majestic volume, at the distance of one hundred and fifty miles above its mouth; see what steamboats already navigate its waters, and the points to which they reach; and listen to the wide plans of the navigators for the use of its most distant upper waters, in British Columbia and Idaho,—sapping the very vitals of British dominion in the North-west, and practically tapping the Pacific railroad as it comes west at Salt Lake for the benefit of Portland and Oregon,—do all this, and we will make our bow together to the Oregonians and their great river.

Only more full surveys can determine the literal correctness of their claims to superior vastness; the Columbia, with its chief division, the Snake, may be anywhere from twelve hundred to two thousand miles in length;—but that it ranks among the three or four great rivers of the world, and that it is the key to vast political and commercial questions and interests,—giving to its line the elements of a powerful rivalry to the great central commercial route of our Continent, of which San Francisco is the Pacific terminus,—no one who examines its position and extent, and witnesses the various capacity of the territory it waters, can for a moment doubt.

As yet, however, the Columbia is most known abroad for the rare beauty and majesty of the scenery developed by its passage through the great Andean range of north-western America. Alone of all the rivers of the West has it broken these stern barriers, and the theater of the conquering conflict offers, as might naturally be supposed, many an unusual feature of nature. River and rock have striven together, wrestling in close and doubtful embrace,—sometimes one gaining ascendancy, again the other, but finally the subtler and more seductive element worrying its rival out, and gaining the western sunshine, broken and scarred and foaming with hot sweat, but proudly victorious, and forcing the withdrawing arms of its opponent to hold up eternal monuments of its triumph.

To witness these scenes has been the main purpose and chief pleasure of a two days' excursion up the stream from Portland. Starting at early morning on a steamboat as capacious and comfortable as the best of those on eastern rivers, and with a company of the leading citizens of Oregon, we soon turned out of the Willamette (twelve miles), and steamed up the broad, deep current of the Columbia. Near at hand was Vancouver, a famous spot in this valley, first as a leading station of the Hudson Bay Company for many years, and since and now as the chief military station of the United States in the interior North-west. Here many of our prominent military men have served apprenticeship,—Grant, Hooker, McClellan and Ingles among them. They are all well remembered in the days of their captaincies here by the old inhabitants. Grant was the same quiet, close-mouthed man then as now, but gave no indication of that great mastery of himself and of others, that he has within these few years so nobly, and to such high purpose, demonstrated. It was while here that he left the army originally, to come back to it in the hour of the Nation's need, a new and nobler man. The present arrangement of the quarters and offices of the post was made under Colonel Ingles' administration, and is both generous and tasteful. It is evidently both a favorite and comfortable military post, and continues to be, as it long has been, one of the "soft places" in the army on this Coast.

Fifty miles of steaming up through heavily wooded banks brought us to the foot-hills of the Cascade Mountains, and soon we were upon the charmed ground. High walls of basaltic rock rose slowly on either side; huge boulders, thrown off in the convulsion of water with mountain, lie lower down the valley, or stand out in the stream,—one so large, rising in rough egg shape some thousand feet up into the air, as to become a conspicuous and memorable element in the landscape. The river gets too fast here, at the Cascades, as they are called, for farther progress by boat; we change to a railway of five miles, along rock and river, at the end of which we come to navigable waters again, and find, to our surprise, another large, and equally luxurious steamer. During these five miles of the Cascades, the river makes a descent of forty feet, half of it in one mile, but it takes the form of rough and rocky rapids, and not of one distinct, measurable fall. The second boat took us from the Upper Cascades to the Dalles, forty-five miles, all the way through the mountains. The waters narrow and run swift and harsh; the rocks grow higher and sharper; and their architecture, by fire and water, assumes noble and massive forms. The dark, basaltic stones lie along in even layers, seamed as in the walls of human structure; then they change to upright form, and run up in well-rounded columns, one after another, one above another. Often is rich similitude to ruined castles of the Rhine;

more frequently, fashions and forms, too massive, too majestic, too unique for human ambition and art to aspire to. Where the clear rock retires, and sloping sides invite, verdure springs strong, and forests, as thick and high as in the valleys, fill the landscape.

At the Dalles lies the second town in Oregon, bearing the name of The Dalles, and holding a population of twenty-five hundred. It is the *entrepot* for the scattered mines in eastern Oregon, for we are now on the eastern slopes of the mountains, and very much also for the Boise and Owyhee mines in Idaho. The miners come in here to winter, send there earnings in here, and buy here many of their supplies. Two millions dollars in gold dust came in here from eastern Oregon and Idaho in the single month of June last. The town is ambitious of that unnecessary adjunct, a mint, and the Oregon politicians have even wheedled Congress out of a preliminary appropriation for one.

The Dalles marks another interruption to the navigation of the river, and another railway portage of fifteen miles is in use. The entire water of the Columbia is compressed for a short distance into a space only one hundred and sixty feet wide. Through this it pours with a rapidity and a depth, that give majestic, fearful intensity to its motion; while interfering rocks occasionally throw the stream into rich masses of foam. Through these second rapids of fifteen miles, the rock scenery at first rises still higher and sharper, and then fast grows tame; the mountains begin to slink away and to lose their trees; the familiar barrenness of the great interior basin reappears; and the only beauty of the hills is their richly rounded forms, often repeated, and their only utility pasturage for sheep and horses and cattle. The fifteen miles of railway, which, with the lower portage of five miles, are built as permanently, and served as thoroughly, with the best of locomotives and cars, as any railroads in the country, landed us on still another large and luxurious steamboat,—"and still the wonder grew,"—built way up here beyond the mountains, but with every appointment of comfort and luxury that are found in the best of eastern river craft,—large state-rooms, long and wide cabins, various and well-served meals. From this point (Celilo), there is uninterrupted navigation, and daily or tri-weekly steamers running, to Umatilla, eighty-five miles, Wallula, one hundred and ten miles, and to White Bluffs, one hundred and sixty miles, farther up the stream. For six months in the year, boats can and do run way on to Lewiston, on the Snake River branch of the Columbia, which is two hundred and seventy miles beyond Celilo, or five hundred miles from the mouth of the Columbia, as White Bluffs, the head of navigation on the main river, is four hundred miles from the mouth.

We spent the night on the boat at Celilo, and during the evening the most of the party went back by rail to The Dalles for speeches to the people from Speaker Colfax and Governor Bross. One of the best bits of fun on our journey was improvised on their return late in the night. Those who had remained on the boat suddenly emerged from their state-rooms, wrapped in the drapery in which they had laid themselves down to sleep, and proceeded to give formal welcome to the entering party. Mr. Richardson addressed the Speaker in an amusing travestie of some familiar points in his own speeches. Mr. Colfax seized the joke, and replied *a la* Richardson with equal effectiveness. The whole scene and performance was picturesque and amusing in the highest degree; and the cabin resounded with boisterous laughter from all sides.

The next morning, we proceeded thirty or forty miles still farther up the river, till we had got beyond all traces of the collision of the stream with the mountain, and the scenery grew tame and common. Then we turned back, having reached a point two hundred and sixty miles above the mouth of the river, and retraced our passage through the mountains, renewing our worship and our wonder before the strange and beautiful effects produced by this piercing of these eternal hills by this majestic river of the West. As a whole, I know no like scenery so grand, so beautiful. It has much of the distinguishing elements of the Hudson in its Palisades, of the Rhine in its embattled, precipitous and irregularly shaped sides, and of the Upper Mississippi in its overhanging cliffs. Each of these holds a beauty that is not here; but the Columbia aggregates more than any one the elements of impressiveness, of picturesque majesty, of wonder-working, powerful nature. I was more enthusiastic over each of those rivers; I saw them with younger and less weary eyes; but this convinces my intellect of its superiority. There is, however, a general uniformity in its characteristics; one five miles repeats another; and once seen, you are indifferent as to a second sight,—before next year, or unless with the accompaniment of new and beloved eyes.

A distinguishing feature in the landscape of this ride up the Columbia,—apart from it, yet bounding it, shadowing it, yet enkindling it with highest majesty and beauty,—is Mount Hood. This is the great snow peak of Oregon, its Shasta, its Rainier, its Mount Blanc. Lying off twenty or thirty miles south of the river, in its passage through the mountains, it towers high above all its fellows, and is seen, now through their gorges, and again at the end of apparent long plains, leading up to it from the river. Most magnificent views of it are obtained through nearly all the sail up and down from Portland. That which Bierstadt has chosen for its perpetuation on canvas, and which is thus familiar to eastern eyes, is the most complete and impressive, and is recognized upon the steamboat. In it, the mountain seems to rise, apart, out from an upward-going plain, snow-covered from base to summit, oppressive in its majesty, beautiful in form, angelic in its whiteness,—the union of all that is great and pure and impressive. Various hights are claimed for Hood, from twelve thousand to eighteen thousand five hundred feet; but it is not at all likely that it exceeds twelve thousand or thirteen thousand feet, or less than Shasta in northern California, and less, also, than Rainier and Adams in Washington Territory.

There is some rivalry among the neighbors of these great snow peaks of the north-western United States as to which is the highest. There are four or five of them from eleven thousand to fifteen thousand feet each, and the last one the traveler beholds seems to him not only the highest but the most beautiful, so engrossing is the view. But the most reliable measurements give Shasta the palm at fourteen thousand four hundred and forty feet, and, until within a year, made it the highest mountain peak in the United States. Last season, however, the explorations of the California Geological Survey brought to knowledge a series of rare snow-covered and granite peaks, among the Sierra Nevadas in southern California and Nevada, one or two of which, at least, mount higher than Shasta, and, for the present at least, may claim to be the highest land in the Nation. One of these peaks was called Mount Tyndall, and is about fourteen thousand five hundred feet high; and another, the very highest, is named Mount Whitney for the head of the Geological Survey of California, and is at least fifteen thousand feet high.

But no mountain peak we have yet passed in our journey is seen to so fine advantage as Mount Hood from the Columbia River,—it is hard to imagine a more magnificent snow mountain; and adding this crowning element to the scenery of the Columbia River, it is probably just to say of it, that this excursion offers more of natural beauty and wonder to interest and excite the traveler, than any other single journey or scene which the Pacific Coast presents, except the Yosemite valley. That must, of course, stand first, unrivaled and unapproachable. But to this I give the second place.

The navigation of the Columbia River is now in the hands of a strong and energetic company, that not only have the capacity to improve all its present opportunities, but the foresight to seek out and create new ones. They are, indeed, making new paths in the wilderness, and show more comprehension of the situation and purpose to develop it than any set of men I have yet met on the Pacific Coast. Organized in 1861, with property worth one hundred and seventy-five thousand dollars, they have now, with eighteen or twenty first class steamboats, the two railroads around the Cascades and The Dalles, and their appointments, warehouses at all the principal towns on the river, including one nine hundred and thirty-five feet long at Cellilo, and real estate in preparation for future growth, a total property of rising two millions dollars, all earned from their business. Besides this great increase of wealth from their own enterprise, they have paid to themselves in dividends three hundred and thirty-two thousand seven hundred and fifty dollars. With wagon roads from The Dalles, from Umatilla, and from Wallula, the river and their boats have formed and still form the cheapest and quickest route for travel or freight from all parts of the Coast to the rich mines of Boise and Owyhee in Idaho, as well as to those in eastern Oregon. Boise

City is two hundred and sixty miles from Umatilla and Owyhee two hundred and ninety miles. The roads from the other points are longer and poorer. So large have been the travel and trade in this direction in the last few years, that the Oregon steam navigation company has carried to the Upper Columbia sixty thousand three hundred and twenty tons in the last four years, beginning with six thousand tons in 1862 and rising to nearly twenty-two thousand tons in 1864. In the same time, their boats have carried up and down on the river nearly one hundred thousand passengers, increasing from ten thousand in 1861 to thirty-six thousand in 1864.

California has at last aroused to the importance of securing this trade, if possible, for herself, and is opening shorter wagon routes to Idaho by way of Chico and Red Bluffs in the upper Sacramento valley, and through Nevada by the Humboldt valley; but the Oregon people are still likely to keep the larger share of the traffic, for their route, though longer, is very much by water, and so cheaper, safer and pleasanter. The Oregon navigation company are also busy with plans for improving their own route. By opening a road one hundred and ten miles long, across a wide bend of unnavigable sections of the Snake River, from Wallula to the mouth of the Powder River, they will again find the Snake River navigable for one hundred and fifty to two hundred miles farther up its course, or into the very heart of the Owyhee and Boise gold basins, and on beyond towards Utah. Then from this new head of navigation on the Snake

River, to Salt Lake, is but one hundred or one hundred and fifty miles more; so that with wagon roads of less than three hundred miles, steam navigation may soon be secured all the way from Salt Lake to the Pacific Ocean in Oregon. Substitute for these wagon roads a railway, or, leaving out the navigation of the upper Snake, and building a railroad five hundred and fifty miles across from Salt Lake through the gold regions of Idaho to Wallula, whence is uninterrupted navigation down the Columbia, and the Pacific Coast is reached by steam through Oregon with less than two-thirds the railroad building required for the central route into San Francisco. The line for this suggested road is easy, crossing the Blue Mountains in eastern Oregon by a very favorable pass, and avoiding by the Columbia River the great work of surmounting the Sierra Nevadas. These are important, pregnant suggestions. The Oregon navigation company is impressed with their significance, and will next spring construct a steamboat on the upper Snake for testing the practicability of that point in the programme. They mean at least to hold their superiority in the commerce of Idaho, and if the Central Pacific railway interest does not push on its work with alacrity, the despised Oregonians may yet show their heels to their California neighbors in the matter of the quickest and cheapest route for travel and freight from the Rocky Mountains to the Coast.

So at the North, into the heart of British Columbia, the Oregon steamboat company are working out a notable plan for extending their operations. By building a wagon portage of one hundred and fifty miles north from White Bluffs, the present head of navigation on the main stream of the Columbia, cutting off a wide and impassable angle of the river, the stream is again struck at a navigable point close to the forty-ninth parallel, and steamers can be run from there one hundred and fifty to two hundred miles north through the series of lakes into which the river widens in that region, away up to the fifty-second and fifty-third parallels, where steamboats were never heard of or thought of, and into the now most famous gold region of British Columbia, the Carriboo country. The steamboat company are already building a steamer in this double upper Columbia, and next season will probably be enabled to inaugurate this capital idea and illustration of their enterprise. Now the Carriboo mines are only reached by way of Victoria, Frazer River, and three hundred to five hundred miles of rough land travel. This new route will bring them into quick and cheap communication with American markets and American impulses at Portland.

In this and other ways, Oregon and its people make a pleasant and promising impression upon us. They lack many of the advantages of their neighbors below; their agriculture is less varied, but it is more sure; mining has not poured such irregular and intoxicating wealth into their laps; they need, as well, a more thorough farming and a more varied industry; they need, also, as well, intelligent, patient labor and larger capital; but they have builded what they have got more slowly and more wisely than the Californians; they have less severe reaction from hot and unhealthy growth to encounter,—less to unlearn; and they seem sure, not of organizing the first State on the Pacific Coast, indeed, but of a steadily prosperous, healthy and moral one,—they are in the way to be the New England of the Pacific Coast. Just now, new and exciting discoveries of placer gold have been made among the head waters of the John Day branch of the Columbia River, in south-eastern Oregon, and extensive improvements are being developed among the quartz mines of the western slopes of the Sierra Nevadas, just off from the Willamette valley; and capital and labor are hastening in both directions: but while there is much to hope from these promises and investments, there is also something to fear for the real growth of the State. The uncertainty, the recklessness, the gambling habit which the varied and fickle results of gold mining throw over the whole business and morals and manners of a community, that is possessed by the passion, are very great obstacles to a real and permanent prosperity, and growth in high civilization. May Oregon steady itself, or be steadied by sufficiently early failure, against such dangers as California's experience has thrown around her condition as a State.

LETTER XIX.

THROUGH WASHINGTON TERRITORY.

OLYMPIA, W. T., July 26.

UNLESS you have been studying geography lately, you will need to open your map to follow us in our journey northward. So near the north-western limit of the Republic and not to touch it; so close to John Bull and not to shake his grim paw, and ask him what he thinks of the preposterous Yankees now; so near to that rarely beautiful sheet of water, Puget Sound, and not to sail through it, and know its commercial capacities and feel its natural attractions,—it would never do. So, two days ago, we put out of Portland, steamed down the Columbia for fifty miles, and up its Cowlitz branch for two miles (all it is now navigable), and landed on the Washington Territory side at two houses and a stage wagon, bearing the classic name of Monticello. Jefferson was not at home; but there was a good dinner with Mr. Burbank, scion of your northern Berkshire Burbanks; testifying, like all the rest of these border settlers, away from schools and churches and society, that there was no such other country anywhere; and that you could not drive them back to the snows and cold winters of "the States."

The next question was, how to put eleven passengers in an open wagon that only held seven, for a ninety-mile and two-day drive across the Territory. It was successfully achieved by putting three of them on saddle horses; and off we bounced into the woods at the rate of three to four miles an hour. Most unpoetical rounding to our three thousand miles of staging in these ten weeks of travel, was this ride through Washington. The road was rough beyond description; during the winter rains it is just impassable, and is abandoned; for miles it is over trees and sticks laid down roughly in swamps; and for the rest,—ungraded, and simply a path cut through the dense forest,—the hight and depth are fully equal to the length of it. Those who worked their passage, by whipping lazy mules whose backs they strode, and paid twenty dollars for the privilege, made the best time, and had the laziest of it. Yet since, I observe, with tender memories of hard saddles, they "stand and wait," instead of sitting upon wooden chairs.

But the majestic beauty of the fir and cedar forests, through which we rode almost continuously for the day and a half that the road stretched out, was compensation for much discomfort. These are the finest forests we have yet met,—the trees larger and taller and standing thicker; so thick and tall that the ground they occupy could not hold them cut and corded as wood; and the undergrowth of shrub and flower and vine and fern, almost tropical in its luxuriance and impenetrable for its closeness. Washington Territory must have more timber and ferns and blackberries and snakes to the square mile than any other State or Territory of the Union. We occasionally struck a narrow prairie or a thread-like valley; perhaps once in ten miles a clearing of an acre or two, rugged and rough in its half-redemption from primitive forest; but for the most part it was a continuous ride through forests, so high and thick that the sun could not reach the road, so unpeopled and untouched, that the very spirit of Solitude reigned supreme, and made us feel its presence as never upon Ocean or Plain. The ferns are delicious, little and big,—more of them, and larger than you can see in New England,—and spread their beautiful shapes on every hand. But the settlers apply to them other adjectives beginning with d, for they vindicate their right to the soil, in plain as well as forest, with most tenacious obstinacy, and to root them out is a long and difficult job for the farmer.

We dined on the second day at Skookem Chuck (which is Indian for "big water,") and came to the head of Puget Sound, which kindly shortens the land-passage across the Territory one-half, and this town, the capital, at night, encountering the usual demonstration of artillery, brass band and banners, and most hospitable greeting from Acting-Governor Evans and other officials and citizens. Olympia lies charmingly under the hill by the water-side; counts its inhabitants less than five hundred, though still the largest town of the Territory, save the mining center of Wallula, way down in the south-east towards Idaho; numbers more stumps than houses within city limits; but is the social and political center for a large extent of country; puts on the airs and holds many of the materials of fine society; and entertained us at a very Uncle Jerry and Aunt Phebe little inn, whose presiding genius, a fat and fair African of fifty years and three hundred pounds, robed in spotless white, welcomed us with the grace and dignity of a queen, and fed us as if we were in training for a cannibal's table.

If there is one thing, indeed, more than another, among the facts of civilization, which the Pacific Coast organizes most quickly and completely, it is good eating. From the Occidental at San Francisco to the loneliest of ranches on the most wilderness of weekly stage routes, a "good square meal" is the rule; while every village of five hundred inhabitants has its restaurants and French or Italian cooks. I say this with the near experience and the lively recollection of one or two most illustrious exceptions, where the meals consisted of coarse bacon, ancient beans and villainous mustard,—and where, if you declined the two former, you were politely requested to help yourself to mustard,—and where, o' nights, the beds could e'en rise and walk with fleas and bedbugs. When the Puritans settled New England, their first public duty was to build a church with thrifty thought for their souls. Out here, their degenerate sons begin with organizing a restaurant, and supplying Hostetter's stomachic bitters and an European or Asiatic cook. So the seat of empire, in its travel westward, changes its base from soul to stomach, from brains to bowels. Perhaps it is only in obedience to that delicate law of our later civilization, which forbids us to enjoy our religion unless we have already enjoyed our victual, and which sends a dyspeptic to hell by an eternal regard to the fitness of things. And certainly the piety, that ascends from a grateful and gratified stomach, is as likely to be worthy as that fitfully fructified by Brandreth's pills.

Is it not a little singular that only our forty-oddth State should bear the name of WASHINGTON? That it was left to this day and to this cornermost Territory to enroll his name among the stars of the Republic's banner? Washington Territory is the upper half of old Oregon, divided by the Columbia River and the fortieth parallel for the southern boundary, and extending up to the forty-ninth, to which, under the reaction from the unmartial Polk's "fifty-four-forty or fight" pretensions, our northern line was ignominiously limited to. Its population is small, less than twenty thousand, and not likely to grow fast, or make it a State for some years to come, unless the chance, not probable, of rich gold and silver mines within its lines should flood it with rapid immigration. But it holds sure wealth and a large future through its certain illimitable forests and its probable immense coal deposits. Of all its surface, west of the Cascade or Sierra Nevada Mountains, not more than one-eighth is prairie or open land; the rest is covered by a growth of timber, such as, alike in density and in size, no other like space on the earth's surface can boast of. Beyond the mountains to the East, the country partakes of the same characteristics as that below it; hilly, barren of trees, unfruitful, whose chief promises and possibilities are in the cattle and sheep line. Its arable land this side the mountains, where the forests are cleared or interrupted, is less fertile than that of Oregon and California; but it sufficeth for its present population, and even admits of considerable exports of grain and meat for the mining populations in British Columbia, and will grow in extent and productiveness probably as fast as the necessities of the Territory require.

LETTER XX.

PUGET SOUND, AND VANCOUVER'S ISLAND.

VICTORIA, V. I., July 28.

WE were a full day and night coming down Puget Sound, on the steamer from Olympia; loitering along at the villages on its either shore, and studying the already considerable development of its lumber interests, as well as regaling ourselves with the beauty of its waters and its richly-stored forest shores. Only the upper section of the southern branch of these grand series of inland seas and rivers, that sweep into the Continent here, and make Vancouver's Island, and open up a vast region of interior country to the ocean, is now called Puget Sound,—only forty miles or so from Olympia north. Formerly the whole confines went by that name; and rightfully it should remain to all which runs up into Washington Territory from out the Strait of San Juan de Fuca, for this has a unity and serves a similar purpose. For beauty and for use, this is, indeed, one of the water wonders of the world; curiosity and commerce will give it, year by year, increase of fame and visitors. It narrows to a river's width; it circles and swoops into the land with coquettish freedom; and then it widens into miles of breadth; carrying the largest of ships anywhere on its surface, even close to the forests' edge; free of rocks, safe from wind and wave;—the home of all craft, clear, blue and fathomless.

It is the great lumber market of all the Pacific Coast. Already a dozen saw-mills are located on its shores; one which we visited was three hundred and thirty-six feet long, and turns out one hundred thousand feet of lumber daily; three ships and two barks of five hundred to one thousand tons each were loading with the product direct from the mill; and the present entire export of the Sound, in prepared lumber and masts and spars, reaches nearly to one hundred millions of feet yearly, and yields at the average price of ten dollars a thousand about one million dollars. San Francisco is the largest customer; but the Sandwich Islands, China, all the Pacific American ports, south and north, and even Buenos Ayres around on the Atlantic, come here for building materials, and France finds here her cheapest and best spars and masts. Much of the shipping employed in the business is owned on the Sound; one mill company has twelve vessels of from three hundred to one thousand tons each. The business is but in its very infancy; it will grow with the growth of the whole Pacific Coast, and with the increasing dearth of fine ship timber in other parts of the world; for it is impossible to calculate the time when, cut and saw as we may, all these forests shall be used up, and the supply become exhausted.

The size of these Washington Territory trees is rather overpowering,—we have not seen the big trees of California yet,—and not daring to trust unaccustomed eyes, we resorted to the statistics of the lumbermen. Trees, six and seven feet in diameter, and two hundred to two hundred and fifty feet high, are very common, perhaps rarely out of sight in the forest; eight feet in diameter and three hundred feet high are rarer, but still not at all uncommon;—the builder of the telegraph line has hitched his wire in one case to a cedar (arbor vitæ) which is fourteen feet in diameter; a monster tree that had fallen,—the forests are full of fallen trees,—measured three hundred and twenty-five feet long; and another tree, at the distance of ninety feet from its root, was seven feet in diameter! Masts for ships are readily procurable, straight as an arrow, and without a knot for one hundred feet, and forty inches in diameter at thirty feet from the base. I stop my figures here, lest my character for truthful reporting grow questionable.

Out of the Sound and straight across the Strait, twenty miles, we encounter the rocky shore of Vancouver's Island; searching along we meet a hidden hole in the wall, and, steaming in, there opens out a little wash-bowl of a bay; and here is Victoria. It is a charming surprise,—the prettiest located and best built town on the Pacific Coast, and next to Portland in size and business,—a healthy copartnership of American enterprise and enthusiasm, and English solidity and holdfastness. The population ranges from twenty-five hundred in summer and dull times (now) to five thousand in winter and the flush season, when the mining across in British Columbia pays well, and the miners come to town to spend their harvest. Out of the town and its trade, the island offers little development; there are some poor-paying gold mines; good bituminous coal is found in abundance, and profitably worked; here and there is farming in patches, which is extending, but most of the food eaten here comes from California and Washington. The whole white population of the island is no more than five thousand to seven thousand, and over these reigns the cumbersome and expensive machinery of an especial English colonial government,—partly appointed by the crown, partly representative,—with a parliament that sat ten months last year; spending four hundred thousand dollars a year, and raising it out of the business of this town by a system of taxation many times more burdensome than our civil war has imposed on our people,—including a tax on all sales, besides special licenses for each particular business, and an income tax on top of all; but giving in return a practically good government, a port free of customs duties, order in the city, and excellent roads into the country.

Over across the Gulf of Georgia the same thing is repeated; there stretches out the vast region of British Columbia, with another seven thousand population, largely mining and American, but scattered from the capital of New Westminster at the mouth of Frazer River, north and east to the Carriboo country and the valley of the Kootenay, five hundred and six hundred miles away; duplicating this formal and expensive machinery of government, with English castles almost for gubernatorial residences, and fifteen thousand dollars a year salaries to live in them with, and a long retinue of imported British officials to match; raising revenue on this side the gulf, however, from customs duties and a fifty cent tariff on every ounce of gold dug, in part; and giving nothing to boast of back but better roads to the mines than the American States offer. The taxation for public purposes in British Columbia swells to the enormous sum of one hundred dollars per head of population, and that in Vancouver's Island to seventy dollars, a year.

The Frazer River gold diggings, in British Columbia, are about worked out now; few besides Chinamen are washing in them this year; and the rush of the white miners is to the more distant and better paying regions of Carriboo and Kootenay, though these, as all others on the Coast, are overshadowed this season by the fame of Idaho and Montana.

Victoria is the chief commercial point for these two British Provinces, and in part, also, for Washington Territory; and much profitable smuggling goes on across these waters and imaginary territorial lines into the United States. There are fewer Americans in Victoria than formerly; they are stepping out, as its prosperity seems waning; but the English element is apparently increasing. The two nations mingle pretty cordially; the Yankees chafe a good deal at the extraordinarily high taxes and the aristocratic government, and even practical John Bull begins to see the ridiculous side of it. More surely than the Canadas, even, when these provinces become really important and worth having, they will be ours. They will drift to the Union by the inevitable law of gravitation, and by the influence of the leaven of American nationality and sentiment, already large throughout their borders, that will grow with their growth, and flavor their whole progress. Three daily papers seem to prosper in Victoria; the stores are exceedingly well built, and, aside from the twenty-five to thirty-three per cent. that are now unoccupied, make a good showing of English goods; "shopping" is cheaper than anywhere in the States; and the whole order of the civilization here has many pleasant points of contrast with other towns on the Pacific Coast.

This, too, is the great depot of the Hudson Bay Company; all their business from the Pacific Coast to the Red River of the North, beyond Minnesota, centers here; and their warehouses of accumulating furs and of distributing goods to pay for them are among the chief curiosities of the place. They do a general trading business wherever they have stations or stores; and you can buy calicoes and cottons, hardware and rum at their counters, as at any old-fashioned country store in New England.

Our day and a half in Victoria has been a very pleasant experience indeed. The Americans gave Mr. Colfax and his friends cordial welcome; the English were no whit less hearty in demonstration of good feeling and respect; there was what the French call a "grand dinner," the eating whereof lasted from seven to ten P. M., and the speaking whereat continued from ten to three A. M.,—the result of which was that all little international differences and accounts were amicably adjusted, Andy Johnson and Queen Victoria were married, and the two grand nations of the Anglo-Saxon race were joined into one overpowering, all-subduing, all-fructifying Republic! "And what a bloody country that would be," exclaimed an enthusiastic Britisher at one of the clock in the morning.

How could the little question as to the title to a group of small islands in this inland sea, and known by the name of the largest, San Juan, be thought of in such a fraternal baptism? And, indeed, by the cool of the morning after, it seems a very small affair. Nothing but wide war between the two countries could ever make it of the slightest practical consequence. The question turns on whether the boundary line runs from strait to gulf by one channel or the other, this side the islands or that. Meantime, each government supports a captain and corporal's guard of soldiers on San Juan,—only distinguishable, probably, one from the other by the blue and the red of their uniforms,—and fraternizing daily, doubtless, over a game of cards and a whisky bottle. All these differences do indeed grow small and unpractical as you get near to them; and it is difficult to appreciate what an excitement and passion one of our generals created up here a few years ago by laying hold on the whole of what the half is a burden. Palpably, by the map, and by the course of ocean travel, the American claim to these islands is the right one; but in view of the certainty of all this apple falling into our lap as soon as it is ripe enough to be really valuable, the present status may as well as not go indefinitely on.

Up here, above the latitude of Quebec and Montreal, we bask in the smile of roses that are denied to you in New England. Mounts Shasta and Hood of California and Oregon are more than rivaled in deep snow fields and majestic snow peaks by Mounts Rainier and Baker of Washington; sailing down Puget Sound, we take in the former from base to three peaked summit of thirteen thousand feet in hight, all aglow with perpetual white,—a feature of deep beauty and impressiveness; along the sea coast, on the opposite side, the hills also rise to the region of continuous snow, and look down bald and white through the long summer days into the tropical flower gardens and orchards and hot streets of Victoria; and here, everywhere under these wintry shadows, reigns a year, that knows no zero cold, and rarely freezing water or snow; that winters fuchsias and the most delicate roses, English ivies and other tender plants, and summers them with rioting luxuriance; that grows the apple, the pear and all the small fruits to perfection, and only cannot grow our Indian corn.

The climate of all this Pacific Coast certainly presents many solaces and satisfactions in comparison with our own New England. I do not wonder the emigrants hither find new health and life and much happiness in its great comparative evenness; but I do not yet recognize that which would compensate me for the loss of our slow, hesitating, coying spring times, our luxuriously-advancing, tender, red and brown autumns, aye, and our clear and crisply-cold winter days and snow-covered lands, with the contrasting evergreens, the illuminated sky, the delicately fretted architecture of the leafless trees, the sunsets, the nerve-giving tonic of the air. Surely there is more various beauty in the progress of a New England year than any which all the Pacific Coast can offer.

LETTER XXI.

SAN FRANCISCO: MR. COLFAX AND HIS RECEPTION IN THE PACIFIC STATES.

SAN FRANCISCO, August 2.

"FRISCOE," as the interior lovingly and for short calls the commercial capital of the Pacific Coast, is a good place to come back to, after dusty stage rides and rolling ocean travel. It is refreshing to stretch on a wide bed at the Occidental, after tangling your legs over night in the corner of a "mud wagon," or cramping them in the narrow berth of a steamer. It is something to miss the punctual Speaker's injunction to be ready at four in the morning, and his quick, cheery voice at quarter before, cautioning us "to be sure and be on hand;" something also to sleep as long as we can, and eat when we have a mind to; much, indeed, to know that no brass bands lie in wait for us, no hoarse cannon hold a horrid welcome for tender nerves, no midnight dinners vex dyspeptic stomachs.

There is real refreshment and rest, always, in the independence and let-you-alone-ativeness of a large city. And Friscoe is, indeed, a good place, *per se.* The Washoe people have their chief incentive to piety in the assurance that thus, when they die, they will come here; just as good Bostonians count Paris their paradise. These bare, brown and white sand hills, that Nature exposes where art has not covered her, all around in San Francisco, furnish no poetical proof of the susceptible Washoe theory; they are just about as far away from all traditional and imaginative ideas of the Garden of Eden as it is possible for ugly fact to be; but the dissimilitude of the "Friscoe" climate to all known anywhere else on the face of the terrestrial globe, may suggest a point on the side of the Washoeites. You cannot palm off old Thomas's almanac on the weather question,—"calculated for Boston, but equally applicable to any other meridian,"—in this town. San Francisco weather is only its own parallel; there is nothing like it, either here on the Pacific Coast, or elsewhere, so far as Bayard Taylor has traveled, or Fitzhugh Ludlow imagined in Hasheesh. It has its summer in winter, and its winter in summer; the ladies go to church and to opera and a shopping, in July and August, clad in heavy furs; overcoats are a daily necessity to every man not lined with a patent air-tight coal stove; and this very day of August is borrowed from the suicide week of November,—I would go "my bottom dollar," as the miners say, that it would snow in half an hour, were I on my native heath. And yet,—ingrate, am I not?—while I write this plaint, I am eating Sweetwater grapes bought in the shops at ten cents a pound, though the season is but just opening; Black Hamburgs are equally cheap and plenty; peaches are ponderous and luscious at fifty cents to one dollar a basket; and pears, plums, apricots, nectarines, figs, blackberries and strawberries (still!) all flood the fruit stores, and are sold at equally low rates.

What gives San Francisco its harsh summer days is, that it is constantly "in the draft." While elsewhere, along shore, the coast hills uninterruptedly break the steady north-west breeze of the summer sea, here they open just enough to let out the waters of the Sacramento River and San Francisco bay, and let in like a tide of escape steam the ocean breeze and mists. When winter comes, the wind changes to south-east, and blows to softer scale, and between showers,—for then comes the rain,—the sky is clearer and the air balmier than in summer. Thus the Friscoe people boast of their winters, and apologize for their summers. Invalids, especially of weak lungs, find the latter seasons very trying here, and flee to the protected valleys inland, where the days are hot and clear, and the nights agreeably cool; and come back here to winter safely and sociably.

Ben Holladay's good steamer Sierra Nevada brought us down from Victoria in less than three days; and we tried the Pacific Ocean and came in by the Golden Gate for the first time. Though no storm raged, the sea did not prove title to the name, but rolled and pitched us altogether unpacifically; and the mile wide gate to San Francisco, guarded by high hills, abruptly opened, and bristling with fortifications, found from us ready answer to its welcome; and we swept around its double corner, and came to wharf in the generous and land-locked bay of San Francisco, with thanksgiving and gratitude, swelling anew and higher to Providence, Captain Conner and Dr. Murdock, as we learned the sad fate of our alternate steamer, the Brother Jonathan, on her passage by us up the route. We passed her and her fatal rock, only an hour or two before their sudden and sad collision; and we readily join, as you can imagine, in the wide tide of feeling that the disaster creates here. The genial old General Wright, long and honorable in service, and beloved throughout the Pacific States, and Mr. Nesbit of the Bulletin editorial staff, we knew, and had experienced their hospitality. Other prominent and beloved citizens went down in that mysterious, sudden wreck.

Speaker Colfax and his friends have now made the round of the Pacific States and Territories, so far as their time will admit. Idaho and Montana they regret not to visit, but they have obtained much intimate knowledge of their characteristics and capacities. A month more remains to them here; and this they spend in excursions to the interior of California,—to the Big Trees, the Yosemite, the Geysers, etc.,—and in more private engagements in this city and State, than they have yet been able to make. The Speaker's public visit, or perhaps more properly his public reception by the people of the Pacific States, may be said to be over. It has been a very remarkable one for its generosity and universality and spontaneity; altogether unexpected to him, and so still more flattering; and greatly creditable to the hospitality and genuine patriotism of the people of these States. I have omitted any record of it, in our progress from town to town and State to State, because the story in all general terms was the same. But now that it is substantially over and the journey completed, it is only simple truth to say that no man ever had such a generous popular welcome on these shores before. From his arrival at Austin in Nevada, where we first struck the spreading tide of Pacific civilization and population, through that State, through California to this city, and again northerly through the State, through Oregon and Washington, and into the British Provinces, up to this time,—a period of six weeks,—his progress through the country has been a continuous popular ovation. Everywhere the same welcome from authorities and citizens, the same unstinted proffer of every facility for the journey, for seeing all parts of the country, all shades of its development: special coaches, special trains and extra steamboats have been at his service; welcome everywhere to confidence, to fullest fact from most intelligent sources; welcome everywhere by brass band, cannon, military escort, public addresses; and everywhere, even to smallest village and tavern collection of neighboring rancheros, the same eager desire to hear the distinguished visitor speak, and eke then for big or little orations from his less distinguished companions.

There is a combination of causes for the marked

demonstrativeness and popularity of this welcome to Mr. Colfax in all this region. Chief, of course, are his conspicuous public position, and the fact that he is the first man high in State who has ever visited the Pacific States for the simple and sole reason of studying their resources and interests, so as the better to serve them in the government; his early and steady friendship and leadership in important legislation at Washington in behalf of all this region; his wide personal popularity among public men and private men, who have ever known him, and the magnetic spread of this popularity along his journey from his intercourse with the people and his speeches to them. We must add to these reasons, now, the newly-developed and hearty sympathy of these western States with the political experiences and interests of the East; their inability to share in the war directly, but their therefore more intensely loyal feeling in regard to it and its issues, and the limited occasion for expressing it. Also, and an important consideration, is the eager looking for larger knowledge and new appreciation of the capacities and interests of these States, in this time of their depression and comparative poverty; and the desire for the spread of such information among the public men, and through the press of the East, as will lead to a fresh emigration and a new supply of capital. It is dull times here; it is flush times in the East; and the West would borrow of our new life and prosperity. Mr. Colfax and his companions were men thought to be in positions to contribute to such results; and part of their welcome, part of the generous confidence and hospitality that have been extended to them, have confessedly been on this ground. Such union of motive, gratitude, appreciation, loyalty, wise and creditable selfishness, have inspired and fed most bountiful welcome and treatment. These western people never do anything by halves; they give of feeling and of time and of money, whenever they are moved, without stint, without calculation.

Mr. Colfax has freely gratified the popular desire everywhere to listen to his voice; no place on his route was too small, no gathering too insignificant, to be turned off with indifference, when such hearty greeting appealed for attention ; and he has spoken, long and short, an average of at least once a day since he left the Missouri River;—some days his speeches number four and five. Never much studied, they were rarely alike in form; never greatly elaborated, they always reached a high level of popular eloquence. The average quality of excellence in all his efforts has surprised me: I doubt if any other of our public men could speak so often and so much, and on such various occasions, and succeed so well in all. The characteristics of his speaking have been practical wisdom or good sense, entire frankness in utterance of opinions, a charming simplicity in his style of oratory, coupled with a ready, clear expression, and a steady, natural enthusiasm, which have kept his hearers in constant sympathy with his individuality. The staple subjects he has treated have been the War and the questions growing out of it, the Resources of the Pacific States and their development, the Mining and the taxation of its results, the Mexican question and the Monroe doctrine, the Future Destiny of the Republic, Mr. Lincoln and his character, the Pacific Railroad, and such local and personal matters as the place and hour suggested.

As to the mines and the taxation of their products, which is a subject of much anxiety in the mining districts, Mr. Colfax has taken the ground that the mineral lands should be thrown open by the government to the free occupation of discoverers and workers, the same as our agricultural lands, and under similar regulations to those the miners themselves have adopted, in the absence of any governmental action, and that the government should not tax the product until it passes, finally, in the form of bullion, into the commercial uses of the world;—the same as it taxes grain only in the form of whiskey and flour, sheep and wool as cloth, and the woods in their last processes of manufacture. He argued this point so justly and strongly that he gained general acquiescence even from the classes who have generally contended that mining should, in no form or stage, be obliged to contribute to the support of the government.

On the Mexican question, he even more bravely set himself against the current of public opinion on this Coast. Here it is popular to talk of "cleaning out" Maximilian in sixty days; of taking up arms for the Juarez government, even if war with England and France should thus be precipitated. Mr. Colfax said distinctly that he had no sympathy with this demand; he believed in the Monroe doctrine, he thought the Juarez was the rightful government of Mexico; but he was for no hasty, no harsh action by our people or government. We should have no new war if it could be avoided honorably; we needed the healing, developing influences of peace; we needed to build the Pacific Railroad, to develop our mines and our manufactures and our agriculture, and to pay our debts,—all which would be forbidden or suffer delay and depression under foreign war; and he believed that with patience and tact, and a generous confidence in our government by the people, the Mexican question would be satisfactorily solved ere long, without any such dire calamity as a new and general taking up of arms by the Nation. Pressing these views constantly and against the popular passion, he has clearly made a strong impression in their favor; leading citizens and prominent journals have responded to his opinions; and he may be said to have worked almost a revolution in the current public sentiment of the Pacific States on this subject; while he has added to the universal respect felt for him personally by his courage in espousing an unpopular view here. His visit may be counted as of real national benefit for the influence of his course in this matter alone.

Mr. Colfax's speeches at Austin, Virginia City, Placerville, Sacramento, San Francisco, Portland and Olympia may be reckoned as his most complete and satisfactory and statesmanlike discussions. That at the dinner table in Victoria, to his combined American and British entertainers, was his finest specimen of popular eloquence; it was well-conceived and tasteful in thought, well-pitched and richly sustained in expression; and its impression upon his audience, one of the most intelligent and critical he has ever addressed, was most decided and gratifying. The leading English gentlemen present were enthusiastic concerning both its matter and manner. It breathed the spirit of peace and fraternal feeling towards the English sovereign and people; while setting forth most effectively the success and destiny of the great American Republic.

Mr. Colfax has indeed gained credit and popularity everywhere on his journey, and his visit here is as likely to prove as valuable to him personally, in his growth as a public man, as it surely will be important and useful in intertwining the bonds of business and of political union, of profit and of patriotism, among the widely separated States of the Nation. Of his companions in his travels, Governor Bross has generally joined him in addressing the popular audiences that have welcomed the party, and Mr. Richardson occasionally, and both with much acceptance. The Governor is sure to gain the cheers of the men, the smiles of the ladies; and Mr. Richardson has charmed all by his cultured sentences and his well-rounded rhetoric.

LETTER XXII.

THE YOSEMITE VALLEY AND THE BIG TREES.

YOSEMITE VALLEY, California, August 11.

THE YOSEMITE! As well interpret God in thirty-nine articles as portray it to you by word of mouth or pen. As well reproduce castle or cathedral by a stolen frieze, or broken column, as this assemblage of natural wonder and beauty by photograph or painting. The overpowering sense of the sublime, of awful desolation, of transcending marvelousness and unexpectedness, that swept over us, as we reined our horses sharply out of green forests, and stood upon high jutting rock that overlooked this rolling, upheaving sea of granite mountains, holding far down its rough lap this vale of beauty of meadow and grove and river,—such tide of feeling, such stoppage of ordinary emotions comes at rare intervals in any life. It was the confrontal of God face to face, as in great danger, in solemn, sudden death. It was Niagara, magnified. All that was mortal shrank back, all that was immortal swept to the front and bent down in awe. We sat till the rich elements of beauty came out of the majesty and the desolation, and then, eager to get nearer, pressed tired horses down the steep, rough path into the Valley.

And here we have wandered and wondered and worshiped for four days. Under sunshine and shadow; by rich, mellow moonlight; by stars opening double wide their eager eyes; through a peculiar August haze, delicate, glowing, creamy, yet hardly perceptible as a distinct element,—the New England Indian summer haze doubly refined,—by morning and evening twilight, across camp fires, up from beds upon the ground through all the watches of the night, have we seen these, the great natural wonders and beauties of this western world. Indeed, it is not too much to say that no so limited space in all the known world offers such majestic and impressive beauty. Niagara alone divides honors with it in America. Only the whole of Switzerland can surpass it,—no one scene in all the Alps can match this before me now in the things that mark the memory and impress all the senses for beauty and for sublimity.

The one distinguishing feature is a double wall of perpendicular granite, rising from a half a mile to a mile in hight, and inclosing a valley not more than half a mile in width on the average, and from ten to fifteen miles in length. It is a fissure, a chasm, rather than a valley, in solid rock mountains; there is not breadth enough in it for even one of its walls to lie down; and yet it offers all the fertility, all the beauties of a rich valley. There is meadow with thick grass; there are groves of pine and oak, the former exquisite in form and majestic in size, rising often to two hundred and two hundred and fifty feet; there are thickets of willow and birch, bay trees and dogwood, and various flowering shrubs; primrose and cowslip and golden rod and violet and painted cup, more delicate than eastern skies can welcome, make gay garden of all the vacant fields now in August; the aroma of mint, of pine and fir, of flower loads the air; the fern family find a familiar home everywhere; and winding in and out among all flows the Merced River, so pure and transparent that you can hardly tell where the air leaves off and the water begins, rolling rapid over polished stones or soft sands, or staying in wide, deep pools that invite the bather and the boat, and holding trout only less rich and dainty than the brook trout of New England. The soil, the trees, the shrubs, the grasses and the flowers of this little Valley are much the same in general character and variety as those of your Connecticut River valleys; but they are richer in development and greater in numbers. They borrow of the mountain fecundity and sweetness; and they are fed by summer rains as those of other California valleys rarely are.

Now imagine,—can you?—rising up, sheer and sharp, on each side of this line of fertile beauty, irregularly-flowing and variously-crowned walls of granite rock, thrice as high as your Mounts Tom and Holyoke, twice as high as Berkshire's Graylock. The color of the rock is most varied. A grayish drab or yellow is the dominant shade, warm and soft. In large spots, it whitens out; and again it is dark and discolored as if by long exposure to rain and snow and wind. Sometimes the light and dark shades are thrown into quick contrast on a single wall, and you know where the Zebra and Dr. Bellows' church were borrowed from. More varied and exquisite still are the shapes into which the rocks are thrown. The one great conspicuous object of the Valley is a massive, two-sided wall, standing out into and over the meadow, yellowish-gray in color, and rising up into the air unbroken, square, perpendicular, for *full three-quarters of a mile.* It bears in Spanish and Indian the name of the Great Jehovah; and it is easy to believe that it was an object of worship by the barbarians, as it is not difficult for civilization to recognize the Infinite in it, and impossible not to feel awed and humbled in its presence.

In other places these mountain walls of rock take similar and only less majestic shape; while as frequently they assume more poetical and fantastic forms. Here and there are grand massive domes, as perfect in shape as your State-house dome, and bigger than the entire of a dozen State-houses. The highest rock of the Valley is a perfect half-dome, split sharp and square in the middle, and rising more than a mile or near six thousand feet,— as high as Mount Washington is above the level of the sea,—over the little lake which perfectly mirrors its majestic form at its foot. Perfect pyramids take their places in the wall; then these pyramids come in families, and mount away one after and above the other, as "The Three Brothers." "The Cathedral Rocks" and "The Cathedral Spires" unite the great impressiveness, the beauty and the fantastic form of the Gothic architecture. From their shape and color alike, it is easy to imagine, in looking upon them, that you are under the ruins of an old Gothic cathedral, to which those of Cologne and Milan are but baby-houses.

The most common form of the rocks is a slightly sloping bare wall, lying in long, dizzy sweeps, sometimes horizontal, sometimes perpendicular, and stretching up and up so high as to cheat the Valley out of hours of sunshine every day. Here huge arches are carved on the face; there long, narrow shelves run midway, along which and in every available crevice, great pines sprout and grow, yet appearing like shrubs against the broad hight of the wall; again, the rock lies in thick folds, one upon another, like the hide of a rhinoceros; occasional columns stand out as if sculptured upon the surface; sometimes it juts out at the top over the Valley like the brim of a beaver; and then it recedes and sharpens to a cone. Many of the various shapes and shades of color in the surface of these massive walls of rock come from the peeling off of great masses of the granite. Frost and ice get into the weak crevices, and blast out huge slices or fragments, that fall in boulders, from the size of a great house down to that of an apple, into the valley below.

Over the sides of the walls pour streams of water out of narrower valleys still above, and yet higher and far away, rise to twelve and thirteen thousand feet the culminating peaks of the Sierra

Nevadas, with still visible fields of melting snows. All forms and shapes and colors of majesty and beauty cluster around this narrow spot; it seems created the home of all that is richest in inspiration for the heroic in life, for poetry, for painting, for imaginative religion.

The Water-falls of the Valley, though a lesser incident in all its attractions, offer much that is marvelous and beautiful. This, however, is the season of their feeblest power. It is in May and June, when their fountains are freshest, that they appear at their best, and assume their proper place in the grand panorama of beauty and sublimity. In the main portion of the Valley, the Bridal Vail is the first conspicuous fall,—now a dainty rivulet starting over a precipice nine hundred feet high, but nearly all lost at once in delicate spray that sways and scatters in the light breeze, and fastens upon the wall, as sign of its being and its beauty, the fabled rainbow of promise. The name of this fall is well chosen; it is type of the delicate gauze, floating and illusory, by which brides delight to hide their blushes and give mystery to their charms. Farther up, before the hotel, you see the Yosemite Fall, perhaps twice the size in volume of the Bridal Vail, but distinguished for its hight,—the greatest hight of any water-fall yet discovered in the world. It is broken about two-thirds the way down its high wall of rock by projecting masses of the mountain, giving it several hundred feet of cataract passage; but counting its whole fall from top to bottom, it is two thousand six hundred feet in hight, which is only fifteen times as high as Niagara Falls! Now, it is a mere silvery ribbon of spray, shooting down its long passage in delicate rockets of whitened foam. Earlier in the season, when ten times the volume of water pours down, it must, indeed, be a feature of fascinating, wonderful beauty.

The Valley above this point separates into two or three narrow canyons, and these are soon walled in by the uprising rocks. At the end of one of these, the main branch of the river falls from its upper fountains over two walls, one three hundred and fifty feet high and the other seven hundred, at points half a mile apart. The lower and shorter fall is called the Vernal, and pours down its whole hight without a break, and forms at the base a most exquisite circular rainbow, one of the rarest phenomena in all nature. The upper fall bears the name of Nevada, breaks as it comes over its crest into a grand blossom of spray, and strikes, about half way down its seven hundred feet, the obtruding wall, which thence offers just sufficient slope to keep the water and carry it in chasing, circling lines of foam to the bottom. This is the fall of falls,— there is no rival to it here in exquisite, various, fascinating beauty; and Switzerland, which abounds in Water-falls of like type, holds none of such peculiar charms. Not a drop of the rich stream of water but is white in its whole passage,—it is one sheet, rather one grand lace-work of spray from beginning to end. As it sweeps down its plane of rock, each drop all distinct, all alive, there is nothing of human art that you can compare it with but innumerable and snow-white point-lace collars and capes; as much more delicate and beautiful and perfect, however, as Nature ever is than Art. For half the distance between the two falls, the river runs swift over a solid plane of granite, clean and smooth as ice, as if Neptune was on a grand sliding-down hill frolic.

The excursion to this head of the chasm from the stopping-place below is through narrow defiles, over fallen rocks, up the sides of precipices, and over perpendicular walls by ladders, for a total distance of about four miles, and is the most difficult and fatiguing one that confronts the visitor; but both in the beauty of its Water-falls, and the new and rare shapes of rock scenery that it offers, it is most richly compensating, and never should be omitted.

The journey hither from San Francisco is both a tedious and an expensive one, and so a barrier to the extensive popular enjoyment of the rare works of nature here gathered. But the number of visitors is rapidly increasing; last year there were in all but one hundred, and already this season over three hundred persons have come into the Valley. Congress has ceded the territory of the Valley to the State of California for reservation and preservation as a spot for public resort and popular enjoyment; and a laudable and promising effort is now making, under the lead of Mr. Frederick Law Olmsted, the manager of the Mariposa estate, to secure an appropriation from the State treasury for improving the means of access, laying out paths among its beauties, and providing cheap yet agreeable accommodations for visitors. This wise cession and dedication by Congress, and proposed improvement by California, also includes the nearest of the groves of Big Trees, which is to be similarly held and protected for the public benefit, and furnishes an admirable example for other objects of natural curiosity and popular interest all over the Union. New York should preserve for popular use both Niagara Falls and its neighborhood and a generous section of her famous Adirondacks, and Maine one of her lakes and its surrounding woods.

The first stage of the journey to the Yosemite is by steamboat to Stockton, up the Sacramento and San Joaquin Rivers, one hundred and twenty-five miles. Next was a stage ride of a day and a half (one hundred miles) up the San Joaquin valley, over now arid plains, waiting for irrigation to be productive, and turning next to the east, among the foothills of the Sierra Nevadas, along the valleys of the tributaries of the San Joaquin, and into and through Mariposa County, seventy square miles of which constitute the celebrated Mariposa estate of General Fremont. Here, at a point near the village of Mariposa, we came to the end of the stage road, and entered upon forty miles of horseback riding, so much farther into the bowels of the Sierras, in order to reach the Happy Valley. Along a narrow trail, climbing up and down steep mountains, by and through close defiles, through continuous forests of majestic pines and firs, rich with yellow-green mosses, up to six and eight thousand feet above the sea level, we rode in single file,—a part of the way by a moonlight that lent indescribable picturesqueness and fascination to forest and ravine, besides frequent doubt as to the trail;—every hour a joy, every hour a fatigue, full of soreness and dirt and merriment; eager for the end, but enjoying every moment of the novel experience, every long mile of the rare road.

Our party had swollen to seventeen, the largest that had ever made the trip, and included five ladies. We had Law Olmsted, creator of New York Central Park, and organizer of the Sanitary Commission; Mr. Ashburner of the Geological Survey corps; Boston lawyers; San Francisco journalists; wit, grace, beauty. We exhausted all the horses of the kingdom of Fremont, and created famine in our path. Lodgings were abundant, however, for whom house and tent did not hold, the wide expanse of heaven safely covered, and the hay-stack warmed. The out-door beds, indeed, came to be at a premium; for in the dry, pure air of this region, there is not only no harm, but actual health in sleeping upon the ground either under tents or wholly in the open air. The mountain pastures,—scattered meadows rich at this season with a vernal green,—furnish mutton sweeter and richer than even English breeders or butchers can give you; the forests yielded their deer, and the rivers their trout to our appetites; the valley has its one vegetable garden,—so that, however our immediate successors shall fare, we have had no complaint to make of the commissary department.

Our companions from San Francisco proved rich

in song and sentiment; good-nature flowed and overflowed; fatigue was forgotten in joke and raillery; and digestion aided by sturdy laughter. We "kept marching through Georgia" with Sherman; we serenaded the "sweet lady" till she must have pined for a chance to sleep; we put John Brown's soul over its familiar road at least twice a day; had "a day of jubilo" with our colored brothers equally often; helped "the turkey gobbler to yank the grasshopper from the sweet potato vine" oftener than he could possibly have been hungry; grew steadily barbaric and dirty; laughed at dignity; and voted form and ceremony a nuisance. But our week in the woods is over, and we turn our faces towards civilization and conformity to-morrow. We shall be glad to see the washerwoman, but we lament that no more, save in memory, shall these eyes behold these scenes of infinite beauty and sublimity.

The name that has attached to this beautiful valley is both unique and euphonious. It rolls off the tongue most liquidly when you get the mastery of its pronunciation. Most strangers render it Yo-se-mite, or Yo-sem-ite; but the true style is Yo-sem-i-te. It is Indian for Grizzly Bear, and probably was also the name of a noted chief, who reigned over the Indians in this, their favorite retreat, and from this chief comes the application of the name to the locality and its marvelous scenery. The foot of white man never trod its limits,—the eye of white man never looked upon its sublime wonders till 1851, when he came here in pursuit of the Indians, with whom the settlers were then in war. The red man had boasted that their retreat was secure; that they had one spot which their enemies could never penetrate; and here they would gather in and enjoy their spoils unmolested. But to the white man's revenge was now added the stimulus of curiosity; and hither he found his way, and, coming to kill and exterminate, he has staid, and will forever henceforth stay, to wonder and worship.

There are but two or three settlers in the Valley. One, Mr. Hutchings, keeps a hotel, and can accommodate a dozen to twenty people at once very comfortably, and is both enterprising and courteous. There are only two paths out of the Valley, one over the mountain to the right, to Coulterville, and the other in the opposite direction to Mariposa. Each are simple trails for foot passengers and horses; and all baggage, all provisions, lumber, etc., have to be packed in on the backs of mules and horses. The mountains close in upon the river so nearly below this spot, that there is no egress or ingress in that way, except for foot travelers, and only with difficulty to them.

Part way in our horseback ride into the Valley, we stopped for a day at a solitary ranch on the South Fork of the Merced, and had generous welcome from its owner, Mr. Galen Clark, an old and intelligent pioneer in this region, and under his pilotage saw the reservation of Big Trees near the border line of Mariposa and Fresno counties. They are but a few miles off the direct road to the Yosemite, and while of the same character, are alike more numerous and larger in individual specimens than the grove of Big Trees in Calaveras County. The latter are the ones first discovered and often described, and are still those most visited; but they lie in an adjoining county, and farther away from the route we took to the Yosemite. Other similar groves to both these two have been discovered within a year or two, and some fifteen or twenty are now known to exist among the forests on the western slopes of the Sierra Nevadas in southern California. They occur along at various points through some hundred miles; and it is quite likely that many more still will be found in the same range yet farther south.

The Big Trees we visited are scattered in groups among the pine and cedar forests through a space of several miles. The collection numbers about six hundred. East of the Rocky Mountains, their pine and cedar companions,—so common all over these hills and in these valleys,—would be the wonder of the States for size and beauty; for they grow to six and eight and even ten feet in diameter, and to two hundred and fifty and three hundred feet in hight. But these mammoths sink to pigmies by the side of the Sequoia Gigantea, which is the scientific name applied to the Big Trees proper. They swell to thirty and forty feet in diameter, and rarely fall below two hundred and fifty feet in hight. Among those we examined are six each over thirty feet in diameter, and from ninety to one hundred in circumference; fifty over sixteen feet in diameter, and two hundred over twelve feet. "The Grizzly Giant," which is among the largest and most noteworthy, runs up ninety feet with scarcely perceptible diminution of bulk, and then sends out a branch, itself six feet in diameter.

But they are even more impressive for their beauty than their bigness. The bark is an exquisitely light and delicate cinnamon color, fluted up and down the long, straight, slowly-tapering trunk, like Corinthian columns in architecture; the top, resting like a cap upon a high, bare mast, is a perfect cone; and the evergreen leaves wear a bright, light shade, by which the tree can be distinguished from afar in the forest. The wood is a deep, rich red in color, and otherwise marks the similarity of the Big Trees to the species that grows so abundantly on the coast range of mountains through the Pacific States, and known generally as the redwood. Their wood is, however, of a finer grain than their smaller kindred, and both that and the bark, the latter sometimes as much as twenty inches thick, are so light and delicate, that the winds and snows of the winter make frequent wrecks of the tops and upper branches. Many of the largest of these trees are, therefore, shorn of their upper works. One or two of the largest in the grove we visited are wholly blown down, and we rode on horseback through the trunk of an old one, that had been burned out. Many more of the noblest specimens are scarred by fires that have been wantonly built about their trunks, or swept through the forests by accident. The trunk of one huge tree is burned into half a dozen little apartments, making capital provision for a game of hide and seek by children, or for dividing up a picnic of older growths into sentimental couples.

Wild calculations have been made of the ages of the larger of these trees; but none now upon the ground date back farther than the Christian Era. They began with our Modern Civilization; they were just sprouting when the Star of Bethlehem rose and stood for a sign of its origin; they have been ripening in beauty and power through these Nineteen Centuries; and they stand forth now, a type of the Majesty and Grace of Him with whose life they are coeval. Certainly they are chief among the natural curiosities and marvels of western America, of the known world; and though not to be compared, in the impressions they make and the emotions they arouse, to the great rock scenery of the Yosemite, which inevitably carries the spectator up to the Infinite Creator and Father of all, they do stand for all that has been claimed for them in wonderful greatness and majestic beauty.

LETTER XXIII.

THE CHINESE: GRAND DINNER WITH THEM.

SAN FRANCISCO, August 18.

I HAVE been waiting before writing of the Chinese in these Pacific States, till my experience of them had culminated in the long-promised grand dinner with their leaders and aristocrats. This came last night, and while I am full of the subject,—shark's fins and resurrected fungus digest slowly,—let me write of this unique and important element in the population and civilization of this region. There are no fewer than sixty to eighty thousand Chinamen here. They are scattered all over the States and Territories of the Coast, and number from one-eighth to one-sixth of the entire population. We began to see them at Austin, in Nevada, and have found them everywhere since, in country and city, in the woods, among the mines, north in the British dominions, on the Coast, in the mountains,—everywhere that work is to be done, and money gained by patient, plodding industry. They have been coming over from home since 1852, when was the largest emigration, (twenty thousand.) A hundred thousand

THE CHINESE HOUSE SERVANTS. 239

in all have come, but thirty thousand to forty thousand have gone back. None come really to stay; they do not identify themselves with the country; but to get work, to make money, and go back. They never, or very rarely, bring their wives. The Chinese women here are prostitutes, imported as such by those who make a business of satisfying the lust of men. Nor are their customers altogether Chinese; base white men patronize their wares as well. Some of these women are taken as "secondary" wives by the Chinese residents, and a sort of family life established; but, as a general rule, there are no families among them, and few children.

The occupations of these people are various. There is hardly anything that they cannot turn their hands to,—the work of women as well as men. They do the washing and ironing for the whole population; and sprinkle the clothes as they iron them, by squirting water over them in a fine spray from their mouths. Everywhere, in village and town, you see rude signs, informing you that See Hop or Ah Thing or Sam Sing or Wee Lung or Cum Sing wash and iron. How Tie is a doctor, and Hop Chang and Chi Lung keep stores. They are good house servants; cooks, table-waiters, and nurses; better, on the whole, than Irish girls, and as cheap,—fifteen to twenty-five dollars a month and board. One element of their usefulness as cooks is their genius for imitation; show them once how to do a thing, and their education is perfected; no repetition of the lesson is needed. But they seem to be more in use as house servants in the country than the city; they do not share the passion of the Irish girls for herding together, and appear to be content to be alone in a house, in a neighborhood, or a town.

Many are vegetable gardeners, too. In this even climate and with this productive soil, their painstaking culture, much hoeing and constant watering, makes little ground very fruitful, and they gather in three, four and five crops a year. Their garden patches, in the neighborhood of cities and villages, are always distinguishable from the rougher and more carelessly cultured grounds of their Saxon rivals. The Pacific Railroad is being built by Chinese labor; several thousand Chinamen are now rapidly grading the track through the rocks and sands of the Sierra Nevadas,—without them, indeed, this great work would have to wait for years, or move on with slow, hesitating steps. They can, by their steady industry, do nearly as much in a day, even in this rough labor, as the average of white men, and they cost only about half as much, say thirty dollars a month against fifty dollars. Besides, white labor is not to be had in the quantities necessary for such a great job as this. Good farm hands are the Chinese, also; and in the simpler and routine mechanic arts they have proven adepts;— there is hardly any branch of labor in which, under proper tuition, they do not or cannot succeed most admirably. The great success of the woolen manufacture here is due to the admirable adaptation and comparative cheapness of Chinese labor for the details. They are quick to learn, quiet, cleanly and faithful, and have no "off days," no sprees to get over. As factory operatives they receive twenty and twenty-five dollars a month, and board themselves, though quarters are provided for them on the mill grounds. Fish, vegetables, rice and pork are the main food, which is prepared and eaten with such economy that they live for about one-third what Yankee laborers can.

Thousands of the Chinese are gleaners in the gold fields. They follow in crowds after the white miners, working and washing over their deserted or neglected sands, and thriving on results that their predecessors would despise. A Chinese gold washer is content with one to two dollars a day; while the white man starves or moves on disgusted with twice that. A very considerable portion of the present gold production of California must now be the work of Chinese painstaking and moderate ambition. The traveler meets these Chinese miners everywhere on his road through the State; at work in the deserted ditches, or moving from one to another, on foot with their packs, or often in the stage, sharing the seats and paying the price of their aristocratic Saxon rivals.

Labor, cheap labor, being the one great palpable need of the Pacific States,—far more indeed than capital the want and necessity of their prosperity,— we should all say that these Chinese would be welcomed on every hand, their emigration encouraged, and themselves protected by law. Instead of which, we see them the victims of all sorts of prejudice and injustice. Ever since they began to come here, even now, it is a disputed question with the public, whether they should not be forbidden our shores. The do not ask or wish for citizenship; they have no ambition to become voters; but they are even denied protection in persons and property by the law. Their testimony is inadmissible against the white man; and, as miners, they are subject to a tax of four dollars a month, or nearly fifty dollars a year, each, for the benefit of the County and State treasuries. Thus ostracized and burdened by the State, they, of course, have been the victims of much meanness and cruelty from individuals. To abuse and cheat a Chinaman; to rob him; to kick and cuff him; even to kill him, have been things not only done with impunity by mean and wicked men, but even with vain glory. Terrible are some of the cases of robbery and wanton maiming and murder reported from the mining districts. Had "John,"—here and in China alike the English and Americans nickname every Chinaman "John,"—a good claim, original or improved, he was ordered to "move on,"—it belonged to somebody else. Had he hoarded a pile, he was ordered to disgorge; and, if he resisted, he was killed. Worse crimes even are known against them; they have been wantonly assaulted and shot down or stabbed by bad men, as sportsmen would surprise and shoot their game in the woods. There was no risk in such barbarity; if "John" survived to tell the tale, the law would not hear him or believe him. Nobody was so low, so miserable, that he did not despise the Chinaman, and could not outrage him. Ross Browne has an illustration of the status of poor "John," that is quite to the point. A vagabond Indian comes upon a solitary Chinaman, working over the sands of a deserted gulch for gold. " Dish is my land,"—says he,—"you pay me fifty dollar." The poor celestial turns, deprecatingly, saying: "Melican man (American) been here, and took all,—no bit left." Indian, irate and fierce,—" D—— Melican man,—you pay me fifty dollar, or I killee you."

Through a growing elevation of public opinion, and a reactionary experience towards depression, that calls for study of the future, the Californians are beginning to have a better appreciation of their Chinese immigrants. The demand for them is increasing. The new State, to be built upon manufactures and agriculture, is seen to need their cheap and reliable labor; and more pains will be taken to attract them to the country. But even now, a man who aspires to be a political leader, till lately a possible United States Senator, and the most widely circulated daily paper of this city, pronounce against the Chinese, and would drive them home. Their opposition is based upon the prejudices and jealousy of ignorant white laborers,—the Irish particularly,—who regard the Chinese as rivals in their field, and clothes itself in that cheap talk, so common among the bogus democracy of the East, about this being a "white man's country," and no place for Africans or Asiatics. But our national democratic principle, of welcoming hither the people of every country and clime, aside, the white man needs the negro and the Chinaman more than they him; the pocket appeal will override the prejudices of his soul,—and we shall do a sort of rough justice to both classes, because it will pay. The political questions involved in the negro's presence, and pressing so earnestly for solution, do not yet arise with regard to the Chinese,—perhaps will never be presented. As I have said, the Chinese are ambitious of no political rights, no citizenship, —it is only as our merchants go to China that they come here. Their great care, indeed, is to be buried at home; they stipulate with anxiety for that; and the great bulk of all who die on these shores are carried back for final interment.

There is no ready assimilation of the Chinese with our habits and modes of thought and action. Their simple, narrow though not dull minds have run too long in the old grooves to be easily turned off. They look down even with contempt upon our newer and rougher civilization, regarding us barbaric in fact, and calling us in their hearts, if not in speech, "the foreign devils." And our conduct towards them has inevitably intensified these feelings,—it has driven them back upon their naturally self-contained natures and habits. So they bring here and retain all their home ways of living and dressing, their old associations and religion. Their streets and quarters in town and city are China reproduced, unalleviated. Christian missionaries make small inroads among them. There is an intelligent and faithful one here (Rev. Mr. Loomis,) who has an attractive chapel and school, but his followers are few, and not rapidly increasing. But he and his predecessors and assistants have been and are doing a good work in teaching the two diverse races to better understand each other and in showing them how they can be of value to one another. They have been the constant and urgent advocates of the personal rights of the Chinese.

The religion of these people is a cheap, showy idolatry, with apparently nothing like fanaticism in it, and not a very deep hold in itself on their natures. "Josh" is their god or idol, and the "Josh" houses are small affairs, fitted up with images and altars a good deal after the style of cheap Catholic churches in Europe. Their whole civilization impresses me as a low, disciplined, perfected, sensuous sensualism. Everything in their life and their habits seems cut and dried like their food. There is no sign of that abandonment to an emotion, to a passion, good or bad, that marks the western races. Their great vice is gambling; that is going on constantly in their houses and shops; and commercial women and barbaric music minister to its indulgence. Cheap lotteries are a common form of this passion. Opium-smoking ranks next; and this is believed to be indulged in more extensively among them here than at home, since there is less restraint from relatives and authorities, and the means of procuring the article are greater. The wildly brilliant eye, the thin, haggard face, and the broken nervous system betray the victim to opium-smoking; and all tense, all excited, staring in eye and expression, he was almost a frightful object, as we peered in through the smoke of his half-lighted little room, and saw him lying on his mat in the midst of his fatal enjoyment.

But as laborers in our manufactories and as servants in our houses, beside their constant contact with our life and industry otherwise, these emigrants from the East cannot fail to get enlargement of ideas, freedom and novelty of action, and familiarity with and then preference for our higher civilization. Slowly and hardly but still surely this work must go on; and their constant going back and forth between here and China must also transplant new elements of thought and action into the home circles. Thus it is that we may hope and expect to reach this great people with the influences of our better and higher life. It is through modification and revolution in materialities, in manner of living, in manner of doing, that we shall pave the way for our thought and our religion. Our missionaries to the Five Points have learned to attack first with soap and water and clean clothes. The Chinese that come here are unconsciously besieged at first with better food and more of it than they have at home. The bath-house and the restaurant are the avant couriers of the Christian civilization.

The Chinese that come to these States are among the best of the peasantry from the country about Canton and Hong Kong. None of them are the miserable coolies that have been imported by the English to their Indian colonies as farm laborers. They associate themselves here into companies, based upon the village or neighborhood from which they come at home. These companies have headquarters in San Francisco; their presidents are men of high intelligence and character; and their office is to afford a temporary refuge for all who belong to their bodies, to assist them to work, to protect them against wrong, and send the dead back to their kindred at home. Beside these organizations, there are guilds or trade associations among the Chinese engaged in different occupations. Thus the laundry-men and the cigar-makers have organizations, with heavy fees from the members, power over the common interests of the business, and an occasional festivity.

The impressions these people make upon the American mind, after close observation of their habits, are very mixed and contradictory. They unite to many of the attainments and knowledge of the highest civilization, in some of which they are models for ourselves, many of the incidents and most of the ignorance of a simple barbarism. It may yet prove that we have as much to learn from them as they from us. Certainly here in this great field, this western half of our continental Nation, their diversified labor is a blessing and a necessity. It is all, perhaps more even, than the Irish and the Africans have been and are to our eastern wealth and progress. At the first, at least, they have greater adaptability and perfection than either of these classes of laborers, to whom we are so intimately and sometimes painfully accustomed.

There are quite a number of heavy mercantile houses here in the hands of the Chinese. The managers are intelligent, superior men. Their business is in supplies for their countrymen and in teas and silks and curiosities for the Americans. They import by the hundreds of thousands, even millions, yearly; and their reputation for fair and honest dealing is above that of the American merchants generally. These are the men, with the presidents of the 'six companies, into which the whole Chinese population is organized, as I have described, with whom Mr. Colfax and his friends dined last night. There were formalities and negotiations enough in the preliminary arrangements of the entertainment to have sufficed for a pacification of Kentucky politics, or the making of a new map of Europe; but when these were finally adjusted, questions of precedence among the Chinese settled, and a proper choice made among the many Americans who were eager to be bidden to the feast, all went as smooth as a town school examination that the teacher has been drilling for a month previous.

The party numbered from fifty to sixty, half Chinese, half white folks. The dinner was given in the second story of a Chinese restaurant, in a leading street of the city. Our hosts were fine-looking men, with impressive manners. While their race generally seems not more than two-thirds the size of our American men, these were nearly if not quite as tall and stout as their guests. Their eyes and their faces beamed with intelligence, and they were quick to perceive everything, and alert and *au fait* in all courtesies and politeness. An interpreter was present for the heavy talking; but most of our Chinese entertainers spoke a little English, and we got on well enough so far as that was concerned; though handshaking and bowing and scraping and a general flexibility of countenance, bodies and limbs had a very large share of the conversation to perform. Neither here nor in China is it common for the English and Americans to learn the Chinese language. The Chinese can and do more readily acquire ours, sufficiently at least for all business intercourse. Their broken or "pigeon" English, as it is called, is often very grotesque, and always very simple. Here is a specimen—a "pigeon-English" rendering of "My name is Norval," etc.:—

My namee being Norval topside that Glampian Hillee,
My father you sabee my father, makee pay chow-chow he sheep,
He smallo heartee man, too muchee take care that dolla, gallo?
So fashion he wantchee keep my, counta one piece chilo stope he
    own side,
My no wantchee long that largee mandoli, go knockee alla man;
Littee turn Joss pay my what thing my father no like pay
That mourn last nightee get up loune, alla same my hat,
No go full up, no got square; that plenty piece
That lobbie man, too muchee qui-si, alla same that tiger,
Chop-chop come down that hillee, catchie that sheep long that cow,
That man, custom take care, too muchie quick lun away.
My one piecie owne spee eye, look see that ladlone man what side
    he walkee,
Hi-yah! No good chancie, findie he, lun catchie my flew:
Too piecie loon choon lun catchie that lobbie man! he
No can walkee welly quick, he pocket too much full up.
So fashion knockee he largee.
   He head man no got shutte far
My knockie he head, Hi-yah! my No. 1 strong man,
Catchie he jacket, long he toousa, galo! You likee look see?

My no likee takee care that sheep, so fashion my hear you got
fightee this side.
My takee one servant, come your country, come helpie you,
He heart all same cow, too muchie fear lun away.
Masquie, Joss take care pay my come you house.

We were seated for the dinner around little round tables, six to nine at the table, and hosts and guests evenly mixed. There was a profusion of elegant China dishes on each table; each guest had two or three plates and saucers, all delicate and small. Choice sauces, pickles, sweetmeats and nuts were plentifully scattered about. Each guest had a saucer of flowers, a China spoon or bowl with a handle, and a pair of chop-sticks, little round and smooth ivory sticks about six inches long. Chi Sing-Tong, President of the San Yup Company, presided at Mr. Colfax's table.

Now the meal began. It consisted of three different courses, or dinners rather, between which was a recess of half an hour, when we retired to an anteroom, smoked and talked, and listened to the simple, rough, barbaric music from coarse guitar, viol drum, and violin, and meanwhile the tables were reset and new food provided.

Each course or dinner comprised a dozen to twenty different dishes, served generally one at a time, though sometimes two were brought on at once. There were no joints, nothing to be carved. Every article of food was brought on in quart 'bowls, in a sort of hash form. We dove into it with our chop-sticks, which, well handled, took up about a mouthful, and, transferring this to our plates, worked the chop-sticks again to get it or parts of it to our mouths. No one seemed to take more than a single taste or mouthful of each dish; so that, even if one relished the food, it would need something like a hundred different dishes to satisfy an ordinary appetite. Some of us took very readily to the chop-sticks; others did not,—perhaps were glad they could not; and for these a Yankee fork was provided, and our Chinese neighbors at the table were also prompt to offer their own chop-sticks to place a bit of each dish upon our plates. But as these same chop-sticks were also used to convey food into the mouths of the Chinese, the service did not always add to the relish of the food.

These were the principal dishes served for the first course, and in the order named: Fried shark's fins and grated ham, stewed pigeon with bamboo soup, fish sinews with ham, stewed chicken with water-cress, sea-weed, stewed ducks and bamboo soup, sponge cake, omelet cake, flower cake and banana fritters, bird-nest soup, tea. The meats seemed all alike; they had been dried or preserved in some way; were cut up into mouthfuls, and depended for all savoriness upon their accompaniments. The sea-weed, shark's fins and the like had a glutinous sort of taste; not repulsive, nor very seductive. The sweets were very delicate, but like everything else had a very artificial flavor; every article, indeed, seemed to have had its original and real taste and strength dried or cooked out of it, and a common Chinese flavor put into it. The bird-nest soup looked and tasted somewhat as a very delicate vermicelli soup does. The tea was delicious,—it was served without milk or sugar, did not need any such amelioration, and was very refreshing. Evidently it was made from the most delicate leaves or flowers of the tea plant, and had escaped all vulgar steeping or boiling.

During the first recess, the presidents of the companies,—the chief entertainers,—took their leave, and the merchants assumed the post of leading hosts; such being the fashion of the people. The second dinner opened with cold tea, and a white, rose-scented liquor, very strong, and served in tiny cups, and went on with lichens and a fungus-like moss, more shark's fins, stewed chestnuts and chickens, Chinese oysters, yellow and resurrected from the dried stage, more fungus stewed, a stew of flour and white nuts, stewed mutton, roast ducks, rice soup, rice and ducks' eggs and pickled cucumbers, ham and chicken soup. Between the second and third parts, there was an exchange of complimentary speeches by the head Chinaman and Mr. Colfax, at which the interpreter had to officiate. The third and last course consisted of a great variety of fresh fruits; and the unique entertainment ended about eleven o'clock, after a sitting of full five hours. The American resident guests furnished champagne and claret, and our Chinese hosts, invariably at the entrance and departure of each dish, invited us, with a gracious bow, to a sip thereof, in the which they all faithfully joined themselves.

The dinner was unquestionably a most magnificent one after the Chinese standard; the dishes were many of them rare and expensive; and everything was served in elegance and taste. It was a curious and interesting experience, and one of the rarest of the many courtesies extended to Mr. Colfax on this coast. But as to any real gastronomic satisfaction to be derived from it, I certainly "did not see it." Governor Bross's fidelity to the great principle of "when you are among the Romans to do as the Romans do," led him to take the meal seriatim, and eat of everything; but my own personal experience is perhaps the best commentary to be made upon the meal, as a meal. I went to the table weak and hungry; but I found the one universal odor and flavor soon destroyed all appetite; and I fell back resignedly on a constitutional incapacity to use the chop-sticks, and was sitting with a grim politeness through dinner number two, when there came an angel in disguise to my relief. The urbane chief of police of the city appeared and touched my shoulder: "There is a gentleman at the door who wishes to see you, and would have you bring your hat and coat." There were visions of violated city ordinances and "assisting" at the police court next morning. I thought, too, what a polite way this man has of arresting a stranger to the city. But, bowing my excuses to my pig-tail neighbor, I went joyfully to the unknown tribunal. A friend, a leading banker, who had sat opposite to me during the evening, and had been called out a few moments before, welcomed me at the street door with: "B——, I knew you were suffering, and were hungry—let us go and get something to eat—

a good square meal!" So we crossed to an American restaurant; the lost appetite came back; and mutton chops, squabs, fried potatoes and a bottle of champagne soon restored me. My friend insisted that the second course of the Chinese dinner was only the first warmed over, and that that was the object of the recess. However that might be,— this is how I went to the grand Chinese dinner, and went out, when it was two-thirds over, and "got something to eat."

LETTER XXIV.

THE GREAT THEME: THE PACIFIC RAILROAD.

SAN FRANCISCO, August 20.

To feel the importance of the Pacific Railroad, to measure the urgency of its early completion, to become impatient with government and contractor at every delay in the work, you must come across the Plains and the Mountains to the Pacific Coast. Then you will see half a Continent waiting for its vivifying influences. You will witness a boundless agriculture, fickle and hesitating for lack of the regular markets this would give. You will find mineral wealth, immeasurable, locked up, wastefully worked, or gambled away, until this shall open to it abundant labor, cheap capital, wood, water, science, ready oversight, steadiness of production,—everything that shall make mining a certainty and not a chance. You will find the world's commerce with India and China eagerly awaiting its opportunities. You will see an illimitable field for manufactures unimproved for want of its stimulus and its advantages. You will feel hearts breaking, see morals struggling slowly upward against odds, know that religion languishes; feel, see and know that all the sweetest and finest influences and elements of society and Christian civilization hunger and suffer for the lack of this quick contact with the Parent and Fountain of all our national life.

It is touching to remember that between Plains and Pacific, in country and on coast, on the Columbia, on the Colorado, through all our long journey, the first question asked of us by every man and woman we have met,—whether rich or poor, high or humble,—has been, "When do you think the Pacific Railroad will be done?" or, "Why don't or won't the government, now the war is over, put the soldiers to building this road?"—and their parting appeal and injunction, as well, "Do build this Pacific Road for us as soon as possible,—we wait, everything waits for that." Tender-eyed women, hard-fisted men,—pioneers, or missionaries, the martyrs and the successful,—all alike feel and speak this sentiment. It is the hunger, the prayer, the hope of all these people. Hunger and prayer and hope for "Home," and what home can bring them, in cheap and ready passage to and from, of reunion with parent and brother and sister and friend, of sight of old valley and mountain and wood, of social influence, of esthetic elevation, of worldly stimulus and prosperity. "Home," they all here call the East. It is a touching and pathetic, though almost unconscious, tribute. Such an one "is going home next spring;" "I hope to go home another year;" "When I was home last;" "I have never been home since I came out;" "I am afraid I shall never go home again;"—these and kindred phrases are the current forms of speech. Home is not here, but there. The thought of home is ever rolled, like a sweet morsel, under the tongues of their souls.

Here is large appeal both to the sympathy and foresight of the eastern States. Here is present bond of union and means for perpetuating it. To build the railroad, and freshen recollection and renew association of the original emigrants, and to bind by travel and contact the children here with the homes and lives and loves of their parents there: this is the cheapest, surest and sweetest way to preserve our nationality, and continue the Republic a unit from ocean to ocean. A sad and severe trial will ensue to the Union if a generation grows up here that "knows not Joseph." The centrifugal forces will ever be in hot action between the far-separated eastern and western sections of the Nation. First among the centripetal powers is the Pacific Railroad, and every year of its delay increases tenfold its burden; every year's postponement weakens in equal degree the influences here by which it shall operate.

What is doing to supply this great want of Pacific progress and civilization and national unity? What are the possibilities and probabilities of the great continental railway? are what you will wish to know from me. Our journey has lain along its most natural commercial route; we started from its eastern terminus on the Missouri border; we kept in the main line of population and travel, which it is desirable for it to follow; we finished our ride upon its beginnings at this end; and we have everywhere had the subject forced upon our thought, and made it constant study. Many of the obstacles to the great work grew feeble in travel over its line. Want of timber, of water, of coal for fuel; the steep grades and high ascents of the two great continental ranges of mountains to be crossed, the Rocky and the Sierras; and the snows they will accumulate upon the track in the winter months,— these are the suggested and apparent difficulties to the building and operating of the Pacific Railroad. There is plenty of good timber in the mountains; and the soft cotton-wood of the Plains can be kyanized (hardened by a chemical process), so as to make sound sleepers and ties. There are sections of many miles, even perhaps of two hundred, over which the timber will have to be hauled; but the road itself can do this as it progresses,—taking along over the track built to-day the timber and rails for that to be built to-morrow. As to water, artesian wells are sure to find it in the vacant desert stretches, which are neither so long nor so barren of possible water as has been supposed.

The fuel question is perhaps more difficult to solve as yet. The Sierras will furnish wood in abundance, and cheaply, for all the western end; we know there is coal in the Rocky Mountains; and we were told almost everywhere over the entire line that it had been, or could undoubtedly be found,—in Kansas, on the Plains, among the hills of the deserts. But suppose the supplies of food for steam have to be carried over a few hundred miles of the road, east and west from the Sierras and the Rocky Mountains; that is not so hard a matter,—certainly nothing to daunt or hesitate the enterprise. We shall soon learn, too, to make steam from petroleum; and that is easily transported for long distances; besides which, prospectors are finding it everywhere from Missouri to Pacific. Build the road, and the intermediate country will speedily find the means for running it.

Now as to difficulties of construction, heavy grades and high mountains, and the winter snows as obstacles to continuous use.

The first third of the line, from the Missouri River to the Rocky Mountains, is mere baby-work. Three hundred men will grade it as fast as the iron can be laid. It is a level, natural roadway, with very little bridging, and no want of water. It is a shame all this section is not finished and running already. The first of January, 1867, ought now to be the limit for its completion. From here to Salt Lake, over the Rocky Mountains, there are apparently no greater obstacles to be overcome than your Western Road from Springfield to Albany, the Erie and the Pennsylvania Central have triumphantly and profitably surmounted. There are various contesting routes; northerly by the North Platte and the South Pass; by the South Platte and Bridger's Pass, which is the route we traveled in the stage;— or more direct still, from Denver through the present gold mining region of Colorado by Clear Creek and over the Berthoud Pass; or again by a kindred route to the last, up Boulder Creek and over Boulder Pass, both these last two entering the "Middle Park" of the Mountains, and through that to the head waters of the Salt Lake Basin. The Berthoud and Boulder Pass routes would probably involve higher grades and more rock cutting, and in winter deeper snows; but they would pass through a richer country, avoid the deserts of the north, and save at least one hundred miles of distance. A new road for the overland stages is this very season being cut through the Berthoud Pass route by the help of United States soldiers from Utah; and the stage line is expected to be transferred to it next spring. But by the Bridger or South Pass routes, the railroad can surmount the eastern slope of the Rocky Mountains with the greatest ease. Our stage teams trotted up the hardly perceptible grades by the Bridger route without any effort. Coming down into Salt Lake Valley, there would be rougher work; but there are several considerable streams along whose banks the track could be brought, I am sure, with no greater labor or expense than has been incurred in a dozen cases by our eastern railroads.

From Salt Lake to the Sierra Nevadas are two routes; southerly through the center of Nevada, and striking Austin and Virginia City, the centers of the silver mining region,—which is the present stage and telegraph route,—and northerly by the Humboldt River. The former would pass more directly through the chief present and prospective populations; but it would encounter a dozen or fifteen ranges of hills to be crossed, and find little wood and scant water. The Humboldt route would be more cheaply built, and goes through a naturally better country as to wood, water and fertility of soil. It is generally conceded to be the true natural roadway across the Continent. The emigration has always taken it. If the railroad is built through it, Virginia City and Austin will be reached by branches dropping down to them through their neighboring valleys.

Now we reach the California border, and the toughest part of the work of the railroad,—the high-reaching, far-spreading, rock-fastened, and snow-covered Sierra Nevadas. But the difficulties here are mitigated by plenty of water and timber, and by the near presence of an energetic population, and are already being practically overcome by the energy and perseverance of the California Pacific Railroad organization. I only wish the East would get to Salt Lake with their rail so soon as the West can and will with theirs. It is not gratifying to eastern pride, indeed, to see how much more California, with its scant capital, its scarce labor, and its depressed industry and interests, is doing to solve this great practical problem of the continental railway, than your abounding wealth and teeming populations of the East, with a great network of railroads from the Atlantic, all needing and professing to seek an outlet west to the Pacific Coast.

Let me state the condition of the work on each end the line.

Congress has given princely bounties to the enterprise, all that could be expected, everything that was asked. Government bonds are loaned to it to the amount of sixteen thousand dollars a mile through the plains and forty-eight thousand dollars a mile in the mountains; besides which half of all the land each side of the road for twenty miles deep is donated outright to the companies doing the work. The Union Pacific Railroad company is recognized at the East, and the Central Pacific Railroad company here, as entitled to this bounty, and are respectively authorized to construct the road from their starting points until they meet. The companies are further authorized to issue their own bonds to an equal amount to those granted by the government, and secure them by a first mortgage; the government loan taking the second place in security.

The business of supplying the populations of Colorado, Utah and Montana,—at least one hundred and fifty thousand persons,—invites the speedy construction of the road from the East. This business for 1864 is estimated at forty million pounds, and for 1865 at two hundred millions, and employed last year nine thousand wagons, fifty thousand cattle, sixteen thousand horses and mules and ten thousand men as drivers, laborers and guards; and the sum paid for freight in the former year is estimated by one authority at enough to build the railroad the entire distance at a cost of forty-eight thousand dollars the mile! And during the months of May and June, this year, counting both the emigration and the freight trains, there passed west over the

Plains full ten thousand teams and fifty thousand to sixty thousand head of stock, according to data furnished from Fort Laramie and the junction of the overland routes on the Platte River. The shipment of supplies for the United States troops on the Plains and in the Mountains this season is alone over eleven million pounds.

All these statistics may not be perfectly accurate; but they have a substantial basis of fact, and with such generous gifts as the government makes, and with such large railway interests behind to be benefited by farther extension of railway lines to the west, they would seem to justify and to demand a rapid construction of the road out from the Missouri River, especially when for the first five hundred to six hundred miles of that road, there is scarcely more required than to scrape a place in the soft soil for sleepers and ties and iron. And yet, though three to four years have passed since the company accepted the bargain of the government and assumed its responsibilities, not a mile of the main road is running from the Missouri west. The lower branch from Kansas City is open to Lawrence, forty miles, and graded to Topeka, sixty miles; but from Atchison and Omaha there is no iron down, and only small sections graded or half graded.

Is it said that by the government flooding the markets with better classes of its securities, there was no sale for the bonds allotted for this work, and so no means for its construction? The reply is that no set of men should step forward to accept this largess and undertake this enterprise, holding such sure profits in its future, that have not at least a million or two of their own to make a beginning with. Has the war absorbed all labor and capital during these years? Other railroads have been built meantime, and labor was cheaper on the Plains than in California. Beside, here are six months since the war ended, and the end witnesses no marked progress, no larger activity, than the beginning.

I know nothing of the men who form the Pacific Railroad Company of the East; I suspect their names are more familiar to Wall street than to the West or the railroad world; but I do know that all I could see or hear of them and their work, along the route of the continental railway, did not indicate either the earnestness or the power that should accompany their position, their responsibilities and their opportunities. After leaving the Missouri River, indeed, they offered no sign of life except in a single small party of engineers in Salt Lake City, who were on a straggling hunt for the best route through the Rocky Mountains, but who seemed to have no proper leadership, and no clear purpose, and in fact confessed that the company had no chief engineer worthy the name or position.

Here in California, however, there is more life and progress. Energy and capital are not perhaps the best directed possible; there has been and still is somewhat of controversy and waste of power as to the true route; but there is earnestness and movement of the right sort, and the track is fast ascending the Sierras on its progress eastward. It has no immediate way business to tempt it but the trade of Nevada with thirty thousand population,—much less, therefore, than that which invites the laying of the rails across the prairies to the Rocky Mountains,—but this business has constructed and amply paid for two fine toll-roads over the Sierras, and was, until a few days ago, building two railroads in their tracks. There being free water carriage from San Francisco to Sacramento, these rival roads (both carriage and rail), have their base at the latter point, and branch off right and left into the mountains, and cross the summit of the latter some thirty or forty miles apart, coming together again at a common point in Nevada on the other side, namely, Virginia City. The distance between Sacramento and Virginia City is about the same, one hundred and sixty miles, by each road; and their rivalry has given excellent accommodations for travel and traffic, and helped to push forward the railroad tracks on both lines.

The original and heretofore most popular wagon road was that by Placerville and Lake Tahoe, over which we came into the State, as already described. The railway track on its line is now laid about forty miles from Sacramento or nearly to Placerville, which is among the foot-hills of the mountains. During the "flush" times of Nevada, 1862 and 1863, the business done over this line was immense; in the latter year about twelve millions dollars were paid for freights alone, the cost of transportation being from five to ten cents a pound,—and the tolls on teams, received by the constructors of the wagon road, amounted to six hundred thousand dollars. The charge for a single team is about thirty dollars; and in 1864, when the business was much less than before, no less than seven thousand teams passed over this Placerville route; carrying all kinds of food and merchandise and machinery over into Nevada, but coming back nearly empty.

As showing how great and wasteful was and still is the cost of doing business in Nevada under such circumstances, it has been carefully estimated that the famous Gould & Curry silver mine at Virginia City would have saved two millions dollars in expenses in a single year, had a railroad been built and running over the mountains. The production of the mine that year was four millions and a half of dollars, but its expenses absorbed three millions and a half, leaving only one million profit to stockholders, against three millions, probably, had there been ready and cheap communication with the San Francisco markets.

The staging and freighting over these mountain toll roads are performed in the most perfect style, however. The freight wagons are bigger and stronger than anything ever seen in the East; generally a smaller one is attached as a tender to the main wagon; ten to twelve large and strong mules or horses, in fine condition, constitute the usual team; and the load ranges from five to ten tons. To each mule in the best teams a large bell is attached, and they are trained to keep step to their music, and so pull and move uniformly. Frequently the road will be filled with these teams for a quarter and a half mile, and the turning out for them is the only interruption to the steady trot or the grand gallop of the six-horse stage teams that, attached to the best of Concord coaches, usually loaded with passengers, go half-flying over these well-graded mountain roads, three to four each way daily. The stage horses are sleek and fat, gay as larks, changed every ten miles, and do their work as if they really loved it. The Placerville road is watered throughout nearly its whole line by sprinkling carts, in the same way as the streets of a city are wet in the dry summer season; and luxurious as this seems and is, —for the dust is otherwise most fearful,—it is found to be the cheapest way of keeping the road itself in good repair. When dry, the heavy teams cut up the track most terribly.

But these horses are running away with the locomotive, which is my main theme to-day. The rival of the Placerville route, though opened since, has won the title and the government bounty of the Pacific Railroad, and has this season pushed its iron track ahead of the former, and so henceforth must have every advantage for both traffic and travel. Indeed, within a few days, its friends have bought a controlling interest in the railway section of the Placerville route, and will probably put a veto upon the construction of the latter beyond that town. It is called the Dutch Flat and Donner Lake route, as well as the Central Pacific Railroad, and lies to the north of the other. Its line was selected by the late

Mr. T. D. Judah, who has left a very enviable reputation in California both for personal integrity and professional ability as an engineer, after a thorough examination of other lines and passes over the mountains; and having gained, mainly by his indorsement, the approval of Congress, and the support and bounty, also, of San Francisco and Sacramento, it has readily achieved these decided advantages over its rival, which has been sustained only by private capital and the profits of its toll-road. Mr. Judah, who died after having established the general route of the Pacific Road and secured its indorsement by Congress, was an assistant engineer in the construction of your Connecticut River Railroad in Massachusetts, and married a Greenfield lady. His reputation is one of the main bulwarks of the friends of his road, in the bitter controversy that has raged between them and the advocates of the Placerville route; and, though this contest now seems nearly over under the triumph of the upper route, many of the most intelligent citizens of the State still contend that the Placerville line is the easiest and safest for the railroad track. Our own superficial examination of the two routes tended to this conclusion, also; but it is too late, now, to argue that question. The Judah or Dutch Flat Route has got the name and the means, and is being pushed over the mountains with commendable vigor and rapidity; and it is wise for California and the country alike to sustain it, and secure its completion as early as possible. This accomplished, the other may and probably will be extended over into Nevada, and already there is agitation to secure government bounty in its behalf.

Our party made a very profitable and interesting excursion over the route of the Central Pacific Road from Sacramento to Donner Lake, on the eastern slope of the mountains, by special train and coaches, and along the working sections on horseback. The track is graded and laid, and trains are running to the new town of Colfax (named for the Speaker), which is fifty-six miles from Sacramento. Grading is now in active progress on the next two sections, to Dutch Flat, twelve miles, and the Crystal Lake, thirteen miles farther, with a force of about four thousand laborers, mostly Chinese. Though these sections are through a very rough and rocky country, the work will certainly be done to Dutch Flat by spring, and Crystal Lake early next fall. Then the rails are within fifteen miles of the summit of the Sierras. The toughest job of the whole line lies in these fifteen miles up, and the three or four miles down to Donner Lake, on the other side. This must hang on for two or three years, it seems to me; there will be some tunneling, probably, and much heavy rock-cutting; for several miles along the summit, which is seven thousand feet above the sea level, the road must apparently be cut into a wall of solid rock, and then be covered by a roof to keep off the snows;—but the later surveys soften the anticipated severity of the work, and the company and its contractors are sanguine of mastering all the difficulties of the summit sections in two years.

The wagon-road goes down from the summit to Donner Lake at the rate of about four hundred feet to the mile, and the railway track will have to be wound in and out on the mountain sides for ten or more miles in order to get ahead two or three, and reach the level of the lake, whence it can be run readily down by the Truckee River into the valleys and plains of Nevada. The road ascends the mountains on this side by a very regular and nearly uniform grade, never exceeding one hundred and five feet to the mile, which is less than the highest grades of the Baltimore and Ohio Railroad, to which the act of Congress limits this road. In going down the other side, no grade will exceed one hundred and five feet, and after reaching Donner Lake the grade will be reduced to forty feet. But the company does not purpose to wait for the full construction of the track over the summit before pushing the work on the line beyond. While that is advanced as fast as possible, they will commence next spring at Donner Lake and proceed down the mountains and out into and through Nevada as rapidly as may be, eager to absorb as much of the whole enterprise, and meet the road coming west at a point as far east as they can.

So far the company have used none of the United States bonds or lands granted by Congress in aid of the work. Some two and a half millions in these bonds are now due. The company can issue an equal amount of their own bonds guaranteed by a preceding or first mortgage; but none of these, also, have yet been used. They also have available a million and a half of other bonds on which the State of California pays seven per cent. interest in gold for twenty years. Here are six millions and a half of good securities now on hand for prosecuting the work, besides what is earned as the road progresses, and the power to anticipate the issue of their own first mortgage bonds at the rate of forty-eight thousand dollars for a mile of mountains and sixteen thousand dollars for a mile of plain, for one hundred miles in advance of construction. The work so far has been done out of about a million of paid-up stock, and subscriptions of the county of Sacramento of three hundred thousand dollars, the county of Placer of two hundred and fifty thousand dollars, and of San Francisco of four hundred thousand dollars, and the profits of that part of the road in running order. Of these sums, nearly half a million is still left, and as the road has gone so far as to substantially secure a monopoly of all the business over the mountains, the profits on its completed section will be constantly increasing. Then, besides all this, there are between eighteen and nineteen millions of the twenty millions capital stock of the road, yet unsubscribed for. Sometime, though not at present, this will be paying property; and it may suffice even now for the profits of the contractors. The company thus feel strong financially, and though much of their securities are not just now marketable except at a discount, they are confident there need be no further delay for the lack of means, and are increasing their working force upon the road as fast as laborers can be had.

All the Chinese that offer, or that can be encouraged to emigrate from home, are employed, and it is expected that five thousand will be at work on the road before the present season closes.

These details are very long, but I trust are not altogether tedious or uninteresting. The theme presses itself upon us more deeply, more solemnly, than any one other offered by our journey and its observations. It is pathetic and painful, as I said in the beginning, in the solicitude and anxiety it awakens here among the people, and which we cannot help but share. There is really nothing unreasonable in demanding that rails should be laid and trains running over half the line between the Pacific Ocean and the Missouri River in two years and a half, over two-thirds of it another year, and the entire distance, unbroken, in five years. There are short sections in the mountains that may require three, or even five years to work them out; but the great bulk of the way can be graded and laid with rails in three years. The California Pacific railroad company, led by some of the best men in the State, with Ex-Governor Stanford for president, say, calmly and distinctly, in their annual report just published, that they will take their completed line into Salt Lake City in three years from date. I believe they can and will do it, with anything like an easy money and labor market. And it is just as practicable for the road from the East to reach the Rocky Mountains in twelve or eighteen months, and to span these mountains in two years more.

Next spring should see as many men at work on

the eastern line as there will be on the western; the fall, fifteen to twenty thousand along its entire route; 1867 should count fifty thousand shovels and picks and drills, leveling the paths for this national highway; and in 1868 the hungry hearts of these people of the Pacific States should dance to the music of a hundred thousand strong,—music sweeter far and holier even than that of all the martial bands of the new Republic.

Men of the East! Men at Washington! You have given the toil and even the blood of a million of your brothers and fellows for four years, and spent three thousand million dollars, to rescue one section of the Republic from barbarism and from anarchy; and your triumph makes the cost cheap. Lend now a few thousand of men, and a hundred millions of money, to create a new Republic; to marry to the Nation of the Atlantic an equal if not greater Nation of the Pacific. Anticipate a new sectionalism, a new strife, by a triumph of the arts of Peace, that shall be even prouder and more reaching than the victories of your Arms. Here is payment of your great debt; here is wealth unbounded; here the commerce of the world; here the completion of a Republic that is continental; but you must come and take them with the Locomotive!

LETTER XXV.

COUNTRY EXCURSIONS: THE GEYSERS: VINE-YARDS, AND AGRICULTURE.

SAN FRANCISCO, August 28.

PERHAPS this is the least pleasant month of the twelve to see San Francisco and California in,—the dryest and dreariest and dustiest, when Nature is at rest; yet we find more to see, more delightful journeys to make into the interior, than we have time for. In every direction, there is a novelty, a surprise for us; everywhere Nature makes strange and fascinating combinations, presents herself in new forms, outrages all our pre-educated ideas as to her laws and habits, and yet everywhere, as ever, is impressive and beautiful. These valleys inside the Coast range of mountains about San Francisco are particularly rich in novelty and beauty, and have been the theater of several very delightful excursions by our party since we came back from the Yosemite. They form the garden of California, agriculturally, and their nearness to the central market, and their fertile soil, have made them to be the best improved and the most steadily progressive in wealth and population of all the interior sections of the State.

California, as you will see by the map, is like a great basin or bowl, between two ranges of mountains. Along the Coast runs one ; and the Sierras, two hundred miles east, separate her from Nevada. The Golden Gate at San Francisco lets in the ocean and out her interial waters ; to the north from that city stretches the Sacramento River and its tributaries through a plain two hundred miles long and forty to fifty wide ; to the south, the San Joaquin (pronounced San Walk-in) repeats the same ; and the two, with all the drainage of the interior, all the inside waste of both ranges of mountains, meet above San Francisco, and spread out into the wide inland bays, twenty to fifty miles long and four to ten wide, that give to that city its beauty, its wealth, and its commerce ; and delaying here, they leisurely balance accounts with the ocean through its narrow gateway.

San Francisco hangs over the edge of its chiefest, largest bay, like the oriole balancing on the crest of his long, pocket nest ; peeping around the corner into the Pacific, but opening wide eyes north and south and east, to the interior. To the north and south, the Sacramento and San Joaquin valleys are shut in by the two ranges of mountains chassezing into each other. And this is California. The side valleys from the Sierras are the field of the gold diggings and the quartz mining ; their mates over the way, inside the Coast range, and among its foot-hills, squeezing first and longest the spongy clouds from the ocean, get the most rain, and are the kindest to the husbandman ; while the broad, intermediate plains along the main rivers, wait somewhat on irrigation or a better understanding of the mysteries of their wealth. Every year's experience goes more and more to prove, however, that nature here does not forbid successful agriculture in withholding rain for six months of the year. The laws of her increase are peculiar; but they are not hard. The vine does not need irrigation, nor the other fruits; and the small grains are natural to hill and plain alike: and all ripen richly under the stimulus of the winter and spring moisture.

Across the bay from San Francisco lies its suburb, Oakland, home of many of its best people. Here is one of the Coast valleys I have mentioned, thick with low-branching evergreen oaks, and softer in sky and air than the city; here is quiet of country and cultivation of town; here grows the "garden sauce" of the metropolis; here are its best seminaries and its hopeful college; here, too, Fred Law Olmsted has planned on a large scale, and with novelties of arrangement befitting the novelties of climate and verdure, a grand rural cemetery; and here Major Ralph W. Kirkham, whom Springfield sent to West Point a generation ago, and has been proud of ever since, has the most elegant house and home to be found anywhere on the Pacific Coast. Down the bay on the San Francisco side, through the San Jose (Ozay) valley and its villages and its culture, and around its base, and back on the Alameda and Oakland shore, forms one of the most interesting of our late excursions. It is a sweep of a hundred miles; but railroads at beginning and end,—the arms which San Francisco is crooking around her intervening waters to stretch out, by way of Stockton, to Sacramento, and there welcome the continental cars,—helped us to make it leisurely in a day.

Many an elegant country home, with orchards and gardens acres wide, showed the overflow of San Francisco wealth, as we rode down the San Jose valley; miles of wheat fields proved how extensive are the plans of agriculture here; busy and prosperous villages told of their sure and steady profit, —quite in contrast with the desolated look of most of the mining towns of the interior; old and tumble-down mission-houses and churches, built of mud and stone, without wood or nails, and neighboring orchards of ancient pear and fig trees, marked the old homes of Catholic and Spanish missionaries among the Indians; modern convents and colleges holding up the cross, proved the presence of the same element, flexible in its character, and now offering perhaps the best education of the Coast to the children of our Puritan emigrants;—everywhere was novelty, on every side beauty, though most of the hills were bare and brown; and only the low, scraggy oaks, making park of field, and the cultivated orchard fed the eye with green. The plain was everywhere yellow with the stubble of grain, or the wild oats that grow spontaneously on unoccupied hill and meadow all over California, or brown with the dry grass, that is hay ungathered, and rich feed still for cattle and horse; and the hills, still of those beautifully rounded shapes, that I first recognized in Nevada, and are ever a surprise and a delight to the eye, wearing the same colors of yellow and brown, blending into each other, and soft and rich under the bloom of a haze that belongs to the season and the shore;—there was no avail in struggling against education and experience,—here was beauty and exhilarating life without rain for many months, without forests, without rivers, without green grass, or flowers.

Similar and prolonged experience, with some added and fresh elements, came from a rapid three days' journey northerly from San Francisco to see the Geysers, or famous boiling springs, and the neighboring valleys famous for farms and fruits and vineyards. Captain Baxter's steamer "Petaluma" took us up through San Puebla Bay, one of the widenings of the outcoming waters of the interior, and Petaluma Creek, to the thriving town of the latter name. I took a sharp look at it because of its persistent desire to steal your neighbor, Rev. Mr. Harding, away from Longmeadow, for its own minister; and found it one of the most prosperous and pleasant of California towns, at the foot of one of the richest agricultural regions of the Coast. The rest of the day we rode through dryest dust and reposing nature, up through the Petaluma valley, and over into that of the Russian River, famous and peculiar here for its especial kindliness to our Indian corn, also for its toothsome grouse, first cousin to our partridge; stopping at the village of Healdsburg for brass band, speeches and supper, and, after a rapid hour's drive by moonlight, at a solitary ranch under the Geyser mountain for the night.

Sunrise the next morning found us whirling along a rough road over the mountains to the especial object of the excursion. But the drive of the morning was the more remarkable feature. We supposed the Plains and Sierras had exhausted possibilities for us in that respect. But they were both outwitted here. For bold daring and brilliant execution, our driver this morning must take the palm of the world, I verily believe. The distance was twelve miles, up and down steep hills, through enclosed pastures; the vehicle an open wagon, the passengers six, the horses four and gay, and changed once; and the driver Mr. Clark T. Foss, our landlord over night and owner of the route. For several miles the road lay along "the hog's back," the crest of a mountain that ran away from the point or edge, like the sides of a roof, several thousand feet to the ravines below; so narrow that, pressed down and widened as much as was possible, it was rarely over ten or twelve feet wide, and in one place but seven feet; and winding about as the crest of the hill ran;—and yet we went over this narrow causeway on the full gallop.

After going up and down several mountains, holding rare views of valleys and ravines and peaks, under the shadows and mists of early morning, we came to a point overlooking the Geysers. Far below in the valley, we could see the hot steam pouring out of the ground; and wide was the waste around. The descent was almost perpendicular;

the road ran down sixteen hundred feet in the two miles to the hotel, and it had thirty-five sharp turns in its course: "Look at your watch," said Mr. Foss, as he started on the steep decline; crack, crack went the whip over the heads of the leaders, as the sharp corners came in sight, and they plunged with seeming recklessness ahead,—and in *nine minutes and a half*, they were pulled up at the bottom, and we took breath. Going back, the team was an hour and a quarter in the same passage. When we wondered at Mr. Foss for his perilous and rapid driving down such a steep road, he said, "Oh, there's no danger or difficulty in it,—all it needs is to keep your head cool, and the leaders out of the way." But nevertheless I was convinced it not only does require a quick and cool brain, but a ready and strong and experienced hand. The whole morning ride was accomplished in two hours and a quarter; and though everybody predicts a catastrophe from its apparent dangers, Mr. Foss has driven it, after this style, for many years, and never had an accident.

The Geysers are exhausted in a couple of hours. They are certainly a curiosity, a marvel; but there is no element of beauty; there is nothing to be studied, to grow into or upon you. We had seen something similar, though less extensive, in Nevada; and like a three-legged calf, or the Siamese twins, or P. T. Barnum, or James Gordon Bennett, once seeing is satisfactory for a life-time. They are a sort of grand natural chemical shop in disorder. In a little ravine, branching off from the valley, is their principal theater. The ground is white and yellow and gray, porous and rotten, with long and high heat. The air is also hot and sulphurous to an unpleasant degree. All along the bottom of the ravine and up its sides, the earth seems hollow and full of boiling water. In frequent little cracks and pin holes it finds vent; and out of these it bubbles and emits steam like so many tiny tea-kettles at high tide. In one place the earth yawns wide, and the "Witches' Caldron," several feet in diameter, seethes and spouts a black, inky water, so hot as to boil an egg instantly, and capable of reducing a human body to pulp at short notice. The water is thrown up four to six feet in height, and the general effect is very devilish indeed. The "Witches' Caldron" is reproduced a dozen times in miniature,—handy little pools for cooking your breakfast and dinner, if they were only in your kitchen or back yard. Farther up you follow a puffing noise, exactly like that of a steamboat in progress, and you come to a couple of volumes of steam struggling out of tiny holes, but mounting high and spreading wide from their force and heat.

You grow faint with the heat and smells; your feet seem burning; and the air is loaded with a mixture of salts, sulphur, iron, magnesia, soda, ammonia, all the chemicals and compounds of a doctor's shop. You feel as if the ground might any moment open, and let you down to a genuine hell. You recall the line from Milton, or somebody: "Here is hell,—myself am hell." And, most dreadful of all, you lose all appetite for the breakfast of venison, trout and grouse that awaits your return to the hotel. So you struggle out of the ravine, every step among tiny volumes of steam, and over bubbling pools of water, and cool and refresh yourself among the trees on the mountain side beyond. Then, not to omit any sight, you go back through two other ravines where the same phenomena are repeated, though less extensively. All around by the hot pools and escape valves are delicate and beautiful little crystals of sulphur, and soda, and other distinct elements of the combustibles below, taking substance again on the surface.

All this wonder-working is going on day and night, year after year, answering to-day exactly to the descriptions of yesterday and five years ago. Most of the waters are black as ink, and some as thick; others are quite light and transparent; and they are of all degrees of temperature from one hundred and fifty to five hundred. Near by, too, are springs of cool water; some as cold as these are hot, almost. The phenomena carries its own explanation; the chemist will reproduce for you the same thing, on a small scale, by mixing sulphuric acid and cold water, and the other unkindred elements that have here, in nature's laboratory, chanced to get together. Volcanic action is also most probably connected with some of the demonstrations here.

There must be utility in these waters for the cure of rheumatism and other blood and skin diseases. The Indians have long used some of the pools in this way, with results that seem like fables. One of the pools has fame for eyes; and, with chemical examination and scientific application, doubtless large benefits might be reasonably assured among invalids from a resort to these waters. At present there is only a rough little bathing-house, collecting the waters from the ravine, and the visitors to the valley, save for curiosity, are but few. It is a wild, unredeemed spot, all around the Geysers; beautiful with deep forests, a mountain stream, and clear air. Game, too, abounds; deer and grouse and trout seemed plentier than in any region we have visited. There is a comfortable hotel; but otherwise this valley is uninhabited. The entire region for two miles in length and half a mile in breadth, including all the springs, is owned by one man, who offers it for sale. Who would speculate in a mundane hell?

Back on the route of our morning ride, we then turned off into the neighboring valley of Napa, celebrated for its agricultural beauty and productiveness, and also for its Calistoga and Warm Springs, charmingly located, the one in the plains and the other close among mountains, and constituting the fashionable summer resorts for San Franciscans. The water is sulphurous; the bathing delicious, softening the skin to the texture of a babe's; the country charming: but we found both establishments, though with capacious head-quarters and numerous family cottages, almost deserted of people.

Past farms and orchards, through parks of evergreen oak that looked as perfect as if the work of art, we stopped at the village of Napa, twin and rival to Petaluma, and from here, crossing another spur of the Coast range, we entered still another beautiful and fertile valley, that of Sonoma.

Here are some of the largest vineyards of northern California, and we visited that of the Buena Vista Vinicultural society, under the management of Colonel Haraszthy, a Hungarian. This estate embraces about five thousand acres of land, a princely-looking house, large wine manufactory and cellars, and about a million vines, foreign and native. The whole value of its property is half a million dollars, including one hundred thousand dollars' worth of wine and brandies ready and in preparation for market. We tasted the liquors, we shared the generous hospitality of the estate, and its superintendent; but we failed to obtain, here or elsewhere, any satisfactory information as to the boasted success of wine-making, yet, in California. The business is still very much in its infancy, indeed; and this one enterprise does not seem well-managed. Nor do we find the wines very inviting; they partake of the general character of the Rhine wines and the Ohio Catawba; but are rougher, harsh and heady,—needing apparently both some improvement in culture and manufacture, and time for softening. I have drank, indeed, much better California wine in Springfield than out here.

The vine and wine interest is already a great one, and is rapidly growing. Nearly all parts of the State are favorable to it; the deserted and exhausted gold fields of the Sierra Nevada valleys and hillsides, as well as the valleys of the Coast range and the southern mountains. Down in Los Angelos County, this season, though the grapes are twice as abundant as last year, the price is treble, because of the increased preparations for their manufacture, and the profit that is sure to be realized from the business when well-conducted. The Buena Vista vineyards have been making part of their wine into champagne the last year, and gratifying results are confidently predicted.

But as doctors never take their own medicines, the true Californian is slow to drink his own wine. He prefers to import from France, and to export to the East; and probably both kinds are improved by the voyages. More French wines are drank in California, twice over, than by the same population in any part of the eastern States. Champagne is mother's milk, indeed, to all these people; they start the day with "a champagne cock-tail," and go to bed with a full bottle of it under their ribs. At all the bar-rooms, it is sold by the glass, the same as any other liquor, and it answers to the general name of "wine" with both drinker and landlord.

From Sonoma, over another hill, to our steamboat of three days ago, and by that back in a few hours to the city. These three days seem long, they have been so rich in novelty and knowledge, in beauty of landscape, in acquaintanceship with the best riches of California. These valleys are, indeed, agricultural jewels, and should be held as prouder possessions by the State than her gold mines. The small grains, fruits and vegetables are their common, chief productions; and the yields are enormous, while the culture and care are comparatively light.

In California, from December till April and May is seed-time; from June till September is harvest. No barns are needed for housing stock; they can roam safely in pasture for the whole year. Neither are they needed for the harvests; threshing and winnowing are done as well in the open field,— sometimes, indeed, by the very machine that reaps, and at the same time,—and the grain is put in bags, and thus transported to the market; all at leisure, for there is no rain nor dew to spoil the crop; it lies safely in any shape in the open field. There is no hot, hurrying work with planting and harvesting, as in the East; no dodging of showers; no lost days during the long summer. Fifty bushels of wheat to the acre is more common here than twenty-five in the best wheat fields of the States, and seventy-five and eighty bushels are often obtained. Barley, which is another leading crop, yields still greater return; an authentic instance of one hundred and twenty bushels to the acre is before me; and crops that would astound an Eastern farmer are often gathered from the droppings of a last year's harvest. A single farmer in the neighborhood of San Jose, with a twelve hundred acre farm, has this year gathered in over fifty thousand bushels of wheat; and the county of Santa Clara, in which this farm is located, lying south fifty miles from San Francisco, and in between two sections of the Coast range of mountains, presents the fol-

AGRICULTURAL RICHES OF CALIFORNIA. 287

lowing aggregates of agriculture: acres fenced in, two hundred and ten thousand; cultivated, one hundred and thirty thousand; grape vines, eight hundred and seventy-nine thousand nine hundred; apple trees, one hundred and twenty thousand; crops this year,—thirty-five thousand tons of hay, one hundred and thirty-five thousand bushels of wheat, one hundred thousand of barley, sixty thousand each of oats and potatoes, and four thousand of corn.

Nothing is wanting to the agriculture of California but a steady and extensive market; she sends north to Washington and the British Provinces; east to Nevada and Idaho; south to Mexico; is even trying China on the west, and with steam navigation hopes for large market for wheat there;— but most of her soil is still unbroken,—her productive power is but suggested, not proven, undeveloped. And still she buys half her butter in the East! Visit ranches in the interior, that boast their cattle by the tens of thousands, and the chances are two to one that neither milk nor butter can be had for love or money!

LETTER XXVI.

OF SAN FRANCISCO: BUSINESS MATTERS.

SAN FRANCISCO, August 26.

THIS is a very ridiculous and repulsive town, in some aspects, and a very fascinating and commendable one, in others, both materially and morally, physically and esthetically. Its youth is its apology in one regard, its wonder and its merit on the other. The location must have been chosen for its water and not its land privileges. It is set upon the inside of a range of the purest sand-hills, six or seven miles wide, blown up from the ocean, and still blowing up, between it and the bay. The main business streets are in the hollows, or on the flat land, made by pulling down the sand from the hills. But go out of these in any direction, and you are confronted by steep hills. Some of these are cut through, or being cut through, others are scaled, to make room for the spread of the town. The happy thought of winding the streets about their sides, which would have made a very picturesque and certainly get-around-able town, came too late. If but the early San Franciscans had thought of Boston, and followed the cow-paths, what a unique, nice town they would have made of this! Only I fear there never was even an estray cow on these virgin sand-hills, as innocent of verdure as a babe of sorrow or vice. The modern American straight line style was the order, no matter what was in front; and the result is that going about San Francisco is all collar and breeching work for man and beast. The consequence is, also, there are only two or three streets that you can think of driving out of town on. The only way to get up and down the others with a horse, is to go zig-zag from one side to the other. Some of the principal residence streets are after this fashion, however; I found our friend, Rev. Horatio Stebbins, of the Unitarian church here, holding on by main strength to a side hill that runs up at an angle of something like thirty degrees. And so they run up and down, and the city is straggling loosely over these hills for several miles in all directions. Some of the highest of the knobs are being cut down, and this leaves the early houses,—that is those built four or five years ago,— away up one hundred feet or more in the air, and reached by long flights of steep steps.

Wherever the hill-sides and tops are fastened with houses or pavements, or twice daily seduced with water, there the foundations are measurably secure; and the deed of the purchaser means something; but all elsewhere, all the open lots and unpaved paths are still undergoing the changing and creative process. The daily winds swoop up the soil in one place and deposit it in another in great masses, like drifts of snow. You will often find a suburban street blocked up with fresh sand; and the owner of vacant lots needs certainly to pay them daily visit in order to swear to title; and the chance is anyway that, between one noon and another, he and his neighbor will have changed properties to an indefinite depth. Incidental to all this, of course, are clouds of sand and dust through all the residence and open parts of the city, making large market for soap and clothes-brushes, and putting neat housekeepers quite in despair for their furniture. Naturally enough, there is a looseness on the subject of cleanliness, that would shock your old-fashioned New England housewives.

But then, as compensation, the winds give health, —keeping the town fresh and clean; and the hills offer wide visions of bay and river, and islands and sister hills,—way out and on with varying life of shipping, and manufactures, and agriculture; and, hanging over all, a sky of azure with broad horizons. Oceanward is Lone Mountain Cemetery, covering one of the hills with its scrawny, low-running, live oak shrub tree, and its white monuments, conspicuous among which are the erections to those martyrs to both western and eastern civilization and progress,—Broderick, the mechanic and senator, James King of William, the editor, and Baker, the soldier. Here is the old Mission quarter, there the soldiers' camp, yonder, by the water, the bristling fort, again the conspicuous and generous Orphan Asylum, monument of the tenderness and devotion of the women of the city, and to the left of that still, the two Jewish Cemeteries, each with its appropriate and tasteful burial chapel. No other American city holds in its very center such sweeping views of itself and its neighborhood.

Then the little yards around the dwellings of the prosperous, even of those of moderate means, are made rich with all the verdure of a green-house, with only the cost of daily watering. The most delicate of evergreens; roses of every grade and hue; fuchsias vigorous and high as lilac bushes; nasturtiums sweeping over fences and up house walls; flowering vines of delicate quality, unknown in the East; geraniums and salvias, pansies and daisies, and all the kindred summer flowers of New York and New England, grow and blossom under these skies, throughout the whole year,—the same in December and January as in June and August, —with a richness and a profusion that are rarely attained by any out door culture in the East. The public aqueducts furnish water, though at considerable expense, and pipes convey and spread it in fine spray all over yard and garden. The result is, every man's door-yard in the city is like an eastern conservatory; and little humble cottages smile out of this city of sand-hills and dust, as green and as yellow, and as red and as purple, as gayest of garden can make them. There is no aristocracy of flowers here; they greet you everywhere in greatest profusion, and are tender solace to homesick heart and cheap and sweet tonic to weary brain.

Kindred contrasts force themselves upon the observant stranger, in the business and social life of the town. Some of the finest qualities are mingled with others that are both shabby and "shoddy." There is sharp, full development of all material powers and excellencies; wealth of practical quality and force; a recklessness and rioting with the elements of prosperity; much dash, a certain chivalric honor combined with carelessness of word, of integrity, of consequence; a sort of gambling, speculating, horse-jockeying morality,—born of the uncertainties of mining, its sudden hights, its equally surprising depths, and the eager haste to be rich,—that all require something of a re-casting of relationships, new standards, certainly new charities, in order to get the unaccustomed mind into a state of candor and justice. People, who know they are smart in the East, and come out here thinking to find it easy wool-gathering, are generally apt to go home shorn. Wall Street can teach Montgomery Street nothing in the way of "bulling" and "bearing," and the "corners" made here require both quick and long breath to turn without faltering.

Men of mediocre quality are no better off here than in older cities and States. Ten or fifteen years of stern chase after fortune, among the mines and mountains and against the new nature of this original country, has developed men here with a tougher and more various experience in all the temporalities of life, and a wider resource for fighting all sorts of "tigers," than you can easily find among the present generation in the eastern States. Nearly all the men of means here to-day have held long and various struggle with fortune, failing once, twice or thrice and making wide wreck, but buckling on the armor again and again, and trying the contest over and over. So it is throughout the State and the Coast; I have hardly met an old emigrant of '49 and '50, who has not told me of vicissitudes of fortune, of personal trials, and hard work for bread and life, that, half-dreamed of before coming here, he would never have dared to encounter, and which no experience of persons in like position in life in the East can parallel.

In consequence partly of all this training, and partly of the great interests and the wide regions to be dealt with, the men I find at the head of the great enterprises of this Coast have great business power,—a wide practical reach, a boldness, a sagacity, a vim, that I do not believe can be matched anywhere in the world. London and New York and Boston can furnish men of more philosophies and theories,—men who have studied business as a science as well as practiced it as a trade,—but here are the men of acuter intuitions and more daring natures; who cannot tell you why they do so and so, but who will do it with a force that commands success. Such men have built up and direct the California Steam Navigation Company, that is to the waters of this State what the Oregon Company is to those of that, commanding the entire navigation and furnishing most unexceptionable facilities for trade and travel; the California and Pioneer Stage Companies, that equally command the stage travel of the Coast; the Woolen Mills of this city; the Wells & Fargo Express Company; the great Machine Shops of Pacific street; the Pacific Mail Steamship Company; and the great private Banking Houses, of which there are many and most prosperous. Much British capital is invested in banking here; nor only in original houses, but through branches of leading bankers in London, India and British Columbia. But chief of the banks is the Bank of California, with two millions of capital, divided into only forty shares of fifty thousand dollars each, and owned by fewer than that number of persons, who represent a total property of thirteen millions (gold). This institution does about half the banking business of the city, and its average cash movement every steamer day, in shipments of bullion and drafts, is five millions of dollars. It keeps the best commercial and financial writer of the Coast in its employ, has agents in all the centers of productive wealth in the Pacific States, invests, directly or indirectly, in most of the leading enterprises of the State, has an eye out for the politics and religion of the country, and to a very considerable extent "runs" California every way.

But there is no institution of the Coast that has interested me more than the Wells & Fargo Express. It is the omnipresent, universal business agent of all the region from the Rocky Mountains to the Pacific Ocean. Its offices are in every town, far and near; a billiard saloon, a restaurant, and a Wells & Fargo office are the first three elements of a Pacific or Coast mining town; its messengers are on every steamboat, and rail-car and stage, in all these States. It is the Ready Companion of civilization, the Universal Friend and Agent of the miner, his errand man, his banker, his post-office. It is much more than an ordinary express company; it does a general and universal banking business, and a great one in amount; it brings to market all the bullion and gold from the mining regions,— its statistics are the only reliable knowledge of the production; and it divides with the government the carrying of letters to and fro.

In the latter respect its operations are very curious. Going along hand in hand with the rapidly changing populations of the mining States, offering readier and more various facilities than the slower-moving and circumscribed government machinery, carrying the goods of the merchant and the bullion of the miner, as well as their letters, it has grown very much into the heart and habit of the people, and even conveys many of the letters upon routes that the government mail now goes as quickly and as safely as the express company, though their cost by the latter is much the greatest. The company breaks none of the post-office laws, but pays the government its full price for every letter it carries. The process is thus: Wells & Fargo buy the post-office envelopes bearing the government stamp, and then put their own stamp or frank upon them, and sell the same for ten cents each; and in these envelopes, thus doubly stamped, all the letters by express are carried. Where the letters are above the single rate, additional government stamps are put on and charged for by the company.

The extent of this business is shown by the facts

that Wells & Fargo bought of the government in 1863 over *two millions* of three-cent envelopes, fifteen thousand of six-cent envelopes, and thirty thousand of ten and eighteen-cent ones, besides seventy thousand of extra three-cent stamps and twelve thousand five hundred of six-cent ditto. In 1864, the business increased, as it has steadily all along, and the three-cent envelopes bought and sold by Wells & Fargo in that year were nearly two and a quarter millions, and the extra stamps about one hundred and twenty-five thousand. Thus all the agencies of Wells & Fargo are private post-offices, doing the business of the government better and more satisfactorily than it does it itself, and paying the government its full price for the same. One long side of the great San Francisco office is devoted to this letter business; clerks wait courteously, and at all hours, on all callers; letters with known or discoverable local addresses are delivered; and for the others, lists of those received each day are regularly posted, so that any one can tell at once, without inquiry, if there be anything for him. The messengers of the company on stages and steamboats receive all letters under the appropriate envelopes, and the facilities of letter carriage they afford are much wider and more intimate than the government gives.

This part of the business of Wells & Fargo is very profitable, and its success, popularity and wide extension, reaching through one hundred and seventy-five different towns and villages, and extending as well to the newest mining regions in Idaho as to the chief cities of California,—even beyond and off mail routes and post-offices,—present very effective practical arguments for the government's giving up wholly its post-office department. The main reason offered against such abandonment has generally been, that the sparsely settled States and widely separated populations could not, by private enterprise, be served with their letters except at high cost; but this experience on the Pacific Coast more than meets this. Private enterprise here does better than the government, and is preferred to it. Wells & Fargo even offered some years ago to do the whole mail service of the Pacific Coast at five cents a letter, provided the franking privilege was abolished. They could doubtless perform it with profit at three cents, and would if the business were all secured to them.

The Wells & Fargo Express is mostly owned in New York, but it is managed out here by men of large business experience and great sagacity, and in its enterprise and popular facilities not only strikingly illustrates but greatly advances the civilization of these States. Often it runs special treasure wagons with escort, and frequently its messengers are exposed to great peril from robbers and Indians. Those from Idaho now have to ride wide awake, day and night, with guns and pistols ready loaded and cocked. The stages on which their messengers and treasure were passing were stopped and robbed on the road eight times during 1864; and several serious robberies have also occurred this year, and in one case a messenger was murdered. The managers of the express are influential leaders and movers in the opening of new routes and in establishing lines of stages; even also are high powers in the construction of railroads.

The success and extent of the Machine Shops and Woolen Manufacture here in San Francisco were also interesting objects of observation. There is no longer use or profit in importing machinery from the East. As good, if not better, is made here, and as cheap; steam engines and boilers of the highest grade; and stamps and crushers and all the various machinery for the mining regions. The machine shops are mostly in a single street, and must employ in the aggregate about one thousand mechanics and laborers. One of the largest and most complete of these establishments is owned and conducted by Mr. Ira P. Rankin, formerly of Boston and Northampton.

There are two large and successful Woolen Mills. The oldest and most successful is the "Mission," the creation of an indomitable Scotch-Yankee, Mr. Donald McLennan, who learned his business among the mills of Middlesex County, Massachusetts, and came out here some eight or ten years ago, with only a few dollars in his pocket, but with a big capital of experience, industry and courage. His establishment is now worth over half a million dollars; consumed last year over one million pounds of wool, and manufactured thirty-two thousand pairs of blankets, near half a million yards of flannels, and over one hundred thousand yards of cloths and cloakings. The wool is all of California growth,—

for this is a large and cheap wool-producing State;—the machinery, which includes eleven sets of cards, thirty-five hundred spindles and fifty broad power-looms, is of the very best and most modern description, from England and the East; and the goods produced are of much variety of grade and style, in order to suit and fill the limited market here. The blankets are the finest made anywhere in the United States, perhaps in the world; certainly there are none in the eastern markets to compare with them either in thickness or softness; and except for the very finest of broadcloths and cassimeres, these mills are fast driving all woolen goods from the East and from Europe out of this market. The army and Indian departments on this Coast have been largely supplied with their blankets and clothing from this establishment during the last four years; and the government officers testify that these goods are of much superior quality to those generally sent from the East.

One of the most interesting features of Mr. McLennan's establishment is that the work is nearly all done by Chinamen, almost three hundred being employed. A few whites are only necessary for the more intricate and skill-requiring processes, and for superintending. The Chinese are found much cheaper of course; indeed the business could not be carried on successfully here but for their labor, which costs but one dollar and twelve cents a day against two dollars and ninety-seven cents for the whites employed; and the superintendent testifies that the difficulties of a first beginning with them were very speedily and fully overcome, and they were found very quick to learn all the details of the work, such as carding, spinning, weaving, finishing and wool-sorting. They live in a large building on the mill grounds, and make the most reliable, constant and valuable of factory operatives.

The first cotton manufactory in California is just finished and going into operation, over the bay in Oakland, and will get its raw material from the Mexican States, for the present at least. Successful experiments in cotton raising on a large scale have been made this season in southern California. —There is a great sugar refinery establishment in San Francisco, drawing its materials for refining from the Sandwich Islands, which are fast coming to be the exclusive source of sweetening for all these States.—There are also extensive lead and iron and glass works. San Francisco enterprise and capital are at the foundation of all these pioneer manufactures; but success will soon extend and multiply them over the State.

I dwell upon these particulars, these illustrations of the enterprise and skill of this city and these States, because they form the promise of the great future. There is a sea-captain in your town, and quite a young man, too, who used to come here for hides, when only a single cabin marked the site of San Francisco. Now it has a population of over one hundred thousand, or nearly a quarter of the whole State; pays half the taxes of the State; has a larger foreign commerce than any city in the Nation but New York and Boston, its customs-revenue for the first six months of this year being three millions and a quarter dollars, and its port clearing two hundred and thirty vessels of one hundred and eighty-three thousand eight hundred and thirty-four tons for foreign ports, and entering one hundred and ninety vessels of one hundred and forty-nine thousand seven hundred and forty-four tonnage during the same time, besides a domestic shipping two-thirds these figures; and soon, within ten years,—struggle as Boston may and grow as she will,—it will divide commercial honors with New York alone. Here is seat of empire, and of population, as great as yours of the eastern States; here the equal arm of the American Nation; and these men and means that I have been describing are the beginnings of the great and majestic end.

LETTER XXVII.

MINING IN CALIFORNIA: ITS VARIETIES, RESULTS
AND PROSPECTS.

MARIPOSA, California, August 28.

WE have been making our final studies of the mining business of the Pacific States here among the mines and mills of the famous Mariposa estate of Colonel Fremont. Thus the occasion is a proper one to sum up my various notes and observations in California on that subject, and so far as possible represent the state of the business in the whole region west of the Rocky Mountains. The gross production of gold and silver by all these States was probably never greater than now. There are no very exact figures to be had; those of Wells, Fargo & Company's Express and the San Francisco mint furnish the best data, and are before me in detail. They indicate a total yield for 1864 of about sixty millions of dollars, and for this year at least an equal, probably a greater sum, perhaps sixty-five or seventy millions. California herself produces now but about one-third of this amount; she has fallen off from forty and fifty millions a year to twenty and twenty-five; while Nevada now offers from fifteen to twenty millions a year, mainly of silver; Idaho and eastern Oregon sent forward nine millions last year, and will probably increase this to twelve or fifteen millions this year; and the British Provinces and Arizona furnish perhaps five millions. The gold of Montana mainly finds its way east through Colorado; but this is the first season of any large production there. But the production of all the States and Territories this side of the Rocky Mountains comes to San Francisco; one-third of it, or about twenty millions, is coined at the United States mint there; and the rest is exported in bars or dust, mainly in bars, to New York, China and England, but chiefly now to England.

The western or California slopes of the Sierra Nevada yield no silver ore,—here the mining is of gold alone, and it is divided into two general classes; that which seeks the metal from the solid rock, or quartz, and that which finds it in sand, gravel, or soil. The former process is the universal and familiar one of all rock mining, following the rich veins into the bowels of the earth with pick and powder, crushing the rock, and seducing the infinitesimal atoms of metal from the dusty, powdered mass.

The accepted theory is that this is the original form or deposit of the precious metals,—that the gold found in gravel, sand or soil,—lying as it does almost universally in the beds of rivers, dead or alive, or under the eaves of the mountains,—has been washed and ground out of the hard hills by the action of the elements through long years. Washing with water is the universal means of getting at these deposits of the gold. But the scale on which this work is done, and the instrumentalities of application, vary, from the simple hand-pan and pick and shovel of the individual and original miner, operating along the banks of a little stream, to grand combination enterprises for changing the entire course of a river, running shafts down hundreds of feet to get into the beds of long ago streams, and bringing water through ditches and flumes and great pipes for ten or twenty miles, wherewith to wash down a hill-side of golden gravel, and get at its precious particles. The simple individual pan-washers have mostly "moved on" for the richer sands of Idaho and Montana; what of this sort of gold seeking remains in California is in the hands of patient and plodding "John Chinaman," who works over the neglected sands of his predecessors, and is content to reap as harvest a dollar's worth a day.

The other means are employed, on greater or less scales of magnitude, by combinations of men and capital. All the forms of gold washing run into each other, indeed; and companies of two or three, sometimes of Chinamen, with capitals of hundreds of dollars, buy a sluice claim or seize a deserted bed, and with shovel and pick and small stream of water, run the sands over and over through the sluice ways, and at end of day, or week, or month, gather up the deposits of gold on the bottoms and at the ends of their sluices. From this, operations ascend to a magnitude involving hundreds of thousands, and employing hundreds of men as partners or day laborers for the managers. Sometimes, too, the enterprise is divided, and companies are organized that furnish the water alone, and sell it out to the miners or washers according to their wants. The raising of auriferous sands and gravel from the deeply covered beds of old streams, by running down shafts and out tunnels into and through such beds, and then washing them over, is called "Deep Diggings," or "Bed-rock Diggings," and in their pursuit the bottoms of ancient rivers will be followed through the country for mile after mile, and many feet below the present surface of the earth. The miners in this fashion go down till they reach the bed-rock, along which the water originally ran, and here they find the richest deposits.

The other sort of heavy gold washing, employing powerful streams of water to tear down and wash out the soil of hill-sides that cover or hold golden deposits, is known as "Hydraulic Mining." This is the most unique and extensive process, involving the largest capital and risk. The water is brought from mountain lakes or rivers through ditches and flumes, sometimes supported by trestle-work fifty to one hundred feet high, to near the theater of operations. Then it is let from flumes into large and stout iron pipes which grow gradually smaller and smaller; out of these it is passed into hose, like that of a fire engine, and through this it is *fired* with a terrible force into the bank or bed of earth, which is speedily torn down and washed with resistless, separating power, into narrow beds or sluices in the lower valleys, and as it goes along these, hindered and seduced at various points, the more solid gold particles deposit themselves. Usually, in large operations of this kind, the main stream of water is divided in the final discharging hose into two or more streams, which spout out into the hill-side as if from several fire engines, only with immensely more force. One of the streams would instantly kill man or animal that should get before it, and frequent fatal or half-fatal accidents occur from this cause. Near Dutch Flat, where extensive hydraulic mining is in progress, a water company taps lakes twelve to twenty miles off in the mountains, and turns whole rivers into its ditches; and as further illustration of its majestic operations, we learned that it spent eighty thousand dollars in one year in building a new ditch, and yet made and divided one hundred and twenty thousand dollars in additional profits that same year. Up near Yreka, in northern California, a ditch thirty miles long, and costing two hundred thousand dollars, was constructed for this business; but in this instance, the enterprise did not prove profitable. Near Oroville, also, are supposed rich gold banks and beds that only lack water for development; but to get this will require ditches costing two hundred thousand dollars. The citizens of the neighborhood are confident it would be a richly-paying investment, however, and say the chief reason why it is not entered upon is the lack of certain laws regulating mining claims, and the conflicts and doubt that are engendered by the neglect of the government to establish the terms of ownership in mining lands.

As it is now, squatter sovereignty is the substantial law of mining properties; prospectors and miners have established a few general rules for determining the rights of each other; and they can occupy and use the properties that they discover or purchase, to a certain limited extent. No one man is allowed to take up more than a certain amount in feet or acres. The government so far has done nothing with these mineral lands, whose fee is still in itself, and gets no revenue from them. Whenever cases of conflict come into court, the regulations of the miners of the district, where the properties are located, have been generally sustained. But the apprehension that the government will yet assume its rights, and establish different rules for the possession and use of these lands, and the uncertainty and controversies growing out of the present loose ways of making and holding claims, are undoubtedly a stumbling-block to large enterprises, and an obstacle to the best sort of mining progress and prosperity all through the mineral country of this Coast.

The returns obtained in some cases of extensive deep diggings and hydraulic mining are very great. A thousand dollars a day is often washed out by a company holding rich soil and employing a large force; and a run of several weeks averaging fifty dollars and one hundred dollars a day to the hand is frequently recorded. A single "cleaning up," after a few weeks' washing in a rich place, has produced fifty thousand dollars in gold dust and nuggets; and in other cases, even one hundred thousand dollars is reported. These are the extreme cases of good fortune, however; other enterprises are run with a loss, or with varying result; but the gold washings, as a general thing, are paying good wages and a fair return to the capital invested.

Of course all these operations create a wide waste wherever they are going on, and have been in progress. Tornado, flood, earthquake and volcano combined could hardly make greater havoc, spread wider ruin and wreck, than are to be seen everywhere in the path of the larger gold-washing operations. None of the interior streams of California, though naturally pure as crystal, escape the change to a thick yellow mud, from this cause, early in their progress out of the hills. The Sacramento is worse than the Missouri. Many of the streams are turned out of their original channels, either directly for mining purposes, or in consequence of the great masses of soil and gravel that come down from the gold-washings above. Thousands of acres of fine land along their banks are ruined forever by the deposits of this character. There are no rights which mining respects in California. It is the one supreme interest. A farmer may have his whole estate turned to a barren waste by a flood of sand and gravel from some hydraulic mining up stream; more, if a fine orchard or garden stands in the way of the working of a rich gulch or bank, orchard and garden must go. Then the torn-down, dug-out, washed to pieces and then washed over side-hills, that have been or are being hydraulic-mined, are the very devil's chaos, indeed. The country is full of them among the mining districts of the Sierra

Nevada foot-hills, and they are truly a terrible blot upon the face of nature. The valley of the Yuba, a branch of the Sacramento, was one of the worst illustrations our journeying has presented; and when we came to the sign over the "grocery" of a now deserted mining camp, indicating that this was "Yuba Dam," we thought of the famous anecdote connected with this name, from its repetition, without the benefit of spelling, to an inquiring colporteur, and were fain to confess that the profane compound fairly represented the spirit of the lawless miner.

The gold quartz mines are mostly in the same neighborhoods with present or past gold-washings; in the hills back and above the rich stream beds and gravel banks. Nevada County in the north, and Mariposa in the south, have been the most famous counties for this interest. The most successful and noteworthy operations of it now are in and around the town of Grass Valley, in Nevada County, which has always been a profitable mining region. It seemed almost the only mining town of importance in California, that we visited, which did not have vacant stores and houses, and show signs of decrepitude. There are now about twenty quartz mills in successful operation in Grass Valley, and the ore they work yields from ten to fifty dollars a ton; occasionally as high as one hundred and two hundred dollars. The cost of mining and working is from six to ten dollars a ton, depending on the facilities of mine and mill. Among the successful miners and capitalists here, is Mr. S. D.

Bosworth, from West Springfield and Springfield, who now occupies the cottage which the notorious Lola Montez built and lived in for several years. She came here to perform for the miners in 1854, and staid to ruin one husband, and change him for another. She led a rollicking life here, and the town is full of scandals concerning her. Intelligent gentlemen who met her confess to her intellectual power and impressive conversation, and to her fascinating manners. Grass Valley also boasts an old horse that goes around alone with a milk-wagon, stopping before the doors of his customers, and nowhere else, and delivering his daily allowances to each with unvarying fidelity. But the really wonderful thing about this story is that Grass Valley should have a population that can be trusted to help themselves to milk, and not take, any of them, more than their allotted share. The mines here are receiving enlarged attention just now, and extensive new investments are being made, both in Grass Valley and the neighboring town of Nevada.

But here in Mariposa County, the interest has a different look, and affairs are in a desperate condition. There are in all ten quartz mills here, all or nearly all on the Fremont estate, but only two or three are now running, and these with moderate results. The villages are decreasing in population; the best people are going away; viciousness of all sorts seems to be increasing; and highway robberies are of almost nightly occurrence. The great Mariposa mining company, formed in Wall street two years ago with a capital of ten millions, a debt of two millions, and not a cent of ready cash,—succeeding to General Fremont's property and his style of doing business,—has come to grief. Its most worthy superintendent and manager, Mr. Frederic Law Olmsted, who was beguiled out here under a gross misapprehension of the situation of affairs, and the duties he was to perform, is going home disgusted, to resume more congenial occupation in the East; the sheriff has been brooding over the estate for six months; and its local creditors are running one or two of its mills and mines, on a close and economical scale,—using up accumulated materials, but laying in no new supplies,—in order to obtain their claims. The ore now being obtained and thus worked returns from seven dollars to ten dollars a ton, which gives a small margin of profit. It is all a sad, vast ruin,—a magnificent gentleman, holding his head high, but wearing his last year's clothes, and dining around with his friends,—a sort of grand land and mine Micawber. There is doubtless life and value, possibly great wealth, in it still, but not of the sort or degree that has been set up for it. Divided up, and conducted by private parties or small companies on a moderate capital, as the Grass Valley mines are, or managed, as a whole even, with an eye to practical results alone, and no such side issues as the presidency, or a grand Wall street stock-jobbing operation, or the control of California politics, depending on it, and drawing its life-blood, the estate may yet have a useful future before it. But the end to it as a grand Principality, as an exhaustless Fountain for political and financial jobbing, seems surely to have come. Indeed, its most striking capacity always has been in carrying an immense, a magnificent indebtedness. A few men are rich from it here and in the East; but their wealth is more from the sale of stock and bonds in New York, than the profits of its mines in Mariposa. The illustration of the whole lies best, perhaps, in the sincere boast attributed to its most gallant but never thrifty original owner. "Why," said General Fremont, "when I came to California, I was worth nothing, and now I owe two millions of dollars!"

There are no very reliable statistics as to the extent of the quartz-mining interest of California, or of its comparative results by the side of the gold-washings. The estimate of a prominent authority before me places the number of quartz-mills in the State at six hundred, their cost at twelve million dollars, and their product, on an average of ten dollars to the ton of ore, at eighteen millions of dollars a year. But these figures are clearly wide of the fact; there can hardly be over one hundred quartz-mills, properly so called, in all California; and they do not divide the State's product with the gold-washers equally. Mining in California, of all kinds, is now much more systematically and intelligently conducted than ever before. It is losing its wasteful, gambling characteristics. In 1862, it apparently had its greatest production; the returns for 1864 were only about half as much; and probably this year will show no gain upon the last. The interest is, on the whole, at the ebb tide. But the risks of the business will henceforth be less than heretofore; the cost of production is cheaper here than in the newer and more remote fields; new and valuable fields are being discovered and opened among the Sierras; and I am inclined to the belief that investments in mining in California can be made with better results, at least with more certainty of profit, if less possible gains, than in any of the fresher and more fashionable regions.

The Idaho mines are perhaps exciting the most interest at present among the people of the Coast; and they are also beginning to divide enticements with those of Nevada and Colorado, for eastern speculators and capitalists. Some reliable facts about them, which I have from original sources, will not be amiss therefore, and serve to complete my general review of the mining developments of this whole region. The Boise Basin district is still rich in gold-washings, and is perhaps the richest region in that respect yet worked anywhere in the West. It has also rich quartz veins, and there are already eight mills in operation there, with eighty-four stamps. South Boise is less rich in placer diggings, but has an even larger development of the quartz interest. The bullion (gold) here holds a large proportion of silver, and is not worth over fourteen dollars an ounce. The Owyhee district borders on Oregon, and its mining wealth runs over into that State. The ore here is like that in Nevada, having more silver than gold in it. There are six mills now in this district, one of them with thirty stamps. The veins in Boise Basin and South

Boise are small, like those of Reese River, in Nevada, opening sometimes as low as four inches, but enlarging generally to four or five feet. The "Mammoth Vein" is from three to twelve feet wide; the ore is generally free and simple, and is worked without roasting. The yield is from forty dollars a ton up; one vein runs from forty to eighty dollars; and others have yielded from two hundred to three hundred dollars a ton. It is not probable that the full value of the ore is obtained by the present means of working, and the tailings are saved.

The country is very barren, having the same general characteristics as eastern Oregon and Nevada. There are some good valleys, and timber is plenty enough for the present save in the Owyhee district. The price of labor is six dollars a day, and goods and provisions are in proportion. The population is made up mostly of the floating mining elements of California, Oregon and Nevada; the men who are always moving on for the newest mines; prosperous to-day, poor to-morrow. The winters in Idaho are severe, and the work in the placer diggings is then suspended. The miners float back to the older towns, to The Dalles and Portland in Oregon, and San Francisco, in the fall, and spend there their summer savings, and start out again in the spring for the old diggings, if no newer and more fabulous ones have been since discovered.

Taking these figures as reliable as statements about mines generally are from those engaged in the business, I do not see that Idaho really offers any better inducements for emigration and capital than Nevada and Colorado. It is probable my statements relate to the best veins, that the average will fall below these rates of production, and that the permanent prosperity of the mining interests and the sure progress of the State will await the profitable working of ores yielding from ten dollars to twenty-five dollars a ton, as is already admitted to be true for California, and for Virginia City, Nevada, and will probably soon be proven in Reese River and in Colorado. And this can hardly be done until quicker and cheaper communication is provided. Only the rare veins, only the choice ore in any of these States can be worked to much profit, so long as all machinery, all food, all goods, used in the business and for the people, have to pay a freight tariff of ten to thirty cents a pound, and labor is from four to eight dollars a day. California has the advantage over her rivals in these respects now; and I repeat that it seems to me mining is likely to be as profitable in this State for the next five years, taking all things into consideration, as in any of the newer regions. The others must wait for the railroad to give real and permanent and steady development and prosperity to greater apparent capacities.

Do not complain, my reader, that this letter is getting dull with dry fact and statistics; consider the mass of figures and "disgusting details" that I have before me, and have spared you, and be grateful: and come now with me, and let us have the sensation of a visit into the abyssmal depths of the mines themselves. Our party have done con-

'siderable of this descending into mines in our progress across the country; for it became occasion of reproach and doubt of our intelligent future judgment, if we failed to go down into every miner's particular pet hole. Over in Austin, we had amusing experience in this regard. We were to stay but three days there. But that is nothing, said the disappointed people; you can't begin to see our mines in that time; you better have staid away. Well, come on, was the reply; show us what you can in three days, and then let us see what is left that is new and strange. So we mounted; and there was an extensive cavalcade of local officials, practical miners, speculators, and genteel bummers generally. We went over and around hills, down into mines, through mills, everywhere that our guides led us; finding naturally great similarity of sights and testimony everywhere. By afternoon, our hosts had dwindled one-half. The next morning, instead of a dozen, we had but three or four guides; at noon, they were reduced to one, and at night we had exhausted not only his strength and patience, but all he had to show us. We had seen Austin and its mines, and had a day to spare!

The newer mines, whose shafts are but fifty or one hundred feet, are descended by a simple rope and bucket, worked by a common hand windlass; older and deeper ones, by the same contrivance, with steam power: if, as is often the case, the vein runs at an angle, or is reached below in that way, a little car runs down a steep track, held and drawn by a heavy rope and steam engine; while other shafts are provided with ladders, winding around, or set perpendicularly up and down. The latest, and safest and readiest contrivance for descending a perpendicular shaft is a cage or box, let down by a rope with steam power, but provided with sharp, opening arms that, in case the rope breaks, will catch into the walls with such power as to hold the cage and its load. Its certainty was proven to us by cutting the rope with an ax, when the cage sent out its fingers and clung midway in its passage. We reached the insides of other mines by long tunnels, running into the veins from the surface, far down the hill-sides on which they were located. The deepest worked mine on the Pacific Coast is in Amador County, this State, and is eight hundred feet down; but some of those over in Nevada are fast approaching this depth; and the latter have the most extensive chambers below the surface of any in the country. The Gould & Curry mine, for instance, has several miles length of tunnels and shafts, and it is a full half day's journey to travel through it entirely.

We entered this mine through a long tunnel, that strikes the vein several hundred feet below the surface. There were half a dozen of us in the procession, each with a lighted candle, which would go out under the out-going draft, and so we soon contented ourselves with grouping along in the dim, cavernous light. It seemed a very long journey, and the nerves had to brace themselves. The most stolid person, stranger to such experience, will hardly fail to find his heart beating a little quicker, as he goes into these far-away, narrow recesses in the bowels of the earth. I never failed to remember the principle that "nature abhors a vacuum," and to wonder if she wouldn't take the present occasion to close up this little one that I was in. At last we reached the scenes of the ore and the work after it; and among these we clambered and wandered about, down shafts to this or that level, and then out on side tunnels through the vein in both directions; up again by narrow, pokerish ladders to a higher set of chambers, in and out, up and down, till we were lost in amazing confusion. Here was, indeed, a city of streets and population far under the surface of the earth. Many of the chambers or streets were deserted; in others we found little coteries of miners, picking away at the hard rock, and loading up cars of the ore, that were sent out by the tunnels and up by the shafts to the surface above. Here, too, was a building in a wide hall under ground, and steam engine to help on the work. Some of the chambers had closed in after being worked out of ore; others have been filled up to prevent caving in and causing great disaster overhead; but many of the open passages were stayed or braced open still with huge frame work of timber; more lumber, indeed, as I have told you, I believe, is used for this purpose in this single mine, than has been put into all the buildings of Virginia City itself, with its ten thousand to fifteen thousand inhabitants. And in many of the passages, such is the outward pressure into the vacuum, that these timbers, as big as a man's body, are bent and splintered almost in two.

Great pine sticks, eighteen inches square, were thus bent like a bow, or yawned with gaping splinters; and the spaces left in some places for us to go through were in this way reduced so small that we almost had to crawl to get along.

Do you wonder that we began to grow weary, and thought we had seen enough? Besides, the mine was oppressively hot and close; the mercury was up to one hundred degrees and more, and the sweat poured from us like water. One of our party grew faint and feeble, and we voted to take the nearest way out. This happened to be the most perilous and trying; but we did not realize that, and our miner guide, unsensitive from experience, did not think of it. So he started us into a long shaft, running straight up and down for several hundreds of feet, dark and damp as night, with no breaks or landing places, and set us going one after another, up a perpendicular ladder fastened to its side. We only took in a sense of the thing after we had got started; each must carry his lighted candle, hold on, and creep ahead; a single misstep by any one, the fainting of our invalid, or of any of us, all weary and unstrung, would not only have plunged that one headlong down the long fatal flight, to become a very Mantilinean cold body at the bottom, but would have swept everybody below him on the ladder, like a row of bricks, to the same destination and destruction. There was, you may well believe, a stern summoning of all remaining strength and nerves, a close, firm grip on the rounds of the ladder, a silent, grave procession, much and rapid thought, and a very long breath, and a very fervent if voiceless prayer, when we got to the daylight and the top. Our part of the shaft and the ladder was about one hundred and fifty feet; it seemed very long; and we were content to call our day's work done when it was over. Brains won the victory over body; but both were weary enough at the end.

But if I prolong this story any further, you will almost wish I had never got out of that shaft!

LETTER XXVIII.

SOCIAL LIFE IN SAN FRANCISCO: THE WOMEN: RELIGION AND MINISTERS.

SAN FRANCISCO, August 30.

You must be a very indifferent sort of person, and have no friends, to escape during the first week of a visit here an invitation to drive out to the Cliff House for breakfast and a sight of the sea-lions. This is the one special pet dissipation of San Francisco, the very trump card in its hospitality. A night among the Chinese houses and gambling holes is reserved as a choice tit-bit for the pruriently curious few; but the Cliff and the seals are for all ages and conditions of men and women. And, indeed, this is a very pleasant, reviving excursion. A drive of five or six miles, along a hard-made road over the intervening sand-hills, brings you out to the broad Pacific, rolling in and out, "wide as waters be." You strain your eyes for Sandwich Islands and China,—they are right before you; no object intervenes, and you feel that you ought to see them. Just at the right, around the corner, is the Golden Gate; and vessels are passing in and out the bay. A rare cliff rock places you beyond the sands, within the ocean; and a fine hotel on its very edge offers every hospitality—at a price.

Out upon half a dozen fragmentary rocks, like solid castles moored in the ocean below and before, are the seals and the pelicans. The rocks are covered and alive with them. You remember Barnum's seals at New York and Boston, don't you?—great sleek and slimy amphibious calves,—all bodies, small heads and short, webby feet,—bobbing up and down in their water tanks, and most making you weep with their large, liquid human eyes, like a hungering, sorrowing woman's? Well, here is their native water and rock; from these rocks they were captured, and here by twenties and fifties you see their relations. Crawling up from the water, awkwardly and blunderingly like babe at its first creeping, they spread themselves in the sun all over the rocks, twenty and thirty feet high sometimes, and lie there as if comatose; anon raising the head to look about and utter a rough, wide-sounding bark; often two or three, by reason of a fresh squatter on their territory, get into combat, and strike and bite languidly at one another, barking and grumbling meanwhile like long-lunged dogs; and again, tired of discord or weary of heaven, they plunge, with more of spring than they do anything else, back into the deep sea. An opera-glass brings them close to you upon the hotel piazza, and there is a singular fascination in sitting and watching their performances. They are of all sizes from fifty pounds weight up to two hundred and three hundred. Sea gulls and pelicans, the latter huge and awkward in flight as turkeys, dispute possession of the rocks; resting in great flocks, or with loud flaps flying around and around, overlooking the water for passing food.

Weary of these sights, the visitor seeks neighboring charming coves among the rocks below, and lies there out of the wind, watching the rolling waves rising and breaking over the island rocks, and sweeping in up the seducing sands to toy with his feet. And again, mounting horse or carriage, he rides swiftly and smoothly along the neighboring broad beach of hard sand for several miles; the unbroken, wide-reaching, long-rolling ocean is before his sight; and his horse's feet dance in merry race with the incoming surf;—and thus solemnly awed with ocean expanse, alternate with dainty titillation of amused senses, he closes his charming half day at the Cliff.

"Society" in this representative town of the Pacific Coast is somewhat difficult of characterization. It holds in chaos all sorts of elements; the very best, and the very worst, and all between. There is much of New York in it, much of St. Louis and Chicago, and a good deal that is original and local; born of wide separation from the centers of our best social civilization; of the dominating materialism and masculineism of all life here; of comparative lack of homes and families and their influences. There are probably more bachelors, great lusty fellows, who ought to be ashamed of themselves, living in hotels or in "lodgings," in this town, than in any place of its size in the world. There is want of femininity, spirituality in the current tone of the place; lack of reverence for women; fewer women to reverence, than our eastern towns are accustomed to. You hear more than is pleasant of private scandals; of the vanity and weakness of women; of the infidelity of wives. "It is the cussedest place for women," said an observant Yankee citizen, some two or three years from home, and not forgetful yet of mother, sister and cousin,—"a town of men and taverns and boarding-houses and billiard-saloons."

Yet there seem to be plenty of women,—such as they are; and Montgomery Street will offer the promenader as many pretty and striking faces, perhaps more in proportion, than Washington Street or Broadway. But the dominating quality, like mercy, is not strained; it savors of the mannishness, the materialism, the "fastness" and the "loudness" of the country; and paradoxical as it may appear, by contrast with eastern society, the men seem of a higher grade than the women,—better for men than the latter as women. Nor is this inconsistent with reason; the men, dealing with great practical necessities and duties, are less harmed, on the whole, by the dominant materialism of life here, than the women, whose pressing responsibilities are lower and fewer;—as a fine, delicate blade is more roughened in cutting the way through bramble and brush than a tough and broader edge.

All which is not only natural, but inevitable. In all new countries, where the first fight is for life and wealth with rough nature, the masculine quality must ever be dominant; and the feminine elements must be influenced by it, more than they influence it in turn. The senses rule the spirit. All civilization, all progress tends to the increase of the feminine element in our nature, and in life; contrast the centuries, and we see it creeping in everywhere, in men and women alike, in religion, in intellectual culture, in art, in social intercourse,—softening, refining, hallowing,—the atmosphere of all modern life pictures. Women, who possess and represent this blossom of our civilization, are by no means wanting here,—no more perfect specimens have I ever met anywhere; tender, tasteful, true; and gaining in aggregate influence over society day by day; but yet not to-day representing or making what is called "society."

The ladies generally dress in good taste. Paris is really as near San Francisco as New York, and there are many foreign families here. But the styles are not so subdued as in our eastern cities; a higher or rather louder tone prevails; rich, full colors, and sharp contrasts; the startling effects that the Parisian demi-monde seeks,—these are seen dominating here. In costliness of costume, too, there is apparent rivalry among the San Francisco ladies. Extravagance is lamented as a common weakness among them, and leading, where fortune is so fickle as here, to many a worse one often. Perhaps in no other American city would the ladies invoice so high per head as in San Francisco, when they go out to the opera, or to party, or ball. Their point lace is deeper, their moire antique stiffer, their skirts a trifle longer, their corsage an inch lower, their diamonds more brilliant,—and more of them,—than the cosmopolite is likely to find elsewhere.

Another "society" item, and we will pass on. The common dining hour being five and six o'clock, the women are denied the esthetic, gossiping tea-party, so peculiar to New England. The "lunch party" is their substitute, and a famous feature of feminine social life it is. The hour is from high noon to two o'clock, when the men are busy at their work, and the women have this dissipation all to themselves. Richer and more various as a meal are the lunches than the teas they substitute; the eating and attendant gossiping often absorb a whole afternoon, leaving the participants appetiteless, it is true, for the family dinner, but with what compensating material for garnishing the meal for the household! I have never even so much as seen through a crack in the door one of these California feminine lunch parties; but confidential confessions lead me to give them a high place in the social features and distractions of the life of the town. And yet for high art in the line of the delicate but industrious scandal-mongering and the virtuous plotting against masculine authority, that we are wont to attribute to these exclusive gatherings of our dear sisters, it does still seem to me that the New England conjunction of twilight and green hyson are much more favorable. Doubtless, these California Eves are bolder in their habits, as becomes their life and the grosser evils they are the victims of; but how much more daintily and delicately the stiletto and the tongue, the knitting-needle and the eye can do their sweet work under a little softening of the shadows and the inspiration of hot tea on a stomach that has already done its duty for the day!

In affairs of public morals, and education and religion, there is much activity in San Francisco, and a healthy progress in the right direction is visibly constant. The New England elements are clearly dominant here and through the whole Pacific Coast region; softened from their old Puritanic habits,—marrying themselves to the freer and more sensuous life of a new country with a cosmopolitan population, but still preserving their best qualities of decency of order, of justice, of constant progress upward in morality and virtue. The "Pikes" were the first people all over this country,—emigrants from Missouri, to which again they had been emigrants from the southern States,—and, joined to some direct importations from the home of the chivalry, they gave tone to society, and law, or rather want of law, to the government of city and State. But the Vigilance Committee revolution of ten years ago,—a mob in the interest of justice and order and morality,—inaugurated a new era. That was the North against the South,—the clash of their civilizations; and the North, seizing the instrumentalities of violence, rose and destroyed violence itself. Since then, there has been a steady, though struggling and sometimes hesitating, improvement in the character of all the life of city and Coast.

Ambition and pride in the things that are respectable and proper are singularly prominent; and men contribute lavishly to build fine school-houses and support churches, whose lives are not especially controlled by the influences that school-houses and churches create. The gamblers give way graciously to the progress towards decency and respectability, and join in outward observance of the Sabbath, help to build churches, and make orderly the street life of the town. It is very interesting to watch the various stages of this progress upward, from the new mining town of one or two years' life, up to San Francisco and Portland, which are the fullest flower of Pacific civilization. The order and decorum of the streets of these two cities are as perfect as those of Boston; the San Francisco police system is admirable, and a woman may walk the streets of this city in the evening, with less danger of insult and annoyance, than in those of Springfield, even.

Money is lavished, even, on the school-houses, which are the most stately and elegant buildings in town, and the schools themselves have all the "modern improvements," good and bad. There is special life, too, in the churches; the Sabbath is certainly as well observed as in New York; the congregations are large, day and evening; the Sunday schools even boast of a larger attendance, in proportion to the population, than those of any other city in the country; new church edifices are constantly going up; and, as your eastern parishes have reason to know, there is an eager seeking of the broadest and best pulpit talent to fill them. The demand seems to be for smart, effective orators, as well as holy men; and the churches are not easily pleased.

Among the "orthodox" preachers, Rev. Dr. Wadsworth, from Philadelphia, perhaps ranks first; ♦and his society, a Presbyterian one, is probably the largest and richest of that order. He is more of a scholar than an orator, however; but is greatly respected and beloved. Just now, Rev. Dr. Scudder, from Boston, is making his debut as pastor of one of the Presbyterian societies, and is drawing large houses. He has a free, \popular, Ward Beecher style of talking in the pulpit, which, if really genuine and natural, will undoubtedly help him to permanent popularity and usefulness here. The Congregational society, that bid so high for Rev. A. L. Stone, of Boston, is still in the market for a first-class preacher. Rev. Horatio Stebbins, of the Unitarian church, which can boast a larger parish income than any society in America, is, of course, chief among the liberals; and his many New England friends will be rejoiced to know that he has won a high position already among the intellectual and religious leaders in California society. Starr King's peculiar popularity and remarkable career here made it hard for any one to come after him in the same pulpit; nobody could fill his place; for that matter, no man was ever great enough to fill anybody's else place: but it was early found that Mr. Stebbins could make a place for himself, and fill it too. And this he has done. His superiority in pure intellectual and spiritual qualities is conceded; and I have heard prominent citizens, with no partial kinship to his church to influence their opinion, speak of him often as the first man in intellect on the Coast. His first year here is now closing, and though his salary is six thousand dollars a year in gold, his friends have just made him up an anniversary gift of four thousand dollars (gold), by way of indicating that they know him and like him, and to repair the damages of his removal from the East.

There is large extra demand upon all the clergymen here for leadership in all literary and moral enterprises, in all matters, indeed, involving the public well-being. Mr. Stebbins has been particularly called upon for public addresses during the past season; and there is also much impatience for his presence and preaching among the liberal religious populations of the interior and of Oregon, where no societies of his faith yet exist,—so that there is an especial need of an able associate and assistant to divide his great and growing field and severe duties with him.*

In the country parishes, particularly in the mining districts, the religious organizations are not so flourishing. The populations have decreased in many cases;—there is nothing more desolate, indeed, than the appearance and prospects of these interior mining villages, the interest, which gave them sudden rise and prosperity, all gone or nearly

* Such provision has since been made by the Unitarian organization in the East, and Rev. Charles G. Ames of Albany has gone out to California for this very purpose. He has excellent qualities for such service, and will admirably supplement Mr. Stebbins' peculiar talents and labors.

spent, and nothing taking its place;—and the ability to fill the churches and pay the clergyman is correspondingly reduced. The people who remain are uniformly generous and self-sacrificing in supporting the institutions of religion, but divided up into the various sects, each with its meeting-house, and its zealous pride of doctrine, no one of them has power to support a minister creditably. Many clergymen are therefore going away, literally starved out; and numerous districts of interior California are actually becoming missionary fields. All this Coast and its interior mining districts have great need to-day of earnest, unsectarian Christian ministers and missionaries. The people are in the main responsive to right appeal; they are eager to develop all the institutions and elements of the best civilization, and will contribute liberally of money, whenever they have it, in aid thereof; but it is no holiday work that invites those who would lead them. The men and women, who engage in it, should come with resolute heart, and the power and willingness to rough it in some respects, and come to stay at least five years,—not for a selfish pleasure trip to see the country, and pay expenses by preaching and prospecting in the mines. This country has had enough of that sort of martyr-missionaries; they are of most profit to the steamship companies; but for men of the other sort, there is no more interesting or fruitful or pressing field of labor, the world over, than this New Nation of our West.

In all these matters, to which I have devoted this letter,—society, manners, morals, education, religion,—the great want, the great reformer, is the Pacific Railroad. These, as much as mines and commerce, await the vivifying and elevating influence of that great instrumentality. Every discussion of the interests and the needs of this half of our Continent ends here. All life on the Coast is a circle leading to that. Everybody here sees this, realizes it, far more painfully than you possibly can in the East. I borrow the philosophical and impressive words of Rev. Mr. Stebbins, in closing his sermon last Sunday, to repeat this idea to you,—to show you how it is felt here, and how you ought to feel it there:—

"The primeval command to 'replenish and subdue' the earth, is promulgated anew to us on these outer borders of the world. We, upon this Coast, need, above all material advantage, as the condition of a noble social life and progress, an unbroken and swift communication by railway and magnetic circuit with the places which we still fondly call our Home. The social effect of such relations would be unspeakable in giving permanence and quiet to society. This longing, that comes like the sigh of the night-wind over the habitations of men, would be hushed. When the continental railway and the ocean line to China shall be complete, the London cosmopolite will make the circuit of the globe in ninety days, and we shall be nourished by the blood of the heart of the world. Intelligence will be increased, society liberalized by intercourse, and extemporaneous adventure driven out by better industries, as in the olden time the temple of God was cleared of money-changers by the presence of a superior spirit. Men have been attracted here by the dangerous and corrupting passion for gold. The inherent tendencies to barbarism in that adventure can be overcome and neutralized only by assimilation with the best forms of society, and bringing these distant places into close proximity with civilization, that the whole world may be tributary of its best things.

"It is not wise for us to flatter ourselves with false appearances or expectations. The bare historic fact is, that no fine state of human society has ever existed over gold mines. And the only ground of expectation we have, that society here will prove an exception to the general law, is, that the compensating influences of a beneficent government and swift communication with the world of mankind will give us the laws, the manners and the religion which no gold-producing country has ever been able to make for itself. Man, here on these shores, contends not merely with the unreclaimed powers of nature, as the pioneer of New England or the Mississippi valley, but natuie herself is dishonest. She bribes and corrupts him, and plays a trick on all his being. She sneers at his industry, makes his business a joke, and his word a lie. The world must be imported here to make nature honest, and outwit her secret arts. Nothing can save us from Spanish decline and Mexic littleness but communication with the world; that rapid and sure intercourse with human society, which assimilates the interests and the life of mankind. And I make this moral predicament concerning the growth and prosperity of our State: That the powers which have made her prosperous thus far have done their best, and that no great impulse of human affairs, having breadth and hight and depth of permanent, untiring progress, can be felt here until the great highways are opened over sea and land; and the world, the many-sided world of industries and arts, and commerce and literature, is imported to us. The primeval command comes to us with the augmented authority of our providential vocation, and is reiterated to us in original sublimity of moral law from every mountain summit which nature raises up as a barrier to our assimilation with the Nation and mankind. It is only by the introduction of new powers that we can conserve those we have. Compared with this all other questions for us are idle. And the people of California can make no better investment of their time, their talents, their money, or their public spirit,—and I would that I could persuade you to believe it and quit all your lesser contradictions,—than in turning all the powers of the State to overcome the barriers which lie between her and the Nation's hearthstone, between her and the heart of the world.

"Human society is made for religion:—for the ends and aims which religion suggests. Whatever promotes the assimilation of mankind, whatever brings nations and peoples into communion, thus supplementing each other in the completeness of humanity, is a step in the advancing kingdom of God. This earth is a musical instrument not yet fully strung. When every Coast shall be peopled, every mountain barrier overcome, every abyss spanned, and the peoples of the earth shall flow together as in prophetic vision to the mountain of the Lord's house, and harmony of common good shall persuade the lion and the lamb; when laws shall be greater than conflict, and order than violence; when manners shall enrobe the races as a garment of beauty, and religion conserve society as virtue conserves the soul,—then this earth shall give its sound in harmony with the infinite intelligence, and the providential purpose shall gleam from every summit as the beacon lights of mankind."

These are, indeed, solemn, majestic truths, most impressively stated. I would that they reach every soul, East and West, and bring forth early, earnest fruit.

LETTER XXIX.

CLIMATE AND PRODUCTIONS: COST OF LIVING:
THE CURRENCY QUESTION: THE MINT.

SAN FRANCISCO, August 31.

THE climate of all this Pacific side of the Rocky Mountains is one in its distinctive qualities. As a change from that of the Atlantic States, there can be no doubt of its beneficial influence upon the health, both because it is a change, and because it is less variable. It offers none of those wide sweeps of temperature that, both in degree and in suddenness, so try a weak constitution, and break down a strong one. Snow and ice are things unknown out of the mountains, in California, Oregon and Nevada. The summer sun is fiercer than in the Middle and New England States; but its oppressiveness is broken by a constant vitality in the air, and uniformly cool nights, that do not accompany your July and August weather in the East. Neither the long summer drouth nor the winter rains appear to be an element of ill health or even of great discomfort to an invalid in themselves. The rains are not oppressive save in the central valley of Oregon; and their chief inconvenience is felt in the mud in the country, as that of the summer's drouth is in the deep and sensitive dust, both making walking and riding off the pavements a great trial to cleanliness and comfort.

But the evenness of the climate and the indescribable inspiration of the air are the great features of life here, and the great elements in its health. There is a steady tone in the atmosphere, like draft of champagne, or subtle presence of iron. It invites to labor, and makes it possible. Horses can travel more miles here in a day than at the East; and men and women feel impelled to an unusual activity. San Francisco, which has the advantage of the interior in a cooler summer, probably offers more working days in the year than any other town or city in America; less occasion for loss from bad weather and consequent ill-health. But this city, though favorable to preserving health, is bad for regaining it. Its doctors say it is the easiest place to keep well in, but the hardest to get well in. They send their invalids into the country.

It is too early yet to determine the permanent influences of the climate of the Pacific Coast upon the race. The fast and rough life of the present generation here is not sure basis for calculation. But the indications are that the human stock will be improved both in physical and nervous qualities. The children are stout and lusty. The climate invites and permits with impunity such a large open-air life that it could hardly be otherwise. There is great freedom from lung difficulties; but the weakness of the country is in nervous affections.

The journey hither is a serious and tedious one,

either by land or water, and no really weak invalid should undertake it. But persons with a tendency to weak lungs, or with a low physical system that is being sapped by our rough eastern changes in temperature, can undoubtedly come over here with advantage, and secure a longer and a heartier life. San Francisco is no place for a weak lung in summer, however; the interior valleys must then be resorted to by those thus afflicted; but in winter this city is as favorable a residence for health as any in the State.

The abundance and variety of fruits and vegetables, and their great size and vigorous health, continue to be a surprise and a pleasure here. No State in the Union has such wealth in these respects as California. Nearly everything that the temperate and torrid zones unite to offer is hers by birth-right or domestication. The southern counties send up figs and oranges and bananas and tenderest of grapes; the northern, apples in abundance; and peaches, strawberries, plums, blackberries and pears come from all. And gnarled or wormy fruit is never seen; everything is round, fair and large. So of vegetables,—the range is wide; only Indian corn is fastidious and requires to be humored; and the size and perfection of shape and vigor of health are uniformly such as are seen in the East only at cattle show exhibitions and in small quantities.

But the fastidious Yankee, who never forgets his home or his mother's pies and preserves, insists that the quality of the fruit and vegetables is below that of the productions of the orchards and gardens of the Middle States and New England,—that there is just a lower flavor and delicacy in them; a sacrifice of piquancy and richness to perfection of shape and bulk. It may be this is only an illustration of that great moral truth that Burton used to impress upon his Chambers street theater audiences, "that the sassengers of infahcy never return;" and yet I am inclined to believe there is really something in it. But he must be an ungrateful churl, however, who is not content with the wealth and variety that nature offers us here for food, and at comparatively low prices, too. The table can be both better and more cheaply spread in nearly all respects here in San Francisco, than in any other American city at this moment. Butter, perhaps, is a weak point, and so is fish; for though the fish of the Pacific are generally the same in species and appearance as those of the East, the quality is confessedly and uniformly below. Everything in the markets, however, is sold by the pound; potatoes and grains and fruit, as well as meat and butter. But this is surely the fairest test. Weight is the finest measure of the real worth of all food; and why should it not be applied to all as to some articles?

The best time to see this country is in the spring. From February to June, when the rains are dwindling away to greet the summer drouth, and vegetation of all sorts comes into its freshest, richest life, then, according to all testimony, is the most charming season for the traveler. All these now bare and russet hills, these dead and drear plains, are then alive with vigorous green, disputed, shaded and glorified with all the rival and richer colors. The wild flowers of California fairly carpet all the uncultivated ground. No June prairie of Illinois; no garden of eastern culture can rival them. For luxuriance, for variety and depth and hight of color, for complete occupation of the hills and the plains, all agree that there is nothing like it to be seen anywhere else in nature. Then, too, the trees are clean and fresh; the live oak groves arè enriched to brilliant gardens by the flowers and grass below; and the pine and fir forests hold majestic yet tender watch over all the various new life of the woods. Those who would visit the Pacific States under the most favorable circumstances, for seeing all their natural beauty, and studying all their improved resources, would do best to come around by sea in February, and go home overland in September or October. That would afford ample time to observe everything leisurely, and at its best estate. After the first two or three days out from New York, the voyage at this season of starting is made under mild and pleasant skies on both sides the Continent.

It is not easy to make any exact comparison between the cost of living here and that at the East. Prices of everything, both here and there, are now much unsettled and fickle; what might be true to-day would be wholly changed next week. Then here, there is a lack of settled and uniform habits or scales of living; an irregular, fitful extravagance prevails; in luck, to-day, a man drinks champagne and flaunts his jewelry at the Occidental; while to-morrow, fortune frowning, he is sponging a dinner and a drink from his friends, and takes a fifty-cent lodging at the What Cheer House. Large profits are generally demanded by the traders; nothing is sold for less than "two bits" (twenty-five cents); and a fifty-cent piece is the lowest coin that it is respectable to carry, or throw to the man who waters your horse. As a general rule, no statement can be more intelligent than that it costs about as much to live in San Francisco in gold as it does in Boston and New York in greenbacks. Food, and consequently board, is cheaper than this here; but dry goods and luxuries are generally more. At the best hotels, the Occidental and Cosmopolitan, the price is three dollars a day in gold, which is the same as the four dollars and fifty cents per diem in greenbacks of your first New York and Boston houses.

The "What Cheer House" is the famous resort for miners and mechanics; and it has made several fine fortunes in furnishing meals and beds at fifty cents each. Some of the features of this establishment are original and noteworthy. It has an especial office for receiving clothes to be washed and mended, a well chosen popular library with five thousand volumes, full files of newspapers and magazines, an extensive and valuable cabinet of minerals, and a beautiful collection of stuffed birds, all for the accommodation and entertainment of its guests. Its reading room is generally well-filled with plain, rough-looking men, each with book or newspaper in hand. The rule of the establishment is for every guest to buy a supply of tickets for meals and lodgings on his arrival, and the proprietor redeems with cash what have not been used up when the customer leaves.

A "drink" at an aristocratic San Francisco bar is two bits (twenty-five cents), at a more democratic establishment one bit (ten cents). There is no coin in use less than a dime (ten cents); one of these answers as "a bit;" two of them will pass for two bits, or twenty-five cents; but the man who often offers two dimes for a quarter of a dollar is voted a "bummer." Some quotations from the retail family markets will still further illustrate the prices of food and living here: butter seventy-five cents a pound, eggs seventy cents a dozen, hams and bacon thirty cents a pound, potatoes one to two and one-half cents a pound, cauliflowers one dollar to one dollar and twenty-five cents per dozen, green peas five to ten cents a pound, apples four to ten cents a pound, peaches five to ten cents a pound, pears three to ten cents, grapes three to ten cents, new figs eight to fifteen cents a pound, dried figs twenty to forty cents, chickens seventy-five cents apiece, turkeys thirty cents a pound, ducks one dollar and fifty cents to two dollars a pair, quails one dollar and fifty cents per dozen, rabbits thirty-seven cents a pair, fresh salmon eight to twelve cents a pound, smelts ten cents a pound, sea bass five to ten cents, codfish ten to twelve cents, oranges four dollars to four dollars and fifty cents per hundred, lard thirty-three cents a pound. French and English dry goods at auction sold like this:—Brussels carpets one dollar and twenty-five cents to one dollar and sixty-seven cents, velvet carpets one dollar and sixty cents to two dollars and fifteen cents, broadcloth two dollars and forty-five cents to three dollars, black silks two dollars and fifteen cents to two dollars and eighty-five cents, plain wool delaines twenty-seven to thirty cents, number five ribbons one dollar to one dollar and seven cents, satinets fifty to sixty-two cents. These latter are wholesale rates, of course, and all the figures quoted are for specie.

My readers will infer, what I think I have not explicitly stated before, that the currency of these States is gold and silver. Paper money has been kept out by the force of a very obstinate public opinion and the instrumentality of State legislation. Our national currency of greenbacks are seen here simply as merchandise; you buy and sell them at the brokers, for about seventy-five cents in coin to the dollar. Of course being made a "legal tender" by United States law, it is competent to pay a debt here with them; but no man who should do this once, without the sum being made proportionately larger of course, could henceforth have any credit or standing in the mercantile community. All large and long credits are now coupled with an express stipulation that they are on a specie footing, and a law of the State, known as the "specific contract act," protects such arrangements. But public opinion so far, and in all the small daily transactions of trade, is the great and controlling law on the subject.

These Pacific States never having had any paper money of their own, and producing plenty of the material for coin, with a mint for its manufacture, it was very natural, though unquestionably selfish and unpatriotic, for them to resist the debasement and supersedure of their currency by the legal tender notes, which the general government resorted to for means to carry on the war. Their motive in excluding them was, of course, to protect their business operations from the dangerous derangements, often spreading a wide financial ruin, that are the common accompaniments of a cheap and abundant currency. But since only activity and prosperity are seen to have resulted in the eastern States,— while depression and dullness have been creeping over affairs in these States,—there has been a gradual change in public sentiment on the subject. Out of San Francisco, and especially in Oregon and Nevada, there is evidently a preponderating feeling now in favor of introducing the national currency. The principal arguments for it are, that the States here ought to share in all the responsibilities of their sisters in the East; if the paper money confers benefits, they should be enjoyed here; if burdens, they too should be assumed by those that are proud to belong to the national Republic. The friends of the introduction also argue that it would make money more abundant and. cheaper, and largely increase the tendency of eastern capitalists to make heavy investments on this Coast, and so give new life and prosperity to all business here.

But San Francisco, as the center of all the business and financial operations of these States, holds all firmly to the present state of things. Her merchants and bankers have prospered all along;

many of them are foreigners, and represent foreign capital; and they are not only content to keep the business of the country on a specie basis, but are determined that it shall be so kept. They argue that these States do not need capital so much as labor; not money so much as emigration; and that while, as matters have now turned out, it might have been well to have accepted the government paper at the start, and gradually come to its influence upon prices and business, as we did in the East, it would create great confusion and disorder to make the revolution at the present time, when there is a difference of fifty per cent. between the two currencies, and the prices based upon them; and, consequently, that it is better to continue as they have begun, and await the return of the currency of the East to the coin standard.

The question is being vigorously discussed; it is, indeed, the only live issue in the politics of these States; but so far San Francisco holds dominance over all the interior, and keeps out the greenbacks. The tendency of opinion and affairs is against her, however; and the day for a change may not be so far distant as it superficially seems. The bankers evidently intend to control the subject; and when they find they must yield, they will lead, and be the first to introduce the paper money. As it now stands, however, the question is a difficult and perplexing one to manage practically. It is even doubtful if the government could spare enough currency from the East to answer for the business of these States, so far away from the financial and government centers that they cannot draw supplies in one or two days, as all your eastern commercial points can. Certainly it will require the co-operation of the government at Washington and of the State governments here, with all the facilities of the bankers of this city, to introduce the change now without great interruption to the progress of trade and possible ruin to many delicate interests. Utah and Colorado have the paper money of the East in use; but all the States and Territories this side of them employ only gold and silver, in sympathy with the fountain head of San Francisco.

Of all the government institutions in San Francisco, the Mint is the most interesting and important. Already it is the great manufactory of coin in the Nation, and its comparative importance in this respect is destined to increase. It coins now about twenty millions of gold and silver a year, against five millions coined at all the other government mints in the country, including the parent mint at Philadelphia. The coinage here for June and July was nearly three millions a month, and the aggregate for this year is likely to go up to twenty-four millions. Mints elsewhere on the Pacific Coast, and in the mining regions, are utterly unnecessary. There is one at Denver in Colorado, but it has nothing to do,—the gold of the Colorado and Montana mines goes right by it, in dust or bars, to New York and Philadelphia. Efforts are making to get mints in Nevada and in Oregon, but they would only prove a waste of money. No local clamor of politicians, seeking home popularity or contractors' jobs for friends, should induce Congress to yield to such demands. Two mints are only needed for the whole country, at New York or Philadelphia, and at San Francisco. The metals, as soon as mined, drift at once to the commercial and financial centers; there only can their true value be known,—there only the use to which commerce may choose to put them. Sometimes, she demands their exportation in bars, and again in coin. Besides, the business of coining is an intricate and delicate one, requiring large responsibilities, expensive establishments, and men of both science and integrity. It should not be needlessly cheapened and scattered. Government may well have assay offices in all the mining districts, acting as branches of the mints, to receive the metals, and give coin or exchange for their full value, minus the bare cost of manipulating, in order to accommodate especially the poorer and smaller miners; but the multiplication of mints, I repeat, is an unnecessary, wasteful, and dangerous operation.

The Mint here is now in charge of one of the best merchants of the city, Mr. R. B. Swain, but it has no adequate accommodations. It is crowded into the back and upper rooms of an old and ordinary block in the principal business street. But provision has been made by Congress for a distinct and appropriate building. The metals are received at the Mint in all manner of half-worked forms, in dust, nuggets, rough bars, silver and gold mixed together, and more or less dross with all. Each parcel is kept distinct, first assayed, to discover its exact value, and then worked over, the dross expelled, and the silver and gold separated. Fire, water and chemicals are the means employed. The processes are simple enough and exquisitely entertaining, as you follow them with eye and intelligent explanation. The results are returned to the owner either in solid bars, bearing official stamp of their value, or in freshly made coin.

Much gold and silver are already exported direct from here to China to settle the balances of trade of both New York and London merchants; and when the Pacific Railroad is done, and the line of steamships to China is running, San Francisco, as the center of the gold and silver producing region of the world, and the half-way house of commerce, will become the great financial and balancing center for all the trade between Europe and America, and Asia.

LETTER XXX.

THE MINING QUESTIONS AGAIN: GENERAL REVIEW.

SAN FRANCISCO, September 1.

I MUST go back to the Mines for a renewed word of caution to the East. You are tempted there with all sorts of seductive ventures in the way of mining in these Pacific States. There are many men, both there and here, busy in working up a *furore* for investments in this business. Every steamer carries speculators and adventurers to the East, with mines to sell,—good, bad and indifferent,—but mostly uncertain. These have often been, and are likely to be, made the basis of joint stock companies of mammoth capitals, yet low-priced shares; their prospects set before the public in flaming advertisements, studded with stunning statements as to the assay of the ore and the assured prospects of the company. It is safe to advise people to put no trust in such enterprises. It is safe to assert that the money made by them will be made out of the stock-buyers, and not out of the mines, and shared by the officers of the company and their friends. Very likely, the latter are in the first instance swindled in the purchase of the mines, and that they are only repeating, in another form and before a larger audience, the game that has been played on them. Most of the mines now being offered to the eastern public are so remotely located, distant from markets, from wood and water, that, even if valuable in themselves, they cannot for many years to come be worked to advantage and profit.

No investments, I repeat, should be made in mines in this region, except after the most intelligent and complete study of the whole subject, and of the merits of the special enterprise offered, either by the capitalist himself, or by some one in whom he can place the most implicit confidence. Not only the mine itself should offer assured evidence of value, and of favorable location, but the capitalist should also be assured of its management here by persons of both intelligence and integrity. This point is as vital as the other, and as difficult, more difficult indeed, to be secured. These qualities of intelligence and integrity are rare here, and command a high price. They can generally do better than to work for other people. Eastern capitalists, investing largely,—and it is certainly best to invest enough to command their personal attention, or not at all,—will always find it wise to send out one of their own number, or a person equally dependable, to oversee the expenditures and direct the financial part of their operations, and let him find here that scientific and practical knowledge on the subject of mining, that he cannot of course possess. This he will obtain in mining engineers of repute, and in old practical miners, the latter most often men who have been foremen or overseers in mines or mills.

The discoverers and prospectors of mines are a class by themselves, and are rarely the right men to work a mine for other people.

I find my conviction of distrust of indiscriminate investments in mining, and my growing conservatism on the whole subject, abundantly confirmed by the experience and testimony of others. There is but one voice among the oldest and best business men of this city,—men who have gone through all the mining excitements of the Coast and shared in them all,—and that is in fullest sympathy with what I have written. Mr. Charles Allen of Boston, the reporter for your Massachusetts Supreme Court, who has followed our party through the Nevada silver and the California gold mining districts, examining them and their operations with even more of strictness and detail, in behalf of eastern clients and capitalists, than we did, I find has written home almost exact transcripts of my conclusions, without any knowledge of what these were. We find them fully confirmed, too, by the printed opinions of Professor Whitney of the California State Geological Survey, on record here. Mr. William Ashburner, who has been the mineralogist of that survey, and is now the confidential mining engineer of some of the most important enterprises and interests on this Coast,—and who is from Stockbridge, (Mass.,) and the son-in-law of Mr. Jonathan E. Field of that town,—acts confidently and cautiously on the same principles, and all his experience justifies their soundness. There is no higher or more intelligent authority on these subjects than he.

None of those who hold these views belittle the mineral wealth of these States. Those who know most about it have, indeed, the largest ideas of its extent and its value. But even thus utterly unable to measure these riches and the amounts to be drawn from them for the use of the world, they have learned how fickle are their individual deposits, how incomplete and uneconomical are present modes of extracting and working them, how remote from supplies are their best fields, and how difficult, almost impossible, has been and still is the reduction of the business of mining to order and legitimacy. Those, too, who have the true interests of these States at heart, who foresee their future, and would have their progress steady and sure, cannot but look upon the invitation of eastern capital hither under false expectations and by deceptive enterprises, with equal sorrow and indignation. The fraud and the injury are as great to the West as the East. Every dollar swindled out of the Atlantic States by speculating adventure on the Pacific loses at least two dollars on the great balance-sheet to this section. It will keep that much, at least, back from legitimate enterprise and investment here. There is field enough on this Coast and the way hither for all the capital and all the labor the East can spare,—legitimate, honorable, profitable field; and so every dollar, every hand turned from this to unremunerative, baseless enterprise, is indeed a double fraud. Sound theories and healthy habits as to mining are fast becoming dominant here; few enterprises, controlled by old miners and long residents, are not now meeting with some degree of success, or carried on with a fair integrity. Only eastern credulity and passion, fed of course by reckless cupidity here, can repeat on a large scale the lamentable experience through which this wisdom has been gained. I warn all whom my words may reach against feeding or yielding to the passion; for they peril in it both their consciences and their cash, and bring injury to the best interests of California and her sister States.

The results of the geological survey of California, under Professor Whitney, just now beginning to come before the public, will aid materially in the dissemination of reliable knowledge on all subjects connected with the State's wealth and the opportunities for its development. That survey is one of the most comprehensive and thorough scientific labors of the description ever attempted in this country; so far as known, its results have challenged the admiration of scientific men everywhere; both its intelligence and its integrity are unimpeachable; and the State of California owes it to her best interests and to her reputation the world over to carry the work through on the high scale with which it has been commenced, disregarding the suggestions of prejudiced ignorance, the clamor of baffled speculation, and the appeal of a narrow economy. No money can be so well expended by California as in telling the world exactly what she is, in whole and in detail; and this is the work that Professor Whitney has carried forward to its near, triumphant completion.

Looking back over our mining experiences, and taking the average testimony of each district as equally reliable, I find myself impressed with the superior richness of the Colorado gold mines. Their ore averaged as uniformly one hundred dollars a ton, as that of Nevada, either Austin or Virginia, or of California does fifty dollars. The extraction is not as complete because of the more intricate nature of the precious deposits; but means to overcome this, though perhaps at enlarged cost, seemed successfully initiated while we were there.

There has been opened a new mining district in California the present season, in the extreme western part of Nevada County, among the higher hills of the Sierras, and near the line of the Pacific railroad, whose ores resemble those of Colorado, both in richness and in peculiarity of combinations, and which, already attracting great attention, seems destined to become both popular and profitable. The poorer portions of the ore of one mine are sold on the spot at forty dollars a ton; and the rest are taken some distance to be worked. But the first and most important step in the successful treatment of all of it is believed to be roasting, which is not a common process in California. A single chunk of ore from this mine was so fat with wealth that it yielded at the rate of over thirty-nine hundred dollars to the ton!

There is even increased doubt and anxiety as to the future of the Comstock Ledge in Nevada, which is the great mineral deposit of the Continent, if not the world. The mines are turning out bullion more richly than in early summer; but they are spending large sums for explorations for new deposits, with results that are, on the whole, disheartening. Dividends are decreasing and stopping; assessments coming; and the stocks are about half the rates in the spring.

The gold and copper mines down in Arizona, along the Colorado River, as it runs between that Territory and California, are also coming more into favor and development. That river offers convenient and cheap access to them; and the chief obstacles, as yet, are the lack of steam communication, the barrenness of the neighboring country, and the hostility of the Indians. Mr. Charles L. Strong, the famous superintendent of the famous Gould & Curry mine in Virginia, until within two years, has just returned from an exploring expedition in that direction, and reports most valuable discoveries of mines, which he has taken up in behalf of some heavy New York capitalists, whom he represents.

From Idaho we hear already of deserted villages and impoverished gold-diggings; successful mining there is fast falling back on the quartz leads; and as a consequence the occupation of the "wandering Jews," the pioneers in gold-hunting, is gone. The experience of the East with oil wells is a fit parallel to the mining experience of the Pacific States. The excitement, the speculation, the lucky hits of the few, the losses and disappointments of the many, the sudden creation of a town with all the elements of civilization, and its almost as sudden desertion for new and more favored localities,—in all these features and in many incidental ones, the history of one experience is counterpart and repetition of that of the other.

COPPER AND QUICKSILVER.

Copper and quicksilver are to be added to the profitable mineral productions of California. The most brilliant success has attended the discovery and working of both these valuable metals, each, however, in a single locality. The copper mines lie in the foot-hills of the Sierras, a day's ride west from Stockton, and the town they have built up is called appropriately Copperopolis. They are being developed very extensively and with much profit; no less than three thousand tons of the ore goes East and to England every month; and an increase from these and other mines to twenty thousand tons a month is predicted by another year. The successful smelting of the ore for the metal is not introduced here yet, except on a small scale. The processes abroad are so much cheaper and more complete that it pays better to ship the rough ore direct.

The great mines of Cinnabar, from which quicksilver is extracted, are those of New Almaden, on the inside of the Coast hills, about sixty miles south of San Francisco; and they have become one of the most curious and interesting objects for visit and inspection in all California. Their discovery and successful working have had a marked influence upon the mining interests of the country, since quicksilver is universally used, and in large quantities, to separate the gold and silver from the particles of dross with which they are bound up in the ore, and the production of the article throughout the world is quite limited. Spain, Peru and Austria only have mines of it besides California; and the New Almaden now controls the prices for the world.

Its present production is four thousand to five thousand flasks a month, worth forty dollars a flask, and the net profits of the operation are about one hundred thousand dollars a month. The history of this property, its discovery and ownership, has been full of romance; there was great dispute over it, a long contest in law, vast sums paid in litigation, and finally a purchase of rival claims. It is now owned by a New York company, with a capital of ten millions, and is a magnificent property. The cinnabar is a red, brick-looking earth or ore, which is dug from its veins like any other ore, fashioned into small squares or bricks, built up into a kiln, and then fire set under and among it; and the precious quicksilver exudes in a liquid stream or vapor, and is caught and bottled for market.

Other cinnabar veins of promise, as other copper mines, are in existence, and to a greater or less extent improved, but these are the distinctive and controlling interests in both metals. In crossing the Rocky Mountains from Denver to Salt Lake City, I remember seeing evidences of generous cinnabar deposits at various points along the North Platte; and the United States are probably destined to be the great producers of quicksilver.

California is not without its petroleum, also: there has been fierce dispute as to its existence; much of furore in the search for it; and much wild speculation, into which the East has been drawn most unprofitably, upon the basis of its discovery in large quantities. That it exists, in greater or less degree, in some form or another, in one or two of the distant Coast counties, may no longer be disputed; but it yet remains to be proven whether it exists under successful commercial circumstances, that is, whether it will pay. I believe there is no well-authenticated case of a flowing well yet; I am sure much more money has been put into the wells than has been taken from them; and I am positive that the only money yet made from petroleum on the Pacific Coast has been made by the land-owners and the speculators. The oil fever has clearly a better basis and a more healthy promise in the East than at the West; and yet, under the influence of rhetorical representations by speculators and their agents, two companies of eastern capitalists have put up large sums of money, and bought a quarter of a million of acres of supposed oil lands in the southern counties of California. Their search for the oil has not had brilliant success yet; and one of the companies has adopted the very sensible plan of turning their land to good account by planting it with grape vines and going into the manufacture of wine. This is not the entertainment to which they invited themselves, but it certainly promises better results. They propose to set out ten millions of vines within two years; and the other company in the same position will probably follow suit with both vines and olives. This is an odd turn for a petroleum speculation to take, but it is fortunate for the true interests of California, and if well followed up will prove remunerative to the victims of the oil fever,—and Professor Silliman's rhetorical report.

LETTER XXXI.

THE FAREWELL FESTIVITIES: POLITICS AND POLITICIANS.

SAN FRANCISCO, September 2.

THERE is something of pathos in the very word parting. Few can confront the fact, can break any experience, from which life has been taken, or to which life has been given, without a flutter in the heart. But this is my last letter from the Pacific Coast. This morning ends the record of the "Colfax party" on this shore: we are closing that wealth of experience which it is difficult to believe has been made ours in only four months' time: host and hostess gather to whelm us with final generosity; to give *coup de grace* to a summer of such hospitality, both of sense and spirit, as was never ours before. Do you wonder we are all a trifle sentimental; and that I would coin my daintiest phrase for the final adieux? Yet the themes left on my note-book are prosaic and practical; and poetry fit to the occasion is felt better than written. Besides, these emotions, voiced to Atlantic shore, would reach unsympathizing ears. So you shall not know these words that are uttered, these scenes that are transpiring, in hotel parlor and steamer saloon, this morning, as guest and host are parting. They belong to those things that should always be taken "during the effervescence."

Our final visit in San Francisco has been crowded with most agreeable attentions, both of a public and a private character. Not half that were proffered could be enjoyed. Excursions to the country, and on the bay; visits to public institutions of the city and neighborhood; the seeing of the Mechanics' Fair, a fine exposition of the manufacturing industry and art ambition of California; addresses here, there, everywhere; private breakfasts and dinners; and a grand final and farewell ball and banquet by the bankers and merchants of the city, at the Occidental Hotel,—this has been the entertainment to which Mr. Colfax and his companions have been invited during the last week. But all are over now,—the Speaker has made his farewell speech; Governor Bross has addressed the last Sunday School; the brass band is hushed,—

"And silence, like a poultice, comes,
To heal the blows of sound;—"

the final photograph is taken,—and rare photographs, indeed, both of faces and scenery, do skill of the artist and clearness of the air combine to produce on this Coast: the tongue has wagged its last good-bye; and the hour of waving handkerchiefs is passing!

Conspicuous among the more private entertainments of the week was a dinner party to Mr. Colfax by the leading banker of the city, and to which were gathered from twenty to thirty of the most noted and notable bankers and business men of the Coast, heads and managers of the great enterprises of the Pacific. It was a rare collection of strong men, real kings in this Israel, and no city of the Atlantic could marshal a superior. The dinner itself was a triumph, was high art itself, in its way. It was said to have never had its equal before in San Francisco; and I certainly never sat through its superior, for richness and rarity, both in its elements and their serving, anywhere.

The farewell ball and banquet was a brilliant fete of a more public character. Two or three hundred ladies and gentlemen joined in the festival; the hotel was surrendered to its accommodation; the tickets were no less than twenty-five dollars in gold; and in aggregate and in detail, in preparation and achievement, it was as elegant and as flattering an entertainment and social compliment as ever city tendered or citizen received. There is more catholicity of feeling as to such amusements among church people here than in the East; dancing is not a sin, even, among the San Francisco orthodox; and the guests were greeted at this ball by the leaders in every good word and work in the town, who, men and women, made themselves gay with its pleasures, and contributed to its brilliancy with their beauty and grace. I had a home pride in recognizing, in the most womanly of the women and the most beautiful of the belles, a daughter and grand-daughter, respectively, of our good old, half-century pastor of Springfield First church, the late venerable and venerated Dr. Osgood. I note, also, as excellent example for eastern evening routs, among which I never saw it, the serving of hot beef-tea, with just a smack of claret in it, as a constant refreshment during the evening. It is a most grateful and delicate substitute for the accustomed spirit and tea and coffee, that leave such wreck of nerves the next day; and it did not on this occasion interfere with the grand banquet of the night, that was the crowning feast of the week.

The politics of these Pacific States are now in hearty sympathy with those which are dominant in the East. Their rescue from the danger of co-operation with the southern rebellion, or the temptation to take advantage of the opportunity and set up a kingdom by themselves, seems to have been almost miraculous, certainly was very narrow. There were strong elements and many circumstances that were leading, or likely to lead, these States in one direction or the other. Had they been enjoying then a vigorous and sure prosperity, the temptation and clamor for independence would, indeed, have been dangerous. But there was here, as in the East, a sudden and contagious uprising of the people for the government and the Union, that swept all discussion before it, and saved these States from anarchy, and the Republic a unit. So marked was the revolution that it seemed almost the work of one man, Rev. T. Starr King, whose voice was first and warmest and truest. But he was rather the leader than the creator of the public feeling; it would have found other prophets, had he been wanting, and groped and stumbled somehow to the same conclusions. Yet his clear, magnetic voice and kindling spirit gave expression and conviction to the slumbering, half-aroused feeling; and to his memory be great glory indeed.

California, Nevada and Oregon are now apparently as fixed and decided in the possession of the republican or Union party, as the average of the States of the East. The type of their public men is also much improved by the change from the old democratic and pro-slavery rule. The lack of personal and political integrity, and of consequent influence, on the part of their representatives in Congress, has confessedly been a chief reason for the want of consideration which these States and their interests have suffered from at the hands of the government. They have never seemed to have the comprehension to see and say what was wanted by their constituents, or the influence to secure it. The new men are not generally conspicuous for intellectual ability; men of that stamp here have too often prostituted their character for gain or pleasure, or are too much absorbed in the great business enterprises of the country to give themselves up to public affairs; but the present representatives at Washington and governors of the States are almost uniformly gentlemen of high personal integrity, great good sense, and large practical qualities for these trusts. Governors Blasdell of Nevada, Low of this State, and Gibbs of Oregon are all of this stamp. They inspire faith and confidence, and give firm hope for States led by them.

Perhaps the most influential, intellectual mind among the Pacific congressmen is that of Senator Stewart of Nevada. He shows qualities of the first order, comprehending the affairs of his section, and stating them with vigorous effect. Mr. Conness, the California senator, is a disciple of Broderick, and possesses great perseverance and force, and a conceded integrity in public affairs, but does not inherit the breadth and commanding qualities of his predecessor and patron. He is too much the victim of his hatreds and his self-conceit for largest power; he is rather the leader of a faction than the senator of a State. His unworthy democratic associate, McDougal, is speedily to be succeeded by a Union man, the canvass for whose selection is now in hot progress. It is impossible yet to say who will be chosen. In intellectual gifts, the most conspicuous candidate has been Mr. John B. Felton, brother of the late President Felton of Harvard College, and a leading lawyer here; but his lack of sympathy with the Union, when it was in peril and its fate doubtful, and his share in private schemes against the public welfare and the public purse, have already stamped his impudent pretensions with defeat. There are half a dozen other candidates, from whom a creditable choice can hardly fail to be made by the next winter's Legislature.

But there is a manifest lack of men of quick perceptions and strong grasp and influence among the politicians of these States. This senatorial vacancy, seeking fitting occupant, would be the occasion for Starr King, were he living; his transference from the pulpit to public life would have been a fitting thing, and greatly to the credit of California. It is interesting to note the sacred fame this man has left here; there is none more sacred in all California history; he is the saint of the Pacific shore. Those who knew him at the East cannot understand it; nor what he was here. He had, in this position, and under the occasion of the war, and the doubtful course of California, a new baptism, a re-creation as man and orator; and his personal influence and political power,—the revolution and development of public opinion that he led,—are among the curious and impressive circumstances in personal history.

California sends three new men of worth to the House this year. Mr. McRuer from the San Francisco district, is an intelligent merchant of Maine and Scotch origin, and is sure to command influence in Washington. General Bidwell from the north, is a farmer of broad acres and capacity, and Mr. Higby is a lawyer from the interior.

Nevada also has a new senator to choose the next year, in place of General Nye, who will probably not be returned again. The politics of Oregon are in danger of a counter revolution, through a large emigration this season from Missouri, Iowa and Illinois, the majority of whom will be of democratic, southern sympathizing. This emigration numbers from seven to ten thousand, men, women and children, and will prove a valuable contribution to the State's population and fundamental sources of wealth, though it imperil the tone of her politics.

Mr. Nesmith, the senator, whose time is about expiring, will hardly be the choice again of either party, for he holds close communion with neither. He is accredited with advocating McClellan before election, and supporting Mr. Lincoln and his policy afterwards. Not a great man, he has sterling qualities of sense and honesty, and has proven a useful legislator. To him is attributed that excellent saying that, on coming to Washington and seeing the august Capitol and the dignified Senate, he wondered how he came to be sent there; but after being there a few weeks, his wonder was still greater how the rest of them got there! Farther north, Washington Territory has testified her sympathy with the new thought and life of the nation, by the choice of a sterling Union man and pronounced republican to Congress.

The loyalty and the patriotism of these Pacific States are surely not less vigorous than those nearer the center of national life. With many the feeling here seems more a passion, a fashion, than a principle, and it is often intolerant and rough towards those who are suspected of opposition. There has, indeed, been less freedom of speech and action in national politics in Nevada and California, during the last year, than in New England. This is explainable, however, by the intenser life of the country, the more passionate habit of the people, and the fact that the supporters of General McClellan here were almost invariably genuine secessionists in heart and often in manifestation. The lines were drawn here more narrowly and distinctly than in the East, where many truly loyal and patriotic men were found voting with the democrats. But if intolerance and injustice are ever excusable, when more so than for a Union endangered, and barely rescued, as it seemed here, from the unholy power of its enemies?

I must linger on the shore for an almost forgotten paragraph about the Indians of the Pacific States. They did not vex our travel this side the Rocky Mountains, as their brethren did on the other; but we saw them constantly in our journeys through the interior. In Utah and Nevada, a poor, dirty, squalid race; apparently inoffensive and incompetent; beggars and poor servants. In California and Oregon and Washington, subdued, and a shade civilized, industrious in small degree, farming a little, fishing a good deal,—hewers of wood and drawers of water,—but fading out fast. Along the Columbia, they were squatted in numbers by the river bank, laying in their annual supplies of salmon, but living for the most part back in the mountains. There is a little war with the Indians in northern Nevada, and the Apaches down in Arizona, a stalwart and fighting race, are making serious trouble, so that troops have been sent to subdue them; but for the rest of the Pacific Coast, the remnants of the Indian tribes are apparently peaceable and disposed to continue so. The testimony is universal in these States that the whites have originated most of the troubles with the Indians. The great Oregon Indian war of some years ago was clearly provoked by whites, as a means of speculating in sup-

THE INDIANS, AND THE "SLANG." 367

plies for carrying on the war against them. The lust of coarse white men for their women; the introduction of whiskey among them; abuse and maltreatment in various ways are the origin of a good many Indian outrages, and these lead into almost necessary wars of extermination. The Indian revenges indiscriminately; when he turns, he falls on innocent as likely as on guilty; and so wars arise, and go on. Often, doubtless, too, is this the case, East and West: mean and sordid whites stir the Indian's blood, teach him the ways of mischief, wherein ignorance and barbarity have made him an apt scholar, and robbery, murder and war ensue in order. The path of government duty is difficult t⁓ trace through such crossing links of crimin⁓¹˙ but the ends of keeping the lines of tr⁓·· the telegraph unbroken, emigration saf zation progressing, are certain. Thes be, even if they oblige the goverr pate the natural extermination of ought not to be necessary, and nf dian department were both vigo administered.

The slang phrases and idioms, among the people of these State some of them quite expressive. those I noticed in Colorado are k section has a set of its own. "⁓ the most common here; it is a s or approval, as the "That's so" of th or "You get" is go, go along, cleaᵢ shout this to their horses. "Get up a

"Get up and Dust," are enlarged, emphasized forms of the same. "You can't prove it by me" is also very common for doubt or disapproval or ignorance; and "None of it in mine" is declination of proffer, and the like, and was probably borrowed from the declination to take "bitters" or any extra fillip in one's drink. "Bilk" stands for a humbug, an imposter, a "poor coot." "On it" is a much-used, condensed, epigrammatic phrase, with varying applications. It signifies, in that line, after something especial, determined, in earnest, and the like. As applied to a woman, it generally means that she is in a wicked way. "Weaken" and "To weaken" are very expressive, meaning failing strength, courage or an[imal spirits] [purp]ose. A man "weakens" is that he is backing civiliz[ation], backing out. The mines furnish many [words], [such as]: "Pan out" for turning out or amounters of water, [a] man will "pan out" good or bad, or [pan]s out" much or little. "Peter out" [for] hing, failing, giving out altogether. [lor]" come from the evidences of [wa]shing sand, and are applied to per[so]nd undertakings. "Corral," from [Spanish] for cattle-guard or high fence, is [long], cornering, getting into control. [Me]n in Nevada say the Montgomery "corralled" all the stock of a cer[tain] uld, therefore, put it up or down as [lingering] beyond my date on these [th]e last gun of the steamer is fired; the [to]hners of good-will and affection are fading from view; the Golden Gate grows wide at our approach; the Golden City sails out into the broad Pacific sea; and we turn our eyes and our thoughts forward for Home. But California and her sister States enlarge upon the inward, the backward vision. It runs quickly and surely to a world-encircling commerce, a world-embracing civilization, an Empire that shall be the glory and the culmination of the American Republic. The share and the duty of the present generation, East and West, in this progress, is the Pacific Railroad. Let them not linger over that!

LETTER XXXII.

THE VOYAGE HOME BY STEAMSHIP AND THE ISTHMUS.

NEW YORK, September 23, 1865.

No one's knowledge of California life is complete, who does not go or come by the steamship and Panama route. It offers as strange and interesting and instructive experience as any other feature of our summer journeyings over the Continent. It is the main, almost sole route for business and pleasure travel between the Pacific and Atlantic Coasts. Two or three thousand persons pass each way by it every month. Where one goes overland, hundreds take this route. There is no ocean steamship route in the world, over which so many people have passed and are passing; none on which the service is so well performed as it has been on a part of this, and promises to be henceforth on the whole; none that introduces the traveler to such novelties of climate and scenery and peoples,—none which affords so varied and unique experiences with nature and human nature. It is as odd and anomalous as nearly everything else is that belongs to California and the Pacific Coast. The stamp of originality imprints itself on all the features of that country and its civilization.

Going to Europe by steamship is ten or twelve days on a rough sea, out sight of land, in the same latitude and climate, in company with two hundred to three hundred people at the outside, who are pretty much like yourself, or at least with whose idiosyncrasies you are more or less familiar. To many this voyage is only a dreary confinement to rolling berth; an imprisonment, without the security of penitentiary. Coming from California by steamer is to this as a kaleidoscope to common spectacles. You have for companions one thousand, more or less,—and oftener more than less,—of the all-est sorts of people. The steamship is larger, more commodious and convenient than any other elsewhere. There are two hundred or more first class passengers, perhaps three hundred second class, and four hundred to five hundred steerage. The latter are quartered forward, deck and hold, and are limited to that portion of the vessel. The first and second classes occupy the center and stern of the ship, and have many rights in common. Both eat in the same saloon, but their meals are served at different hours. The staterooms of the first class are on deck; the berths of the second class are below: perhaps the chief distinction, however, is that the first class dine at four, and the second at one. They mingle very much together on deck, and morals and manners are generally as good in one set as the other. The food is good, even luxurious, and nearly equal to first class hotel fare: beef, mutton, pork and poultry are carried on board alive, and the butcher has his daily slaughtering to do, to keep this army of hungry boarders in meats.

The crowd is the only source of standing discomfort. We are as thick as flies in August; four and five in a state-room; we must needs divide into eating battalions, and go twice for our meals: would we have chairs to sit in shade around the decks, we must buy and bring them: there is no privacy; gamblers jostle preachers; commercial women divide state-rooms with fine ladies; honest miners in red flannel sit next my New York exquisite in French broadcloth:—and as for the babies, they fairly swarm,—the ship is one grand nursery; and like the British drum-beat, the discordant music of their discomfort follows sun, moon and stars through every one of every twenty-four hours. There were at least one hundred of them on our ship; and new and kinder notions of old King Herod prevailed among suffering passengers. The new historian Froude makes saint and anchorite of wife-changing, woman-killing Henry the Eighth: why should not some ambitious rival, gaining new light from the California voyage, make public benefactor of baby-slaughtering Herod?

We go out the Golden Gate into the Pacific ocean, and turn down along the shore. It is three thousand miles, or fourteen days, from San Francisco to Panama; from latitude thirty-eight degrees to seven degrees, from temperate to tropic. There is rarely any rough sea in this part of the trip; for most of the way, the steamer keeps in sight of the land; some captains on the route make straight lines and go across the mouths of gulfs and bays and other indentations of water into land,—and so sometimes meet severer sea and storm; but our accomplished Captain Bradbury of Golden City finds economy of coal, equal progress, and greater pleasure to passengers in following the Coast around,—and so we kept company with rock and mountain and verdure for at least eleven of our fourteen days. For much of the way, we were within rifle shot of land; we could see the different kinds of trees, houses and men, and study geography to perfection; it was like sailing down a broad river or through a pond, for often, by days together, the water was as mirror for smoothness; and only once or twice, and for a few hours then, were sensitive stomachs upbraided and upheaved for Neptune's sake. Indeed, it is steamboating, rather than steamshipping, on the Pacific side; and the boats can be and are larger,—up to four thousand tons in capacity and four hundred feet in length,—than on the Atlantic, with wide and convenient guards along the deck, that are forbidden in rougher seas.

The Coast hills along California make rough and barren work of the shore view; but as we get down to Mexico, the hills open and become clothed with rich green. The weather, never cold, grows hot; flannels come off; the fortunate in white linen blossom out in spotless garb; the close and crowded state-rooms turn out their sleepers on to the cabin floors, the decks, everywhere and anywhere that a breath of air can be wooed; babies lie around loosely and *au naturel;* you have to pick your way at night about the open parts of the ship, as tender visitor to battle-field at Gettysburg. The languor of the tropics comes over you all; perspiration stands in great drops, or flows in rivulets from the body; a creamy, hazy feeling possesses the senses; working is abandoned; reading becomes an effort; card-playing ceases to lure; dreaming, dozing and scandal-talking grow to be the occupations of the ship's company,—possibly scandal-making, for the courtesans become bold and flaunt, and the weak and impudent show that they are so.

Half way down, at the end of first week, we stop at Acapulco, the chief Mexican port on the Pacific Coast, founded by Spain, and famous in the days of her prosperous American commerce. It lies beautifully, under the hills, back of an island, which forms exquisite and safe bay. Here we taste of tropical life on shore; here we sample the Mexicans and Mexican Republic. It is a pitiful civilization that they present, and not very inspiring of sympathy or hope. The Mexican population is several thousands, and there are only two or three families of whites. The Mexicans are a mulattoish race, an apparent cross between Indians and negroes, with here and there a vein of Spanish blood. Indolence and incompetency mark their life and character. The principal local industry appears to be the supplying of the passengers on the steamships, that stop here, going either way, for coal and provisions, with fruits and fancy shell-work. The houses are low, adobe, and with thick walls, and whitewashed on the outside; the streets no wider than a generous city sidewalk; the plaza or church square opens broad but barren,—and here is the market-place,

THE EVENING AT ACAPULCO. 375

where, from little stands or on the pavement, the simple wares and food and fruits and fancy shells of the people, are offered for sale by gross women, dreary old hags, or precocious girls; and chaffering goes on day and evening with citizen and stranger. A few of us landed and spent the evening on shore; and it was a weird scene that the market-place presented under rude and scant torch-light. Occasionally we found a comely girl among the stands, with rounded arm and bright eye, and such usually got the best bargains from our party. A trick of the trade is to make you a present of some petty article, even to force it upon you, with flattering manner and speech,—and then to expect gallant and munificent return in coin. This is type of tropical trading the world over, and in all ages, I believe. Did not Abraham or other of the old prophets buy land for burial place for his kindred under such embarrassing circumstances? Close and heavy was the evening's heat; and the people, not busy trading with the Yankees, laid around loose in hammocks, or on the floors of piazza, thinly raimented, stolid, indifferent and indolent.

Mr. Colfax and some of his friends went to call on General Alvarez, the Mexican (Juarez) commander of all this region, and by the help of an interpreter had some talk with him. The general has reputation as one of the best men of his party; he seemed substantial and sensible in mind; and for his body was a big, burly negro. We met at his place a younger and livelier representative of the Mexicans, a member of the Liberal Congress, who spoke with zeal and intelligence of his country and its cause, and was disposed to upbraid Mr. Colfax a trifle for not more heartily espousing their side against Maximilian, in his California speeches. Such men as these two inspire some interest and faith in their country; but the general effect of all we saw and learned at Acapulco was not very encouraging. Without our aid, directly or indirectly, we were assured by American residents, there was little hope for the Mexican resistants to Maximilian's authority. The interference of the United States in some form or another was his fear and their faith. Acapulco itself alternates in possession between the two parties. A French man-of-war comes into the harbor; General Alvarez and his followers retreat into the back country; and the Frenchmen possess a barren town. They go away, and the Mexican leaders come back. Either way, there is little difference in affairs; there is no commerce save such as the American steamships make, and this goes on uninterruptedly. Though Acapulco is the largest town in the west of Mexico, its chief Pacific port, there is not a single road out from it to the interior; there is no ingress or egress save on foot or horseback; no other means of communication between it and the capital. The town has no wheeled vehicle of higher pretensions than a wheelbarrow. What can be done for a people who, with two hundred years and more of contact with civilization, can do no more for themselves? It was season of religious festivity when we were there; and a third distinguished personage we met at Alvarez's head-quarters was a fat old mulatto priest, who had come in from the interior to preside at the church ceremonies, and had brought along with him for Christian solace and refection, for himself and followers, a couple of hundred rare fighting cocks!

When we returned to the steamer, there was still a crowd of little boats along and under her sides, filled with Mexicans of all ages, sexes and conditions of raiment; with their stocks of fruits, cigars, eggs and shells; fitfully lit up with pine torches; and engaged in noisy traffic with the passengers on the decks far above. It was not possible for many of the passengers to go on shore, and the Mexicans were not allowed to come on to the ship; so with mingled shoutings of English and Spanish, and by the help of baskets and long ropes, the exchange of coin and commodities went on for hours. Oranges and bananas and limes were the principal fruits, and were alike fresh and cheap; and large supplies were taken in by both passengers and the ship's steward. It was interesting and exciting interruption to the monotony of the voyage to make this stop at Acapulco; and to passengers coming down the Coast, it gives the first close observation of tropical life and vegetation. Here were the groves of palm, of banana, of cocoa-nut; here, luxuriant in the open air, the broad leaves and rich colors of many plants that are seen in the temperate latitudes only in hot-houses; here, fresh from trees, on the trees, were the delicious fruits that come to us at home only after long voyages, and often stale and tasteless.

On down the Coast again, by Mexico, out of

sight, of course, but not out of thought of its mammoth volcano, Popocatapetl, the highest known mountain of North America, (seventeen thousand seven hundred and eighty-three feet); across the gulf of Tehuantepec; by Guatemala; by its wonderful and beautiful volcanic mountains, peaceful now, but exquisite in outline, perfect in cone-shapes, and rising to thirteen thousand and fourteen thousand feet in hight; by San Salvador; amused with the lively little flying fishes that single or in shoals skipped from wave to wave, flashing in the sunlight, as dexterous boy skips bright stone over the water, and awed with tropical lightning that made the heavens all aglow with wide and frequent flashes; by Nicaragua, where the opposition line of steamers, as yet weak, stop, and their passengers cross to Atlantic waters; then Costa Rica; steering easterly all this while to keep the tapering Continent; last New Granada; and on early morning at close of fortnight, rounding into the wide, warm bay of Panama, where the narrow neck of land, that connects and divides two seas and two Continents, confronts us. It is a charming scene, as we go by the richly-green islands of the bay, one with thriving-looking town at its base, another holding sacredly exclusive the sad burial-place for strangers and travelers, another the depot for the steamships, others undisputed with luxuriant and grasping nature, and anchor, amid all, in front of the quaint old city of Panama. The harbor itself is center for wide commerce North and South, gathering here to cross the Isthmus, and reach American and Euro-

DEATH ON SHIPBOARD. 379

pean centers; but a bad bar forces the slow use of lighters for passengers and freight.

We left the steamer one less than came upon it. There was a death among the steerage passengers, two days before reaching Panama; but the body was brought on, and lies now in the lonely strangers' cemetery out in the bay. Poor fellow! He was eager to go "home" to die. That hope buoyed him up, as it keeps alive a feeble, struggling lady in the cabin: but disease was too strong for even this tonic,—and now he lies buried, afar from kindred, dependent upon strangers for the last offices, and bearing, painted on the simple board above his grave, these more sympathetic than coherent lines, the composition of one of the ship's guard:—

> Death chanced to roam o'er
> the ocean's breast,
> And spied a hapless wander-
> -er wanting rest,
> Who from the western land of
> gold returning
> To see his childhood's home
> was yearning.
> But unpitying death, with
> resistless stroke,
> The casket of his soul broke ope,
> And set forth to another home
> From whence again it ne'er
> will roam.

We spent the day from early morning till late evening upon the Isthmus. By grace and gold, a few passengers were landed at once at Panama, which gave us several hours there for breakfast, for sight-seeing, for shopping, before the great crowd of our company, the baggage and the fast freight could be transhipped, and the trains for their conveyance over to Aspinwall be made ready. Panama we found to be only an improvement over Acapulco; it mingled more modern quality with its as ancient features; the streets were broader; the houses of two stories; and carts and rickety omnibuses, and a fine carriage or two, as well as retail stores by Jews or Yankees, and large warehouses under English or American superintendence, showed the innovations and elevations of commerce. There was a flavor of Spanish about everything, however; the food, the churches, the stores, the town generally; decayed, effete, luxuriant, tropical Spanish. The natives were a good deal mixed, wearing all the mulatto shades; the women flaunting in narrow, sleazy white gowns, rich with wide negro ruffles and furbelows; and the children rollicking in single, short, wide chemises, or unblushing and bold with utter freedom of covering. The churches, ancient, cheap and moss-grown, won no veneration except for their antiquity; they told of no interest in religion; of nothing but a tawdry, vulgar fanaticism; a lazy, cock-fighting priesthood, and an indifferent parish. We found the bats flying about in the arches above and behind the altar, and priests and boys firing guns at them among the poor tinselry of the worship, with results more damaging to "bell, book and candle" than birds. The things to buy here at Panama are fine linen lawns for ladies' dresses; they are delicate and pretty, and, Panama being a free port, cheap; besides which they are rarely to be had in New York, or other northern cities. Our passengers also found some bargains in other linen goods and under clothing; and their wardrobes were sensibly improved, without corresponding benefit to Uncle Samuel's customs revenue.

At mid-day, the long and crowded passenger train started Across the Isthmus,—treasure and baggage waited for a second,—and we had that ever-memorable ride, in the experience of all who have ever made this trip, between the Continents, from ocean to ocean, in the very fullness of the tropics, over rails fairly built upon human bodies, so fatal was the miasma of the country to nearly all classes of imported laborers. The road is fifty miles long, and the run is made in two to three hours. Monopolizing the commerce of all the Pacific Coast of both North and South America, the gateway for all travel from Continent to Continent, it is a rich possession to its owners. The fare for this two hours' ride is no less than twenty-five dollars, and freights are correspondingly high. The sleepers and ties of the track are of lignum-vitæ wood, the telegraph posts of cement, as thus only are both protected from rot and insect. The road is well appointed in other respects, and the service unexceptionable.

But the ride was rare revelation. All was substantially new and strange to our unused northern eyes; and we stared and wondered and absorbed through all this tropical passage. The sun was not fierce; one will suffer more from heat in a ride from Springfield to New York of a dry and dusty August day; but the warmth was deep and high,—it lay in thick, heavy, sensuous folds in the air,—it did not fret, but it permeated and subdued and enriched. With Nature, it was season of rest,—colors were dulled from the spring and early summer hues,— but what quantity! what ripeness and fullness, what luxuriant, wanton rioting! There was no limit to variety or aboundingness of tree and shrub, and plant and flower and grass. Waste and robbery, there could not be in such abundance; the vacancy of to-day's ax or fire is filled to-morrow; only daily use of hatchet and scythe keeps open path. Palms everywhere, singly and in groves, with great rough fruit, rich in oil; ferns as trees and in forests; clusters of bananas as big as an honest two-bushel charcoal basket, yet hidden by the generous leaves of their tree; bread-fruit and cocoa-nuts ripening and rotting out of reach of man or beast; tall oaks and short oaks; little trees and big trees of every family, interlaced so closely that you could not tell where one begun and the other left off; vines, tender and strong, marrying everything to everybody, running up, and running down, and running around, dropping down lines straight and stiff like ropes, all through the woods, making swings everywhere, but permitting no place for their play; great, coarse, flaming flower, and delicate, tender microscopic blossom holding up its cup by roadside, between rails, on every hand; occasionally bright plumage of gay bird fluttered across the vision among the thick foliage, and hid behind leaves so wide and long that we knew why Adam and Eve needed no tailor or mantua-maker,—one would suffice for all ordinary length of nakedness:—thus and more like it and continuously was our ride across the Isthmus.

At frequent intervals along the road are well-built stations with handsome yards and gardens and American occupants. Adjoining, and at other points, we passed crowded negro hamlets and villages; their houses frequently thatched both on top and side with the generous leaves of the adjoining forests, and their food the easy-growing fruits and vegetables of the tropics. What work they will do the railroad probably furnishes. The mark of the white man is among them; if dead, he yet liveth in the blood of the native; but the habit of the negro is dominant. The climate and their rude wants invite a lazy, sensual life, and such is theirs. There is small expenditure for clothes; boys and girls, even of full-growth, stroll freely about before the passing trains, and among their fellows, with not a rag of clothing to their bodies; and the men, when they do work, strip as fully to the task.

We pass by the thick and sinuous Chagres River, up and down which in flat-boats the early passengers by this route were pushed by the negro; along whose banks in this slow and painful passage did many lie down to die; and out of whose fetid breath came many a long-lurking and finally fatal fever. The passage is now made so quickly in the cars, that there is little danger at any season of taking the fever of the country. Exposure to the rain, or imprudence in eating, added to a system receptive of disease, are quite likely to bring it on; but persons in ordinary health and taking reasonable care of themselves need have no apprehensions. As a precaution, many travelers by this route take small doses of quinine for a day or two before reaching the Isthmus and a day or two after passing it. In this way the system is pretty surely toned up against the feverish tendencies of the passage.

We came into Aspinwall, in the first rain storm that we had felt since rain and hail pelted us so mercilessly on the Plains near Fort Kearney, most four months ago, and found that a dreary new town of one street, lined with hotels and shops and Jamaica negroes and negresses. These people are proof against this climate; they luxuriate and thrive from the start here, and it was due to their importation that the railroad was finally completed, as it was, after all other importations, white and black alike, had fallen in their tracks along its line of rotting nature, stirred to revengeful miasma by shovel and pick.

Aspinwall has no past like Panama, no present and no future but what the railroad and steamships make for it. There was a political revolution and civil war in progress on the Isthmus as we came through; but what it was all about, nobody could intelligently tell us; and we were not half so excited by the fact as we should have been over the ebullition of a neighboring volcano,—the latter being the more strange and interesting event here in Central America than the former. The town had little to interest us; plenty of tropical fruits and imported liquors; plenty of cheap stores, but no "bargains," and not a wanting watch crystal on the Isthmus! So we were glad when the baggage was all on board our new steamer, and the gun summoned us to follow it to our places.

The steamship service on the Atlantic side, between Aspinwall and New York, has been very poor for years; a disreputable monopoly, and greatly aggravating the perils and discomforts of the California voyage. But lately the management has been changed, and the service much improved; and we were in the luck to connect with a new and elegant steamship, on her first voyage, and under command of that Nestor of Isthmus-going sailors, Captain Tinklepaugh. The discomfort of a crowd continued and increased, for the vessel was of less size than that of the Pacific side; and we missed the shambles and the butcher's shop before getting through, for the meats for the round trip on this side, covering twenty days' time, are taken out of New York on the ice. But in all other respects the accommodations and service were beyond criticism; and old travelers on the route reported the improvement from the sad past beyond description.

Good fortune attended us, too, in the weather; the September equinoctial was past due, but we escaped even the breath of it. The Caribbean Sea forgot its accustomed crispness and spared our stomachs and appetites. Threading our way through the West India Islands; stopping at none, and catching glimpse of but few; passing near but outside Cuba, and waving our hands to its eastern shores, we swept up on calm waters, under summer skies, into the broad Atlantic; caught the Gulf Stream and crossed it; cherished our fears of a rough time "off Hatteras," and woke to pass the dreaded spot on the smoothest sea of all; and, our steamer being fast and on her trial trip, and winds and seas favoring from first to last, we disposed of our two thousand miles, and swept into never more beautiful New York harbor on soft September morning, and up to the dock, in just six days and a half from Aspinwall, this being the shortest trip ever made by any vessel.

Though one day longer on the Pacific side than usual, the whole journey from San Francisco to New York was thus accomplished in twenty-one days. The whole distance is five thousand miles; with fine weather and crowding the steamers up to their fullest power, it can be passed over in eighteen or nineteen days; but the trip is ordinarily extended to twenty-two to twenty-four days. The tropical weather kept with us until within two days of New York, and indeed is the usual experience of two-thirds to three-fourths the voyage, on both Coasts, whatever the season. On this side no land is seen from leaving the Isthmus till Cuba, and none again till the Jersey shore is sighted as New York is neared.

The whole line of this service, on both sides the Continent, has now passed into the hands of the Pacific Mail Steamship Company, heretofore controlling only the steamers on the Pacific Coast. This event is hailed with delight by all California travelers, old and new. The Pacific Company is the most notable triumph of our American steam marine, and is as popular as it has been successful. No passenger steamships in the world are larger or more elegant than theirs; no service more satisfactory to the public. They have within a year put three new and mammoth vessels on the Pacific portion of the line, and new and larger and better steamers than have ever been employed on this side will be at once placed in the service to connect with them. A uniform excellence in accommodations will be maintained on both sets of steamers; and for the first time in the history of California emigration and commerce, their facilities will be somewhat commensurate to their extent and importance, and the voyage will invite rather than deter the traveler.

For the past few months, the tide of travel has been greater from than to California; the larger prosperity of the East has invited home the unsuccessful there; but this is not likely to continue. The general flow must be the other way. And with these more agreeable facilities, and a widening curiosity and interest in the region of the Pacific Coast, there will soon grow up a large pleasure travel from the Atlantic States to those of the Pacific. The public and the Pacific Steamship Company are both fortunate in the new arrangement, and the prosperity of the latter is likely to be still more conspicuous. The owners and chief managers are in New York; though all its heavy interests and property have been till now on the Pacific Coast; and now it has added still further to its undertakings the proposed line of steamships between San Francisco and China. Larger and stauncher ships, if possible, will be built for this service, than are run on the Coast; the line is to commence with 1867; and the event will mark a new era in the commercial history of the Pacific and the Republic. So fortunate has this steamship company been, though it lost one of its best vessels (the Golden Gate) three years ago by fire, that its three new ships on the Pacific Coast, costing a million of dollars each, were all built out of the profits of insuring its own property. Its steamers will henceforth run three times a month between California and New York, and the fares for passengers are established at three hundred and fifty dollars for first-class, two hundred and fifty dollars for second, and one hundred and twenty-five dollars for steerage. These rates seem high; but they include board and the passage across the Isthmus, and are really but a little higher in proportion than the steamship rates to Europe, while the expenses in the latter service are much less. All the coal, for instance, used by the Pacific steamers, has to be carried way around Cape Horn from the East. No adequate source of supply has yet been developed on the Pacific Coast.

The point where relief and improvement are most needed, it seems to me, on this great thoroughfare of continental travel, is in the over-crowding of the steamers. I know they must carry large numbers in order to support such fine vessels and such an expensive service; but they surely do not need to carry more than can be comfortably accommodated with state-rooms and berths. There should be a limit set to the number going on each steamer, which for no reason should be exceeded. If three steamers a month will not accommodate the passengers applying, then run four or five,—one a day, if necessary. First-class passengers ought not to exceed three to a state-room ; that is a crowd ; more is indecent. If the Pacific Mail Steamship Company would preserve their reputation and continue their substantial monopoly of this great traffic, they will have to make reform here,—to put no more passengers on their boats than they have comfortable accommodations for ; to have boats of uniform capacity on each side the Isthmus, and to insure to all who take tickets through just what they pay for. There is moral unhealth in this heterogeneous mixture of humanity that flows back and forth in such close communion from California. The strong and the true are only made wiser for the experience ; but the vain and the weak, the susceptible and unsettled are only and often contaminated. Everything that the Steamship Company and its officers can do to ameliorate these inevitable incidents of such democracy of company in such pent-up quarters; to restrain and punish the wicked; to protect the weak; to make the long and tedious voyage on shipboard comfortable and tasteful to all, seems to have been and to be done, except this of preventing an indecent over-crowding of state-rooms and saloons.

—But the summer's journey is ended ; and my garrulity over its experiences and observations must cease. It has been a rare experience ; a rare opportunity, happily achieved by and for us all. We have gone together from ocean to ocean, across a Continent, up and down a Continent ; from longitude one degree to longitude thirty-four degrees; from latitude fifty degrees to latitude seven degrees; traveling in all some twelve thousand miles, half by sea, nearly a third by stage, and the balance by railroad and river; crossing the great mountain ranges of the Continent; exploring the forests, the mines, the commerce of a new world; seen and learned the field of a new empire; enjoyed the most generous of hospitality in every possible and imaginable form; and are back in our homes in a trifle more than four months from the day of leaving them. All without the accident of a finger's scratch; all without breaking for a moment the harmony of our personal circle. We part here; we lay off the robes of honored guests, that were so unexpectedly laid upon us, and so richly endowed through all our long journey; we return to our accustomed lives; but we come back with fuller measure of the American Republic and larger faith in its destiny. For myself, this summer bears greatest increase for my knowledge and my life; it will be perpetual pleasure to have had it; it will be great glory to have contributed in any degree by these letters to a knowledge by the American People of the real breadth and capacity, the necessities and the possibilities of the American Nation.

SUPPLEMENTARY PAPERS.

I.

THE MORMONS.

THEIR PRESENT ATTITUDE TOWARDS THE GOVERNMENT.

SINCE our visit to Utah in June, the leaders among the Mormons have repudiated their professions of loyalty to the government, denied any disposition to yield the issue of Polygamy, and begun to preach anew, and more vigorously than ever, disrespect and defiance to the authority of the national government. They seem to be disappointed and irate that their personal attentions and assurances to Mr. Colfax and his friends did not win from them more tolerance of their peculiar institution, and something like espousal of their desire for admission as a State of the Union. New means are taken to organize and drill the militia of the Territory, and to provide them with arms, under the auspices and authority of the Mormon church; and an open conflict with the representatives of the government is apparently braved, even threatened. I make these illustrative quotations from speeches and sermons by prominent church leaders during August and September :—

From Heber Kimball, first Vice-President of the Church.

The next army that comes here, I want you women to meet,—all armed with brooms and pop-squirts and hot water, to squirt hot water all over 'em. We had a good time with the last army that came here, and I guess we'll have it with the next one! Greet them, sisters, with a shower of suds; with even the half of a scissors about eighteen inches long. And you, brethren, grease your old firelocks. And you, sisters, grease your old firelocks, too. Arm even with cornstalks, everybody. In the "States" they do it between the ages of eighteen and forty-five. Out hyere, I suppose we might do so between the ages of ten and one hundred and eighty. Broomsticks and mop-handles, brethren, and pails of hot water, my dear sisters, if you can't do any more. If a dozen of our women were in the South, the time of that war, with pails of hot water, they could have licked the northern army.

We believe what Christ taught,—the commandments he gave. He said: "Thou shalt not interfere with thy neighbor's wife, nor his daughter, his house, nor his man-servant, nor his maid-servant." Christ said this; but our enemies don't believe it. That was the trouble between the North and the South. The abolitionists of the North stole the niggers and caused it all. The nigger was well off and happy. How do you know this, Brother Heber? Why, God bless your soul, I used to live in the South, and I know! Now they have set the nigger free; and a beautiful thing they have done for him, haven't they? I am what you might call a son of the veterans. My father bled in the revolution for our liberties. I, his son, have been five times robbed and driven out by Gentile persecutors,—I and my brothers Charles and Samuel. They threaten to come here and destroy us. Let them come. I am the boy that will resist them.

From George A. Smith, another Vice-President.

He said the Lincoln administration did not want peace with the South, but wanted to destroy and devastate all the good southern people, and, that in order to do so, the party in power had laid aside the Constitution entirely, and were the main ones who rebelled, and the South was right. He said the northern army burned and destroyed everything in the South, and abused, by force, all their women, and said they would be here some day to treat the *fair women* of Utah in like manner, and that all, both old and young, should have plenty of arms, and when they approached, God would fight the battles and the Saints would be victorious! He said our government was not at peace; and he damned it and hoped to see the day when it would sink to hell; that nothing in the shape of a free government could ever stand on North American soil that was opposed to Mormonism and polygamy!

From Brigham Young, himself.

He said if they undertook to try him in a Gentile court, he would see the government in hell first, and was ready to fight the government the rub. That he had his soldiers and rifles and pistols and ammunition and plenty of it, and cannon too, and would use them. He was on it! The governor of this Territory was useless and could do nothing. He (Brigham) was the real governor of this people, and by powers of the Most High he would be governor of this Territory forever and ever, and if the Gentiles did not like this, they could leave and go to hell! He said that nine-tenths of the people of the Territory were southern sympathizers; that the North was wrong, and this people sympathized with the South.

SUPPLEMENTARY PAPERS: THE MORMONS. 393

Much of this demonstration is probably mere bravado; means to arouse the ignorant people, excite them against the government, make them still more the fanatical followers of the church leaders, and also to intimidate the public authorities, and induce them to continue the same let-alone and indulgent policy that has been the rule at Washington for so long. The government always seems to have demonstrated just enough against the Mormons to irritate them and keep them compact and prepared to resist it, but never enough to make them really afraid, or to force them into any submissive steps. The bristling attitude of the saints has ever had the apparent effect to qualify the government purpose, and make it stop short in its proceeding to enforce the laws and national authority. It is no wonder, therefore, that they repeat their frantic and fanatic appeals to their people, and their defiance to the government, and grow more and more bold in them. They find that it works better than professions of loyalty and half-way offers of submission, one bad effect of which, for their own cause, is of course to demoralize their followers, and weaken their own authority over them.

There is no evidence yet of any change in the policy of the executive authorities at Washington. While the new federal Governor of the Territory, Mr. Durkee from Wisconsin, the federal judges, and the Superintendent of Indian Affairs are both anti-Mormons and anti-polygamists, all or nearly all the other federal officers in the Territory are both leading Mormons and practical polygamists,—the postmasters, collectors of internal revenue, etc. The postmaster of Salt Lake City is one of Brigham Young's creatures, and editor of the Mormon daily paper there. The returns of internal revenue in the Territory are found to be, proportionately to similar populations and wealth, quite small; and there are reasons to believe that the taxes are not faithfully assessed and collected. General Connor, who has been returned to his old place, as military commander of the district of Utah alone, is assigned a force of only one thousand soldiers; though he asked for and expected to have five thousand. The lesser number, remote from all possible reinforcement, is entirely inadequate to support the Governor and judges in any exercise of authority that they may dare to undertake, and that the Mormons may chose to resist. One thousand soldiers could very readily be "wiped out,"—which is a favorite phrase of the saints towards their enemies,—by a sudden uprising of the fanatical followers of Brigham Young and his apostles.

17*

Excuse for such uprising is in much danger of being developed from the growing strength and impatience of the anti-Mormon elements in society at Salt Lake City, and the reckless, desperate character of some of those elements. Miners from Idaho and Montana have come into that city to winter, to spend their profits, if successful, or to pick up a precarious living, if unlucky. Many discharged soldiers also remain there or in the neighboring districts. The growing travel and commerce across the Continent floats in other persons, "good, bad and indifferent" as to habits and self-control. Other accessions to the "Gentile" strength and agitation are constantly being made. The merchants of that class are increasing and becoming prosperous; those who have been silent and submissive under the Mormon hierarchy, dare now to demonstrate their real feelings, under the protection of sympathy and soldiers; the "Daily Union Vedette" continues to be published as organ of the soldiers and other "Gentiles," and is bold and unsparing and constant in its denunciations of the Mormon church and its influences; Rev. Norman MacLeod, chaplain of the soldiers, and pastor of the Congregational society in Salt Lake City, has returned from a summer's trip to Nevada and California, with funds for building a meeting-house, and increased zeal against the Mormons; a "Gentile" theater has been established; various social organizations, in the same interest, are increasing, and growing influential over the young people; General Connor himself, his fellow-officers and soldiers are all bitter in their hatred of the Mormons, and eager for opportunities to subdue them to the governmental authority; Governor Durkee seems less disposed to be tolerant of the Mormon control and the Mormon disrespect to federal authority, than his predecessors generally have been; and the judges, goaded, like all the rest of the "Gentiles," by Mormon insults and Mormon defiance, and their own incapacity, under government neglect, to perform their duties, more than share the common feeling of antagonism to the church leaders.

Thus the two parties are growing more and more antagonistic, more and more into a spirit of conflict. Thus, too, while are rapidly aggregating and operating the means by which the Mormon problem is ere long to be solved, even without the special help or interference of the government, are also coming into life the elements and the danger of a more serious and personal collision, in which the Mormons, from their numerical superiority, would most probably be successful, and, quite likely, wreak terrible vengéance on their enemies. Of course, such a result would evoke full retribution on their own heads; for then people and government would arouse, and enforce speedy and complete subjugation.

But these threatened and dreaded results ought to be and can be avoided. The government has now the opportunity to guide and control the operation of natural causes to the overthrow of polygamy and the submission of the Mormon aristocracy, without the shedding of blood, without the loss of a valuable population and their industries. The steps to this are, first, a sufficient military force in the Territory "to keep the peace;" to protect freedom of speech, of the press, and of religious proselytism; to forbid any personal outrages on the rights of the Mormons; and to prevent any revenges by them upon the "Gentiles." And next, the supplanting of all polygamists in federal offices by men not connected with that distinctive sin and offense of the church. These steps, wisely taken, firmly administered, would rapidly give the growing anti-polygamous elements such moral power, as would ensure speedy and bloodless revolution. It may not be wise or necessary, at least at present, in view of past indulgence, to undertake to enforce the federal law against polygamy; that may be held in abeyance until the effect of such proceedings as have been indicated is fully developed. In short, I would change the government policy from the "do-nothing" to the "make-haste-slowly" character; I would have its influence decidedly and continuously felt in the Territory against the crime of polygamy.

Neglecting to do this, there is danger of anarchy and deadly conflict springing up on that arena; there is also sure prospect that the people of the country at large will, in their impatience and disgust, force upon Congress such radical measures against the Mormons, as are, in regard to our past neglect and the present opportunity of peaceful revolution, to be almost as deeply deprecated. In either event, the responsibility will rest heavily and sharply upon the President and his Cabinet, who are permitting the affairs of the Territory to drift on in the present loose and dangerous way, either ignorant of, or indifferent to, the rapidly developing social conflict there.

DEFENSE OF POLYGAMY.

My readers may be interested to know the reply of the Mormons to my letters on the subject of Polygamy. The Deseret News, the official organ of the church, had such a reply in August, from which I quote:—

"As a people we view every revelation from the Lord as sacred. Polygamy was none of our seeking. It came to us from Heaven, and we recognized in it, and still do, the voice of Him whose right it is not only to teach us but to dictate and teach all men, for in His hand is the breath of the nostrils, the life and existence of the proudest, most exalted, most learned or puissant of the children of men. It is extremely difficult, nay utterly impossible, for those who have not been blessed with the gift of the Holy Ghost, to enter into our feelings, thoughts and faith in these matters. They talk of revelation given, and of receiving counter revelation to forbid what has been commanded, as if man was the sole author, originator and designer of them. Granted that they do not believe the revelations we have received come from God. Granted that they do not believe in God at all, if they so desire it. Do they wish to brand a whole people with the foul stigma of hypocrisy, who, from their leaders to the last converts that have made the dreary journey to these mountain wilds for their faith, have proved their honesty of purpose and deep sincerity of faith by the most sublime sacrifices? Either that is the issue of their reasoning, or they imagine that we serve and worship the most accommodating Deity ever dreamed of in the wildest vagaries of the most savage polytheist. Either they imagine that we believe man concocts and devises the revelations which we receive, or that we serve a God who will oblige us at any time by giving us revelations to suit our changing fancies, or the dictation of men who have declared the canon of revelation full, sealed up the heavens as brass, and utterly repudiate the interference of the Almighty in the affairs of men. By the first of these suppositions we would be gross hypocrites; by the other grosser idiots.

"Know, gentlemen of the press and all whom it may concern, that though a repugnance to this doctrine may be expressed by one in a thousand of the people whom you call 'Mormons,' he is not one, nor recognized as such by that religious community of which he may be called a member. If one revelation is untrue, all are untrue; if one was revealed by God, all have their origin in the same Divine source."

The News goes on to declaim that greater purity, better morals accompany Polygamy than Monogamy, and adds:—

"As well might it be said that the affection of the parent must be confined to one child, and that the affection of a united family could not reciprocate that of the parent, or jealousy would creep in, bitterness of thought be engendered and the finer feelings and susceptibilities be blunted, is that one man cannot entertain for and extend affection to more than one woman, or that his affection could not be reciprocated by more than one without the same results being called into existence.

"The presumed misery consequent upon polygamy is advanced

as one of the strongest arguments against it. Upon what is it based? Some person met and conversed with some other person who did not enjoy that amount of happiness in polygamy, which they desired to realize. Who does in any condition of life? How many monogamic wives curse the hour they ever entered the bonds of wedlock? There is no argument in it, nor can an argument be logically based upon it. It is a statement, and can be met by a counter statement which the experience of this united people can indorse, they having had a practical acquaintance with, and an experience in, the workings of both forms of marriage. Take fifty polygamic families indiscriminately from this community, and the same number in the same manner from any other community in the world, and there will be found more conjugal unhappiness in the latter than exists in the former."

The Mormons point lustily to the incontinence and license that exist in society, where one man to one wife is the rule, as practical argument in favor of their system. It is their final and favorite appeal, and always very satisfactory—to themselves. They hold that there is more real purity and order, in the intercourse of the sexes, in society based upon Polygamy, than in that where Monogamy is the law, and license the practice.

A SPECIMEN OF MORMON PREACHING.

This extract from a late Sunday discourse in the Salt Lake City Tabernacle by Heber C. Kimball, the first Vice-President and chief prophet of the church, is a fair specimen of a good deal of the preaching of the Mormon bishops. I have reports of other sermons by Brigham Young himself and others, so absolutely filthy in language, that they cannot be reproduced in print anywhere :—

"Ladies and gentlemen, good morning. I am going to talk to you by revelation. I never study my sermons, and when I get up to speak, I never know what I am going to say only as it is revealed to me from on high; then all I say is true; could it help but be so, when God communicates to you through me? The Gentiles are our enemies; they are damned forever; they are thieves and murderers, and if they don't like what I say they can go to hell, damn them! They want to come here in large numbers and decoy our women. I have introduced some Gentiles to my wives, but I will not do it again, because, if I do, I will have to take them to my houses and introduce them to Mrs. Kimball at one house, and to Mrs. Kimball at another house, and so on ; and they will say Mrs. Kimball such, and Mrs. Kimball such, and so on, are w——. They are taking some of our fairest daughters from us now in Salt Lake City, damn them. If I catch any of them running after my wives

I will send them to hell! and ladies you must not keep their company, you sin if you do, and you will be damned and go to hell. What do you think of such people? They hunt after our fairest and prettiest women, and it is a .amentable fact that they would rather go with them damned scoundrels than stay with us. If Brother Brigham comes to me, and says he wants one of my daughters, he has a right to take her, and I have the exclusive right to give her to who I please, and she has no right to refuse; if she does, she will be damned forever and ever, because she belongs to me. She is part of my flesh, and no one has a right to take her unless I say so, any more than he has a right to take one of my horses or cows.

"All the federal Governor has to do is to pay the legislature and administer justice. Are the Governors our masters? No, sir; not for me; they are our servants. We have our apostolic government. Brigham Young is our leader, our President, our Governor. I am Lieutenant-Governor. Aint I a terrible feller? Why, it has taken the hair all off my head. At least it would, if I hadn't lost it before. I lost it in my hardships, while going out to preach the kingdom of God, without purse or scrip.

"[To the Gentiles.] Oh, don't be scart at me! Come up to my house and see me. I will give you some peaches, and make you happy. I have two sons abroad preaching the kingdom of God. Brother Byrd says they are good boys. It makes me proud to hear it. I want the time to come when I can send out fifty sons to preach, all at one lick. Come up and see me. I will give you some peaches. I will give you some apples. I would give you some meat if I had it, but I am about out."

THE EMIGRATION OF 1865.

The Mormons boast of one thousand emigrants from Europe this season, proselyted and shipped by their missionaries abroad. Most of them are English and Norwegians, simple, ignorant people, beyond any class known in American society, and so easy victims to the shrewd and sharp and fanatical Yankee leaders in the Mormon church. Education, common schools are among the first of reformatory means needed in Utah.

II.

MINES AND MINING.

THE MINES IN MONTANA.

MR. ALBERT D. RICHARDSON of our summer party, who remained behind to visit Montana and Idaho, writes from Virginia City, Montana, October 28th, as follows:—

"Montana is very promising,—richer, I think, than any of our other gold or silver States or Territories. The placer diggings are paying largely, and the quartz seems to me richer than anything else I have seen; and a good many mills are coming in. But there are lots of Montana people in New York to sell leads, many of whom ought to be sent to the penitentiary for obtaining money under false pretenses. 'Beware of Wild-Cat' should be written over every article published on quartz-mining, in letters so large that he who runs may read, and the wayfaring man, though a fool, may not invest therein."

From other sources are gathered the following facts: Alder Gulch is the theater of the original and most extensive gold-mining in Montana. Virginia City is the first and largest town here. About thirty millions of gold have been taken in the various diggings of the gulch; and the quartz mines at its head among the hills are now very popular and promising. The present population of the Alder Gulch region is about fourteen thousand. About one hundred and forty miles north and east, more immediately among the Rocky Mountains, is the second center of development and population; and Helena is its chief town, with about five thousand inhabitants. Neighboring valleys and gulches are also rich in gold and silver, both washings and quartz. Many millions of treasure have already been obtained from this section of the Territory. And the country is described as very picturesque and beautiful. It is watered by the head streams of the Missouri River,—the Jefferson and Gallatin Rivers, and their tributaries,—and Fort Benton, the head of navigation on the Missouri, is but one hundred and seventy-five miles east from Helena.

The maps give but inadequate idea of the divisions of Idaho and Montana, and their chief districts of gold and population. Montana lies along upon the Rocky Mountains, above Colorado and Utah, mostly on the western slopes, but still going over into the eastern valleys, whose waters feed the Missouri River, and find their way to the Atlantic Ocean. Idaho lies beyond Montana to the west, among the Blue Mountains, and the upper waters of the Columbia River, or its Snake River branch. The population of each Territory is fickle; it has probably been from twenty thousand to twenty-five thousand each, during the past summer; but in the winter these figures will be reduced one-third to one-half.

THE UNCERTAINTIES OF MINING.

From a Lecture in San Francisco by PROFESSOR J. D. WHITNEY *of the State Geological Survey of California.*

It is a fact, that extremely few metalliferous veins are equally rich for any considerable distance, either lengthwise or up and down; the valuable portions of the ore are concentrated in masses which are frequently very limited in extent, compared with the mass of the vein, in which they are contained.

It is a fact, that indications of valuable ores on the surface do not always, nor once in a hundred times, lead to masses of ore beneath the surface of a sufficient extent and purity to be worked with profit. There are, literally and truly, thousands of places in New England where ores of the metals, including silver, copper, tin, lead, zinc, cobalt and nickel, have been observed; many of these have given rise to mining excitements, and have been taken up, worked for a time, abandoned, taken up again, abandoned again, off and on for the last fifty or even a hundred years, and always with partial, and usually with a total, loss of the money invested. There may be one solitary mine in Vermont which is paying a small profit to the shareholders; but with the exception of this, and a few mines of iron ore on the border of Massachusetts and Connecticut, there is not one which has not cruelly burned the fingers of those who have meddled with them.

Even on Lake Superior, that region which is commonly appealed to as made up of solid copper, there have been many hundreds of companies formed, and at least a hundred mines opened and worked more or less extensively; but for ten years after mining had begun to be actively carried on there, only two of the mines had paid back to the stockholders one cent of dividend. Even in England, it is the opinion of Mr. Hunt, the Keeper of Mining Records, who has devoted many years to the investigation of the statistics of this branch of the Nation's wealth, that mining for the metallic minerals, with the exception of iron, is not on the whole remunerative. There is a wonderful fascination about the mining business, which seems to blind the eyes and bewilder the senses of those who come within the sphere of its influence. The organ of hope seems to swell up and predominate over all the others:—what phantasmagoria will men not follow, if there is any metallic luster about it!

If the California capital, which has been wasted in foolish mining enterprises in this State and on its borders during the past three years, would, as I fully believe, have paid for a railroad to Washoe; then California is the poorer by a railroad to Washoe, with double track and rolling stock complete, than it would have been, had not recklessness and ignorance diverted capital from this great enterprise.

THE MINING LAWS AND THEIR OPERATION.

From the Letters of MR. CHARLES ALLEN, *Lawyer, of Boston.*

The method of establishing mining laws strikes one who is accustomed to the settled usages of older countries as very peculiar. At the outset the miners of a particular region get together, of their own motion, fix the limits and name of their district, and establish a series of rules, which may be altered in methods therein prescribed, for the location, holding and working of mines. The fundamental idea which runs through all of these rules is, that he who finds a mine shall have the right to locate upon the ledge a certain number of feet in his own name, after which other locations may be made by anybody. In practice the discoverer usually locates a number of claims in the names of his friends. The validity of these locations depends upon doing upon the ledge a certain amount of work within a certain time. Provisions are also inserted which are designed to meet such contingencies as can be foreseen; but, although the general principles are in accordance with just views of what is right, it is of course impossible to provide for every condition of things; and, besides, the rules themselves are expressed in language not always clear. An immense amount of litigation is sure ultimately to ensue, and there is no place in the world, I suppose, where the lawyers' fees, absolute or contingent, are so large as in mining regions. Questions of fact constantly arise, whether enough work has been done to hold a claim, and whether two veins which appear on the surface to be different do or do not in fact ultimately run into each other. If they do come together, the oldest location prevails.

It is well understood that there is a government title, which, if ultimately insisted on, is beneath all titles to mining property. But it is so plain, both as a matter of justice and policy, that this title will never be insisted on, that I do not regard it of essential importance in considering the practical question of investing money in mines. This question is not very well understood yet at the East, or even in Congress. But the leading considerations are so just that they will be understood before final action is taken. The miners' rules have been recognized in State courts as valid and having the force of law; and, after a vigorous contest in Congress, a law was finally passed at the last session, which provided that "no possessory action between individuals, in any of the courts of the United States, for the recovery of any mining title, or for damages to such title, shall be affected by the fact that the paramount title to the land on which such mines are is in the United States, but each case shall be adjudged by the law of possession." It should be added that the miners' rights are superior to all other rights of property except the government title. The survey, location and ownership of a piece of land as real estate gives no right, under the miners' laws, to the minerals which it contains.

HOW THE METAL IS EXTRACTED FROM THE REESE RIVER QUARTZ.

From MR. CHARLES ALLEN'S *Letters from Nevada.*

After the quartz has been extracted from the mine, it is taken to the mill, broken into pieces of from half a pound to two pounds in weight, thoroughly dried by the application of heat, and then crushed to powder in the mill. Various machines are advertised for crushing quartz, which their inventors and proprietors say will accomplish great results, but none of them are yet in practice and successful use at Reese River, or anywhere else that I know of. The process universally resorted to in Nevada is the old stamp mill. This process is simply the dropping of heavy weights upon the quartz, which s placed in dies prepared to receive it. Five stamps are usually arrayed side by side, weighing from five hundred to seven hundred pounds each. They are raised a distance of from eight to ten inches, and dropped from sixty to eighty-five times a minute. A wire sieve is placed upon each side of the dies, through which the powdered quartz escapes into a receiver, from which it is taken to a furnace, where it is subject to the action of a stream of flame from five to eight hours, during which time it is constantly stirred. As this flame carries off some silver bodily, it is made to pass through a long chamber, and exposed to cooler air before reaching the chimney, so that the silver can be saved. After being roasted, the pulverized quartz is ready for amalgamation. At the Midas Mill, which is considered to be the best mill at Reese River, the amalgamation is done by the Freiburg barrels, into which loose and irregular pieces of iron are placed for the purpose of mixing the quicksilver with the pulp, (as the pulverized quartz is called,) and which are then revolved over and over. In other mills, the pulp is put into tubs, and stirred in water for nearly an hour, and then the quicksilver is applied, and the mass is stirred by means of iron flanges for three hours. About seventy-five pounds of quicksilver are allowed for one thousand pounds of pulp. After this, the water is drawn off, and a process like the distillation of cider brandy is resorted to for the purpose of saving the quicksilver, and the amalgam, composed of silver and quicksilver, is squeezed, to get out the quicksilver, after which it is put into the retort, and upon being subjected to heat more quicksilver passes off in fumes, and is saved, and the crude bullion which is left is ready to be taken to the assay office. This is substantially the process used at Reese River, where dry crushing is necessary, on account of the presence of the baser metals. In Virginia and its vicinity, where the ore is of a different character, and far less rich, it is crushed wet, and not roasted, and the expense is much less.

EASTERN INVESTMENT IN REESE RIVER MINES.

From the Letters of MR. ALLEN *of Boston.*

Boston has already invested a million of dollars in the Reese River mines. Will these investments pay? In reply to this question, it may be said in general terms that those who expect to get back their money speedily will be disappointed, and that a large share and perhaps the bulk of them will probably never get back their money at all. I have made some inquiry with a view to ascertain how many out of the seven thousand mines within this (Austin) the richest district have already paid their actual working expenses; and my conclusion is, that this is true of not over thirty. Of course, this is not a fair test for so new a country. Good mines do not ordinarily pay until the water level is reached; and much work must be done before that. Many good mines here have been so far worked that they are now apparently on the point of paying a profit. Besides, some very rich mines have been badly managed. The above fact, therefore, is not mentioned as affording a fair test for the future. Still it is worthy of the attention of those who consider a silver mine as sure to bring immediate profits.

It is perfectly surprising to observe the recklessness with which investments in silver-mining property have been made at the East. Prudent, sagacious, and experienced persons, who would not pay ten thousand dollars for a country house, or five hundred dollars for a horse, without careful consideration and examination, appropriate much larger sums to the purchase of mining interests, merely upon the representations of the sellers. This has been done, and will be again. Of course, when capitalists are so ready to part with their money, swindling transactions will be frequent. Some purchasers that I have heard of will never be able to find their property at all. Others have paid very large sums for what could be purchased here for very small sums. A leading citizen of this place remarked to me, "I do not see why eastern gentlemen who have surplus funds will invest them in our mines, while there are faro banks at home." This is an extravagance; but it is, after all, not altogether inapplicable to those who undertake to realize profits here, without taking the ordinary business precautions.

GENERAL ROSECRANS ON THE MINES OF NEVADA.

General Rosecrans, who has spent much time this summer in the Reese River country of Nevada, as the representative of a Boston mining company, offers the following conclusions as the result of his observations:—

1. The number of lodes of silver ore is almost unlimited in Nevada, and no part of the State shows more lodes or richer ores than Reese River.
2. Therefore many of great richness of ore must remain utterly without value, present or prospective, for years to come; hence, not every "large" lode, however promising the ore, should be purchased.
3. No reduction works should be erected upon a single lode, however promising, lest the at least temporary failure of an adequate supply of ore should entail losses upon the company.
4. Only those mines which have several lodes in such proximity to each other as to be easily and economically worked by the same superintendent, and with a single set of machinery for pumping water and hoisting the ore, are likely to be truly successful.
5. This is the more important in this country, where the whole surface of the country is a net-work of small rich lodes, running parallel to and crossing each other in every direction, and often only a few feet apart, because these spurs and cross-cuts add to a company's chances of increased profit and success, and give it moreover all the benefit of its own draining, shafting, tunnelling and ventilation.
6. Whoever buys single mines,—mines far apart, or high in the hills and of difficult access,—must expect to lose money by them, or to hold them as "permanent investments."
7. It ought to be known by the public that much of the mining is at present *speculative*, and most of the money that is made off unfortunate purchasers of mines, at high prices, goes into the hands of "middle men," who are quite willing to profit by the losses of both capitalists and miners.

Such is the feverish eagerness of the poor locaters and proprietors, that they hasten to give deeds in fee to some adventuring speculator, who starts for the East to sell their mines for all they can get, regardless of what becomes of the mine or the purchaser.

But on the question of the *really almost unlimited* quantity of the precious metal in Nevada, and of the existence of the necessary salt, water, fuel and other necessaries for their mining and reduction in such a way as to amply remunerate well-directed capital, I entertain no doubt, nor do I think any other attentive observer would. Really all that Bishop Simpson said about the quantity of silver in this State, fanciful as it may appear to those who have not been here, is no exaggeration.

III.

MR COLFAX'S SPEECHES.

THIS record of the remarkable Summer's Journey Across the Continent would be incomplete, without some portion, at least, of the many and valuable public speeches on the route, by MR. COLFAX, whose high public position and wide personal popularity made the trip so conspicuous, and gave all its participants such rare advantages. These speeches are but generally described in the Letters; and the extracts that follow,—only too limited by the confines of the volume,—relate almost solely to special themes connected with the development and civilization of the Mountain and Pacific States:—

MR. LINCOLN'S MESSAGE TO THE MINERS.

From MR. COLFAX'S *Speech at Central City, Colorado, May* 27.

He had come in part to bring a message from our late President,—that noble man, so pure, so patriotic, so forgiving, the most lovable of all men, whose tender heart bore no ill-will, who never answered railing with railing; on the very night he was seeking to soften the fate of the fallen enemies of the country, struck down by the assassin. The crime towered in its infamy, but its purpose was not accomplished. It was intended to weaken the Nation, but it made the Nation stronger. It had placed Abraham Lincoln on the very pinnacle of fame. He did not die because he was Abraham Lincoln, but because he represented the Nation's contest with and victory over treason. We might engrave his name on marble,—it would crumble; we might inscribe it on Mt. Blanc, where that living wall four thousand feet in hight overlaid a portion of the mountain eleven thousand feet high,—that granite spire would moulder in fragments round the base of its pedestal before the name and memory of Abraham Lincoln would be forgotten.

Said Mr. Lincoln to me, when I called the day before his death, to say good-bye:—"Mr. Colfax, I want you to take a message from me to the miners whom you visit. I have (said he) very large ideas of the mineral wealth of our Nation. I believe it practically inexhaustible. It abounds all over the western country, from the Rocky

Mountains the Pacific, and its development has scarcely commenced. During the war, when we were adding a couple of millions of dollars every day to our national debt, I did not care about encouraging the increase in the volume of our precious metals. We had the country to save first. But now that the rebellion is overthrown and we know pretty nearly the amount of our national debt, the more gold and silver we mine, makes the payment of that debt so much the easier. Now, (said he, speaking with much emphasis,) I am going to encourage that in every possible way. We shall have hundreds of thousands of disbanded soldiers, and many have feared that their return home in such great numbers might paralyze industry by furnishing suddenly a greater supply of labor than there will be demand for. I am going to try to attract them to the hidden wealth of our mountain ranges, where there is room enough for all. Immigration, which even the war has not stopped, will land upon our shores hundreds of thousands more per year from overcrowded Europe. I intend to point them to the gold and silver that waits for them in the West. Tell the miners from me, that I shall promote their interests to the utmost of my ability; because their prosperity is the prosperity of the Nation, and (said he, his eye kindling with enthusiasm,) we shall prove in a very few years that we are indeed the *treasury of the world.*"

That evening he (Mr. Colfax) had called again and was with the President half an hour just before he started for the theater, to which he had been invited to accompany him. But he expected to leave Washington the next morning, and having other engagements for the evening, he could not go. The President was still in the highest spirits in the evening. As he was departing for the theater, accompanied to the door by Mr. Ashmun of Massachusetts,—the last walk to the door of the Executive Mansion he was ever to take,—as they were shaking hands, a thought seemed to strike the President, who repeated in a condensed form what he had just delivered to us, thus showing how important he held it, and said to him, "Don't forget, Colfax, to tell those miners that that is my speech to them,—a pleasant journey to you. I will telegraph you at San Francisco,—good-bye,"—the last good-bye of his life. These words he brought were the last words of the President on public subjects before the bullet of the assassin crashed through his brain. It showed that amid the exultation consequent on the grandest consummation of the dearest wishes of the President and the Nation, the interests of the great West, particularly of the miners, were uppermost in his thoughts. These words were true, prophetic.

THE RESPECTIVE DUTIES OF GOVERNMENT AND PEOPLE—SUGGESTIONS TO THE MORMONS.

From Mr. Colfax's *Speech at Great Salt Lake City, June* 12.

I have had a theory for years past that it is the duty of men who are in public life, charged with a participation in the government

SUPPLEMENTARY PAPERS: SPEECHES. 407

of a great country like ours, to know as much as possible of the interests, development, and resources of the country whose destiny, comparatively, has been committed to their hands. And I said to my friends, if they would accompany me, we would travel over the New World till we could look from the shores of the Pacific towards the Continent of Asia, the cradle of the human race. And, therefore, we are here, traveling night and day over your mountains and valleys, your deserts and plains, to see this region between the Rocky Mountains and the Pacific, where, as I believe, the seat of Empire in this Republic ultimately is to be.

Now, you who are pioneers far out here in the distant West, have many things that you have a right to ask of your government. I can scarcely realize with this large assembly around me, that there is an almost boundless desert of twelve hundred miles between myself and the valley of the Mississippi. There are many things that you have a right to demand; you have created, however, many things here for yourselves. No one could traverse your city without recognizing that you are a people of industry. It happened to be my fortune in Congress to do a little towards increasing the postal facilities in the West, not as much as I desired, but as much as I could obtain from Congress. And when it was proposed, to the astonishment of my fellow-members, that there should be a daily mail run across these pathless plains and mighty mountains, through the wilderness of the West to the Pacific, with the pathway lined with our enemies the savages of the forest, and where the luxuries and even the necessaries of life in some parts of the route are unknown, the project was not considered possible; and then, when in my position as Chairman of the Post-Office Committee, I proposed that we should vote a million of dollars a year to put that mail across the Continent, members came to me and said "You will ruin yourself." They thought it was monstrous, an unjust and extravagant expenditure. I said to them, though I knew little of the West then compared to what I have learned in the few weeks of this trip, I said, "The people along the line of that route have a right to demand it at your hands, and in their behalf I demand it." Finally the bill was coaxed through, and you have a daily mail running through here, or it would run with almost the regularity of clockwork, were it not for the incursions of these savages. And here let me say, by way of parenthesis, that if I ever had any particular love for "the noble red man," it is pretty much evaporated during this trip. I do not think as much of him as I did. They were looking down from the hills at us, as we have since learned; and had it not been that Mr. Otis and I had our hair cut so short at Atchison, that it would not have paid expenses to be taken even by an Indian, they might have scalped us.

You had a right to this daily mail, and you have it. You had a right, also, to demand, as the eastern portion of this Republic had, telegraphic communication speeding the messages of life and death, of pleasure and of traffic; that the same way should be opened up by that frail wire, the conductor of Jove's thunderbolts, tamed down and harnessed for the use of man. And it fell to my fortune to ask it for you; to ask a subsidy from the government in its aid. It was but hardly obtained; yet, now the grand result is achieved, who regrets it,—who would part with this bond of union and civilization? There was another great interest you had a right to demand. Instead of the slow, toilsome and expensive manner in which you freight your goods and hardware to this distant Territory, you should have a speedy transit between the Missouri valley and this intramontane basin in which you live. Instead of paying two or three prices,—sometimes overrunning the cost of the article,—you should have a railroad communication, and California demanded this. I said, as did many others in Congress, "This is a great national enterprise; we must bind the Atlantic and Pacific States together by bands of iron; we must send the iron horse through all these valleys and mountains of the interior, and when thus interlaced together, we shall be a more compact and homogeneous Republic." And the Pacific Railroad bill passed. This great work of uniting three thousand miles, from shore to shore, is to be consummated, and we hail the day of peace, because with peace we can do many things as a Nation that we cannot do in war. This railroad is to be built, this company is to build it; if they do not, the government will. It shall be put through soon; not toilsomely, slowly, as a far distant event, but as an event of the decade in which we live. * * *

And now, *What has the government a right to demand of you?* It is not that which Napoleon exacts from his officers in France,— which is allegiance to the Constitution and fidelity to the Emperor. Thank God, we have no Emperor nor despot in this country, throned or unthroned. Here, every man has the right, himself, to exercise his elective suffrage as he sees fit, none molesting him or making him afraid. And the duty of every American citizen is condensed in a single sentence, as I said to your committee yesterday,—not in allegiance to an Emperor, but *allegiance to the Constitution, obedience to the laws, and devotion to the Union.* [Cheers.] When you live to *that* standard, you have the right to demand protection; and were you three times three thousand miles from the national capital, wherever the starry banner of the Republic waves and a man stands under it, if his rights of life, liberty and property are assailed, and he has rendered *this* allegiance to his country, it is the duty of the government to reach out its arm, if it take a score of regiments, to protect and uphold him in his rights. [Cheers.]

THE MINES AND THEIR TAXATION.

From Mr. Colfax's *Speech at Virginia City, Nevada, June* 26.

I know that in all these mining regions, there is some distrust and alarm, in regard to the taxation of the mines; and I came here this evening to this balcony, that I might tell you frankly what I believe myself, about this interesting subject, whether it agrees with your views, or does not agree with them,—for I can only speak to you those words that I sincerely believe. I take it for granted, in the first place, that everybody in this broad land has, directly or indirectly, to aid in the payment of our national debt; that debt which has been accumulated for the salvation of our country; a debt which, great as it is, is small in comparison with the value of the great interests which were saved by its incurring. For though it has cost much to save this country, it will prove in the end that it has cost less to save than it would have cost to lose the country. The question is, how shall this burden be adjusted? For it is the duty of the statesman to adjust that burden with equity to all the interests in the land. I came from my home on this long journey, not for pleasure and relaxation alone, but for instruction; that I might see with my own eyes the improvement in the West, the interests and resources of the country on this side of the Continent, its wants and what it had a right to demand of legislation. Having been in the past,—and I do not speak of it boastfully, for I believe you all know what I have done for western interests in the past,—having been in that past a sincere and earnest friend of western interests, I thought that a personal visit to this interesting region of the Republic, now being developed rapidly, and to be developed with tenfold rapidity in the years which are to come, now that peace has returned to our land, might make me a more intelligent and useful friend and advocate of western interests than ever before.

In the first place, I believe in a fable that I read in my younger years, the moral of which was that you should never kill the goose which laid the golden egg. On the contrary, you should encourage the goose to lay more eggs of that kind. [Applause.]

I think that is a principle you will all agree in. We are having an immense immigration from Europe. It was scarcely checked by the war, even with all the threatening of a draft hanging over the immigrant,—a threat which the potentates and powers of Europe published throughout their lands, and had described with exaggerated terrors. The subjects in Europe were told that our country was racked with civil strife, was going down into anarchy and ruin; that the great institutions of American liberty were overthrown, and that we were to be consigned to constant intestine war hereafter. In spite of all these prophecies of evil, immigrants poured in upon us, even during the war, by thousands and tens of thousands. They will come by hundreds of thousands hereafter. They have to go somewhere in this broad land. When they arrive on our shores from overcrowded Europe, they should be pointed to this western realm of country, filled with the precious metals, open for all men to come and prospect and gather for themselves. I want no fetters of restriction placed upon the mining prospector who is willing to pursue his hazardous vocation. On the contrary, I would encourage him, and I would encourage others to come hither and follow his example, by extending every reasonable inducement. And I think we have a precedent in our legislation, which justifies us in throwing open all these lands to whomsoever may choose to come here to dig for silver and for gold. If you will look at the policy of our country, which, after years of stormy contest in Congress, was finally settled in regard to our agricultural lands,—a policy that will never be repealed,—you will find a policy which is the truest and wisest that a great country could adopt in order to have its people tilling the soil, becoming producers of national wealth, adding to our agricultural resources, calling our people away from the crowded cities to make them tillers of the soil of the Republic. That policy is to give them an estate at a nominal price, throwing open our public lands to them, that they may become owners of the soil they till and have a stake in the prosperity of the Nation. That is the great object sought to be obtained, and which is obtained, by the provisions of the homestead law. If that is the just policy in regard to the agricultural lands, it is equally just in regard to the mineral lands. Because the man who goes, enjoying the benefits of the homestead law, to till the soil, is assured of success. He knows, judging by all ordinary calculations, that when he turns over the greensward with his plow and puts in the seed, it will return him ten, twenty or fifty fold. But the miner, on the contrary, knows that his vocation is a hazardous one; and if there should be a priority of benefits to either, I would hold out rather more inducements to the miner upon the mineral lands, than I would to the tiller upon the acres of agricultural lands. [Applause.] But I believe in assimilating the policy. If it is right in the one case it is right in the other, and upon that rock of right I plant myself in that policy. [Applause.]

But the homestead law says that this land shall only be given to the farmer upon condition that he will occupy and improve the land himself. If he abandon the land, he loses it. If he attempts to hold it as a non-resident, he loses it. He must go on and add to the national wealth by his industry; and upon that condition he receives the land at a mere nominal fee for the patent granted to him, after five years occupancy, by the government. That seems to be the correct policy, and that should be the policy in regard to the mineral lands. While the right of discovery and occupancy should be protected by the government, when mineral discoveries, or what are supposed to be such, are abandoned, they should not be held to the exclusion of those who might be willing to work the abandoned claims. That is a doctrine which is based upon the principles of justice, I think.

Now, my friends, in regard to taxation, I have precedents which will be familiar to you when I quote them. And I speak of these things because I would, as far as possible, impress on your minds those precedents, as I believe them to be right, and that your senators, and that your representatives may place your claims and your demands in the Capital at Washington, not upon the basis of a bonus to the miner, but upon the basis of justice as compared with other interests in the land. Let us examine the principles of the tax bill which we have framed. I know that it is a heavy and onerous tax bill. Nothing in the shape of a tax bill is calculated to be popular. Government can never get that class of bills exactly correct; and I would not claim that this one is exactly correct, although I believe it is as nearly equal in its burdens as possible. In that tax bill you will see illustrated the policy of Congress, which has been to put the tax as far away as possible from the first production of the soil. Let us take, for instance, the article of wood. There is nothing in the tax bill levying a tax on wood growing in the forest or cut down by the forester; but when the wood is manufactured into a buggy, into a wagon, into cabinet-ware, or into any other kind of work made of wood, then the tax accrues for the first time upon the manufactured article, whatever it may be, and not until then. It is so with wool. There is no tax in the national tax law on the wool upon the sheep's back; there is no tax upon it after it is clipped from the sheep's back and packed up in bales in the store of the wool merchant or sheep raiser. But when the wool is manufactured into woolen goods, then it is taxed,—not until then. The same principle applies to tobacco, which I presume you know is very heavily taxed. Now, I don't suppose that any of you drink whiskey. [Laughter and cries of "No, no!" "never!"] But if you do drink whiskey,—which I don't,—you will realize that every glass of whiskey which you drink and pay for, contributes a portion to the revenues of the general government, whether you like it or not. Now I take all my vice out,—(I think every man is guilty of at least one vice,—I don't believe there are any perfect men,—I believe the ladies are about all perfect, Heaven's last best gift to man, but I believe that all men are addicted to one vice or another)—I take my vice out in tobacco, in smoking. I take my cigar, and have the satisfaction of thinking that by every one I smoke I am aiding somewhat in the support of the general government. If any of you take patent medicines, you are entitled to feel the same interest and satisfaction in the operation. [Laughter.] You will see on the outside label a stamp of from two to four cents. So much is contributed to the general government from that particular source. But, to resume seriously: There is no tax upon tobacco in the leaf, nor is there any tax upon the corn out of which the whiskey is made. When the corn is manufactured into whiskey, then the government puts the tax on the whiskey. When the tobacco is manufactured into cigars or plug, then the tax is put on. This is the policy of the general government in this respect. There is only one exception to it. That is cotton. Cotton is taxed when it is produced in the field. There is a reason for that. Cotton used to be king. We concluded that we would see if we could not in this Republic dare to tax the king. That is the only exception in the tax law. In every other case the tax is put away from the produce until the article is manufactured or ready for consumption.

You understand already what I am going to say to you. That is just my theory in regard to the taxation of the precious metals. Don't embarrass the men who are taking the precious metals out of the mines; but when these metals are assayed, when they enter as bullion or coin into the monetary wealth of the country, then they will be taxed, and then they should be taxed, and then, whether you like it or not, they must be taxed. [Great applause.] I think that is the true basis to put this whole question upon in Congress, and, presented in that way, I believe that you can command success and that regard for your interests which you need and justly require.

THE PACIFIC RAILROAD.

From MR. COLFAX'S *Speech at Virginia City, Nevada, June* 26.

A VOICE.—"How about the Pacific Railroad?"

In regard to the Pacific Railroad, I can only turn to my record on that subject. I believe the Pacific Railroad to be a national and political and military necessity. I believe that there should be a railroad binding this great Continent together with its iron bands. It is riveted and banded together now by mountain and river and plain, upon which are written: "What God has joined together let no man put asunder." And when the tide of immigration poured across these Plains and made these States of the Pacific Coast, looking out over the slope of the Sierras across the Pacific Ocean to the birthplace of mankind, the Continent of Asia, I believed it was our duty, the duty of those of us living in the older States, to make the means of transit between the Pacific and Atlantic States not a slow and toilsome journey by ox or horse or mule team, but by the iron horse that we have in all other portions of the land. Years and years ago, before there was a Pacific Railroad bill passed in Congress, I was its earnest advocate. When men talked about the amount of money that would have to be paid by the general government in the building of a line of road, I said that was not an iota in the balance in comparison with its national benefits. Since that time the necessity for it has been enhanced. It is needed for the development of this mineral wealth. Go with me to Austin, where I saw their seams of silver with my own eyes. There are mines there which would be sources of wealth on either side of the Sierra Nevadas. Many of them, besides those now being worked, could be developed, but cannot be now. Why? Because of their distance from their base of supplies; because of the great cost of freight,—of machinery. But when we have a Pacific Railroad opening to this vast interior region, with all its enormous resources, then the mining pioneers of our country will be able to work with great profit the mineral lands which cannot now be worked at all. It will pay back to our national treasury far more than the bonus which may be given to aid in the construction of such a railroad or railroads; it will add to our national wealth; besides being a bond of union, firm as the eternal hills, over which the tracks will run. And I believe that it is about to come, and come rapidly, if continued peace enables us to devote the energies of the country to it.

THE REPUBLIC AND PEACE—THE MEXICAN QUESTION.

From MR. COLFAX'S *Speech at San Francisco, July* 8.

So much for the past and present of our country. Now, what of its future? Providence hides destiny from individuals.

"Heaven from all creatures hides the book of Fate;
All but the page prescribed,—the present state."

But Nations can predict their destiny for themselves. It is beyond the limit of mortal conception to compass the grandeur of the future of our Nation, if prudence guides its course. Napoleon has said in his day, after a bloody war, that his empire was peace; we can more truly say that this Republic is peace. Peace is the mission of Freedom, and Freedom is the primal principle of the American Republic. It is not by the glory and triumphs of aggressive war that its destiny is to be realized, but by peace.

I am here among you people of California apparently a welcome guest. You have placed full confidence in my honesty of purpose, and I would not appear before you to speak only those words which you would applaud, when I really differed from you. I know how you feel on the Monroe Doctrine and driving out Maximilian. [Tremendous applause.] I do not agree with you on these subjects; I will be frank with you. I am opposed to war for any purpose, or for any cause, except for the vindication of the national honor, or the salvation of the Union. [Applause.] I am for such a war, if it should occupy four, ten or forty years; but to war in any other cause, that can be honorably avoided, I am opposed. You people of California have not seen the horrors and desolations of war around your own doors; you have not seen the hundreds and thousands of friends, neighbors and countrymen torn, mangled, dead and dying on the cold earth moistened by their blood; you have not seen the long string of ambulances carrying the mangled, groaning, suffering thousands as they have been carried to the hospitals to die, or to suffer mutilation even worse than death, that cause vigorous, industrious men to become burdens on society for life; you have not seen and could not have heard of half the horrors of war. Oh, it is a fearful thing to rush into war, except for the preservation of one's country. Such a war is as sacred as the war against the Saracens to save the sepulchre of the Savior from the pollution of the Infidel. I am for no war with any Nation, if that war can by any honorable statesmanship be avoided, even if by saying so I shall be driven into private life. I am a believer in the justice and patriotism and republicanism of the Monroe Doctrine. [Tremendous applause.] But I am not for war with France and England on that question now, with its renewed destruction of our commerce; its rivers of blood, and its millions of added debt. I want the Pacific Railroad built, instead of the laurels of victory on fields of carnage and of death. I want the progress and blessings of peace, instead of more hecatombs of piled up dead, and hundreds of millions more of debt. I want the prosperity and developments of peace. I do not object to the principles of the Monroe Doctrine. I admire the courage and patriotism of Juarez and his patriot bands in defence of their native land. I do not think Maximilian is the rightful ruler of Mexico. [Enthusiastic applause.] But I object to rushing into a foreign war ere we have scarcely ended our domestic one, to drive him out. I believe that diplomacy can effect the purpose better. Time may settle it for us, if we are but patient and firm. When you have a President in the chair, who is such a believer in the Monroe Doctrine as Mr. Johnson, whose sentiments expressed in the Senate of the Nation on this question, leave us in no doubt where he stands. Trust him, then, to effect this object. His patriotism no one can doubt. Faithful among the faithless, he stood by his country when every other southern senator faltered or deserted.

Remember that his chief adviser is W. H. Seward, whom God has spared from the bloody harvest of the assassins who thought to gather the lives of six of the truest in the land, but reaped with their murderous sickle but one. Trust him! His diplomacy has more than once saved the country from a foreign war, and will solve this question successfully without war. We are strong enough as a Nation to gain our own ends without wars. Let us stand by and trust in the government, in Johnson, in Seward, in Stanton and their faithful associates, and all will be well. [Applause.]

CALIFORNIA'S PAST AND FUTURE.

From MR. COLFAX'S *Speech at San Francisco, July 8.*

You, as a people, are most deeply interested in the future progress and prosperity of our common country. Less than twenty years ago,—and what a little time it appears,—this great city of San Francisco was not; its site was scarcely known. But gold was discovered, and hither came adventurous pioneers with their caravans, laden, not with the spices and perfume of Asia, nor like the caravans of the Indies, with their wealth, but with their wives, children, and household goods, wending their way over the sandy deserts, or scaling craggy passes through the mighty mountain ranges that separate you from your sister States on the Atlantic side of the Continent. These were men of energy and of iron will; and it needs both to travel two thousand miles over such a country, and to brave the blood-thirsty savages on the way. They were men of faith, tried in the ordeal of adversity, and profited by its lessons. It was such men who founded your State, it was such men that saved it from the grasp of slavery, which its advocates had already fastened upon it. It was by their means that she entered the glorious sisterhood of States, clothed in the golden robes of Freedom. If with such a foundation, with the example of such men before you, you are but true to yourselves, it is beyond the power of language to picture the glory of your future. Your city is destined to become the New York of the Pacific, commanding much of the trade of China, Japan, India, Australia, Mexico, South and Central America, while your store of mineral wealth, and the richness and variety of your grain and fruit, and the energy and enterprise of your people, must make your future great and glorious. Then the interest taken in the departures of your semi-monthly steamers, will be lost in the continued daily departures of many to all parts of the globe. And now, as I say to you good-night, let us all rejoice together, that, from Orient to Occident; from sea to sea; from the Atlantic seaboard, where the masts of our commerce are like the trees of the forest, across valley and river, over the vast mountains that lift their mighty forms as sentinel watch-towers of our inheritance; to the Golden Gate; from the frozen North to the sunny South, we have now, and shall have in all the coming centuries, but one Nation, one Constitution, one Flag, and one glorious Destiny!

AMERICA AND BRITAIN.

From MR. COLFAX'S *Speech at Victoria, Vancouver's Island, July* 27.

You have given me a welcome that is truly gratifying. I see around me not only American citizens, but the officials, civil and military, and the subjects of that great and good woman, Queen Victoria. Although I am a republican in every sinew and fiber, I never think of her without my heart flowing with gratitude. When our country was in imminent peril, and when Great Britain and America, the representatives of a common lineage, a common language, and, if such it can be called, a common religion, were almost embroiled in mortal conflict on the Trent difficulty, Queen Victoria stepped in and demanded of her ministers that the character of their missives should be conciliatory; that it should not be repulsive to the United States, but should enable the American people to comply with the request without any sacrifice of honor. On that occasion she proved her wisdom, her sagacity, and her kindness. * * * * * *

I know there are difficulties between the United States and Nations on the other side of the Atlantic, but these can be safely confided to the sagacity and wisdom of the respective governments. We Americans should never forget, so long as we speak the same tongue, how much we owe to the people of the British Isles,—in science and art; in history and literature; in poesy and song. We claim an equal share in the fame of Shakespeare and Milton, Cowper and Pope, Gibbon and Macaulay, Newton and Rosse. * * *

The people of Great Britain respect the memory of Wilberforce. I think it was Macaulay who said of that great man, when he ascended to the judgment-seat of God, that he held in his hands the shackles of a hundred thousand of his fellow-beings. We had another name hallowed in all our memories, and never to be forgotten in connection with the emancipation of the slaves,—the name of a great and good and kind-hearted man,—Abraham Lincoln,—who, taking the helm of State, never despaired of our great Republic, proving himself the faithful and indomitable pilot, steering through good and ill the Ship of State. While he stood at the helm, he was the greatest and purest and best in the land; and when he went above, he took with him the fetters of a down-trodden and oppressed race, which no power on God's footstool could ever again place on their enfranchised limbs. The whole civilized world now sees that when ingrates and rebels lit the torch of civil war, they also lit the funeral pyre of the institution of slavery. Let me not be misunderstood; I believe that this war will open a new era for the genial and fertile land of the South. The honorable gentleman here sketched in glowing language the peculiar advantages of the South, saying that it held three great keys of the country,—Hampton Roads, the keys of Florida and New Orleans; and that, with free and paid labor to replace that enforced system of labor which had been a blight to mankind,—for with Lamartine he believed that God never allowed a chain to be bound round the limbs of the slaves, without forging the other end round the neck of the oppressor,—the fortunes of the country would again be in the ascendant. If our people were only faithful to themselves, to their institutions, to the country, they would merit and attain to the grandest destiny that lay in the womb of time for any Nation on the globe. Instead of thirty-six stars, a whole galaxy of blazing orbs would spangle that glorious field of blue. The star of Washington Territory,—that only Territory that has been named after the great and immortal statesman,—would shine there; the stars of Idaho, of Montana, of Colorado, of all the Territories, would shine on that glorious flag, and all these noble States would revolve round the central government as one central sur — distinct as the billows, but one as the sea!

FAREWELL SPEECH,

At the Parting Banquet in San Francisco, September 1.

Ladies and Gentlemen:—The brevity that an occasion like this commands, impels me to omit much that rises before my mind as I stand before you. But the kind and generous hospitalities of which we have been the recipients, culminating in this brilliant testimonial, which is at once a reception and a farewell, and the very cordial and complimentary address to which I have just listened, forbid that I should remain entirely silent.

Just two months ago, after journeying over thousands of miles of mountains and valleys and deserts and plains, your honored Mayor, and a Committee of your Supervisors met us in the cabin of the steamer "Chrysopolis," and gave us an official welcome to this seven-hilled city. Since then, in all our travels upon this Coast, we have been accustomed to speak of San Francisco as a home. And now, though I came here a stranger and a traveler, I feel like one who is indeed about to leave his home and hearthstone. [Applause.]

When on Saturday morning, I sail out through the Golden Gate upon the broad ocean, and see headland and cliff recede from view, I shall feel, as now, the inward struggle between the joy with which I think of the home and the many friends of many years, and the regret with which I leave the home I hope I have in the hearts of new friends here.

Our party came hither to learn, by actual observation, more of this Pacific portion of the Republic, its resources and its wants; and you can testify that the grass has not grown under our feet. We have seen your varieties of mining,—placer, hydraulic and quartz. We have seen many of your rich agricultural valleys,—the Sacramento, San Joaquin, San Jose, Petaluma, Russian River Napa, Sonoma, Alameda, and others. We have traveled on nearly every mile of your two hundred to three hundred miles of railroads, closing with the delightful excursion to-day on the Alameda Railroad, for which we were indebted to its president, Mr. Cohen. We have visited, or passed through, over half of your cities and towns. We have enjoyed visits to your great national curiosities, the world-renowned Yosemite Valley, to be visited by thousands hereafter, instead of scores, if California, by wise legislation, appreciates the gift of it from the general government,—the Big Trees, the Geysers, and your neighbors, the Sea Lions.

We have examined, with interest, many of your manufactures, and reared as I was, in the school of Henry Clay, to believe in American manufactures, I am prouder of the suit in which I am clothed to-night, of California cloth, from wool on the back of California sheep, woven by the Mission Woolen Mills, and made here, than of the finest suit of French broadcloth I ever owned. [Applause.] I would urge you, in these last words, to foster manufactures, which are the backbone of national or State prosperity and independence. Even if they should not be profitable as a pecuniary investment, every triumph of mechanical or manufacturing industry here, is another spoke in the wheel of your progress. Develop and foster commerce on your great Pacific sea; for Raleigh spoke truly when he said, "Those who command the sea, command the trade of the world; those who command the trade of the world, command the riches of the world, and thus command the world itself." [Applause.]

But the moments sweep by, and I must not detain you longer. There have been weary hours in all this incessan' journeying, but they have been happy and golden hours, too; happy, because full-freighted with hospitality and feasts to the eye and the mind; golden, because filled with recollections that will never die; friendships never to be forgotten till this heart ceases to beat; affectionate regards more priceless than the wealth of Ormuz and the Ind; and memories enshrined in the soul forever. [Applause.]

Hoping I have a happy God speed from you all on the long journey before me, I must now say farewell,—no, not farewell, for that seems for life, and

"Farewell, farewell, is a lonely sound
   That always brings a sigh;
   But give me rather, when true friends part,
   That good old word, good-bye."

And thus, to friends of other years, whom I have met here so happily again, and to the newer friends I have found in your midst, I bid you, one and all, not a life-long but a regretful Good-Bye.

IV.

IDAHO AND ITS MINES.

WITH AN ACCOUNT OF THE OVERLAND JOURNEY FROM OREGON TO SALT LAKE CITY.

THE following letter concerning Idaho Territory, its mines and miners, and the routes through it, was written for the Editor of this Volume by a distinguished and intelligent citizen of Oregon, who has just traveled leisurely through that country, and properly completes the observations and information as to the Pacific States and Territories, which the book has undertaken to give. The letter will be found very interesting, and its facts are reliable :—

SALT LAKE CITY, October 1, 1865.

The route from Oregon to Salt Lake, through Idaho, a distance of over eight hundred miles, presents occasional rare scenic views and interesting objects. We left The Dalles, at the eastern slope of the Cascade Mountains, in the gray of early morning, and a ride of thirteen miles over Oregon's longest railroad, at the base of towering rocky bluffs which there line the southern bank of the Columbia, along the narrow gorges of the river, worn deep into the hard basalt, sometimes so near the edge as to reveal the dark surface of the river, far down below; then so closely to the mountain bluff that it seemed to overhang and threaten with its fall,—brought us to Celilo, the depot of the Oregon Steam Navigation Company's (conveniently abbreviated to O. S. N. Co.) boats on the Upper Columbia. Here we were transferred to one of their comfortable steamers, in which we made the trip to Wallula, a distance of one hundred and twenty-three miles, much of the way against a strong current, in about twenty hours. The country along this portion of the river is I the main uninviting. It consists of bald and mostly barren hills, or sandy flats. Here and there along the way, on either side, at long intervals are small streams putting into the river, and draining proportionately small valleys, upon which are scattered settlements. But the great surface of the country is unoccupied and unsusceptible of settlement.

At Wallula we took seats in the stage for Walla Walla, the site of the old fort of that name, and a pleasant, thrifty town of fifteen hundred or two thousand inhabitants. A disastrous fire had, a few weeks before, swept away near one-half of the village, but it was rapidly being rebuilt. This region has in former years been the scene of Indian troubles, and Walla Walla is a point of historic interest with officers of the old army. Probably half of their number have sometime visited the post, while not a few have been stationed there, and have participated in the Indian wars the surrounding country has been the theater of.

The valley of the Walla Walla consists of uplands, valuable for grazing, but too arid for cultivation, interspersed with bottoms or low-lands, mostly farmed without irrigation, and some of which are of surpassing fertility. The corn, small grains, root crops, melons, squashes, etc., which were growing or standing harvested upon the ground, might be safely compared with the richest productions of the Mississippi valley. But these lands are limited, and the best portion of them claimed, and, where for sale, held at high figures for a new country.

The country along the route from Wallula comprises little but alkali plains, covered with sage brush, with an occasional fertile spot, upon which usually is located a stage station, and cultivated a bountiful garden. This region, like all that east of the Cascade range, is exempt from the winter rains of western Oregon and California. The winters are dry and cold, though much milder and accompanied with less snow than in like latitudes east of the Rocky Mountains.

At Walla Walla, going east, is commenced the overland stage ride. This is the starting point proper of Thomas & Ruckel's stages for the Boise mining region, connecting there with Holladay's line for Salt Lake and Missouri River. The distance from Walla Walla to Boise City is about three hundred and fifty miles. Another line of stages leaves the Columbia at Umatilla Rapids, twenty-two miles below Wallula, connecting at Uniontown, situated at the southern end of Grand Ronde valley. Messrs. Thomas & Ruckel have constructed a road across the Blue Mountains, over which their stages pass. It is new, in perfect repair, and one of the best mountain roads upon the Continent. A ride upon it over the Blue range is surpassingly grand, and an event to be remembered and enjoyed for a lifetime. Sometimes you pass high up along the very edge of a deep ravine, where a capsize on the wrong side would precipitate you hundreds of feet into the rocky gorge below; again, you are upon a lofty mountain top, where the scenery, as far as vision can reach, is as wild and beautiful as eye ever rested upon; then you are in the bottom of a deep gorge, where mountains above you covered with immense forests tower almost out of sight; now you find yourself in a natural park, stretching miles away, studded with bright yellow pines and carpeted with luxuriant grass. Thus the panorama is ever changing, ever inspiringly grand and enchanting.

The first day's ride brought us to the Warm Springs, where the proprietors of the stage line are erecting a substantial hotel and other buildings suited to a watering and bathing place. Here are three springs of sulphur water, of just the right temperature for bathing, gushing out from the rocky sides of the mountain. In one of them I enjoyed a delightful bath, and here I found some rheumatic acquaintances being cured of their malady by the healing virtues of the medicinal waters which nature has so lavishly provided.

The Blue are often pronounced "the best mountains in America;" the most gradual of ascent, with the best soil, grass and timber. Upon their highest summits, where the timber is not too thick to permit their growth, the finest quality and greatest quantity of natural grasses are found.

The second day's ride took us through the Grand Ronde valley, a beautiful, level tract of country, from forty to fifty miles in length and twenty or thirty in width, surrounded on every side with mountains. It is a pleasant spot to look upon, but too much elevated for general agricultural value. For years the emigrant to Oregon has passed through this valley on his weary way to the Willamette. Occasionally a late party would winter here, on account of the abundant grass, and resume their journey in the spring. But all were deterred from settling by the long winters and late and early frosts. Since the discovery of gold in Idaho, the only line of travel from the West and North has been through this valley. This gives a high value to the hay which, in lavish abundance, is cut here. Consequently many, who in former years passed neglectfully through here, returned and settled in Grande Ronde. But they will be compelled to depend mainly upon their herds and hay, for the late springs and early falls render the production of anything else difficult and uncertain. We passed through in early September, and the country had already been visited with a light snow, and frosts so heavy that all tender vegetation was completely killed. Fields of wheat were green and unharvested.

Passing out of the Grand Ronde through the only "gap" in the surrounding hills, we enter Powder River Valley, less in size than Grand Ronde, and nearly valueless for farming or grazing. A few settlers are found here, but the valley is mostly destitute of grass, and covered with sage brush. In this valley, yet in Oregon, we stopped a day to visit the Rockfellow gold mine, owned by Colonel Ruckel. It is seven miles from the stage road, a quartz mine, exclusively gold-bearing, and of a very high grade of fineness. The product coins over nineteen dollars per ounce. It is apparently a very rich mine, and, so far as indications point, of probable permanency. It is pretty well opened, and is being successfully worked under the superintendence of Captain Laban Coffin, an old Massachusetts skipper, from Nantucket, I believe; at any rate, from some bleak country down that way.

Farther on, and over a generally barren country, we cross Snake River at Old's Ferry,—the proposed starting point of the Oregon Steam Navigation Company's new line of steamers, which are expected to ascend the river from there two hundred miles,—and are in Idaho. A continued ride over a similarly valueless country, spotted with indifferent ranches, about thickly enough for stage stations, and we reach Boise City. Time from Walla Walla, two and a half days; fare, sixty dollars, coin, except upon "opposition days," when it is forty dollars.

Here ends the Thomas & Ruckel Stage Line. The proprietors are characters and powers in this country. George F. Thomas is of Irish extraction, if not of birth. He may not know whether the latter or not; certainly he doesn't care. Formerly he was a knight of the whip in Georgia. Drifting to California, with the early adventurers to that country, after the discovery of gold, he became a large stockholder in the California Stage Company, and was for some years its Vice-President. In that capacity he established the line from Sacramento to Portland in Oregon, residing in the latter State the while. Upon the discovery of gold in Idaho in 1862, he sold his interest and resigned his position in the California Company, and removed to Walla Walla, from whence he ran stages, as the constantly shifting tide of mining travel demanded. Afterwards, Colonel Ruckel joining him, they extended their line to Boise City, constructing, at a heavy outlay, the Blue Mountain road. He is a sensible, whole-souled, hospitable "Irish gentleman," fond of a quiet glass, a good story or joke, and said to be the best judge of the horse on the Pacific Coast. Colonel J. S. Ruckel went early from New York to California, and thence to Oregon, without means, but with great resources in business ability and energy. Alone, unaided, he constructed the first railroad in the Territory, along the Cascades, and built the "Mountain Buck," which was among the first steamers to navigate the waters of the Columbia. Afterwards he merged railroad and steamboat in the Oregon Steam Navigation Company, a corporate body with two millions capital stock, and owning all the steamers and controlling all the business of the Columbia River. He became a prominent member of the company, for some time its Superintendent, and lastly its President. He has now left it, however, and is devoting his wealth and energy to mining and staging.

Idaho Territory has an area of one hundred and twenty-five thousand square miles, and is bounded on the north and east by British Columbia and Montana, south by Utah and Nevada, and west by Oregon and Washington. Idaho is an Indian word, signifying "the gem of the mountains." It was chosen by the early gold hunters as an appropriate name for the embryo State in the mountains, then extending both sides of the Rocky range. But a comparatively small portion of its vast surface is susceptible of tillage, and mining must ever continue its principal interest. The population of the Territory is now probably about twenty-five thousand. It has been more; but as the richest placer diggings are exhausted, other and richer localities are sought. About half of this population has been contributed by Oregon; the remaining half must be about equally divided between California and Nevada, and the States east of the mountains. In the mountains a great depth of snow falls in the winter; but the climate is milder than in like latitudes and altitudes on the Atlantic side.

Boise City, the capital of the Territory, is, for a mining region, a substantial, steady-going little town. It contains some ten or twelve hundred inhabitants, comprising a number of families, and affording tolerable society. It is the depot for all the mining region so far discovered in southern Idaho. Here are some large stocks of mining goods, and here, and through here, all the mining towns and camps obtain or receive their supplies. There are no mines immediately about the town, nor, indeed, nearer than twenty-five miles. It is located upon the west bank of the Boise River, a moderate stream which marks a fertile but narrow valley, in which nearly all the grain and vegetables, thus far raised in southern Idaho, are produced. This product, however, does comparatively little towards supplying the miners. The bulk comes from Oregon, with an occasional venture of salt and vegetables from Utah.

Idaho City is some thirty-five miles north of Boise City, and you are taken there in the stages of Henry Greathouse, a brother of Ridgley Greathouse, who was convicted at San Francisco of attempting to fit out a pirate vessel, discharged under the amnesty proclamation of Mr. Lincoln, afterwards re-arrested, taken to New York and confined in Fort Lafayette, from which he made his escape and fled to Europe, where he now is. His brother, Henry, is understood to hold southern sympathies, but never talks of public affairs. He is a quiet, hard-working man, drives a coach himself, when necessary, and has accumulated a good deal of money. The town is situated in what is termed the "Boise Basin," between Moore and Elk Creeks, branches of Boise River, and is the largest town in the Territory. It is in the midst of an important placer district, and contains from five to seven thousand inhabitants, on week days, and from ten to fifteen thousand on Sundays. For Sunday is a populous and profitable day with a mining town. On that day all the miners for miles around visit the town to purchase supplies, exchange greetings, gamble, guzzle, and indulge in the dissipations of mining metropolitan life. Idaho City, seen on Sunday, is a very different town from the Idaho City of any other day. There is no store, shop or business place of any character closed on that day. It is altogether the busiest of the week with shopkeepers, victualers, gamblers and whiskey dispensers.

Idaho City is built in and over the mines, and one-third or one-half of the buildings in the place have been already mined under; nearly all undoubtedly will be. In a mining country the miner is king, and his will is the law. If he finds "pay dirt" under a house, he locates and records his claim, and commences to undermine it, without saying "by your leave" to owner or occupant. Of course, as he digs, he props up the building so that it may not fall upon his head; that secure, he troubles himself no further. When a claim is worked out, he leaves it without filling under or further propping up the house. If it falls, it concerns not him. The city or territorial authorities have enacted laws forbidding the undermining of buildings without making them permanently secure from fall. But the miners elect the officers and compose the juries that administer the law; it is unnecessary to add, the miner wins the suit. Several have been commenced and prosecuted, but with no other result. The same is the case with regard to the streets; where the miner's claim leads across, up or down one, across, up or down he goes, wherever "pay dirt" points, and the public can repair or abandon the road, as they find most convenient or profitable.

About two months prior to our visit, Idaho City had been almost entirely destroyed by fire, occasioning an estimated loss of one million five hundred thousand dollars. Already the town had been rebuilt with a better class of wood buildings than before, interspersed with a number of brick blocks. The recuperative energies of a flourishing mining town are extraordinary.

The "Boise Basin," as it is called, is a sink or depression in the mountains; higher mountains surrounding constitute the basin's "rim." I do not know the extent of the basin, but should think it to be from thirty to forty miles in length, and perhaps a little less in width. Over this are scattered placer mines of varying extent and richness, the most important of which are those in the vicinity of Idaho City. There are, however, other placers and other towns of consequence, not far distant, in the surrounding country. One of the latter bears the euphonious name of "Hog 'em," said to have been derived from the swinish propensities of its early proprietor.

These placer mines are of considerable extent, and more than fair productiveness. They are of three classes: the first and richest being the "Creek diggings," comprising the bed of the creek and its low banks; the next and less productive, though yielding from ten dollars to fifteen dollars per day to each miner when supplied with water, includes the higher bank; the third consists of hill diggings beyond, still poorer, but paying for working when water can be had. The Creek diggings, best and longest supplied with water, have been generally worked out, and, of course, with them has gone the cream of the mines. An unusual rise of Moore and Elk Creeks last spring brought down the "tailings" from the mountains, and buried the claims below ten or twelve feet deep, and all summer the miner has been compelled to "strip" this surface off before being able to work his claim. The bench and hill diggings, with here and there the exception of a gulch, down which the melting snows have poured torrents, remain generally undisturbed. They depend mainly upon the melting snows and spring rise for water. The consequence is, the mining season for anything but Creek diggings is short, not exceeding two or three months of each year.

We were in the Basin in the month of September, the dull season. Probably at that time ten thousand persons were employed in placer mining. In the spring the number has heretofore been larger, and will again be, if other excitements and discoveries do not further draw off the population. Already, it was said two thousand persons had left for the Blackfeet Mines, and if the reports of rich discoveries there were confirmed, a stampede in the spring was predicted.

I have no means of ascertaining accurately the product of the Idaho gold mines. The known amount deposited for coinage in the San Francisco mint for the year ending December, 1864, was reported at three million five hundred thousand dollars; and San Francisco estimate placed the total amount for that year at six million dollars. That is probably not above the actual product. But mining there is, as everywhere else, a precarious business, a life of excitement, and not seldom non-success. A few acquire sudden riches; the many make a living.

In and around the Boise Basin are many gold-bearing quartz leads, some thought to be rich and extensive, but few, if any, yet fully proved to be so. Several mills are at work upon some of them, but none that we saw are so far developed as to satisfactorily demonstrate their richness. Among the apparently promising leads we visited were three lying near together in the Summit Flat District, distant some fifteen or eighteen miles from Idaho City. They are called the ' Mammoth," " King," and " Specimen" Ledges, and are owned by Messrs. Jackson, Humason and Bibb. They are gold mines only, and not extensively developed; yet reasonably promising so far as they have been worked. There has been an eight-stamp water-mill running upon the ore of one of them for a year, and, from the proceeds of it, they had purchased and were erecting a ten-stamp steam-mill, expecting to have it running by the beginning of winter. They were without capital, except as they dug it from the mine, and were therefore compelled to work slowly. The country about the Flat is liberally supplied with water and timber, which makes working the mines easier and cheaper.

South Boise, distant about sixty miles, is a more recent discovery, and is thought to be richer in quartz than the Basin. The discoveries there are mostly silver.

The Owyhee mines are situated in the mountains of that name, about sixty miles south of Boise City, to reach which you are compelled to pass over the worst alkali road in Idaho. There is a line of stages running there from Boise City. We found two little towns, Ruby and Silver Cities, extending more than a mile along the narrow gulch in which are limited placer mines. The Owyhee mines are almost wholly silver-producing, and there can be little doubt that the district is, as a whole, rich in this metal. There are some valuable ledges there, and many worthless ones; some honest and some bogus, wild-cat companies. The only mine which has been fully proven rich is the "Oro Fino," and, perhaps, the "Morning Star," owned by Moore & Fogus. Upon the first ledge they have excavated a tunnel six hundred feet long, and sunk a connecting shaft, also upon the ledge, over one hundred feet. All the way they find it rich and wide, and improving in both respects as they go in and down. On the "Morning Star," they have sunk a shaft about one hundred feet, and thus far find the ledge yielding well.

There are doubtless many other valuable ledges there, but none have been so fully tested. Some New York companies are putting up large mills, and twenty or thirty are on the way. Some ledges, little prospected, may prove rich. Others, doubtless, will be found worthless. Some interests, valuable and valueless, are claimed by those who have failed to comply with the mining laws of the Territory, and consequently they have no title. Many were talking about going East to sell their mines, and, if they can raise the passage money, a goodly number will be in the eastern cities before long, with Idaho mines and mining stock for sale. Some of this species of property will be genuine; much of it will possess no known or probable value. Purchasers should be well assured of the standing and repute of parties with whom they deal and upon whose representations they rely. If not, they had better personally inspect, or employ some reliable agent to do so, before they purchase mining property.

The Owyhee district is sparsely supplied with wood, and water is not abundant. There will be fuel enough for some years, but if the district proves as rich as it is expected to, it must become exhausted at no very distant period. Probably before that time coal will be discovered.

Illustrative of mining life are the experiences and conditions of some acquaintances I found in Idaho. One was an excellent gentleman, a lawyer of learning and ability, who once held an important appointment connected with the United States courts of one of the Pacific States. He is a graduate of Harvard, son of a wealthy Bostonian, who desires him to travel. In pursuance of such request, accompanied with unlimited letters of credit, he spent last fall and winter at the Sandwich Islands. Now he was in the Boise Mines, in miner's garb, with pick and shovel, hard at work upon a not over-remunerative claim.

Another acquaintance had, in years agone, fallen heir to a sawmill in California, by the death of a brother. The mill soon in-

SUPPLEMENTARY PAPERS: IDAHO. 427

volved him beyond his ability to pay, and was sold, leaving him in debt. He remained in that unpleasant condition until the spring of 1863, when, with a small steam saw-mill that he could have almost packed upon a wagon, he went to Idaho City. I met him last month, just on the eve of leaving for the Atlantic States with fifty-five thousand dollars in gold.

A third I had known in early times on the Pacific Coast as a man of wealth. In dissipation he had squandered the most of it. Going early to Boise he soon made another "raise," and was worth forty or fifty thousand dollars n gold. Now he was "flat broke." Cards, whiskey and women were the rocks upon which he had a second time wrecked. The son of a New England deacon, and graduate of a New England orthodox Sabbath school, was keeping a stylish drinking saloon, and living with a commercial miss, with whom, owing to the scarcity of clergymen or other persons qualified to perform the service, he had never married. When I meet his relatives they always inquire after his welfare, and, anxiously, if "he continues to love the Lord and grow in grace."

A leading clergyman of a popular denomination built a church at Idaho City, and occasionally preached in it on Sunday; and being engaged in merchandising, it was said his clerks kept his store open, the while. At the time we were there, preaching had been suspended and the church rented to the United States for a court-room; and the only time we visited it, Chief Justice McBride was trying a murderer therein.

Captain Fiske relates finding in Idaho a Mr. Murphy, who endeavored to sell him a mine he owned for twelve thousand five hundred dollars. Captain Fiske declined to buy, and, a few months after, Murphy sold the property to New York capitalists for one hundred and seventy-five thousand dollars. A few weeks before I was at Owyhee, an acquaintance, in company with another, discovered a silver lead. He sold his half for eleven hundred dollars. While we were there, one-fifth of the same half was sold for thirty thousand dollars, gold. A friend who, burnt out by fire and washed out by flood, became bankrupt in the Willamette Valley, went to Boise in 1862 or '63. Now he is joint owner in four stores and stocks of goods, a fast freight and passenger stage line near four hundred miles long, a large hotel, and much other property. A good many others, who went there in indigent circumstances, I also found had "held their own" remarkably.

The stage line from Boise City to Salt Lake, three hundred and seventy miles,—fare one hundred dollars, gold,—is owned by Ben Holladay. It traverses a barren country, covered with the interminable sage, and inhabited only by coyotes and wolves. We pass within two miles of the celebrated and not long ago discovered Falls of Snake River, greater than those of Niagara, but could not visit them without remaining over a day, and running the risk of finding a crowded coach on the morrow. Unless I shall some time chance to pass that way again, I shall never cease to regret that we did not remain and visit that world-wonder. A little farther on, at the last crossing of the south fork of the Columbia, we found quite a large river abruptly bursting from out a mountain side. It ran, cold and clear, a short distance, and added its waters to those of the Snake.

The Boise end of this road has sometimes been visited by "road agents," as highwaymen are called in the mines. They infest all the roads leading from Boise. The day before we left Boise City, the stage-coach was robbed by them. Among the passengers was a miner with eight thousand dollars in gold, the savings of two years' labor in the mines. He had been in town several days, inquiring whether it was safest to go to the States by way of Walla Walla or Salt Lake. Probably his inquiries led to the robbery of that particular coach by some villains of the town. They usually go in parties of about a half dozen, disguised and armed with double-barreled shot-guns, and, springing suddenly from an ambush, rarely fail to succeed in stopping the coach and robbing the passengers. If resistance is not made, they do not usually add murder to their crime. When their depredations become frequent, the community generally rise and hunt them like wolves, shooting and hanging them wherever found. Order then succeeds, as long as the fright continues. These depredations become every year less frequent, and the danger is not now considered great.

These vast sage plains! Is it not possible that sometime in the ages to come, as soon, perhaps, as they will be required for settlement, timber may cover them, rains and rivers follow, and population swarm?

At Bear River we paid for our breakfast in greenbacks, being the first place at which we found them circulating as currency. Here the stage line merges with Holladay's line from the mining regions of Montana, and continues eighty miles to Salt Lake. A short distance brought us into prosperous Mormon settlements, through which we continued to pass until night rolled us into this chief city of the "Latter-Day Saints."

V.
THE YOSEMITE VALLEY.

ITS MARVELS AND ITS BEAUTIES SCIENTIFICALLY DESCRIBED.

From PROFESSOR J. D. WHITNEY'S *Geological Reports—Volume II.*

THE Yosemite Valley is situated on the Merced River. It is about one hundred and forty miles in a direction a little south of east from San Francisco. It is nearly in the center of the State, north and south, and exactly midway between the east and west bases of the Sierra, here about seventy miles wide.

The valley is a nearly level area, about eight miles in length and varying from half a mile to a mile in width. For the lower six miles its course is from north-east to south-west; the upper two miles are nearly at right-angles to this, the angle of the bend being at the spot where the Yosemite Fall comes over the precipice on the north side. Below the expanded portion of the valley, the Merced enters a terribly deep and narrow canyon, which is said to be inaccessible, and which we had no time to explore.

The peculiar features of the Yosemite are: first, the near approach to verticality of its walls; next, their great hight, not only absolutely, but as compared with the width of the valley itself; and, finally, the very small amount of debris, or talus, at the bottom of these gigantic cliffs. These are the great characteristics of the valley throughout its whole length; but besides these, there are many other striking peculiarities, and features both of sublimity and beauty which can hardly be surpassed, if equalled, by those of any mountain scenery in the world.

Tutucanula (Great Jehovah,) or El Capitan, is an almost vertical cliff of naked, smooth granite. From its edge down to the valley below is about three thousand three hundred feet; it is usually called three thousand six hundred feet, which may be the extreme hight of its slightly rounded summit. It is undoubtedly one of the grandest objects in the Yosemite, and it would be difficult to find anywhere in the world a mass of rock presenting a perpendicular face so imposing and elevated. The pile of debris at its base is so insignificant in dimensions, compared with the cliff itself, that it is hardly noticed at all from some points, in a general view of the valley, and this is one of the most striking and unique features of the scene, for it is a condition of things of the rarest possible occurrence. We know of nothing like it in any other part of the world.

The Bridal Veil Fall, of which the Indian name is "Pohono," is about one thousand feet in hight, and, during the season when the stream is fed by the melting snow on the mountains above, it is a wonderfully beautiful object. The body of water is not large, but is sufficient to produce the most picturesque effect. As it is swayed backwards and forwards by the varying force of the wind, it is continually altering its form, so that it seems, especially as seen from a distance, to flutter like a white veil; hence the name, which is both appropriate and poetical.

Proceeding up the valley, we find, a little above the Bridal Veil Fall, and on the same side, the prominent and massively sculptured pile to which the name of Cathedral Rock is given. It was not measured by us, but it appears to be about three thousand feet in hight. Behind this are the "Cathedral Spires," two slender and beautiful columns of granite, on the same gigantic scale as everything else in this region, and which here are passed almost unnoticed, although, by themselves, in other parts of the world, they would be considered objects of the greatest interest.

A couple of miles farther up the valley, and on the other side, is the next cluster of peaks, a triple row of summits rising in steps one above the other; these are called the "Three Brothers." From the highest of these, nearly four thousand feet above the valley, there is the finest view which can be had of the Yosemite itself and the whole surrounding region up to the crest of the Sierra.

Opposite the Three Brothers is a prominent point, which stands out near the angle where the valley makes its most distinct turn, and which, from its fancied likeness to a gigantic watch-tower, is called "Sentinel Rock." As seen from the south-west, it is a group of cliffs, of which the outside one has quite the form of an obelisk, very regular and beautiful, for at least a thousand feet down. The entire hight of the Sentinel above its base is a little over three thousand feet.

Three-quarters of a mile south-east of the Sentinel is the Dome of the same name, four thousand one hundred and fifty feet high, and one of the most perfect of the dome-shaped masses of granite so peculiar to the Sierra Nevada. Its horizontal section is nearly circular, and its slope very regular and uniform on all sides. From its summit the view is, of course, extremely grand; it is especially fine in the direction of the Obelisk Group of mountains, and it commands the canyon of the south fork of the Merced,—"Illilouette," as it is called by the Indians. From this point the glacial phenomena, and especially the regular and extensive moraines, of that valley are finely displayed. The profile of the Half Dome is best seen from the Sentinel Dome.

From near the foot of Sentinel Rock, looking directly across the valley, we have before us, if not the most stupendous feature of the Yosemite, at least the most attractive one, namely, the Yosemite Fall. About the time of full moon, and in the month of May, June,

SUPPLEMENTARY PAPERS: THE YOSEMITE. 431

or July, according to the dryness and forwardness of the season, is the time to visit the Yosemite, and to enjoy in their perfection the glories of its numerous water-falls. Those who go later, after the snow has nearly gone from the mountains, see the streams diminished to mere rivulets and threads of water; they feel satisfied with the other attractions of the valley, its stupendous cliffs, domes and canyons, and think that the water-falls are of secondary importance, and 'hat they have lost little by delaying the time of their visit. This is not so; the traveler, who has not seen the Yosemite when its streams are full of water, has lost, if not the greater part, at least a large portion, of the attractions of the region, for so great a variety of cascades and falls as those which leap into this valley from all sides has, as we may confidently assert, never been seen elsewhere,—both the Bridal Veil and the Nevada Fall being unsurpassed in some respects, while the Yosemite Fall is beyond anything known to exist, whether we consider its hight or the stupendous character of the surrounding scenery.

The Yosemite Fall is formed by a creek of the same name, which heads on the west side of the Mount Hoffman Group, about twenty miles north of the valley. The volume of water varies, of course, with the season; at the ordinary stage of summer, through the months of June and July, it is about twenty feet wide and two feet deep, on the average. From the edge of the cliff over which it is precipitated to the bottom of the valley, the perpendicular distance is, in round numbers, two thousand five hundred and fifty feet. Professor Brewer's measurement gave two thousand six hundred and forty-one, and that of Mr. King two thousand five hundred and thirty-seven, the difference being due to the circumstance that the lip or edge is a gradual curve, and so highly polished that a near approach to, or a precise definition of, the place where the perpendicular portion of the fall commences is impossible.

The fall is not in one perpendicular sheet. There is first a vertical descent of fifteen hundred feet, where the water strikes on what seems to be a projecting ledge; but which in reality is a shelf or recess, almost a third of a mile back from the front of the lower portion of the cliff. From here the stream finds its way in a series of cascades down a descent equal to six hundred and twenty-six feet perpendicular, and then gives one final plunge of about four hundred feet on to a low talus of rocks at the base of the precipice. As these various falls are in one vertical plane, the effect of the whole from the other side of the valley is nearly as grand, and perhaps even more picturesque, than it would be if the descent was made in one sheet from the top of the cliff to the bottom. The mass of water in the fifteen hundred foot fall is too great to allow of its being entirely broken up into spray, but it widens very much as it descends, and as the sheet vibrates backwards and forwards with the varying pressure of the wind, which acts with immense force on this long column of water, the effect is indescribably grand, especially under the magical illumination of the full moon. The cliff a little east of the edge of the Yosemite Fall rises in a bold peak to the hight of three thousand and thirty feet above the valley; it can be reached through Indian Canyon, a little farther east, and from here a magnificent view of the whole region may be obtained. The ascent to the summit of the upper fall and the return to the valley may be made in one day, but only by good mountain-climbers.

About two miles farther up from the falls just noticed, the main valley of the Yosemite comes to an end, and runs out into three distinct canyons, each of which, however, has new wonders to disclose. The Merced River keeps the middle one of these, and its course here is about the same that it was below, or nearly west. In the left-hand, or north-westerly canyon, the Tenaya Fork comes down; in the right-hand one, the south fork or the Illilouette. Following up the Tenaya Fork, we have on the right hand, just at the entrance of the canyon, that grandest and loftiest mass of the Yosemite Valley, called the Half Dome. This has been in sight, however, through all the upper part of the valley, above the Yosemite Falls, and is a conspicuous point from all the region around. It is an inaccessible crest of granite, rising to the hight of four thousand seven hundred and thirty-seven feet* above the valley, the face fronting towards Tenaya Creek being *absolutely vertical* for two thousand feet down from the summit. The whole appearance of the mass is that of an originally dome-shaped elevation, with an exceedingly steep curve, of which the western half has been split off and has become engulfed. Hence the name, which is one that seems to suggest itself at first sight of this truly marvelous crest of rock. From all the upper part of the valley, and from the hights about it, the Half Dome presents an aspect of the most imposing grandeur; it strikes even the most casual observer as a new revelation in mountain forms; its existence would be considered an impossibility if it were not there before us in all its reality; it is an unique thing in mountain scenery, and nothing even approaching it can be found except in the Sierra Nevada itself.

The North Dome, on the opposite side of the valley of Tenaya Creek, is another of these rounded masses of granite, of which the concentric structure, is very marked. It is three thousand five hundred and sixty-eight feet in elevation above the valley, and is very easy of ascent from the north side. At the angle of the canyon, appearing as a buttress of the North Dome, is the Washington Column, a grand, perpendicular mass of granite, and by its side the Royal Arches, an immense arched cavity formed in the cliffs by the giving way and sliding down of portions of the rock, the vaulted appearance of the upper part of it producing a very fine effect.

Farther up the canyon of Tenaya Creek is a little lake, called Tisayac; it is surrounded by the most picturesque cliffs, having the giant Half Dome overhanging its eastern side.

The canyon of the Merced, above the Yosemite Valley proper, rises very rapidly for the distance of about two miles, when it attains the level of the surrounding plateau. In this two miles the river descends one thousand nine hundred and eighty feet, making, besides innumerable cascades, two grand falls, which are among the

*There is a difference of one thousand feet in two scientific measurements of this peak; one, and the latest, by Professor Brewer, makes its hight nearly SIX THOUSAND *feet above the valley.* S. B.

greater attractions of the Yosemite, not only on account of their hight and the large body of water in the river during the early part of the season, but also because of the stupendous peaks and cliffs by which they are surrounded.

The first fall reached in ascending the canyon is the Vernal, or Piwyac. It is a simple perpendicular sheet, four hundred and seventy-five feet in hight, as nearly as we could determine, the blinding spray at the bottom rendering exact measurements impossible. The rock behind the Vernal Fall is a perfectly square cut mass of granite, and it is wonderful to see how little any eroding effect of water can be traced in its outline. It would seem as if causes now in action had nothing to do with the formation of this step in the descent of the Merced down to the valley below.

Ascending to the summit of the Vernal Fall by a series of ladders, and proceeding a mile farther up the river, passing a series of rapids and cascades of great beauty, we come to the last great fall of the Merced, namely, the Nevada, or the "Yowiye," of the Indians. The total descent, from the edge of the Nevada Fall to that of the Vernal, is eight hundred and ninety-four feet; of which six hundred and thirty-nine, as near as we could determine, is in one perpendicular sheet. The Nevada Fall, however, has a peculiar twist in it, near the summit, caused by the mass of water falling on a projecting ledge, which throws it off to one side, adding greatly to the picturesque effect. This fall is certainly to be ranked as one of the very finest cataracts in the world, taking into consideration its hight, the volume and purity of the water, and the whole character of the scenery which surrounds it, Mount Broderick alone being an object of which the fame would be spread world-wide, if it were not placed as it is, in the midst of so many other wonders of nature.

There are also grand cascades in the South Fork Canyon, the scenery through the whole of which is little inferior to that of the other portions of the Yosemite; but, amid so many objects of attraction, few visitors find time to examine this canyon, especially as the trail by which it is reached is a rough and difficult one.

In the angle formed by the Merced and the South Fork Canyon, and about two miles south-southeast of Mount Broderick, is the high point, called the "South Dome," and also, of later years, "Mount Starr King." This is the most symmetrical and beautiful of all the dome-shaped masses around the Yosemite; but it is not visible from the valley itself. It exhibits the concentric structure of the granite on a grand scale; although its surface is generally smooth and unbroken. Its summit is absolutely inaccessible.

Having thus briefly noticed some of the more prominent objects of interest about the Yosemite, we may add a few words in regard to the valley itself. This is an almost level area, the fall from one end to the other of the valley proper being only about fifty feet. The width of the bottom-land, between the slopes of debris at the base of the cliffs, is only about half a mile; below El Capitan, however, it is nearly twice as much. Its smooth surface and brilliant color, diversified as it is with groves of trees and carpeted with showy flowers, offer the most wonderful contrast to the towering masses of neutral and light purple-tinted rocks by which it is surrounded.

Its elevation above the sea is, according to our measurements, four thousand and sixty feet; and the cliffs and domes about it are from seven thousand to nine thousand in altitude above the sea-level.

All will recognize in the Yosemite Valley a peculiar and almost unique type of scenery. Cliffs absolutely vertical, like the upper portions of the Half Dome and El Capitan, and of such immense hights as these, are, so far as we know, to be seen nowhere else. The dome form of mountains is exhibited on a grand scale in other parts of the Sierra Nevada; but there is no Half Dome, even among the stupendous precipices at the head of King's River. It is natural to ask, then, how these vertical cliffs have been formed, and to what geological causes does the Yosemite Valley owe its existence?

Most of the great canyons and valleys of California have resulted from denudation. The long-continued action of the tremendous torrents of water, rushing with impetuous velocity down the slopes of the Sierra, has excavated those prodigious gorges, by which the chain is furrowed to the depth of thousands of feet. But these eroded canyons, steep as they may be, have not vertical walls; neither have their sides the peculiar angular forms which the mass of El Capitan, for instance, has, where there are two perpendicular surfaces of smooth granite meeting at right-angles, and each over three thousand feet high.

Farther investigations are needed to discuss the theory of the formation of the valley with scientific intelligibility; but it may now be stated, that it appears to us probable that this mighty chasm has been roughly hewn into its present form by the same kind of forces which have raised the crest of the Sierra and moulded the surface of the mountains into something like their present shape. The domes, and such masses as that of Mount Broderick, we conceive to have been formed by the process of upheaval itself, for we can discover nothing about them which looks like the result of ordinary denudation. The Half Dome seems, beyond a doubt, to have been split asunder in the middle, the lost half having gone down in what may truly be said to have been "the wreck of matter and the crash of worlds." It has been objected to this view, by some of the corps, that the bottom of the valley, in places where an engulfment must, according to this theory, have taken place, seems to be of solid granite, when there should be an unfathomable chasm, filled now, of course, with fragments, and not occupied by a solid bed of rock. To this it may be replied, in the first place, that the masses which have been engulfed may have been of such enormous size as to give the impression, where they are only imperfectly exposed, of perfect continuity and connection with the adjacent cliffs. But, again, this grand cataclysm may have taken place at a time when the granitic mass was still in a semi-plastic condition below, although, perhaps, quite consolidated at the surface and for some distance down. In this case it is not impossible, certainly, that the pressure from above may have united the yielding material together, so that all traces of the fracture would be lost, except in that portion of it which affected the upper crust. If the bottom of the Yosemite did "drop out," to use a homely but expressive phrase, it was not all done in one piece, or with one movement; there are evidences in the valley of fractures and cross-fractures at right-angles to these, and the different segments of the mass must have been of quite different sizes, and may have descended to unequal depths.

In the course of our explorations, we obtained ample evidence of the former existence of a glacier in the Yosemite Valley, and the canyons of all the streams entering it are also beautifully polished and grooved by glacial action. It does not appear, however, that the mass of ice ever filled the Yosemite to the upper edge of the cliffs; but one of our corps thinks it must have been at least a thousand feet thick. He also traced out four ridges in the valley which he considers to be, without a doubt, ancient moraines. One of these ridges is a low and narrow band of fragments of rock and rounded boulders, extending from the base of the Half Dome in a curve down the valley, and up again to the debris under the Washington Column. This seems to be the terminal moraine of the Tenaya Creek glacier.

A well-defined medial moraine extends from the foot of the western end of the Half Dome out into the valley, in a slight curve. Another one was formed between the glaciers descending from the canyon of the Merced and the south fork, and remains now as a large pile of debris extending down the valley.

A terminal moraine extends across the Yosemite Valley from the cliffs just below the Bridal Veil Fall, curving down the river on the south side and up again on the north until it meets the talus about a quarter of a mile below El Capitan, thus forming a complete barrier across the valley. It is not very conspicuous, rising only about twenty feet above the general level, yet it seems to mark an important change in the character of the talus at the foot of the cliffs of the Yosemite. Above it the quantity of debris accumulated in this position is exceedingly small; indeed, there is in some places actually none at all, the lower edge of the cliff meeting the floor of the valley, with hardly a fragment of rock lodged in the angle; below the moraine, on the other hand, the debris piles are extensive, uniting at the river, and extending high up the cliffs on each side.

It seems not unlikely that this moraine may have acted as a dam to retain the water within the valley, after the glacier had retreated to its upper end, and that it was while thus occupied by a lake that it was filled up with the comminuted materials arising from the grinding of the glaciers above, thus giving it its present nearly level surface.

It is evident, from the fresh appearance of large masses of debris along the sides of the valley, that these materials are now accumulating with considerable rapidity; and when we consider how small the whole quantity of talus is, as compared with the hight and extent of the cliffs, we are forced to the conclusion that the time which has elapsed since the Yosemite was occupied by a glacier cannot have been very long. It would seem that there are strong reasons for believing that a great change in the climate of California may have taken place within the historical period. We know that such a change has occurred, as there is abundant evidence to prove that the precipitation of moisture in the Sierra Nevada was once vastly greater than it now is; but to the cause of this change we have as yet no clue.

VI.

"THE BIG TREES."

THE GROVE IN CALAVERAS COUNTY.

The following exact and scientific measurements of some of the largest of the BIG TREES in the grove in Calaveras County, California, were made in August, 1865, by Dr. CHARLES T. JACKSON of Boston, Massachusetts, and Mr. JOSEPH B. MEADE of Stockton, California. It will be seen that none of these are so large in circumference and diameter as the "Grizzly Giant" and some of its companions in the less-known and less-visited grove near Mariposa, as described in Letter XXII of this volume:—

"We were provided with a Sir H. Douglass reflecting semi-circle, a reflecting level, and a measuring tape, and by means of these instruments have made quite accurate measurements. The horizontal point, or level, was first ascertained on each tree by means of the reflecting level, and the angle was measured to that point, and the difference of level was corrected for in each case. By means of the tape the base lines were determined, and the circumference of each tree at least six feet above the ground, or where the tree took its proper form, was measured. Sir H. Douglass' reflecting semi-circle is made so as to protract the angles, and it carries also a scale for measurement of the sides of the triangles protracted. In several instances we repeated the measurements, with different bases, especially in those where too high an angle introduced the error of refraction of the glass of the mirrors.

Names of the Trees.	Hight in feet.	Circumference six feet above the roots.
T. Starr King,	366	50
General Scott,	327	45
General Jackson,	320	42
Two Sentinels (front of hotel),	315	—
Salem Witch,	310	—
Trinity,	308	48
Mother of the Forest,	305	63
William C. Bryant,	305	49
Henry W. Beecher,	291	45
Granite State,	286	50

Names of the Trees.	Hight in feet.	Circumference six feet above the roots.
General Washington,	284	52
Abraham Lincoln,	281	44
Bay State,	280	48
Old Kentucky,	277	45
Empire State,	275	50
Andrew Johnson,	273	22
Daniel Webster,	270	49
Mother and Son,	269	64
Edward Everett,	265	46
Pride of the Forest,	260	50
Vermont,	259	41
John Torrey (nobis),	259	35
Arbor Vitæ Queen,	258	31
Beauty of the Forest,	258	—
Henry Clay,	241	44

"We measured the following large pines near the hotel:—

P. Englemanni, or yellow pine,	232	27
Another,	220	19
P. Lambertiana, or sugar pine,	165	—

" The big stump covered by the Stump House has a mean diameter of twenty-three feet one and one-third inches, and its least possible age is one thousand three hundred and eighty years, allowing only ten annual rings per inch. The extremes are ten and sixty, and computing the mean thirty-five per inch, the tree will be four thousand eight hundred and thirty years old."

THE SPECIES AND THE NAME.

A California journal accompanies the above with these notes upon the scientific status of the Big Trees:—

For several years after their discovery there was considerable difference of opinion among scientific men as to the true position which the tree occupies in the botanical system. Soon after its discovery, an English botanist, supposing it to be a new species, named it "Wellingtonea Gigantea;" which, however, a patriotic American proposed the more appropriate name, "Washingtonea Gigantea." It was subsequently named "Tuxodium Gigantium," by Messrs. Kellogg & Behr, in a paper read before the California Academy of Natural Sciences, in May, 1855. In the succeeding August, Dr. Torrey, the distinguished American botanist in a communication to Silliman's American Journal of Science, settled the matter to the satisfaction of the whole scientific world by placing it, where it undoubtedly belongs, in the same *genus* as the redwood,—which was already known as the "Sequoia,"—and this being a larger species than any previously known, was very properly called the "Sequoia Gigantea."

VII.
CALIFORNIA'S WEALTH.

STATISTICS.

From an Agricultural Address by Dr. Holden *of Stockton*, 1865.

The State of California, with a length of 570 and an average breadth of 230 miles, embraces 89,685,515 acres adapted to agricultural purposes, besides 29,000,000 acres of swamp or "tule" land, thousands of acres of which are now being reclaimed, and much of it producing unparalleled crops of vegetables, grass and fruits. The area of the valley land is 30,000,000 acres, making, with the mountain land, a total of 100,000,000 acres suitable for agriculture and grazing. Of this there is under fence over 6,000,000 acres, of which 178,960 acres (in 1860) produced 3,068,093 bushels of wheat; 154,690 acres produced 4,639,678 bushels of barley; 37,620 acres produced 1,263,459 bushels of oats. This year, as near as can be ascertained up to the present date, four times the above amounts of cereals have been raised. Fruit trees and grape vines in 1860 numbered 6,000,000. These have quadrupled up to this time. Stock of all kinds in 1860 numbered 1,577,980; horses, 157,700; cattle, 722,374; sheep, 491,794; goats, 12,743; swine, 165,921; mules, 47,000; poultry, over 80,000. At the present time there are over 2,000,000 sheep, and in no part of the world do they do better, or can they be raised at a less cost. The French and Spanish Merinoes, the Southdown, the Cotswold, and other varieties, have been imported from the Atlantic States, France, Spain and Australia, and prosper as well as in their native countries. Wool is fast becoming an important article of export, over 7,000,000 pounds having been shipped last year. Besides the inexhaustible gold mines, which embrace over 44,000 square miles, minerals and metals of almost every kind have been found. Silver, copper, platina, iron, quicksilver, antimony, tin, arsenic, cobalt, manganese, lead, coal, ochres, saltpetre in large quantities, lime, gypsum, freestone, marble, granite, borax and brimstone are found in quantities to supply the world. Petroleum has been recently discovered in several sections of the State, and bids fair to be of great value, thus adding another item to our wealth and commerce. Over $1,000,000,000 of gold have been exported since 1856.

VIII.

THE GOLD MINES OF CALIFORNIA
AND THE
SILVER MINES OF NEVADA.

THEIR HISTORY, CONDITION AND PROSPECTS.

THE following elaborate and authentic Paper on the Gold Mines of California, and the Silver Mines of Nevada, particularly those upon the celebrated Comstock Vein in Virginia and Gold Hill, is by Mr. WILLIAM ASHBURNER, the confidential mining engineer of the leading bankers of San Francisco, and the Mineralogist of the California State Geological Survey. It will be found most full and exhaustive on the subjects which it treats, and as intelligent as it is reliable in its statements; and the Editor commends it, with confidence and with pride, to all parties interested in the development of our great mineral resources, as a faithful guide and instructor both in their theoretical study and their practical operations:—

MR. SAMUEL BOWLES,—*My Dear Sir:—*

INTRODUCTORY.

The redundancy of currency in the eastern States has stimulated enterprise, during the last few years, in all branches of industry, and the discovery of silver bearing veins in Nevada has afforded a field for speculation in mining properties, such as has never before been witnessed in the United States.

Several millions of dollars have already been invested by eastern people, some of them persons of small means, in the mines on this Coast; and I purpose in the following pages to show briefly the present situation of the two important interests of gold and silver, as exemplified by the quartz mines of California and the Comstock vein of Nevada.

We are all familiar with the excitement caused by the discovery of gold in California during the spring of 1848. For many years subsequent to that event, the tide of emigration flowed steadily hither, bringing an adventurous population from all parts of the world, attracted solely by the desire of reaping the advantages supposed to be possessed by those engaged in mining for the precious metals. The scene of their operations extended along the western slope of the Sierra Nevadas, rarely reaching into the mountains for more than twenty-five miles from the lower foot hills, being limited on the south by Mariposa County, and on the north by Siskiyou. This district, which is about two hundred and fifty miles in length, forms what is known as the gold region of California, and in it are those great placers which, in spite of prophesies of early exhaustion, are still continuing to furnish an annual supply of gold, amounting to more than forty millions of dollars.

QUARTZ MINING IN CALIFORNIA.

In addition to this, the quartz mining interest has been gradually developed, so that now, although the gross amount yielded by the mines of this nature, does not compare very favorably with that afforded by the placers, it is, and promises to continue for many years to come, to be, one of the most important interests of the State. It affords a fine field for the investment of capital, when guided judiciously, and the significant fact of but few of these mines having as yet found their way into the hands of eastern proprietors, shows in what manner they are regarded here. The principal quartz mining districts of California are in Mariposa County, Tuolumne, round about Sonora, Amador County, near Jackson, Nevada County, where the celebrated mines of Grass Valley are situated, Sierra and Plumas counties.

The mining of quartz for gold in California dates back as far as the summer or autumn of 1850, when a small mill was constructed in Mariposa County. The year following, quartz mining was commenced in Grass Valley, and has been continued with the greatest success in that locality ever since. Here are now, without any doubt, the richest gold mines in the world, and they are yielding regularly from two hundred and fifty thousand dollars to three hundred thousand dollars a month, which is nearly one-third the total production of gold from the quartz mines in California. There are probably at the present time from seventy-five to one hundred mills in successful operation throughout the State, yielding annually about eight millions of dollars worth of gold. The veins which furnish the quartz for these mills, are generally situated in the immediate neighborhood of rich placers; they have, for the most part, a dip and direction nearly coincident with the stratification; their workable width varies from a few inches to thirty or forty feet, though it invariably happens that the wider the vein, the poorer it is. The rock in which they are encored is either slate, granite or greenstone, and it is difficult to state which of these three formations is most prolific, and the best adapted for gold producing veins; for we have, in each of them, mines which have been worked for years, and are

SUPPLEMENTARY PAPERS: GOLD MINES.

still continuing to yield apparently as well as ever. The Princeton mine on the Mariposa estate is in slate, and is now down to a depth of more than six hundred feet; it has already yielded about three million of dollars worth of gold, and it is by no means certain that this mine is now exhausted, although the yield is very much less than it was formerly.

The history of every quartz mine, which has been worked for any length of time, will show great changes in the yield of rock from month to month; or, perhaps, from year to year; and it is not yet proved that, in the more permanent veins of California, the percentage yield of the quartz is less at great depth than nearer the surface. There appears to be no general rule governing the distribution of gold in the body of the vein, and after working for months with a regular yield, suddenly, without any apparent cause, the quartz will become nearly barren, and destroy well arranged plans, as was the case with the Princeton mine in December, 1864, when, after having for some time afforded rock which was gradually increasing in value until it yielded forty dollars per ton, it suddenly fell off, without giving any warning, to six dollars. This was the immediate cause of the failure of the Mariposa Company.

Near Jackson, in Amador County, the mine of Hayward & Co., affords an interesting example of the success, which sometimes attends deep quartz mining. The vein, upon which it is situated, has been worked for the last ten years with varying success. The results obtained, during the first few years of its history, were anything but encouraging, and work was prosecuted in depth almost against hope. Since 1860, however, the mine has yielded with the greatest regularity, and now at a depth of nine hundred and sixty feet, the quartz is said to be of as good and in some places of even a better quality than that found nearer the surface. Geologically, this vein is one of great interest. It is situated at the junction of the slates and greenstone, and is of the nature of a contact deposit. The length of underground workings is between five hundred and six hundred feet, and in one place, the vein has been worked to a width of forty feet.

In the neighborhood of Grass Valley the veins are in greenstone, and their width is very much less, as a general thing, than those which are found in the slates. Still their greater richness enables them to be worked with large profits. Two of the most famous mines of this district are the Massachusetts Hill and Allison Ranch. The first of these is from a vein of about one foot or fourteen inches in width, and has produced, in connection with its continuation the Gold Hill vein, upwards of seven millions dollars worth of gold; while the Allison Ranch had produced, between the spring of 1857, and the winter of 1861, from a vein which will only average ten inches in width, some eight hundred and fifty thousand dollars, and since that time probably as much more. In the more northern part of the State, in Plumas County, are some very successful mines, which are situated in the granite formation; and although this district has been worked for only a few years, the veins give good indication of permanence, and excellent results may be expected from this almost "unprospected" region.

COST AND PROFITS OF GOLD MINING IN CALIFORNIA.

The profits realized from quartz mining adventures, besides depending in a great measure upon the absolute yield of the rock, are affected by the cost of extraction from the mine, which, when the wall rock is hard and the vein narrow, runs up sometimes as high as twenty-six dollars a ton. No general average can be given for this item, and every mine is governed by circumstances peculiar to itself. It is different, however, with regard to milling; here we have accurate data to follow, which are not much affected by change of locality. It is rare that the expense of treating the quartz, after it leaves the mine, exceeds three dollars per ton in a steam mill, and in some mills, which are moved by water power, this item is only about seventy cents a ton. As a general thing, however, it may be considered that it requires quartz yielding eight dollars a ton, when both the mine and mill are situated under favorable conditions, to cover the expense of mining and milling. Therefore, when the vein is of moderate size, say five or six feet in width and water power can be employed, quartz yielding ten dollars per ton may be regarded as valuable, and affording a certain profit.

In 1861, the production of the quartz mines throughout the State was about six millions of dollars; this year it will probably be eight millions of dollars; and the total production in gold of the American possessions on the Pacific Coast will not be far, in round numbers, from fifty millions of dollars.

SILVER MINING IN NEVADA.

As I before remarked, the best of these mines in California have heretofore been owned, almost exclusively, by Californians, who are well acquainted with their value, and therefore comparatively little eastern capital has been invested in them. It is not so, however, with the silver mines of Nevada; and at present a very large proportion of the stock of the incorporated companies, working upon the Comstock vein, is held in the Atlantic cities. I have consequently thought it well to devote far more space to these mines, than to those which possess at present merely a local interest for the public.

Although since the discovery of silver in Nevada, several districts have sprung rapidly into notice, and enjoyed an ephemeral notoriety the "Washoe" region still maintains its pre-eminence, and there seems every reason to suppose that the supremacy which it now enjoys will not be seriously interfered with by any of the districts of less repute. The average monthly production of the four principal mining centers of Nevada has been, during the first nine months of the present year, very nearly as follows; and this shows better than any other means their relative importance:—

Washoe (Virginia and Gold Hill districts), . $1,236,275
Austin (Reese River district), ... 75,000.
Aurora (Esmeralda district), ... 19,000
Unionville (Humboldt district), ... 1,282.

THE COMSTOCK LODE AND ITS PRODUCTS.

From the time of the first discovery of the Comstock lode in 1859, the annual production of silver continued to increase regularly until within the last few months, when the yield of the Virginia and Gold Hill districts began to diminish very materially, and grave apprehensions have been excited in the minds of many persons, lest these mines were giving out, and fears were entertained that they would cease to pay their expenses.

The decrease in the production of the mines of Nevada was most marked between the months of May and July, when the falling off was nearly eighteen thousand pounds avoirdupois, or about nine tons, and the value of the bullion forwarded to San Francisco, during the quarter ending September 30th, was about one million dollars less than that of the previous quarter. The approximate yield of all these mines for the first nine months of this year has been nearly as follows:—

	Pounds avoirdupois.	Value.
January,	54,123,	
February,	59,106,	$4,434,669.
March,	64,737,	
April,	61,179,	
May,	58,453,	$4,261,811.
June,	49,979,	
July,	41,526,	
August,	44,927,	$3,224,951.
September,	40,278,	

The principal cause of the large yield for the month of March was the discovery and opening up in the "Yellow Jacket" mine, of a valuable deposit of ore, which lasted into June, but since that time the production of this mine has decreased considerably. In nearly every mine on the Comstock, from the "Ophir" to the "Belcher," the lower workings show ore which is of a poorer quality and much inferior in quantity to what was found in some of the upper levels. In view of these facts, it becomes an interesting matter to ascertain what are the probabilities of discovering new and valuable deposits, as the explorations are continued in depth, and also what quantity of ore now exists in the upper works, which are now furnishing nearly all the daily supplies.

Both these questions are exceedingly difficult to decide. In forming an opinion with regard to the first, we must reason entirely from analogy and apply to Washoe the experience acquired by mining in other countries; and the difficulties which surround the latter are also great, owing to the peculiar and irregular manner in which these deposits of ore occur; therefore, what follows with regard to the present condition of these mines must be regarded more as the expression of a personal opinion, rather than an infallible conclusion the correctness of which may at any time be destroyed by the dis covery of new bodies of ore in ground heretofore unexplored. It is only by repeated examinations, made at short intervals of time, that a true idea can be obtained of the value of the daily or weekly developments made in the progress of working one of these mines.

It has never been the policy of any of the companies of Virginia and Gold Hill, to keep reserves of ore on hand, which would furnish supplies when any particular deposit was exhausted. They consulted, merely, what appeared to them to be the interest of the moment, and assumed that each new body of ore, which they met in the progress of working, was inexhaustible. Thus a result, which was easy to foresee, has now taken place. Nearly all the mines on the Comstock, from the "Ophir" to the "Belcher," find themselves, almost simultaneously, either without ore in their lower works, or else what they have is of such inferior quality that they are obliged to await the result of future explorations. To use a Mexican term, they are no longer in *bonanza*.

It may be well, before speaking of any individual mine, to describe, without too much detail, some of the peculiar features of the Comstock lode, as shown by the extensive workings which have been made upon it during the last five years. The Comstock vein is situated on the eastern slope of Mount Davidson, at an elevation of some six thousand three hundred feet above the level of the sea, and about one thousand eight hundred feet above the valley of the Carson River, while the mountain rises behind it on the west to a hight of one thousand six hundred feet. Directly on its course lie the cities of Virginia and Gold Hill. The vein is formed in a fissure at the junction of two formations of different lithological characters, and has a direction very nearly north and south. The Western Country rock, as it is termed, and which forms the foot wall of the vein, has a dip towards the east of from forty degrees to sixty degrees, and is a greenstone porphyry, containing a large proportion of hornblende, hard and compact in its texture. The Eastern Country consists of a much softer feldspathic porphyry, devoid of hornblende. As we proceed eastward from the vein, this feldspathic porphyry is overlaid by trachyte. In some places, particularly opposite the northern portion of the vein, this porphyritic belt is of great width, and in front of the "Ophir" and "California" mines, it is probably two thousand feet wide. As we go south, however, towards the Gold Hill claims, it becomes narrower, until opposite the "Yellow Jacket," its width scarcely exceeds five hundred feet. Still farther south, it rapidly widens again, and in front of the "Uncle Sam," it is at least one thousand feet wide. The greenstone porphyry of the Western Country is recognized as being eminently a mineral bearing formation, and possesses a striking resemblance, in its lithological characters, to the rock that encases the veins of some of the most noted silver producing districts of any of the world, which, after being successfully worked for many centuries, e obtained a conspicuous celebrity, and are still regarded as persistent, continuing as they do to furnish their metalliferous tents to as great a depth as has yet been attained by mining.

On the surface of the ground, the vein appears in places to be lit up and broken into several distinct portions. In the mines of

Virginia, the most eastern of these bodies is nearly vertical for several hundred feet below the surface, while in many of those in Gold Hill, it is sensibly parallel to the more western body, which everywhere lies upon the hard compact country rock, and dips with great regularity towards the east. The western body, being as a general thing more metalliferous, is not so liable to be affected by atmospheric agencies, and on account of its greater hardness has preserved a marked prominence above the surface of the ground, while on the other hand, the more eastern and mineral bearing portion of the lode is comparatively soft and friable, and has generally been degraded to the level of the surface of the ground, and in some places it is completely covered by detritus. The distance, which separates these two principal bodies, is sometimes as much as six hundred feet, as is the case back of the "Ophir," where the prominent croppings are known as the Virginia, and are quite non-metalliferous. Back of the "Gould & Curry," the croppings are known as the "El-Dorado" vein. As these are all, so far as yet explored, non-productive masses of quartz, they possess no value for mining purposes; still, owing to the fact that they were more marked and prominent, "locations" were made upon them, at an earlier date than upon the richer portions of the lode; and although these bodies, which appear separate and distinct near the surface, converge towards each other and meet, forming one vein at an inconsiderable depth, much litigation to the Virginia companies was caused by this apparent plurality of veins, and has given rise to many suits involving the question of "one or two ledges." All recent developments have, however, gone to prove that, although on the surface, there are many bodies of quartz, more or less metalliferous, separated from each other by clay and fragments of porphyry, these blend together on descending, and form one and the same vein.

Towards the west the main vein becomes incorporated with a large mass of quartz, associated with a reddish brown ferruginous clay, which has caused the name of the "red lead" to be given to this portion of the mine. Occasionally this "red lead" is impregnated with small quantities of sulphuret of silver, but in the "Ophir" it has never been found of a sufficient amount to pay for working. As we proceed south, however, this "red lead," in many places, proves productive, as in the "Gould & Curry" and "Savage" mines, but it is, even here, separated by a considerable distance from the most western body, which is still barren.

In the "Chollar" and Gold Hill claims, the back vein or Western Country ore begins to prove productive, though the more eastern body continues to preserve its superiority. The large space, which separates the most easterly portion from the back vein, is filled with bodies of quartz, separated from each other by fragments of porphyry, technically termed "horses," which are frequently of great size, and have been detached from the two walls. These "horses" are surrounded by seams of clay of various colors and thicknesses, and, in consistency, resemble that which forms the eastern and western selvages of the vein.

The mines extend along the course of the Comstock vein for a distance of more than two miles. It is not in every place where explorations have been undertaken that they have proved profitable; in some, ore has been found of the greatest richness near the surface; in others, it is only at considerable depth that anything of value has been discovered; while elsewhere works, after having been prosecuted for months, have been abandoned as hopeless. This is the history of all mineral bearing veins in other countries. Some portions are rich and valuable, while others are barren and worthless; and certainly there is no silver producing region in the world, that has ever yielded so large an amount of bullion in so short a space of time, as that district on the Comstock, lying between the "Ophir" on the north, in Virginia, and the "Belcher" on the south, in Gold Hill.

In the working of these mines, however, no regular system of exploitation has ever been pursued; so that, in the wide space between the eastern and western walls, many valuable deposits were overlooked in the progress of working, and since the lower levels have in some cases ceased to prove profitable, the upper works have been more thoroughly prospected, and generally with very excellent results.

THE GOULD AND CURRY MINE.

The "Gould & Curry" Company have a location of twelve hundred feet upon the course of the vein, or rather their stock represents this number; but in reality the whole actual length of the claim is only nine hundred and sixty feet, owing, I believe, to an error of measurement between the original bounds. Of this nine hundred and sixty feet, no more than about four hundred feet of the southern end has ever been productive ground; and, although the balance has been thoroughly prospected on the north, towards the "Best" and "Belcher," it is an accepted conclusion that no reliance can be placed upon this portion of the claim, as furnishing any supplies of ore in the future, unless at a much greater depth than has yet been obtained. The ore producing portion of this mine has been hitherto confined to that triangular space comprised between the surface of the ground, the "El-Dorado" vein, as indicated by the croppings, and the eastern clay selvage, a short distance west of the Bonner shaft. The main workings of the mine were upon an exceedingly rich body of ore about three hundred and fifty feet long, and which extended to the south end of the company's claim, where it adjoins the "Savage." This deposit was formerly worked with the greatest extravagance, and, until the management of Mr. Bonner, absolutely no works of exploration had been kept in advance of those of extraction, so that, when he took charge of the mine in June, 1864, he found himself with apparently nothing to work upon, and only those portions of the older works, which were considered as being exhausted, from which to draw his supplies of ores, and these, owing to ineffective timbering, were rapidly caving in. He immediately commenced prospecting the ground below the "adit level," and also in the neighborhood of the old workings. He was fortunate to discover, in many parts of the mine which had been entirely abandoned, comparatively small bodies of ore of inferior richness to those which formerly rendered this mine so celebrated; and it is these which have kept the works in existence since that time. He also commenced a new shaft outside the limits of the vein on the east, for the purpose of prospecting the ground to a much greater depth than had been attained by any previous exploration. This shaft is now six hundred and thirty-five feet below the D street tunnel, but its bottom is not yet in the vein. Only one drift has as yet been run from the shaft west towards the vein. This is at a depth of two hundred feet below the adit. Although the fissure is filled with barren, unproductive matter, where it is intersected by this drift, it is still of good width, and is not far from one hundred and thirty feet between the two walls. The work of sinking this shaft still further, and developing the ground by means of drifts, is being continually prosecuted.

All the ore that is now being taken from this mine comes from the croppings or the upper levels on both sides of the old workings, and discoveries have frequently been made in this unexplored ground, which were not anticipated, so that it is impossible to predict with any degree of certainty how long these supplies will last; but there is very little doubt that there is sufficient ore in the mine, and in sight, to continue the present monthly production of about four thousand five hundred tons for at least four months. Other deposits may be met with which will furnish supplies for a longer time; but this is all that can be relied upon with certainty. The affairs of the company, both above and below ground, appear now to be managed with skill and economy, and afford a striking contrast to what was formerly the case, during the first years of the history of this mine.

Immediately adjoining the "Gould & Curry" on the south is the "Savage." The principal workings in this mine have been upon a continuation of the rich body of ore found in the "Gould & Curry." In this latter mine, the deposit had a general dip towards the south of about twenty degrees, and, although the most valuable portion was some distance north of the boundary line, it still continued to furnish a large amount of rich ore. The greater bulk of this has now been worked out, and explorations are being prosecuted on every side of the old workings, where there is any prospect that deposits may have been overlooked. As a general thing, these have been very successful, and several bodies of ore have been discovered within the last few months, the existence of which was not suspected, while the mine was in more prosperous circumstances. The lowest workings are four hundred and forty-five feet from the surface, and the body of ore which has been laid open has not yet been sufficiently developed to enable me to form a positive opinion, with regard to its value and probable duration. As yet, however, there are no such indications as would lead one to suppose that this body of ore will prove anything like so valuable and extensive as those found in the upper works.

THE OPHIR MINE.

In the "Ophir" mine, the appearance of the lower workings is gloomy in the extreme. The main shaft is now down to a depth of five hundred and eighty-six feet from the surface. At the bottom of this, there is a sump twenty-one feet deep, making in all a depth of six hundred and six feet from the surface. At the ninth level or five hundred and eighty-six feet from the surface, the fissure is twenty-two feet wide, but contains no ore, and is filled with clay and fragments of porphyry; in fact nothing of value has been discovered in this mine in the progress of sinking below the level of the seventh gallery, or for a distance of one hundred and sixty-seven feet. All the ore, which is now being extracted, amounting to from forty to fifty tons a day, is taken from the upper works near and above the seventh level. How long these supplies will last, it is utterly impossible to predict. Two years ago those persons who were most familiar with this mine were unable to see ore for more than eight months' supply; and since that time the production, although greatly diminished, has been maintained so as to pay all ordinary expenses. It is obviously, however, a mere question of time, and a few months more work must exhaust all the ore above the level of the "Latrobe Tunnel," so that the final prospects of this mine are entirely dependent upon what will be met with after sinking still farther to the east.

OTHER LEADING MINES.

Like the "Ophir," "Gould & Curry" and "Savage," the "Chollar-Potosi" company have been obliged to commence and sink a new shaft in the Eastern Country, some distance to the east of the vein, in order to avoid the great expense of working in the hard Western Country. It is expected that by means of this shaft, when completed, the vein can be developed to a depth of at least eight hundred feet. The principal exploitations in this mine are in what are known as the old Bajazet workings, about one hundred and forty feet south of the north line of the claim. Here the pay seam varies in width from ten to twenty-five feet, and has been developed on a face of nearly one hundred and thirty-five feet. About forty tons a day are being extracted from this portion of the mine, which is worth forty dollars a ton. About thirty-five tons a day are now being taken from workings at a depth of one hundred and fifty feet from the surface, which are being continued upwards. This body is now eight feet wide and some two hundred and fifty feet in length, and there seems every probability that there is now sufficient ore in sight, of an apparent average value of thirty-five dollars a ton, to last nearly a year. The lowest workings in this mine are at a depth of four hundred and eighty-five feet; and on the lower levels the ore is still of an excellent quality, so that there is a fair prospect of these works continuing to furnish ore to a considerably greater depth than has yet been attained.

The "Hale & Norcross" company, whose claim adjoins on the north, is now down to a depth of seven hundred feet, and in drifting south they discovered an excellent deposit of ore which, however, was found to be upon the ground of the "Chollar-Potosi." This was at a depth of one hundred and sixty-five feet below the lowest workings of this latter company.

The profits of the "Chollar-Potosi" mine for the month of September last, were seventeen thousand two hundred and forty-one

SUPPLEMENTARY PAPERS: SILVER MINES. 449

dollars, and were realized from the sale and milling of about four thousand two hundred tons. The ore yielded in the mill from thirty-three dollars to forty dollars per ton.

In the "Imperial" mine, the lower station is five hundred and eighty-seven feet from the surface. The present daily extraction from this mine is now about one hundred tons, worth say thirty-five dollars a ton. Seventy feet above the lower station in the old workings, there are supplies of ore for perhaps six weeks; and in the lower works, the pay seam has a mean width of about twenty-seven feet, and continues through the whole length of the claim, or seven hundred and eighteen feet. This will probably furnish ore enough for from four to six months' workings. No works of prospecting in depth are being carried on, and the shaft is in such bad condition, that, should the coming winter prove wet, serious apprehensions would be entertained of a cave, which would oblige work to be suspended. It is contemplated to sink a new shaft, some distance to the east of the present one in the solid Eastern Country; but it has not yet been commenced.

The lower works of the "Empire" do not present so good an appearance as those of the "Imperial." The fifth and lowest station is at a depth of six hundred and fifteen feet. Between the second and third stations, all the ore has been worked out; between the third and fourth, nearly all, except what has been left to support its shaft; and between the fourth and fifth, there are about fifty-six feet of ore that is undisturbed. With the exception of what may be ultimately met with in sinking still farther, the main reliance of this mine is from a body of unexplored ground within one hundred and thirty feet of the surface. This is about one hundred and eighty feet high, seventy-five feet long and fifty feet wide, and I understand that, since I examined the mine, this ground has afforded some good ore. Preparations are being made for sinking still farther, but a wet winter will be likely to affect disastrously this mine, as well as all others in Gold Hill proper.

THE FUTURE OF THE COMSTOCK MINES.

Now what are the probabilities of finding new deposits of ore in these mines, as the works are pursued in depth? It is now an accepted conclusion by all those persons, who have examined the matter carefully, and have had the most experience in geological as well as general mining matters, that the Comstock is a fissure vein of extraordinary width and productiveness, and, consequently, reasoning from analogy, we have great right to assume that ore exists and will ultimately be found at as great a depth as it is possible to extend underground workings. In fact, there is no instance, where a well defined fissure vein has been found terminating entirely in depth; and although nothing is more frequent in the progress of working than to meet with barren zones of unproductive matter, their metalliferous contents have never been exhausted at any depth, which has yet been obtained by mining. The limit to the successful working of one of these veins appears to be fixed entirely by the increased cost of extraction of the ore, and pumping the water from the lower levels, and consequent reduction of the profits. There is a point, of course, where, in the absence of new discoveries of increased value, the receipts will exactly counterbalance the expenses of working; and then soon these latter will exceed the former.

Nearly all the silver producing mines of Mexico are upon fissure veins, and the principal one of them, the "Jeta Madre" of Guanaxuato, has many points of resemblance to the Comstock. It has been actively worked for more than a hundred and twenty-five years, and in the year 1803 the depth attained in one mine upon its course, "the Valenciana," was about twelve hundred feet, which is below the point at which nearly all the mines in Mexico cease to pay a profit on account of the largely increased expenses of working. But owing to the great width of this vein, which does not, however, exceed that of the Comstock, works have been successfully continued to a depth of two thousand feet, and it is now the deepest mine on this Continent. During its history, there have been periods of profound depression, and the rich bonanzas, which gave it a prominent celebrity throughout Mexico, and have made it an historical mine, were at times replaced by ore of merely average value, and occasionally by vein matter that was entirely unproductive; still, work was prosecuted in depth, and the discovery of new deposits rewarded the efforts and enterprise of the owners.

Nearly every mine of importance in the world will show a similar record. In fact, all indications with regard to the continuance of mineral deposits, and the discovery of new ores of increased richness, are acknowledged to be of a doubtful character; and there seems to be no department of human science, which will enable us to fix with certainty the limits of possible success or possible disappointment; and thus it is only after long and fruitless explorations that we can decide whether labor should cease, and the works be abandoned.

The Freiberg mines in Germany present another interesting example of veins of this character continuing in richness to a great depth. The mean depth to which they have been worked is now about twelve hundred feet, and although continually increasing, it does not appear that there has been any falling off during long periods in the average yield of the ores for the last three centuries.

The silver mines of Andreasberg in the Hartz have been worked since 1520, with varying success and profit. At the beginning of the present century, the workings were down to a depth of one thousand five hundred feet, and since that time a depth of two thousand five hundred feet has been attained. Although it is now generally conceded that these famous mines have become exhausted, the cause appears to be entirely owing to the fact of the lodes and mineral bearing portion having been intersected by a cross vein of an older geological formation, consisting of schist and barren clay; and the probability of this being ultimately the case has been known and predicted for years. In Hungary, the silver and gold mines of Schemnitz have been worked since the year 735, and accurate records with regard to their seasons of success and depression extend back as far as the latter part of the fifteenth century. Although the ore is much inferior in richness to that even now being taken from the Comstock, the limits of depth to which they have been successfully worked would seem to have depended entirely upon the increased cost entailed by the pumping of water; but the utmost confidence has always prevailed with regard to the continuance of ore to any depth that it might be possible to carry the underground explorations; and works of great expense have been undertaken on several occasions to drain the mines by means of adits. The first of these was commenced about three hundred and fifty years ago, another forty years later, which was not completed for two hundred and seventy years, and still more recently, in 1782, a new tunnel was commenced, and not yet terminated, which will be about nine miles in length and had already cost in 1850 over a million of dollars. This, when completed, will enable the mines to be worked to a depth of fifteen hundred feet. The total length of the adits, which have been constructed for the purpose of draining these mines during the last three centuries, is not less than forty miles.

Works like these, involving so much time, labor and expense, are never undertaken without securing beforehand the best mining talent, which the country affords, and all go to prove that the utmost reliance is placed on the continuance of these veins in depth, and that the great object is to secure economy of working, so as to enable greater profits to be realized from the treatment of the ores.

Within the last five years upwards of thirty-five millions dollars worth of bullion have been taken out and thrown upon the markets of the world, from the mines of Virginia and Gold Hill, in Nevada; and if we consider the wasteful extravagance of the methods formerly employed for working the ores, it is safe to assume that not more than sixty per cent. of the value of the precious metals was secured, and consequently ore containing silver and gold to the amount of nearly sixty millions dollars has been extracted from the mines of a district not more than two miles in length. The "Gould & Curry" alone has furnished fourteen millions dollars, and although we must not estimate the present value of a mine from what it has produced, yet it would be assuming the occurrence of a most extraordinary natural phenomenon to suppose that all this vast amount of mineral wealth had been segregated within a space of three hundred and fifty feet in length, by less than five hundred in depth, and that no more remained behind to reward future explorations. In view of these facts, although nearly every mine on the Comstock has passed through a rich body of ore or bonanza, we have strong reasons for presuming that other deposits will be met within the limits of profitable working. The average depth of these mines is not yet more than five hundred feet, and ores yielding thirty-five dollars per ton will allow works to be carried to a depth of from one thousand to one thousand two hundred feet, and still leave a small margin for profit.

As a general thing, these mines have been worked heretofore, not so much with reference to the permanent interests of the stockholders, as for the purpose of raising the market value of the stock. With this view, it has frequently happened that circumstances deeply affecting the interests of the mines have been concealed from the public, and the policy has hitherto been to increase the production as largely as possible, in order to enable certain persons to realize immediately great profits from the sale of their stock, rather than await the slower and perhaps more hazardous return which it was expected would be afforded by dividends. This is the only excuse, or rather reason, why, in the midst of mines yielding so enormously, no proportion of the gain in their more prosperous days was ever devoted to the purposes of exploration, and the necessity of keeping these works in advance of those of extraction seems never to have entered the minds of those persons who were called upon to fill the positions of trustees to the various companies, until the receipts began to be inferior to the expenses. A very different policy from that which prevailed heretofore now governs the administration of these mines, and the experience that has been gained during the last five years is beginning to show itself in more economical management and better divided labor. Easy access can be obtained to the mines, and the financial position of the companies can generally be ascertained without difficulty. In very many ways, the situation of these companies is much more satisfactory than it was two or three years since. The titles to their mining ground have, as a general thing, been perfected, although frequently at an enormous expense, and now the profits accruing from the working of the ores can be devoted either to the payment of dividends, or to the farther development of the mines; and those who are familiar with the frightful expenditures, which have been incurred for litigation, being in some cases more than the total receipts from the mines themselves, are able to form some idea what an important item of expense has ceased to exist. Again, many of the companies, that were accustomed to employ outside mills for working their ores, now possess mills of their own, in which the cost of treatment is barely one-half what it was formerly.

In addition to these important gains, the influence of which is already being felt, several projects have been set on foot that cannot fail, when completed, to increase the value of the mining properties upon the course of the Comstock vein, by enabling the companies to work their ores much more cheaply, and realize profits from those which are now of too low a grade to be extracted from the mine or treated in the mills. At the head of these enterprises is without doubt what is known as the "Sutro Tunnel." This is a project for draining the mines upon the Comstock by means of an adit some three and one-half miles in length, and which will strike the vein at a depth of nearly one thousand nine hundred feet below the outcrops. Its importance cannot be too highly estimated as affording a permanent, economical drainage to such a great depth, and it is to be hoped that the projectors of this scheme will meet with the encouragement which they deserve.

I am Yours Very Respectfully,

WILLIAM ASHBURNER,

Mining Engineer.

SAN FRANCISCO,
November, 1865.

www.ingramcontent.com/pod-product-compliance
Lightning Source LLC
Chambersburg PA
CBHW030322020526
44117CB00030B/520